HTML FOR DUMMIES®

2ND EDITION

by Ed Tittel and Steve James

IDG Books Worldwide, Inc.
An International Data Group Company

Foster City, CA ♦ Chicago, IL ♦ Indianapolis, IN ♦ Braintree, MA ♦ Southlake, TX

HTML For Dummies,® 2nd Edition

Published by
IDG Books Worldwide, Inc.
An International Data Group Company
919 E. Hillsdale Blvd.
Suite 400
Foster City, CA 94404

Library of Congress Catalog Card No.: 96-75002

ISBN: 1-56884-647-9

Printed in the United States of America

10 9 8 7 6 5 4 3 2 1

2E/RR/QT/ZW/IN

Distributed in the United States by IDG Books Worldwide, Inc.

Distributed by Macmillan Canada for Canada; by Computer and Technical Books for the Caribbean Basin; by Contemporanea de Ediciones for Venezuela; by Distribuidora Cuspide for Argentina; by CITEC for Brazil; by Ediciones ZETA S.C.R. Ltda. for Peru; by Editorial Limusa SA for Mexico; by Transworld Publishers Limited in the United Kingdom and Europe; by Al-Maiman Publishers & Distributors for Saudi Arabia; by Simron Pty. Ltd. for South Africa; by IDG Communications (HK) Ltd. for Hong Kong; by Toppan Company Ltd. for Japan; by Addison-Wesley Publishing Company for Korea; by Longman Singapore Publishers Ltd. for Singapore, Malaysia, Thailand, and Indonesia; by Unalis Corporation for Taiwan; by WS Computer Publishing Company, Inc. for the Philippines; by WoodsLane Pty. Ltd. for Australia; by WoodsLane Enterprises Ltd. for New Zealand.

For general information on IDG Books Worldwide's books in the U.S., please call our Consumer Customer Service department at 800-762-2974. For reseller information, including discounts and premium sales, please call our Reseller Customer Service department at 800-434-3422.

For information on translations, contact Marc Jeffrey Mikulich, Director, Foreign & Subsidiary Rights, at IDG Books Worldwide, 415-655-3018 or fax 415-655-3295.

For sales inquiries and special prices for bulk quantities, write to the address above or call IDG Books Worldwide at 415-655-3200.

For information on using IDG Books Worldwide's books in the classroom, or ordering examination copies, contact the Education Office at 800-434-2086 or fax 817-251-8174.

For authorization to photocopy items for corporate, personal, or educational use, please contact Copyright Clearance Center, 222 Rosewood Drive, Danvers, MA 01923, or fax 508-750-4470.

 is a trademark under exclusive license to IDG Books Worldwide, Inc., from International Data Group, Inc.

About the Authors

Ed Tittel

Ed Tittel is the coauthor of numerous books about computing and the World Wide Web, including *The Foundations of World Wide Web Programming with HTML and CGI*, and *World Wide Web Programming Secrets* (both books' authors also include Mark Gaither, Mike Erwin, and Sebastian Hassinger). These days, Ed's aiming his efforts at Internet programming-related topics, both as a writer and as a member of the NetWorld + Interop program committee.

Ed has been a regular contributor to the trade press since 1987, and has written over 200 articles for a variety of publications, including *Computerworld*, *InfoWorld*, *Maximize*, *I-way*, and *NetGuide*. He's a columnist and contributing editor for *Windows NT* magazine, and works for several online 'zines, including *WebSite* and *Webster*.

These days, Ed enjoys working at home, where his real job is keeping Dusty, his large and rambunctious Labrador retriever, company. When he's not pounding the keyboard, he's either out walking Dusty, playing pool, or cooking up something in his kitchen for friends and family.

Contact Ed at `etittel@zilker.net` or visit his Web site at `http://www.lanw.com`.

Steve James

Steve James is a long-time computer industry writer who's covered the documentation needs of organizations as diverse as the U.S. Army Corps of Engineers and the Psychological Corporation. He's also the coauthor, with Ed Tittel, of *ISDN Networking Essentials* and *PC Telephony*, from AP PROFESSIONAL (1995 and 1996, respectively).

A former biological researcher, Steve has concentrated his efforts in one computer-related operation or another for the past fifteen years. Along the way, he's fathered more than 50-odd manuals and other lengthy works of technical prose and has made some excellent friends, too.

Currently, Steve divides his time between the keyboard, his family, and the great outdoors, where the thrill of competitive bicycling continues to lure him, despite his accelerating decrepitude.

Contact Steve at `snjames@wetlands.com`.

Welcome to the world of IDG Books Worldwide.

IDG Books Worldwide, Inc., is a subsidiary of International Data Group, the world's largest publisher of computer-related information and the leading global provider of information services on information technology. IDG was founded more than 25 years ago and now employs more than 7,700 people worldwide. IDG publishes more than 250 computer publications in 67 countries (see listing below). More than 70 million people read one or more IDG publications each month.

Launched in 1990, IDG Books Worldwide is today the #1 publisher of best-selling computer books in the United States. We are proud to have received 8 awards from the Computer Press Association in recognition of editorial excellence and three from Computer Currents' First Annual Readers' Choice Awards, and our best-selling ...*For Dummies*® series has more than 19 million copies in print with translations in 28 languages. IDG Books Worldwide, through a joint venture with IDG's Hi-Tech Beijing, became the first U.S. publisher to publish a computer book in the People's Republic of China. In record time, IDG Books Worldwide has become the first choice for millions of readers around the world who want to learn how to better manage their businesses.

Our mission is simple: Every one of our books is designed to bring extra value and skill-building instructions to the reader. Our books are written by experts who understand and care about our readers. The knowledge base of our editorial staff comes from years of experience in publishing, education, and journalism — experience which we use to produce books for the '90s. In short, we care about books, so we attract the best people. We devote special attention to details such as audience, interior design, use of icons, and illustrations. And because we use an efficient process of authoring, editing, and desktop publishing our books electronically, we can spend more time ensuring superior content and spend less time on the technicalities of making books.

You can count on our commitment to deliver high-quality books at competitive prices on topics you want to read about. At IDG Books Worldwide, we continue in the IDG tradition of delivering quality for more than 25 years. You'll find no better book on a subject than one from IDG Books Worldwide.

John J. Kilcullen

John Kilcullen
President and CEO
IDG Books Worldwide, Inc.

Acknowledgments

Our biggest thanks go to our readers, who helped make the first edition a howling success. Their feedback has helped improve this second edition of the book! We have way too many people to thank, so we would like to start out by thanking everybody who helped us that we don't mention by name. Actually, we couldn't have done it without you, even if we don't mention you here! Thanks for all the help, information, and encouragement.

Ed Tittel: I want to share my thanks with a large crew. First off, there's my family: Suzy, Austin, Chelsea, and Dusty — you were there for me when it counted. Thanks! Second, a talented crew of technical people helped me over a variety of humps, large and small. I would like to specifically mention Mark Gaither, Michael Stewart, Claire Sanders, Sebastian Hassinger, and Mike Erwin. You guys are the greatest! Third, there's a whole crowd of other folks whose information has helped me over the years, especially the originators of the Web — most notably, Tim Berners-Lee and the rest of the CERN team. I'd also like to thank the geniuses, sung and unsung, at NCSA, Netscape Communications, and anyplace else whose Web collections I visited, for helping pull the many strands of this book together. I'd also like to thank Steve James for sticking with me from the first edition to the second! Finally, I'd like to thank my lucky stars for making it possible for me to work at home and make writing a part of my daily routine.

Steve James: First and foremost I have to thank Ed Tittel for asking me to coauthor this book with him. He has been my inspiration and mentor in this, my first venture into the world of book publishing. My eternal gratitude to my understanding family, Trisha, Kelly, Chris, and Randle-Ann (cattus extraordinarius) for putting up with my writer's quirks and schedule, especially during late-night work sessions. My appreciation to Mark Gaither for his excellent technical editing and UNIX HTML tools screen shots, and Jeff Evans for providing Macintosh HTML tools screen shots and advice. And last, but certainly not least, my thanks to all of the HTML tool developers and HTML Web page authors on the Net for selflessly providing fantastic tools, information, and Web pages for the WWW community to enjoy.

Together, we want to thank the editorial staff at IDG Books Worldwide, especially Jennifer Ehrlich, one of the best Project Editors we've ever had the chance to work with; Leah Cameron, our Copy Editor; Amy Pedersen, the lady who made it all happen; Diane Steele, who let us keep this "strange torpedo" moving; and all the other editorial and production folks at IDG.

Please feel free to contact either of us, care of IDG books, IDG Books Worldwide, Inc., 919 East Hillsdale Blvd, Suite 400, Foster City, CA 94404. Ed's e-mail address is etittel@zilker.net; Steve's is snjames@wetlands.com.

(The publisher would like to give special thanks to Patrick J. McGovern, without whom this book would not have been possible.)

Credits

Senior Vice President and Publisher
Milissa L. Koloski

Associate Publisher
Diane Graves Steele

Brand Manager
Judith A. Taylor

Editorial Managers
Kristin A. Cocks
Mary Corder

Product Development Manager
Mary Bednarek

Editorial Executive Assistant
Richard Graves

Marketing Assistant
Holly Blake

Editorial Assistants
Constance Carlisle
Chris Collins
Kevin Spencer

Acquisitions Assistant
Gareth Hancock

Production Director
Beth Jenkins

Production Assistant
Jacalyn L. Pennywell

Supervisor of Project Coordination
Cindy L. Phipps

Supervisor of Page Layout
Kathie S. Schnorr

Supervisor of Graphics and Design
Shelley Lea

Reprint/Blueline Coordination
Tony Augsburger
Patricia R. Reynolds
Todd Klemme
Theresa Sánchez-Baker

Media/Archive Coordination
Leslie Popplewell
Melissa Stauffer
Jason Marcuson

Project Editor
Jennifer Ehrlich

Copy Editor
Leah P. Cameron

Technical Reviewer
James Michael Stewart

Project Coordination Assistant
Regina Snyder

Graphics Coordination
Gina Scott
Angela F. Hunckler

Production Page Layout
Cameron Booker
Linda M. Boyer
Kerri Cornell
Anna Rohrer
Kate Snell

Proofreaders
Melissa D. Buddendeck
Joel Draper
Jennifer Kaufeld
Betty Kish
Christine Meloy Beck
Gwenette Gaddis
Dwight Ramsey
Carl Saff
Robert Springer

Indexer
Sharon Hilgenberg

Cover Design
Kavish + Kavish

Contents at a Glance

Cartoons at a Glance

By Rich Tennant
Fax: 508-546-7747
E-mail: the5wave@tiac.net

page 7

page 55

page 171

page 291

page 273

page 321

page 243

page 357

Table of Contents

Introduction

● ●

*W*elcome to the wild, wacky, and wonderful possibilities inherent in the World Wide Web. In this book, we introduce you to the mysteries of the Hypertext Markup Language used to build Web pages, and we initiate you into the select, but growing, community of Web authors.

If you've tried to build your own Web pages before, but found it too forbidding, now you can relax. If you can dial a telephone or find your keys in the morning, you too can become an HTML author. (No kidding!)

In this book, we take a straightforward approach to telling you about authoring documents for the World Wide Web. We try to keep the amount of technobabble to a minimum and stick with plain English as much as possible. Besides plain talk about hypertext, HTML, and the Web, we include lots of sample programs and tag-by-tag instructions for building your very own Web pages.

We also include a peachy diskette with this book, that contains each and every HTML example in usable form and a number of other interesting widgets for your own documents. In addition, this diskette also includes the magnificent and bedazzling source materials for the *HTML For Dummies*, 2nd Edition, Web pages, which you might find to be a source of inspiration and raw material for your own uses! We also throw in lots of HTML tags and extensions to satisfy your hunger for HTML knowledge.

About This Book

Think of this book as a friendly, approachable guide to HTML and to building readable, attractive pages for the World Wide Web. Although HTML isn't hard to learn, remembering all the details needed to write interesting Web pages can be difficult. Some sample topics you'll find in this book include the following:

- ✔ the origins and history of the World Wide Web
- ✔ designing and building Web pages
- ✔ creating interesting page layouts
- ✔ testing and debugging your Web pages
- ✔ mastering the many aspects of Web publication

Although you might think that building Web pages requires years of training and advanced aesthetic capabilities, we hasten to point out that this just ain't so. If you can tell somebody how to drive from their house to yours, you can certainly build a Web document that does what you want it to. The purpose of this book isn't to turn you into a rocket scientist; it's to show you all the design and technical elements that you need to build a good-looking, readable Web page and to give you the know-how and confidence to go out and do it!

How to Use This Book

This book tells you what the World Wide Web is all about and how it works. Then it tells you what's involved in designing and building effective Web documents to bring your important ideas and information to the whole wide world, if that's what you want to do.

All HTML code appears in monospaced, screened type like this:

```
<HEAD><TITLE>What's in a Title?</TITLE></HEAD>...
```

When you type in HTML tags or other related information, be sure to copy the information exactly as you see it between the angle brackets (< and >) because that's part of the magic that makes HTML work. Other than that, you find out how to marshal and manage the content that makes your pages special. And we tell you exactly what you need to do to mix the elements of HTML with your own work.

Due to the margins in this book, some long lines of HTML markup, or designations of World Wide Web sites (called *URLs,* for Uniform Resource Locators), may wrap to the next line. On your computer though, these wrapped lines appear as a single line of HTML, or as a single URL, so don't insert a hard return when you see one of these wrapped lines. Each instance of wrapped code is noted as follows (with the subsequent lines a bit shorter):

Code wraps—
do not insert
hard return

```
http://www.infomagic.austin.com/nexus/plexus/lexus/sexus/
     this_is_a_deliberately_long.html
```

HTML doesn't care if you type tag text in uppercase, lowercase, or both (except character entities, which must be typed exactly as indicated in Chapter 6 of this book). In order for your own work to look like ours as much as possible, you should enter all HTML tag text in uppercase only.

Assume Makes an A** Out of U & Me

They say that making assumptions makes a fool out of the person who's making them and the person who's the subject of those assumptions. Nevertheless, we're going to make a few assumptions about you, gentle reader:

- ✔ You can turn your computer on and off.
- ✔ You know how to use a mouse and a keyboard.
- ✔ You want to build your own Web pages for fun, profit, or because it's part of your job.
- ✔ You have a working connection to the Internet.
- ✔ You have one of the many fine Web browsers available.

You don't need to be a master logician or a wizard in the arcane arts of programming, nor do you need a PhD in computer science. You don't even need a detailed sense of what's going on in the innards of your computer to deal with the material in this book.

If you can write a sentence and know the difference between a heading and a paragraph, you can build and deploy your own documents on the World Wide Web. If you have an imagination and the ability to communicate what's important to you, you've already mastered the key ingredients necessary to build useful, attractive Web pages. The rest is details, and we help you with those!

How This Book Is Organized

This book contains eight major parts. Each part contains two or more chapters, and each chapter contains several modular sections. Anytime you need help or information, just pick up the book and start anywhere you feel like it, or use the table of contents and index to look up specific topics or keywords.

Here is a breakdown of the eight parts and what you can find in each one:

Part I: Building Better Web Pages

This part sets the stage and includes an overview of and an introduction to the World Wide Web, its history, and the software that people use to mine its treasures. It also explains how the Web works, including the Hypertext Markup Language to which this book is devoted, and the server-side software and services that deliver information to end-users.

HTML documents, also called Web pages, are the fundamental units of information organization and delivery on the Web. Here, you also learn what HTML is about and how hypertext can enrich ordinary text. You can also work through a primer on basic Web page layout and design to help you begin the process of building your own HTML documents.

Part II: A Tour of HTML Basics

HTML mixes ordinary text with special strings of characters, called *markup*, that instruct browsers how to display HTML documents. In this part of the book, you find out about markup in general and HTML in particular. This includes logical groupings for HTML tags, a complete dictionary of HTML tags, and an equally detailed discussion of HTML character entities. By the time you finish with Part II, you should have a good overall idea of what HTML is and what it can do.

Part III: Advanced HTML

Part III takes all the elements covered in Part II and puts them together to help you find out how to build commercial-grade HTML documents. This includes building complex pages, developing on-screen forms to solicit information and feedback, and creating clickable image maps to let graphics guide your user's on-screen navigation. Finally, you get a chance to examine the work being done to extend HTML beyond its standard definitions.

Part IV: Beyond HTML? CGI Programs and "Real" Applications

Much of the real power of the World Wide Web lies in its ability to support user interaction and to link all kinds of server-based programs into attractive, visually-appealing documents that are easy to understand and control. In this part of the book, you go behind the scenes on your Web server to understand how the Web can absorb and handle input from users and interact with them. By the time you finish this section, you should understand how open–ended and powerful your Web documents can be.

Part V: Call the Exterminator! Debugging Web Pages

Once you build your HTML documents, the real fun begins as your work meets the ultimate test: what users like or don't like about it. As you get ready to release your Web site to a possibly indifferent world, you need to be prepared to catch and kill potential bugs yourself. You also need to be armed with strategies to enlist user feedback, to help you effectively communicate online, and to avoid having to deal with too many problems once you take your work public. Part V gives you the information you need to produce and maintain quality pages.

Part VI: Going Public: Serving Up Your Web Pages

After you test and debug your work, it's time to publish your documents. In this part of the book, you find out how to blow your own horn and let the world know, not just where your pages are, but why they're worth a visit. You also prepare yourself to deal with the potential onslaught of users and to decide whether you want to put your pages on somebody else's Web server or build your own.

Part VII: It's Tool-time! HTML Development Tools and More

When it comes to building HTML, you can do it alone, with only your trusty text editor. But it doesn't have to be that way: In Part VII, we expose you to the many different tools available to help you build the Web pages of your dreams and to manage those pages once they're built. Along the way, you get a chance to see what's available for UNIX, Macintosh, Windows, and other computing platforms by way of HTML editors and related tools and Web servers and related services.

Part VIII: The Part of Tens

In the concluding part of the book, we sum up and distill the very essence of what we've presented. Here, you get a chance to review the top dos and don'ts for HTML markup, to rethink your views on document design, and to catch and kill any potential bugs and errors in your pages (before anybody else sees them). Finally, you end your adventure by revisiting your Web server situation as you reconsider whether you should place your pages on an Internet provider's Web server or build a Web server of your very own.

Icons Used in This Book

This icon signals technical details that are informative and interesting but not critical to writing HTML. Skip these if you want (but please, come back and read them later).

This icon flags useful information that makes HTML markup, Web page design, or other important stuff even less complicated than you feared it might be.

This icon points out information you shouldn't pass by — don't overlook these gentle reminders (the life you save could be your own).

Be cautious when you see this icon. It warns you of things you should or shouldn't do; the bomb is meant to emphasize that the consequences of ignoring these bits of wisdom can be severe.

When you see this spider web symbol, it flags the presence of Web-based resources that you can go to and investigate further. You can also find all these references on the *Jump Pages* on the diskette that comes with this book!

Where to Go from Here

This is the part where you pick a direction and hit the road! *HTML For Dummies, 2nd Edition* is a lot like the parable of the seven blind men and the elephant: It almost doesn't matter where you start out, you look at lots of different stuff as you prepare yourself to build your own Web pages. Who cares if anybody else thinks you're just goofing around — we know you're getting ready to have the time of your life.

Enjoy!

Part I
Building Better Web Pages

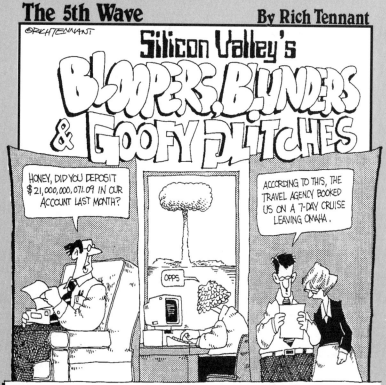

In this part . . .

HTML stands for HyperText Markup Language. It's a driving force behind the myriad of colorful interactive screens of text, graphics, and multimedia — called Web pages — popping up all over the place today on the World Wide Web (known as WWW or W3). Before you can understand the ins and outs of building Web pages, you need to learn a little about the World Wide Web and the Internet universe in which it lives.

Part I is your introduction to the WWW and includes a quick review of Web basics, along with a blisteringly short history of the Web and how it works. This coverage will be old hat for seasoned Internauts, but should provide some background information for those less well-traveled in Cyberspace. By the time you make it through the first three chapters, you should have a good understanding of what the Web is about, why HTML is important, and what it can (and can't) do.

Along the way, you should also gain an appreciation for the vast skeins of knowledge, wit, folklore, esoterica, and information already strung through the WWW. It's humbling to think that your own work with HTML may someday result in stringing that web just a bit further!

Chapter 1

The Web's THE Place to Be!

· ·

In This Chapter

▶ Defining the World Wide Web

▶ Examining other Internet search tools

▶ Making the most of the Web — browsers and search tools

▶ Examining Web background and terminology

▶ Looking at exploding Web growth

▶ Interpreting Web pages

▶ Accessing the Web

· ·

*T*o understand HTML, you first have to understand the environment that it serves and the world in which that environment operates. HTML is a text-based markup language that provides the underpinnings for one of the most exciting information search and navigation environments ever developed: This environment is called the World Wide Web (Web, WWW, or W3, for short). The Web represents a major step forward in making all kinds of information accessible to average folks like you and me.

From Small Things, Big Things Sometimes Come

Tim Berners-Lee and his colleagues at the European Laboratory for Particle Physics (CERN) in Geneva, Switzerland, had no idea what they were starting when they began hacking together their ideas for the Web back in March of 1989. Nevertheless, they succeeded in starting a strange and wonderful thing that has taken the whole Internet community by storm. Their mission was to build an online system for ordinary users to easily share data, without having to master arcane commands or esoteric interfaces. By 1992, users outside CERN were creating Web pages, and developers were creating powerful, graphical browsers for a broad range of desktop computers and workstations. By 1993, the Web had emerged as the most popular tool for Internet *surfing*.

What's in the words?

As you read through this book, you'll probably encounter some words of Web jargon that you don't recognize along the way. You'll also encounter a fair number of acronyms, like HTTP, that may not make a lot of sense to you, either. Don't worry, this is pretty normal when tackling a new subject in the computer world, where gibberish is the norm and acronyms proliferate like mushrooms! The good news is we've included a glossary at the end of the book that contains definitions for most terms that you may not know and for all acronyms that we could find herein. Therefore, if you see a word you don't know, check the glossary: You may find enlightenment there! If not, drop us an e-mail and make us explain the word to you; maybe we don't know what it means either!!

To get started surfing, you need a way to access the Internet, a Web browser, and information about where to enter the Web. After that, you can scan the information that shows up on your screen and follow chains of information for the rest of your life (without ever again having to come up for air).

But wait a minute! Before you get lost in its infinite strands, you may want to consider a few more details about the Web's workings. (But don't let us stop you from trying it out — just check in right here when you come back!)

What is the Web, and where is it strung?

By now, you probably have a vague idea that the Web is a vast, amorphous blob of text, image, audio, and video data that is scattered across networks and computers worldwide. Hence comes the name, World Wide Web.

And now, a word from our sponsor . . .

According to Tim Berners-Lee, one of the Web's chief architects (and a founding father for the original development at CERN), the World Wide Web is "the universe of network-accessible information, an embodiment of human knowledge. . . . It has a body of software, and a set of protocols and conventions. W3 uses hypertext and multimedia techniques to make the Web easy for anyone to roam, browse, and contribute to." (From a Web page written by Berners-Lee that you can find at `http://www.w3.org/pub/WWW/WWW/` entitled *The World Wide Web*). By working with HTML, you too can roam, browse, and contribute to the Web!

Before the Web: Other Internet Navigation Tools

To understand the extraordinary impact of W3, you may want to look at previous Internet navigation tools. These other tools require considerably more user expertise than do Web browsers. While you're taking the trip down memory lane, please keep the following in mind: Although Web browsers supplant the functionality of many navigation tools, they work with these tools as well. Through HTML links, browsers call on other services to locate and retrieve files, messages, and other goodies from the vast Internet storehouse.

FTP (no, it's not about delivering flowers — that's FTD!)

FTP (File Transfer Protocol) is a cross-platform tool for transferring files to and from computers anywhere on the Internet. *Cross-platform* means that you don't have to use the same kind of computer operating system to access files on a remote system. Figure 1-1 shows a graphical FTP menu; notice the PC file system on the left (what's on your machine) and the remote file system on the right (what's on the FTP server). By navigating the directories, you can copy files between the two systems, as your access rights allow. (In English, *navigating the directories* means finding the location in a file system where the files you're after reside; and *access rights* refer to your ability to see, copy, delete, or write files within the FTP server's directories.)

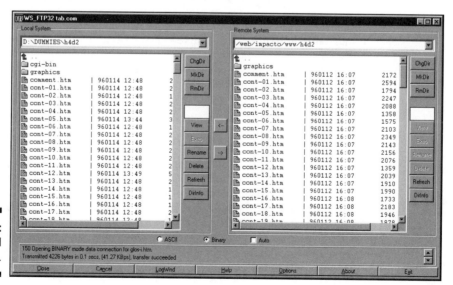

Figure 1-1:
A graphical view of FTP.

Burrowing around in Gopherspace

Gopher is the creation of a team of dedicated programmers at the University of Minnesota, home of "The Golden Gophers." More than just a totemic animal, Gopher is a good tool to use when browsing for files on the Internet. Gopher servers are extensively interlinked, much like the Web. In addition, all Gopher interaction occurs through a consistent menu interface that makes all systems look alike. (See Figure 1-2.) You can search by keyword or filename, so that you have more flexibility in finding your way around.

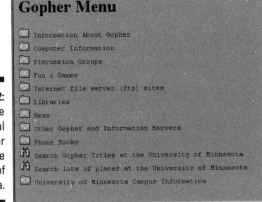

Figure 1-2:
The
primeval
Gopher
at the
University of
Minnesota.

The beauty of mailing lists and electronic mail

A little-known bit of trivia is that much information on the Internet is available through e-mail and through tools like FTP and Gopher. By stating the proper requests to the right e-mail servers — thereby accessing mail service programs such as *listserv* and *majordomo* — users with sufficient savvy can get to just about anything on the Internet.

Usenet

Usenet is a worldwide message system, where anyone can read and post articles. Usenet organizes its articles into named groups by topic and focus. These groups have varying degrees of internal organization — from strict moderation to freeform conversation. In some cases, you can approach Usenet with a specific question and come away with an answer immediately, but other queries can go unanswered for weeks on end. Persistence, coupled with an appreciation for Usenet's workings and *netiquette,* is your key to success. (Figure 1-3 shows a listing of Usenet messages.)

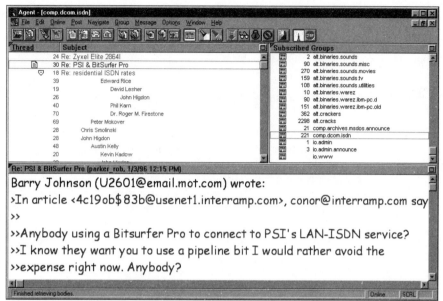

Figure 1-3:
A listing of
Usenet
messages.

Wide-Area Information Service (WAIS)

WAIS (pronounced "ways" or "wase") is one of a handful of Internet search tools that can spread itself across the network to scour multiple archives and handle multiple data formats. It searches tirelessly throughout the entire Internet for the information you request. WAIS can help you find things, especially when you're not sure of precise filenames, menu entries, or other name-specific information.

To learn more about the Internet, take a trip to your local bookstore. You'll find no shortage of Internet-related titles there. (We counted over 100 on our last visit!) You should pay particular attention to John R. Levine, Carol Baroudi, and Margaret Levine Young's *The Internet For Dummies*, 3rd Edition and Levine and Young's *More Internet For Dummies*, 2nd Edition, (both published by IDG Books Worldwide, Inc., 1995).

Why is the Web a "Big Deal"?

We hope that you can come up with answers to this question on your own by now. But we'll run this one down, just to be sure: The World Wide Web is a major development in information access on the Internet. W3 is a big deal because it covers an astonishing amount of ground; it makes finding the way around huge collections of data easy and intuitive for users; and it hides most of the ugly details of how to grab and use information on the Internet.

Any one reason would make the Web important and useful; all of them together make it a genuine step forward in the way we use and share information as a part of our daily lives.

Of Browsers and Search Tools

For most end users, their Web access software — called a *browser* or a Web client — is the most important piece of Internet software that they use. Today, you can find many browsers for PCs running Windows, a more limited selection for DOS-only machines, and several options for the Macintosh, UNIX machines, and other platforms. All graphical Web browsers share a common, point-and-click approach to interacting with information. Even character-based browsers, like Lynx, still make it easy to pick and follow links by selecting the appropriate highlighted text. In the next few paragraphs, we give you a cursory look at browsers.

Lynx

Lynx is a text-only Web browser. That is, it cannot display or deliver graphical or multimedia elements (although it can be configured to display graphics using an external file viewer on appropriate systems). Even so, Lynx provides useful Web functionality for users on so-called *dumb terminals* because it supports keyboard navigation and boldface display of hypertext links (which is where we think that the program got its name: Lynx = links; get it?). Figure 1-4 shows a sample Lynx display.

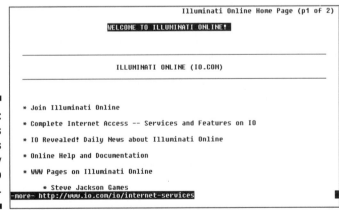

Figure 1-4: Lynx uses text displays effectively for Web pages.

Netscape

Netscape, the brainchild of Marc Andreesen, is the Internet's most popular graphical Web browser. It offers clear evidence of its developer's wisdom and experience, and it includes some advanced features not found in other Web browsers. The list of features, advancements, and add-ons to Netscape is a list that boggles the mind — with additions made almost daily. Available both as shareware and in a commercial release, Netscape provides one of the best and most popular Web interfaces that we've encountered anywhere. See Figure 1-5 for a look at Netscape's welcome screen.

Internet Explorer

You can get Internet Explorer, Microsoft's entry into the Web browser arena, in the Plus! add-on package for Windows 95. However, you can obtain the most recent release from the Microsoft Web site at `http://www.microsoft.com`. (We're told that Microsoft is planning to release 16-bit versions that run on Windows 3.1, 3.11, and Windows for Workgroups; they're even planning a port to NT. Perhaps by the time you read this, you can find all these elements at the Microsoft Web site.) Although it's a new player in this game, Internet Explorer has already made significant wrinkles in the Web community. Like Netscape, it has proprietary HTML tag elements in its list of features. The Internet Explorer is quickly becoming a popular interface to the Web and promises to cover Windows users of all stripes soon!

Figure 1-5: Netscape is used by over 70 percent of Web surfers.

Mosaic

Mosaic is a graphical Web browser developed by a team of programmers at the National Center for Supercomputing Applications (NCSA). One of the original programmers, Marc Andreesen, eventually left NCSA to form his own Internet service company — Netscape. Mosaic was the first graphical browser for the Web, and it continues to hold its own against the *newbie* browsers. You can find many flavors of Mosaic today, including ones for X Windows (primarily for UNIX systems), Microsoft Windows, and the Macintosh. Mosaic was the first *full-featured* graphical browser and has spawned many clones.

Uniform Resources on the Web

The most significant feature of the World Wide Web is its ability to shield and even protect users from the harsh UNIX environment of the Internet. With the Web, locating information is greatly simplified. You find Web resources identified with special names — called *URLs* or *Uniform Resource Locators* — which describe the protocols that you use to access the resources and point to the resources' Internet locations.

URLs hold the keys to the Web

As you examine a URL for a specific HTML file, it looks something like this:

```
http://www.w3.org:80/hypertext/WWW/Addressing/Addressing.html#spot
|—1—|———2———| 3 |————————4————————|———5———| - 6 -|
```

This URL is composed of six parts that work as follows:

1. **Protocol/data source:** For network resources, this part is usually the name of the protocol used to access the data that resides on the other end of the link. The syntax for this part of the name is as follows:

   ✔ **ftp://** — points to a file accessible through the File Transfer Protocol.

   ✔ **gopher://** — points to a file system index accessible through the Gopher protocol.

   ✔ **http://** — points to a hypertext document (typically, an HTML file) accessible through the HyperText Transfer Protocol.

   ✔ **mailto://** — links to an application that allows you to compose a message to send through e-mail to a predefined address.

- **news://** — points to a Usenet newsgroup and uses the Network News Transfer Protocol (NNTP) to access the information.

- **telnet://** — links to a remote log-in on another Internet computer, typically to select from a predefined menu.

- **WAIS://** — points to a Wide-Area Information Server on the Internet and provides access to a system of indexed databases.

- **file://** — indicates that the file is local and is not a public Web page (that is, not available outside your directory or local network). Use this syntax for local data (typically, HTML files from your desktop machine's hard disks or other drives), but note that the syntax can vary from browser to browser. If you're desperate for a more complete discussion of accessing local files, see the sidebar "URL syntax and punctuation for local file access."

2. **Domain name:** The domain name for the Web server where the desired Web page or other resource resides.

3. **Port address:** In most cases, the default port address for HTTP is *:80* (and you can omit it), but you may see URLs with other numbers in use; this number identifies the process address that a Web session needs to connect with. In general, if a number appears in the URL, it's a good idea to include it (even if the number is the default *:80*).

4. **Directory path:** The location of the Web page in the Web server's file system.

5. **Object name:** The actual name of the HTML file for the desired Web page or the name of any other resource that you require.

6. **Spot:** Sometimes, getting users to the HTML file isn't enough: You want to drop them at a particular location *within* the file. By preceding the name of an HTML *anchor* with a pound sign (#) and tacking it onto the HTML file name, you can direct a browser to jump right to a specific location. Using this structure is especially handy for larger documents, where readers might otherwise need to do quite a bit of scrolling to get to the right information.

Making those URL keys fit

All in all, the most important thing to remember about URLs is to enter them *exactly as they're written* because they don't work if they're not exactly correct. When you use a Web browser, cutting and pasting URLs into a hotlist, bookmark, or text file is better than writing them out by hand because you reduce the possibility of a transcription error.

URL syntax and punctuation for local file access

When trying to access local files, you can first look for a menu selection in your browser that lets you search your local file system (like "Open File" or "Open Local File"). If that doesn't work, we've had pretty good results with the following approach:

```
file:///<drive ID>|<directory spec>/
   <filename>
```

Notice the three forward slashes after the colon. After the drive ID (which would be a letter for DOS or the volume name for Macintosh, NetWare, and so on), use a vertical

bar character (|) in place of a colon. Then, when specifying the directory path (spec), use forward slashes (/) to separate directory levels. Follow the path with the exact name of the file, and you should be able to access it with your browser.

If the preceding strategy doesn't work for you, look in your browser's Help file for enlightenment: Often, it's just waiting a few screens away. Search on a phrase such as "Open File" or "Open Local File," and you should get the information that you need.

For more information on URLs, consult this URL:

```
http://www.w3.org/hypertext/WWW/Addressing/Addressing.html
```

This resource describes the details for URL syntax and supported protocols and points to specifications and other documents on the subject. A word to the wise: The CERN site gets a lot of traffic, so you may get *timed out* trying to connect. (In English, *timed out* means that you wait forever, and then your browser tells you that it can't retrieve the page!) We've had good luck getting there on off-hours, like 3 a.m. eastern standard time.

Danger! Explosive Growth

The word *exploding* conjures up an image of something that isn't safe to crawl onto, but exploding is just what the Web is doing in terms of growth. Even though its introduction (in 1991) makes it one of the newest Internet applications around, the Web has already become the most popular Internet application of all time. According to the work of one Web aficionado, former MIT student Michael Gray (now a principal at net.genesis, a successful Internet consultancy), the Internet has an annual growth rate of over 1,000 percent (or it increases 10 times each year, if you like smaller numbers)!

Wherever you get your statistics about W3, you find the unanimous opinion that Web usage is growing dramatically and user ranks are swelling robustly. The only real question then becomes, "How can I possibly manage to find what I really need out there on the Web?" For Web publishers, this question translates into, "How can I let the people know where my pages are?"

Following are the URLs for the references that we mentioned here:

✔ Michael Gray's "Growth of the Web"

```
http:/www.netgen.com/info/growth.html
```

✔ A good general source for Web and Internet statistics with links to most other Web and Internet surveys and statistics worth mentioning (including "official" and personal efforts in that direction)

```
http://WWW.Stars.com:80/Vlib/Misc/Statistics.html
```

✔ We also recommend that you check out the Graphics, Visualization, and Usability Center's fourth WWW User Survey at

```
http://www.cc.gatech.edu/gvu/user_surveys/survey-10-1995/
```

A Scintillating Survey of the Web, Worldwide

At this point, you should have some idea about the Web's origins; now you can take a quick look at some of the many treasures that W3 offers.

Jumping-off points galore

Every browser comes with a predefined home page; many offer excellent starting points for your Web travels. Three browsers in particular — Netscape, Internet Explorer, and NCSA Mosaic — offer outstanding home pages with "Starting Points," topic indexes, and search capabilities to help you locate items of interest. However, the Web is a mystical thing — whose circumference is nowhere, and whose center, everywhere — so no "perfect starting point" really exists.

Search pages, anyone?

You can find a variety of search pages on the Web. These pages provide a link to background applications that can examine loads of data repositories on the Internet and, based on keywords that you supply, can return URLs matching the topics that you want.

The major search pages are nicely represented in a number of places, but we find the Yahoo! "Searching the Web" page to be most useful. The URL for this page is

```
http://www.yahoo.com/Computers_and_Internet/Internet/World_Wide_Web/
Searching_the_Web/
```

Try it on for size; pick a search engine and try a search with a term of particular interest. (For best results, pick something specific like *coriander,* instead of something general like *spices.*)

As you travel around the Web, pay attention to page layouts and to the use of indexes, graphics, and hotlists. You can glean a great deal from these examples, both good and bad. You can also select View Source from your browser's menu to see the HTML code that represents each of these pages!

Under the Hood: How the Web Works

Now that you know what the Web is, where it came from, and what a big deal it has become, it's time to start grappling with how W3 actually works. Despite the volume of connected information and the different ways of presenting and delivering that information, the Web works through a basic set of mechanisms.

The Web is more than just the browser that you use on your desktop. The hidden structure of the Web is just as important as the utility that you use to access it. The Web has two labor-handling divisions: storage/retrieval and display/input. The Web *server* (located elsewhere on the network) typically handles the storage and retrieval part. The browser on the user's workstation (sometimes called a *client*) handles the display of information and recognition of input, when appropriate.

In the grand scheme of the computer world, this approach to handling information delivery is called *client/server computing.* Client/server has become an industry buzzword; nevertheless, the approach does confer some appreciable benefits:

✔ Because this approach divides the processing load, clients can concentrate on providing the best possible interface to users. Also, the client's concentration simplifies the offering of cool graphical displays and powerful visual controls.

✔ Likewise, servers can concentrate on maximizing their ability to service lots of requests; the division of labor lets the Web servers handle tens of thousands of resource requests per day.

✔ Another benefit of the client/server split derives from the location where the server stores the information that clients use: Residence on a server makes information ideal for sharing; permits better control over the data; and lets information providers decide how much power and capability that they want their servers to provide.

✔ By keeping dollars and data concentrated in one place — namely, at the server — the client/server approach helps to maximize performance on the server (where it's going to do the greatest good for the most users). The server environment also ensures information protection through backups, more rigorous control of data access, and accurate logging of request statistics (known as *hits*).

In short, clients handle the job of user interaction, and servers tackle the rapid retrieval and delivery of information. Client/server capabilities are well-realized on the World Wide Web, which features powerful, graphical clients (browsers) and fast, powerful servers. By working together, these elements contribute to the Web's burgeoning popularity.

Networking Takes Protocols

In diplomatic circles, a protocol is a set of rules that keeps professionals, friends and enemies alike, from making fools of each other (or themselves). For networks, methods of bulletproof communication are equally necessary and appreciated. Thus, you shouldn't be surprised to learn that the rules and formats that govern the methods by which computers communicate over a network are also called *protocols*.

How Webs talk: the HyperText Transfer Protocol (HTTP)

HTTP is an Internet protocol for a specific application — the World Wide Web. It provides a way for Web clients and servers to communicate with one another, primarily through the exchange of messages from clients (like "Give me this." or "Get me that.") and servers (like "Here's the page you asked for." or "Huh? I can't find what you're looking for.").

Acronymophobes, beware!

One thing you've got to realize, if you're going to become a real WebMaster, is that when you climb onto the Web, you're joining the Internet community. If there's ever been an unabashed bastion for acronyms — those multiletter combinations that nerds use to refer to things like personal computers (PCs), a disk operating system (DOS), random-access memory (RAM), or a compact disc, read-only-memory (CD-ROM) — it's with the Internet crowd.

Because we're talking about Web lore, the term *WebMaster* is a ubiquitous name for a person who holds the Web protocols on high, is a

veteran of the Web trenches, and lives, eats, and breathes the Web. You might be lucky and good enough to be called a WebMaster yourself — someday!

So, if your most fiendish nightmare is of drowning in a bowl of alphabet soup, maybe you'd better rethink your Web-oriented efforts! That's because networking in general, and the Internet in particular, is a field that revels in acronyms. When it comes to discussing Internet protocols, you'll find no better gathering spot for bizarre alphanumeric combinations.

To fully understand HTTP, you need to fully understand TCP/IP. A longish sort of acronym, *TCP/IP* stands for Transfer Control Protocol/Internet Protocol, which is the name given to the full set of protocols used on the Internet. But to begin writing good Web documents, you don't need to know much about either topic. However, we have included a list of reference materials for you masochists out there.

Welcome to the Nebulous Zone . . .

It's a place where different kinds of computers can freely exchange information with one another, where mere implementations bow to the demands of an all-encompassing standard. TCP/IP is a world unto itself: More bits use TCP/IP in a day on today's Internet than are required to store every piece of printed material known to mankind before 1950.

When it comes to TCP/IP, there's a lot to learn and a lot to know. Covering TCP/IP in any depth is way beyond the scope of this book. Therefore, we'd like to give you some choice references:

- The Internet is the subject of at least two other . . . *For Dummies* books: *The Internet For Dummies*, 3rd Edition (IDG Books Worldwide, Inc., 1995) by John R. Levine, Carol Baroudi, and Margaret Levine Young; and *More Internet For Dummies,* 2nd Edition (IDG Books Worldwide, Inc., 1995) by Levine and Young. Both books are a good place for beginners to start investigating the basics of TCP/IP.

- John Quarterman and Smoot Carl-Mitchell are the authors of *Practical Internetworking with TCP/IP and UNIX* (Addison-Wesley, 1993). This book is aimed at the system or network administrator for a TCP/IP network who wants to understand how and why things work.

✔ *TCP/IP For Dummies* by Marshall Wilensky and Candace Leiden (IDG Books Worldwide, Inc., 1995) is a great place to continue your TCP/IP investigations. In addition to covering the topic in wonderfully amusing detail, the book provides a gentle introduction to TCP/IP that is hard to beat.

✔ Matthew Flint Arnett is the first in a series of 14 coauthors for *Inside TCP/IP* (New Riders Press 1994), another book aimed at helping those who must run a TCP/IP network or internetwork, or those who must oversee an Internet connection.

✔ O'Reilly & Associates covers TCP/IP with a Nutshell handbook for UNIX system administrators, *TCP/IP Network Administration*, by Craig Hunt.

✔ A truly definitive look at TCP/IP comes from Douglas E. Comer, author of *Internetworking with TCP/IP*, a 3-volume set (Prentice-Hall 1991, 1991, 1993; Volumes 2 and 3 were authored with David L. Stevens). Comer's books are widely regarded as the best general references on the subject.

✔ Another comprehensive 2-volume treatise on TCP/IP, called *TCP/IP Illustrated, Volumes 1 and 2* is available from W. Richard Stevens (assisted by Gary R. Wright on the second volume, Addison-Wesley 1994). These books are more up to date than Comer's, and they offer detailed "war stories" taken straight from life on the Internet. For a reference that brings many salient TCP/IP details together in one place, this set is a good choice.

✔ The ultimate authority on TCP/IP comes from a standards body called the Internet Architecture Board (IAB). Within the IAB, the Internet Engineering Task Force (IETF) drafts and maintains Internet standards of all kinds, including those for protocols, in the form of numbered documents called "Requests for Comment" (RFCs). See Table 1-1 for more information on the IETF RFCs.

For a listing of all the current protocol-related RFCs, consult RFC 1720 "Internet Official Protocol Standards," which is available in at least three ways. (If 1720 isn't current anymore, it'll tell you it's been made obsolete by a new document, and you can follow a link to the new reigning standard.)

If you take the time to poke around in the RFC collection, you'll be going straight to the horse's mouth, where TCP/IP and related matters are concerned!

Table 1-1	Three methods for examining RFCs
Service	*Method*
e-mail	Send e-mail to `mailserv@ds.internic.net` and type **file/ftp/rfc/rfc1720.txt** in the message body
FTP	Anonymous FTP to `ds.internet.net` (password = your e-mail address). Look in directory rfc/ for the file named rfc1720.txt

(continued)

Table 1-1 *(continued)*

Service	Method
Web	`<URL: http://www.cis.ohio-state.edu/htbin/rfc/rfc1720.html>` for the contents of RFC 1720 `<URL: http://www.cis.ohio-state.edu/hypertext/information/rfc.html>` has general RFC information

The straight dope on HTTP

Protocols that link clients and servers together must handle requests and responses. Consequently, you'll not be surprised to know that information exchanges on the Web happen in four parts, all classed as specific message types for HTTP.

- **Connection:** Occurs when a client tries to connect to a specific Web server (your browser may display a status message such as `Connecting to HTTP Server`). If the client can't make the connection, the attempt usually times out and the browser displays a `Connection timed out` message.

- **Request:** The client asks for the Web resource that it's looking for. The request includes the protocol to use (which indicates the type of resource), the name of the object to find, and information about how the server should respond to the client.

- **Response:** Now it's the server's turn. If the server can deliver the requested object, it responds with a delivery in the manner requested by the client. If it can't deliver, the server sends an error message explaining why not.

- **Close:** After the server transfers information in response to the request, the connection between client and server is closed. You can easily reopen the connection with another request — for example, by clicking on a link in the current object — that jumps you back to reestablish the connection.

After it completely transfers the requested object, HTTP has done its job. Then the browser must interpret and display what the server delivered, and another strand in the Web unfurls.

HTML: Hypertext Markup Language

After the Web server returns the response to a Web request, the browser takes over to interpret and display the information.

HTML is a *markup language* that describes the structure of a Web document's content plus some behavioral characteristics. All Web browsers are able to understand and interpret this standard language. HTML is a subset of a larger markup language, SGML, called Standard Generalized Markup Language. (That's as much as you need to know about SGML in order to write Web documents.)

HTML is a way of representing text and linking that text to other kinds of resources — including sound files, graphics files, multimedia files, and so on — that allows the concurrent display of different kinds of data and lets different resources augment and reinforce one another.

As delivered by a Web server, HTML is nothing more than a plain text file that includes two kinds of text:

- ✔ **The content**: Text or information for display or playback on the client's screen, speakers, and so on
- ✔ **The markup**: Text or information to control the display or to point to other information items in need of display or playback

Also, a browser must be prepared to convert a third kind of data — encoded files — and to hand them off to the right kind of helper application. This hand-off may involve a graphics program for an icon or image, a sound player program to handle audio, a video player program to play back a video file, or any other program necessary to reproduce a particular kind of information.

HTML files include both control information (tags) and content (text), which together describe the appearance and contents of Web pages. The HTML language also provides the mechanisms for tying in other Internet protocols and services on the Web — like FTP, Gopher, Usenet, e-mail, WAIS, telnet, and HTTP — so that Web pages can deliver many kinds of resources.

Accessing the Web

The crucial ingredient in gaining access to the Web — the one that lives up to the "World Wide" in its name — is the attachment to the Internet. In fact, the biggest constraint on your enjoyment of the Web is likely to be the size of the pipe that connects you to the Internet (and it to you). The term *pipe* refers to how much data the connection between you and the Web server can accommodate; like a water pipe, the more capacious the connection between you and your server, the faster things can move. Because waiting for screens to complete is a big drag, the faster the data goes, the better you'll like it!

Following are the two basic ways to go for your Internet link-ups:

- ✔ Over the telephone system and into another computer or network that's connected to the Internet
- ✔ Over a network and onto the Internet (or onto another computer that's properly connected)

You need to contact your ISP (Internet service provider) to get detailed information on how to maximize your speed and access to the Web.

Chapter 2

Getting Hyper

• •

In This Chapter

▶ Understanding basic HTML concepts

▶ Linking up the strands in the Web

▶ Looking for hypertext examples

▶ Getting past hypertext — to hypermedia

▶ Going for the graphics

▶ Dealing with multimedia display/playback

▶ Bringing multiple media together on the Web

• •

*T*he real secret behind the Hypertext Markup Language is that there is no secret: Everything's out in the open in an HTML document, just waiting for the right interpretation. The beauty of HTML is its simple content — just a stream of plain characters — which makes virtually any text editor a potential HTML generator. The challenge of using HTML is working with its sensitivities. That is, HTML relies on the order in which its characters occur and the way that they're used to produce the right results.

Even though HTML can be forgiving (when you use *some* browsers to view documents with *certain* omitted or misstated elements), the best way to use HTML is to understand and work within its structure. Because your readers can use so many different browsers, the only way to get consistent Web page appearance and behavior is to know the rules for creating HTML documents and to use them to your readers' advantage!

This chapter presents the fundamental ideas behind HTML and introduces the concepts and operation of hypertext. Along the way, we hope that you begin to appreciate some of the basic principles behind building well-structured, readable Web pages.

HTML Basics

HTML stands for HyperText Markup Language. Its name reflects the two key concepts that make it work (and that make the World Wide Web such an incredible phenomenon):

- **Hypertext:** A way of creating multimedia documents; also a method for providing links within and between documents

- **Markup language:** A method for embedding special tags that describe the structure as well as the behavior of a document (not a way of discussing a preschooler's efforts with crayons on the wall!)

The simplicity and power of HTML markup let anyone create Web documents for private or public use. The power of hypertext, with its built-in support for multimedia and document links, creates the threads that compose the incredible breadth and reach of the Web. Making Web documents is so easy and straightforward that anyone can do it — as long as you can play the game by its rules.

Of Links and Sausages

HTML supports links within the same document and to completely different data elements elsewhere on the Web. Both types of links work the same way: You simply put the correct HTML tags around text or graphics to create an *active* (linked) area. Then when readers visit your Web site and click on the active area, they're transported to another spot within the same file, to another document in the same Web, or off to another place somewhere out on the Net. Figure 2-1 shows the *HTML For Dummies Hotlist* that includes links to several Web resources. (They're the items beneath the heading "Here are a few of our favorite Web spots:".) Each of these links can carry you off to a valuable source of information.

The method of indicating a link varies from one browser to the next, but all browsers give some kind of visual clue that you're selecting an active area of the screen. You may see text underlined in a bright color, the font changed to bold, or a graphic outlined in a contrasting color. You may see image maps without direct visual clues other than a changing set of coordinates (in the browser's status line) that correspond to the location of your mouse cursor on-screen. Using this type of link is a bit like playing an adventure game: You're not always sure where you're going or what you'll find after you get there!

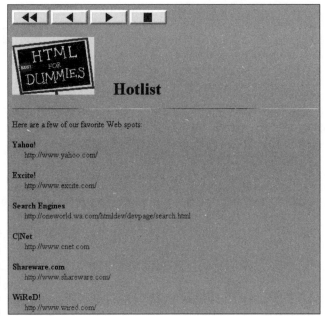

Here are a few of our favorite Web spots:

Yahoo!
http://www.yahoo.com/

Excite!
http://www.excite.com/

Search Engines
http://oneworld.wa.com/htmldev/devpage/search.html

C|Net
http://www.cnet.com

Shareware.com
http://www.shareware.com/

WiReD!
http://www.wired.com/

Figure 2-1:
A simple
HTML link
example.

Jumping around inside documents

One variety of link connects points inside the same document; such links are called *internal anchors*. WebMasters often use this kind of link from a table of contents (at the top of an HTML file) to the related sections throughout the document. Also, you can use this method to jump directly to the start of the document from its end; it beats the heck out of scrolling up through a long file.

This points to a key advantage of hypertext — namely, the capability to circumvent the linear nature of paper documents by providing rapid, obvious ways to navigate within (or among) documents. Sure, you can do the same thing with the table of contents or the index of a paper book by looking up and flipping the pages yourself (what a pain!). Hypertext automates this task for you, so that you can effortlessly jump around inside and between documents by creating links that are a snap (or actually, a click) to use.

Jumping across documents (and services)

By using a combination of links and Uniform Resource Locators (URLs), HTML can link your page to other Web pages, no matter where they are on the Web. Because URLs can reference a variety of protocols and services on the Internet (not just other HTML files), you can link through telnet, WAIS, Gopher, FTP, Usenet newsgroups, or even e-mail.

The same hypertext technology that lets you jump around inside a document also lets you reach any other resource available through the Web, as long as you know its exact URL (address). HTML's simple, text-tagging technique erases the difference between *here* and *there*. With a single click of the mouse or selection of the right text field, you are there, or the information is here. . . . Anyway, you get it.

Creation of the Web as we know it today comes from the work of individual Web weavers who include links to other documents from their Web sites. That is, the documents may constitute the Web, but the links among the documents reveal the Web's true power. Those links make up the strands in the Web that tie people, ideas, and arbitrary locations together.

Whenever you reference a URL in an HTML document, try to cut and paste that URL from a browser if at all possible. You'll save time on typing — some URLs can get pretty long — and even better, you'll be sure to get the reference right. For an additional check, test the URL with a browser to make sure that it's still valid before you copy it.

You've Used Hypertext, without Even Knowing It

At this point, you may be saying something like, "What is this hypertext stuff?" Although you may see hypertext as strange and exotic, you're probably much more familiar with it than you think. Your own desktop computer undoubtedly contains several hypertext applications that you use regularly.

For example, if you're a Microsoft Windows user, every time you run the Windows Help utility, you're using a hypertext application. Figure 2-2 shows a Microsoft Windows Help screen. Notice the buttons near the top of the screen: "Help Topics," "Back," and "Options." These buttons work much like the navigation tools for a Web browser; they can let you return to where you've been (Back), or examine the range of available links within a document (Help Topics). The underlined phrases (such as, "taskbar") are links to text within the help system. They work much like the HTML links via your browser.

Macintosh users can identify HyperCard or SuperCard as forms of hypertext; others will have to take our word for it and not assume that these are games of chance! Here again, these applications have concepts in common with the Web: some kind of home page, various navigation tools (shaped arrows and specific commands), multimedia data, and plenty of links to select.

Likewise, UNIX users who are familiar with FrameMaker or other multimedia authoring tools can find some common ground with the Web's hypertext capabilities. Once again, the concepts of a home page, document navigation

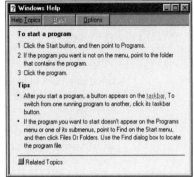

Figure 2-2:
The
Microsoft
Windows
Help engine
is a
well-known
example of
hypertext.

and linkage, and integrated multimedia help to realize the notion of hypertext and how it operates.

The difference between the preceding examples and the Web is the kinds of links that they support: Only the Web offers the capability of jumping across the Internet and following links to other Web documents and servers. Enabling this feature is what gives HTML its unique value and, of course, what's made the Web possible.

Beyond Text, There's Multimedia

If you include nontext files (such as sound, graphics, and video) in Web pages, you must employ a certain amount of alchemy. Shipping Web information in a format called *MIME* (Multipurpose Internet Mail Extensions) makes it possible for a Web server to deliver multiple forms of data to your browser in a single transfer. Actually, MIME is a technique designed to bundle attachments within individual e-mail files. The following paragraphs tell a little more about how this works.

After a MIME file with attachments shows up at your workstation, additional processing begins immediately. The text portion of the message file arrives first. It contains the text-only HTML page description and lets the browser get right to work building and displaying the text portions of the page. Because the text arrives first, you may see placeholders or icons for graphics when you first see the Web page. Then the graphics or other forms of data replace these place-holders after their related attachments arrive.

While the user views the Web page, the browser receives attachments in the background. As they come in, the browser identifies these attachments by a file type or by description information in the attachment tag (as specified by the MIME format). After the browser identifies a file, it can handle the file's playback or display. Table 2-1 shows a list of common file types used on the Web, including expansions for the inevitable acronyms that such files often entail.

Table 2-1 Common Sound, Graphics, and Motion-Video Formats on the Web

Extension	Format	Explanation
Sound Formats		
RA	RealAudio	Used with RealAudio Web Server and RealAudio Player add-on for browsers.
SBI	Sound Blaster Instrument	Used for a single instrument with Sound Blaster cards (multiinstrument: IBK).
SND, AU	8 kHz mulaw	Voice-grade sound format used on workstations (such as Sun, NeXT, HP9000, and so on).
WAV	Microsoft Waveform	Sound format used in Windows for event notification.
Still-Video (Graphics) Formats		
GIF	Graphics Interchange Format	Compressed graphics format commonly used on CompuServe, easy to render multiplatform. Can be interleaved or not, depending on how image is created.
JPEG, JPG	Joint Photographic Experts Group	Highly compressed format for still images, widely used for multi-platform graphics.
PDF	Portable Document Format	Adobe's format for multiplatform document access through its Acrobat software.
PS	PostScript	Adobe's type description language, used to deliver complex documents over the Internet.
XBM	X-Window Bitmap	Image bitmap used by X-Windows, primarily on UNIX workstations.
Motion-Video Formats		
AVI	Audio Video Interleaved	Microsoft's Video for Windows standard format; found on many CD-ROMs.
DVI	Digital Video Interactive	Another motion-video format, also found on CD-ROMs.

Extension	Format	Explanation
FLI	Flick	Autodesk Animator motion-video format.
MOV	QuickTime	Apple's motion video and audio format; originated on the Macintosh, but also available for Windows.
MPEG, MPG	Motion Picture Experts Group	Full-motion video standard using frame format similar to JPEG with variable compression capabilities.

Several Web sites contain large amounts of information on file formats and programs.

✔ **Common Internet File Formats:** Contains an annotated list of audio, graphic, and multimedia file formats with links to applications that use them.

```
http://www.travelresource.com/form-pc.html
```

```
http://www.travelresource.com/form-mac.html
```

✔ **GRAPHICS:** Maintained by Martin Reddy at the University of Edinburgh, this site contains "everything you ever wanted to know" about graphics and links to additional resources.

```
http://www.dcs.ed.ac.uk/%7Emxr/gfx/
```

✔ **Multimedia File Formats on the Internet:** A Beginner's Guide for PC Users, by Allison Zhang.

```
http://ac.dal.ca/~dong/contents.htm
```

Hyperhelpers: useful "helper" applications

When referenced by a Web page, nontext data shows up as attachments to the HTML file. Sometimes the browser itself handles playback or display, as often is the case for simple, two-dimensional graphics (including .GIF and .JPEG files). Even so, these may be handled by other applications (especially when using character-mode Web browsers like Lynx).

But when other kinds of files show up and need special handling capabilities (beyond the scope of most browsers), the browser hands off the files to other applications for playback or display. These *helper* applications have the built-in smarts to handle the formats and processing necessary to deliver the contents of specialized files on demand. The process normally works something like this:

✔ The browser builds a page display that includes an active region (under-lined or outlined in some way) to indicate the attachment of a sound, video, or animation playback.

✔ If the user selects the active region (the link), the browser calls on another application to handle playback or display.

✔ The other application takes over and plays back or displays the file.

✔ After the helper completes the display or playback, the browser reasserts control, and the user can continue on (or select the active region again, and get another playback or display).

A standard part of browser configuration supplies the names and locations of helper programs to assist the browser when such data arrives. If the browser can't find a helper application, it simply doesn't respond to an attempt to display or play back the requested information.

For example, WPlany and Wham are two common shareware sound player applications for PCs running Windows. As part of their configuration or setup, most browsers supply a method for linking particular file types (like the .SBI and .WAV file extensions common on the PC) with a helper application.

By establishing an association between the sound playback application (WPlany or Wham) and the related audio file extensions (.SBI and .WAV), the browser automatically launches the application you designate when it encoun-ters files with those extensions. This causes the sounds to play (which, we assume, is a good thing!).

For comprehensive listings of PC, Mac, and UNIX helper applications and links to their sources, start your search at one of the following URLs:

```
http://www.travelresource.com/help.html
http://charlotte.acns.nwu.edu/internet/helper/
http://www2.netscape.com/assist/helper_apps/index.html
http://wwwhost.cc.utexas.edu/learn/use/helper.html
```

Some useful helper applications for Windows include

✔ **For still graphics:** Lview is a good, small graphics viewer that can handle .GIF, .PCX, and .JPEG files. It also supports interesting image editing capabilities. (See Chapter 9 for more details.)

✔ **For video:** You'll want to use QuickTime for Windows (for QuickTime movies) or MPEGplay for .MPEG video files.

✔ **For PostScript viewing:** Ghostview for Windows works with a companion program called Ghostscript that allows users to view or print PostScript files from any source, including the Web. Because so many documents on the Internet have the PostScript format, we find these to be useful programs.

All in all, a good set of helper applications can make your browser even more effective at bringing the wonders of the Web to your desktop. With the right help, your browser can play back or render just about anything you'll run into!

The value of visuals

Without a doubt, graphics add impact and interest to Web pages, but that extra punch doesn't come without a price. You can easily get carried away by the appeal of pictures and overdo their use on your Web page. (Overdoing applies as much to the small images that you use as buttons and visual on-screen controls as it does to large images that help to dress up the Web page.)

Therefore, when you use graphics, remember these two important things:

- ✔ Not everybody who reads your page can see the graphics. Readers may not see the graphics because they use a character-mode browser (that can't display them) or because they switch off their graphics display (a common option on most Web browsers to conserve *bandwidth,* or their ability to move data, and improve response time).

- ✔ Graphics files — even compressed ones — can sometimes be quite large, often ten or more times greater in size than the HTML file that they're attached to. Moving graphics across the network takes time and consumes bandwidth. Also, it penalizes users with slower modems far more than those attached directly to the Internet.

Sometimes graphics are essential — for example, when you are using a diagram or illustration to explain your material. In other situations, impact is important — such as on a home page, where you'll be making a first impression. Under these circumstances, using graphics is perfectly appropriate, but be sensitive to the different capabilities and bandwidths of your readers.

Following are rules of thumb for using graphics effectively in your Web pages. (As you examine the work of others, see what happens to your attitude when you find that they violated these rules.)

- ✔ Keep your graphics small and uncomplicated whenever possible. This reduces file sizes and keeps transfer times down.

- ✔ Keep file sizes smaller by using compressed formats (like .GIF and .JPEG) when you can.

- ✔ Create a small version (called a *thumbnail*) of your graphic to include in your Web page. If you must use larger, more complex graphics, link the created thumbnail on your Web page to the full-size version of the graphic elsewhere. This linking spares casual readers the impact of downloading the larger version every time they access the page (and keeps Internet usage under better control, making you a better *netizen!*).

✔ Keep the number of graphic elements on a page to a minimum. Practically speaking, this means at most two or three graphic items per page, where one or two items are compact, iconlike navigation controls and another is a content-specific graphic. Here again, the idea is to limit page complexity and to speed up transfer times.

Sometimes, the temptation to violate these rules of thumb is nearly overwhelming. If you must break the rules, be sure to run your results past some disinterested third parties. (You'll learn more about testing techniques in Part V of this book.) Watch them read your pages if you can. Listen carefully to their feedback to see whether you've merely bent these rules or broken them to smithereens!

Also, remembering that not everybody who accesses the Web can see your graphics should help to keep you humble. For readers who don't have access to graphical browsers, try to think of ways to enhance their reading experience even without graphics.

Mavens of multimedia

The rules that go for graphics go *double* for other forms of multimedia. If graphics files are large when compared to HTML text files, then sound and video files are HUGE. They are time dependent; therefore, the longer they play, the bigger they are, and the longer the browser takes to download them to your computer. Although they're appealing and definitely increase the interest level for some topics, sound and video files are not germane to most topics on the Web. Use them sparingly or not at all, unless your Web site is an Internet radio show or movie theater.

With the advent of the smaller, faster display and interactivity tools for the Web (such as Java, VRML, and Shockwave), the Web will undoubtedly use more and more multimedia applications. Java *applets* work with Netscape, Mosaic, and other browsers to allow quick display of animated graphics and other special effects. VRML (Virtual Reality Modeling Language) is similar to HTML but provides 3-D viewing capabilities and more. Shockwave is the name of Macromedia's plug-in to Netscape 2.0 that allows Director movies to play inside Web pages. The use of these tools goes far beyond the scope of this book, but you can look forward to using them in your second generation Web page. If you're interested in these tools, you can get more information at the following URLs:

Java — Sun Microsystems

```
http://www.javasoft.com or http://java.sun.com
```

VRML

```
http://www.vrml.org/
```

Shockwave — Macromedia

`http://www.macromedia.com`

 Once again, the trick is to make large files available through links instead of including them on pages that everyone tries to download. Labeling such active regions with the file's size is also a good idea so that people know what they're in for if they choose to download. (For example: `Warning! This points to a 40K sound byte of a barking seal.`)

Bringing It All Together with the Web

Let's get down from multimedia hyperspace and back to the cyberspace world of your future Web page. Now that you understand the basic concepts behind the Web and HTML and have met (briefly) some tools of the trade, you need to read the following paragraph carefully. It embodies the essence of your Web pages.

The three most important factors in building good Web pages are content, content, and content. (Get the idea?) If the content is well-organized, engaging, and contains links to interesting places, your Web site can be a potent tool for education and communication. If your Web site is all flash, sharing it can be an exercise in sheer frustration (and humiliation for the WebMaster . . . that's you!). Therefore, if you put your energy into providing high-quality content and link your readers to other high-quality, content-filled pages, your Web site will be a howling success. If you don't, your site will be the electronic equivalent of a ghost town!

In the next chapter, you'll discover what's involved in using — and building — documents for the Web. Just fly into our parlor for a look at what's in (and on) a Web page.

Chapter 3

What's in a Page?

*T*he trick to understanding HTML lies in knowing how to separate the two components of the HTML file: the *content* and the *controls*. (Controls are also known as *tags* or *markup*.) You can present the majority of *content* in a plain text (ASCII) file with no tagging whatsoever. When you look at an HTML source file, you see *markup* in the file that doesn't show up when your browser displays the page. (It's the characters that show up inside the HTML bracket markers (<>) that control the way characters appear on the screen; if you're puzzled, don't worry — you see plenty of examples throughout the rest of this book.) Even though markup doesn't show up on-screen, it is crucial to controlling how Web pages look and act.

The really interesting parts of HTML are the combinations of markup and content such as the commands used to title pages or control textual guide-posts — headers, graphics, lists of elements, and so on. Before you can read, write, and understand HTML, you must be able to mentally separate the structure of a document from its controls.

Building good Web pages requires that you not only understand the distinction between content and controls but also use it for its best effects. In this chapter, you'll begin to appreciate the components of a Web page, and you'll find out how to bring these pieces together to create readable Web documents.

It's All in the Layout

The human eye and brain are marvelous instruments. They are capable of scanning incredible amounts of material and zeroing in on the things that are most important to the reader. As a Web page designer, your mission (should you decide to accept it) is to aid the reader's eye in locating the page's salient features quickly and efficiently. Nothing communicates this concern — or your lack of it — more quickly than a document's layout.

The layout is the overall visual arrangement of the elements in your document. Layout isn't concerned with the placement of individual text elements on a page. Instead, layout involves the number of elements on a page, how they're arranged, and how much white space is around them.

The layout of a document — whether a Web page, a letter to your sister, or an advertisement in a magazine — is a crucial part of communicating with the reader. For materials where reader interest is mandatory, layout may not appear to be important at all (this may explain why tax forms are so boring to look at). For documents where interest must be generated, layout is almost as important as the information that the document delivers.

Think of all the boring textbooks that you've slogged (slept?) through, with pages and pages of text and the occasional graphic crammed between two half-page paragraphs. By comparison, think of a magazine or television advertisement that you've seen recently. The people who designed the advertising grabbed your interest by creating eye-catching images, by using appealing language, and by delivering arresting combinations of elements.

When it comes to building Web pages, your job can be as challenging as the one faced by advertising designers. You shouldn't assume that your material is of such great interest to the world that your Web pages can stress content at the expense of layout. You are competing with millions of Web sites on the WWW. Even if your site's content is completely unique, you can encourage your readers to visit more often and to link your site to theirs by making the layout as inviting as possible.

Because attention to layout adds to the accessibility of any document, you do your readers a service by building a good layout: At the same time that you make your page more pleasant to read, you deliver the content quickly and effectively, which is everyone's desire in the information age.

What Are You Trying to Say?

As markup languages go, HTML is fairly simple and easy to learn. Unfortunately, this fact creates a nearly overwhelming temptation to rush out and start building Web pages right away. In fact, you're probably wondering when we're going to get around to putting HTML tags on text, aren't you?

Well, whether you're an individual trying to share information with others or an organization trying to advertise its products and services, the impetus to publish online ASAP is powerful. Nevertheless, we advise you to step back and do a little analysis and design work, instead of trying to build "killer Web pages" on the fly.

Who's listening?

Knowing your audience is a critical requirement for building Web pages that people can use. If you don't know who you want visiting your Web site and why you want them to visit, you're just putting together a *vanity page* that a few Web surfers may pass through once. Don't get all bent out of shape — vanity pages comprise the majority of the personal pages on the Web. If you really have a reason for your Web site, you want to know how to emphasize it to your potential readers.

It's important to start your Web document's design based on certain assumptions about your audience. Although this is true for advertisements and for encyclopedias, the focus on form and excitement is a little more intense and urgent for ads than it is for encyclopedias. You could do worse than to create the initial interest and impact of an advertisement, but you'll want to go farther than most ads go to deliver the depth of content that your audience is most likely to want, even if it isn't entirely encyclopedic in nature.

How can you get to know your audience? Think of it as a form of hunting: Identify your target group and then start hanging around their haunts, whether in cyberspace or in the real world. Watch and listen to them. When you recognize their interests, you can target their needs and duly consider the factors that can hook them into your content. You must deliver solid, usable information to your target group so that they come back for more and spread the word about what you have to offer.

Design springs from content — and intent

Web pages built around long documents with complex ideas take more forethought and are more difficult to design. That's a big surprise ... NOT. Short, single-concept documents are easy to make into good Web pages ... not necessarily true either. No matter how long, short, complex, or simple your content is, you still need to follow this basic principle: Design springs from content, as form follows function. Also, remember the audience that you intend to reach; emphasize the high points that your research shows to be of interest to your potential readers.

Creating an outline before you start writing (or programming in HTML, for that matter) is usually sufficient to help you organize your information. An outline helps you to determine the order of topics and the need for graphics, sound, or other multimedia information. It also gives you a blueprint to follow as you construct the document that expands the outline.

Identifying the topics and major elements of your document highlights the relationships between those components (and possibly between the components and other information sources on the Web). Therefore, outlining your content plays a key role in establishing links and presenting your readers with visual clues on how to read and navigate the information in your document.

The intent behind a document — to inform, educate, persuade, or question — plays a major role in your design.

- ✔ If your goal is to inform, you are less inclined to include numerous eye-catching displays and more inclined to direct readers' vision to the highlights of the information that your document contains.

- ✔ If your goal is to persuade or sell, you try to hook the readers' attention with compelling visuals and riveting testimonials, and then you follow through with the important details.

- ✔ If your goal is to question something, you raise the issues to be queried early on and provide pointers to additional discussion and related information afterward.

In each case, the goal behind the document strongly conditions its execution and delivery. That's why understanding your intent is so important to building the right kind of document.

Establish your key messages

At the beginning of your document design process you need to answer the question at the head of this section — "What Are You Trying to Say?" Approach this task by outlining the key ideas or messages that you want to convey; put the most important ones first. Then follow each main idea with any relevant information that makes your case, proves your point, or otherwise substantiates what you're saying.

If you follow this exercise carefully, you find much of the content emerging gracefully from your outline. The important relationships among the various elements of your document (and other documents) more or less establish themselves as you work your way through the outlining process.

Think about superstructure and information flow

Superstructure refers to the formal mechanics of how you communicate a document's organization and navigation. It includes elements such as

- ✔ a table of contents
- ✔ a set of common controls
- ✔ an index
- ✔ a glossary of technical terms

In short, the superstructure is the wrapping that you wind around your content so that readers can find their way to the information they want and understand what they're reading or viewing. For any given document, you may not need every element of superstructure, but for most documents — especially longer ones — some elements of superstructure are helpful, and others are absolutely essential.

The TOC (table of contents)

From a lifetime of exposure to printed materials, we've come to expect a table of contents that lays out the topics and coverage at the beginning of most documents. The beauty of hypertext is that you can build links that take readers directly from any entry in the TOC to the corresponding information in the document. Thus, the TOC becomes not just an organizational map for your document, but a convenient navigation tool.

Common controls for all screens

To promote readability and familiarity within your Web site, include common controls in each individual document. These common controls can be a set of clickable icons: to page backward or forward, to jump back to the TOC, or to return to your home page. If you include a search tool for keywords in the document, make the tool accessible from any point in any of your documents. Whatever you do, establish a common look and feel for your pages; then your readers can navigate much more easily. Consistency may be "the last refuge for the unimaginative," but it does promote familiarity and ease of use!

An index or a search engine

Helping readers locate keywords or individual topics can ensure that they get the best use from your content. Another great thing about hypertext is that an old-fashioned index may be unnecessary. Because all your content is online and accessible to the computer, you can often replace the functionality of an index with a built-in search engine for your Web pages.

Chapter 14 presents a discussion of search engines, including tools that you can use to provide index capabilities for your documents.

A glossary helps manage specialized terms and language

If you're covering a subject that's full of jargon, technical terms, or other forms of arcane gibberish (beloved by experts and feared by newcomers), try to include a glossary with your Web pages. Fortunately, HTML includes a text style specifically built for defining terms, which helps you to construct a glossary whenever you need one. You'll still have to come up with the definitions yourself — unless you can find a Web site with a glossary that you can link to your page. That's the beauty of the Web!

Grab the audience's attention . . .

If you've ever had the pleasure of viewing a movie at a THX-equipped theater, you're probably familiar with the phrase "The Audience Is Listening." It comes up at the conclusion of the THX demonstration, which usually happens immediately before the feature presentation.

The THX demonstration consists of the simple "THX" graphic that fills the entire screen. A loud, sustained orchestral chord, overlaid with a powerful pipe-organ note, accompanies the graphic. The musical effect starts quietly, builds to a peak over 20 seconds, and then fades away on a low pedal-tone that you swear moves the entire theater. The sensation is similar to standing at the end of the runway while a jet fighter comes toward you and takes off over your head at 200+ mph. It definitely (and almost deafeningly) gets your attention. Having raised the audience nearly out of its seats, the demonstration concludes with the words "The Audience Is Listening."

Even though we don't recommend this audio effect for most Web pages, we do encourage you to grab your readers' attention when they first glimpse your page. Nothing does this as effectively as a tasteful image coupled with a brief, compelling introduction to your page. Include information that tells why your page is important, what it contains, and how to get around. Get your readers interested, get them oriented, and then they'll be hooked!

They're after the goods . . . don't get in the way!

After you have your readers' attention, help them to get to the real content of your Web site easily. Your superstructure should be visible, but don't let it get in the way. If you include pointers to direct your readers to more-detailed content, make the pointers obvious and easy to distinguish from the rest of the page. An overly complicated design, layout, or information flow can prevent easy access to the information.

This advice translates into some important rules of thumb, particularly for introductory materials. Keep your welcoming (home) page simple and elegant. Use short, direct sentences. Keep your focus on the topic(s) at hand. Use the superstructure to emphasize your content. For a complex Web site, you can include a link to an "About this site" page for those who want to understand the site's structure and function.

What should they remember?

A well-known educational principle reports that people exposed to new materials generally remember ten percent of the content — at best. When designing your Web documents, keep asking yourself, "What ten percent do I want my readers to remember?" This question helps you focus on the really important ideas so that you can direct the audience to them and reinforce them throughout your Web pages.

Also true, if somewhat sad, is that most readers remember a limited volume of material as well. Remembering ten percent of the concepts in a document doesn't translate into remembering ten percent of its overall content: Would you remember ten out of a hundred pages in a document that you'd never seen before? This sometimes means presenting less information than you may otherwise be inclined to convey, in the interest of concentrating on what's really important. Therefore, save yourself some time and trouble, and concentrate on the important stuff right from the outset!

Don't be too ambitious in your document's coverage: Strongly related concepts linger in memory far better than loosely linked or unrelated ones. As with so much else in life, sticking to your focus is a key ingredient for successful communication.

Meet the Elements of Page Design

Okay, you've been exposed to some important design concepts for building Web pages. At this point, you should be ready to meet the elements that make up an HTML document. These elements may sound familiar because many are integral parts of any well-written document. Others may be less familiar, perhaps because of the terminology or because the concepts — like hypertext links — don't correspond to normal printed materials.

Nevertheless, the following are the building blocks that make up Web pages. After we give you a tour of these basic elements, we conclude with a discussion of information flows and design elements for Web documents.

Tagging text

Including tags along with text is what separates HTML from any ordinary ASCII file. In HTML, tags are enclosed within angle brackets: for example, a document head is indicated with a `<HEAD>` tag. Most HTML tags travel in pairs, so that the `<HEAD>` tag marks the beginning of a document head and a corresponding `</HEAD>` marks its end.

Some tags include particular values, called *attributes*, that help describe a pointer or a reference to an external data element. Other attributes label information to be communicated back to a Web server; still others add to the physical description of a display object (for example, the alignment or dimensions of a graphical element).

Attributes provide the source and destination information for links within and across documents: These link attributes (usually called *link anchors* or *anchors*, for short) describe the relationship between two named locations in the Web, whether the locations are in the same document or are in different documents.

A linked location is indicated by a document reference (for access to other documents), a location reference (for a point inside the same document), or a combination of the two (for a point inside another document). For more information on such links, please read about <BASE>, <A> (anchor), and <LINK> tags in Chapter 5.

Many HTML tags require that certain attributes be specified, others can take on optional attributes and values, and still others never acquire attributes. You'll find out how to tell the difference as you discover the elements of document design presented in this book.

Titles and labels

Every HTML document should have a title that serves to identify it to the readers. Also, titles have three other important aspects:

- ✔ You can save titles in hotlists, which makes them a navigation tool for readers who use hotlists.
- ✔ Titles allow Web walkers to decipher what HTML documents are about, which makes the corresponding entries that these walkers create search databases more accurately and usefully.
- ✔ Titles help you manage your documents, especially when they're complex and voluminous.

When you display a Web document, the title typically shows up in the window's title bar. Figure 3-1 shows the viewing window for an HTML Style Guide with the title, "Style Guide for online hypertext," prominently displayed.

Labels aren't required, but they're a good document-organizing tool. Labels help identify sections or topic areas in a document and provide better navigation for readers, especially when you use them for links. As you'll see in Parts III and IV of this book, if you use the NAME attribute inside an anchor, you can direct an HTML link to a named section in a document as well as to the head of that document. Anchors also signal to other browsers, "Hey, if you want to point to me, reference me by my anchor's NAME attribute."

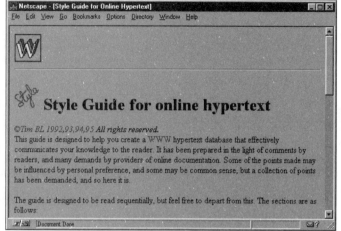

```
<A NAME="Mexican Dove">Linda Paloma</A>
```

If some author, or even the original author, wants to link to the `Linda Paloma` area of the current document, all they need to do is create an HTML link definition by using the anchor's NAME (in this case, `"Mexican Dove"`).

Text and hypertext links

Anyone writing HTML has only one kind of link available — a unidirectional association between a source and a target. But this one kind of link has four purposes in HTML files:

- ✔ **Intradocument linking** provides a way to move from one location to another location inside the same document.

- ✔ **Interdocument linking** provides a way to move from one document to another document.

- ✔ **Linking to an *agent* program** that acts on behalf of the Web server provides a way for a document to handle a query or provide a service (such as information gathering).

- ✔ **Linking to a nontext object** provides a way to access a graphic, sound, video, or other multimedia file.

Interestingly enough, the links from inside HTML files to other types of data — like sound, graphics, motion video, and so on — are what enable the hypertext aspects of HTML. Along with these external links, HTML's inter- and intradocument links create the connections that compose the Web. Remember, no matter how they're used, links contribute to the Web's appealing look and feel.

Using graphics effectively

First impressions are critically important; therefore, you want to use your most potent, eye-catching images on the initial page that your readers see. However, bigger images mean longer download times — especially for dial-in users. You must balance the trade-off between the positive impact of a catchy image and the negative impact of *wait time*. (And you must realize that some readers have no graphics capabilities at all!)

What does all this mean for effective use of graphics?

- ✔ Use graphics only when they add to the impact, intelligibility, or value of a page. A picture can be worth a thousand words — by providing a flowchart of a complex process, for example. But if the related words are only tangential to the content, an image may end up detracting from your document's ability to communicate with its readers.

- ✔ Keep your graphics as small as possible, both in terms of image space and file size. The two are related, but you can reduce file sizes by using .JPEG (with more data compression) to render large images from relatively small files. Be sure to check the image on a lower-resolution display and adjust the compression almost to the point where resolution begins to suffer.

- ✔ Insert a *thumbnail* version of a large graphic (if you must use it) and link it to the full-size version. Also, tell users the file size of the full version, so that they can decide how badly they want to see it (translation: how long they want to wait).

- ✔ Keep the number of graphical elements per page to a minimum. Each graphic adds to the time that is needed to build a page. If you must use numerous graphical elements on a page, keep them small in order to minimize transfer time. In other words, multiple icon-sized elements on a page are fine; more than one or two large graphical elements typically is not.

Overcoming two-dimensional thinking

Although hypertext is new and exciting, the legacy of thousands of years of linear text is difficult to overcome. In other words, even though document designers can do incredibly nifty and creative things with linking and hypermedia, they have to fight the nearly overwhelming tendency to make their documents read like books. You must exploit the hypertext capabilities of HTML displays and links in appealing and useful ways, or your Web pages won't live up to their potential or the expectations of your readers.

In the sections that follow, you have a chance to examine some common organizational techniques for building Web documents; you also encounter documents that can exist only on the Web.

Stringing pages together the old-fashioned way

Some pages demand to be read in sequence: for example, those presenting a narrative that builds on previous elements. In such a case, string the pages together as shown in Figure 3-2. If you have a document of five pages or more — if you believe Tim Berners-Lee in his *Hypertext Online Style Guide* — you should chain them together sequentially anyway.

Figure 3-2:
Chain pages together to read them in sequence.

The nice thing about hypertext is that you can chain pages together forward and backward; then you can easily "turn" pages in either direction. Don't be afraid to include other appropriate links in this basic structure (such as links to other HTML documents, a glossary, or other points inside your document).

Hierarchies are easy to model in HTML

If you commonly construct documents from an outline, a hierarchical approach to document links should immediately make sense. Most outlines start with major ideas and divisions that you refine and elaborate on to wind up with all the details of a formal document. Figure 3-3 shows a four-level hierarchical document structure that organizes the entire work.

HTML itself has no limits on the levels of hierarchies that you can build; the only limit is your (and your audience's) ability to handle complexity. For both your sakes, we suggest keeping the hierarchy from getting too big or too deep.

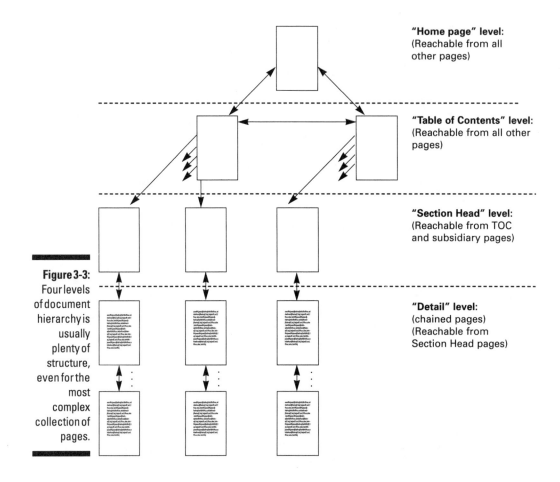

"Home page" level:
(Reachable from all other pages)

"Table of Contents" level:
(Reachable from all other pages)

"Section Head" level:
(Reachable from TOC and subsidiary pages)

Figure 3-3:
Four levels of document hierarchy is usually plenty of structure, even for the most complex collection of pages.

"Detail" level:
(chained pages)
(Reachable from Section Head pages)

Multiple tracks for multiple audiences

It isn't unusual to build a document that includes different levels of information to meet the needs of different audiences. By using HTML, you can easily interlink basic introductory documents (like a tutorial or technical overview) with more pointed, in-depth reference materials. That way, you can design a home page that points beginners to a tutorial and leads them through an overview before assaulting them with the down-and-dirty details of your "real" content.

This kind of organization, depicted in Figure 3-4, lets you notify experienced readers how to bypass the introductory materials and access your in-depth content directly. Such an approach lets you design for multiple audiences without doing a lot of extra work.

The organization in Figure 3-4 differs somewhat from that depicted in Figures 3-2 and 3-3. It emphasizes the links between related documents more than the flow of pages within those documents. In fact, the kind of document pictured in Figure 3-4 would probably combine elements from both a linear and a hierarchical structure in its actual page flows. The tutorial section would be read from front to back (or at least a chapter at a time), but the reference section would be consulted by topic (and only rarely read all the way through).

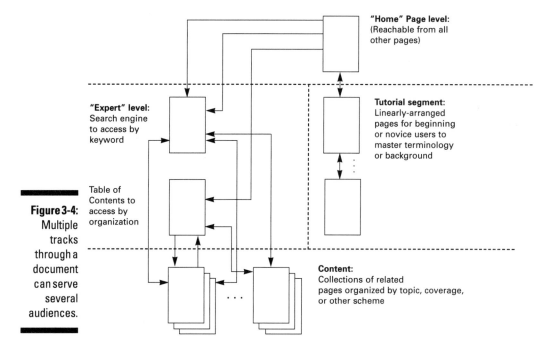

"Home" Page level:
(Reachable from all other pages)

"Expert" level:
Search engine to access by keyword

Table of Contents to access by organization

Tutorial segment:
Linearly-arranged pages for beginning or novice users to master terminology or background

Figure 3-4:
Multiple tracks through a document can serve several audiences.

Content:
Collections of related pages organized by topic, coverage, or other scheme

A bona fide Web wonder: the "hotlist" or "jump page"

Some of the best resources we've located on the Web consist of nothing more than a list of annotated references to other documents. The lists usually relate to one or more specific topics. You can see this kind of document structure in Figure 3-5, which shows a single page pointing off to multiple pages in various locations. In this example, the picture fails to do complete justice to the concept. For a better illustration, you need to look at a real Web page. Consequently, we advise you to check out the URL listed below — it's quite convincing as an example of what a good hotlist can do!

There are more good hotlists on the Web than you can shake a stick at. Of course, we suggest that you start by looking at the *HTML For Dummies Hotlist* Page.

```
http://www.outer.net/html4dum/hotlists.htm#top
```

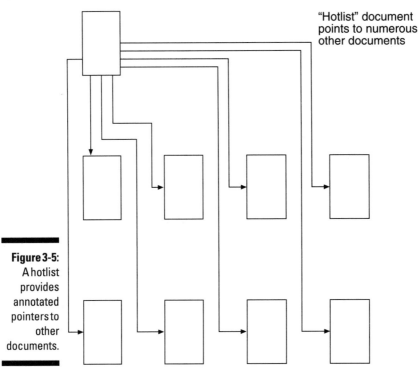

"Hotlist" document points to numerous other documents

Figure 3-5:
A hotlist provides annotated pointers to other documents.

Extending the Web, a piece at a time

Another kind of Web page solicits input from readers who, by their input, help to create an open-ended document. Readers contribute comments, additional text, and hypermedia or add to an ongoing narrative. The structure of such a document is hard to predict and, therefore, hard to depict. Suffice it to say that this kind of Web document can grow like a colony of coral, more by accretion than by prior organization or design.

For an example of this kind of living, ongoing document, consult the following URL.

http://bug.village.virginia.edu/

WAXweb is a hypermedia implementation of a feature-length, independent film, *WAX or The Discovery of Television Among the Bees* (David Blair, 85:00, 1991). WAXweb is a large hypermedia database available over the Internet. It features an authoring interface that lets users collaborate in building onto the story. WAXweb includes thousands of individual elements, ranging from text to music, motion videos, and video transcriptions of motion picture clips. For users with VRML-capable browsers, WAXweb also offers a pretty nifty VRML implementation, as well.

The only limitations on how you structure documents are those imposed by your need to communicate effectively with your audience. After you realize that, you can use the various page-flow and organizational techniques that we've outlined here for their best effects.

Now that you know the first building blocks of Web-page design — layout and organization — it's time to initiate you into the world of markup languages. In Chapter 4, you discover what HTML looks like and how you use it to structure a document. Here comes the good stuff!!

Part II
A Tour of HTML Basics

"HELLO, SMART-HOME MAINTENANCE? CAN YOU SEND SOMEONE OUT - OUR DEN IS ACTING REALLY STUPID."

In this part . . .

OK, this is where things really start to get interesting. In this part of the book, you get to know — and hopefully, love — the syntax and capabilities of the HyperText Markup Language. You begin with a general look at what markup languages are all about to help you better understand what's behind the strange sequences of characters that make HTML do its thing.

Then you get a look at the whole set of markup tags that make up HTML, from A to V. Sorry, there's no markup these days that starts with any of the remaining letters of the alphabet — W, X, Y, or Z — except for some codes that are now obsolete. While you're learning about each tag, you get a chance to examine its syntax, attributes, and how it relates to all the other tags. You also see examples for most tags, including the occasional screen shot that shows how they display.

After you've worked your way through the tags, you find out how HTML represents special characters, including the symbols that ordinarily indicate to browsers that they're part of the markup language itself. You continue your tour with a table of character codes that covers everything from A to Z, and ~ to |, and way beyond, as we take you through the ISO-Latin-1 character set for HTML. By the time you're through, you'll have seen most of what there is to see under the HTML 2.0 umbrella.

Then, we conclude the part with two chapters on building HTML documents, to help you put all this terminology and the library of HTML's markup tags to work. In Chapter 7, we start you out gently and show you how to build a basic Web page. Then in Chapter 8, we turn up the heat and show you how to add a little flair and impact to your Web pages. By the time you finish this part of the book, you not only know about the HTML markup language, you have had a chance to see it in action and try it out for yourself!

Chapter 4
What's a Markup Language?

In This Chapter

▶ Defining HTML markup conventions

▶ Understanding HTML's roots

▶ Introducing the basic HTML control characters, elements, attributes, and entities

*I*n this chapter, you'll finally see what HTML looks like. You'll begin to appreciate what's involved in a markup language and start to understand how to use HTML to create your own Web pages. Because this chapter is an overview, you won't be able to run right out and start building pages after you read it, but you should have a pretty good idea of the pieces and parts that make HTML do its thing.

A Markup Language Is Not a Form of Graffiti

HTML represents a way to take ordinary text and turn it into hypertext, just by adding special elements that instruct Web browsers how to display its contents. These special elements are called markup tags.

The purpose of a markup language is to give either machines or humans clues about the structure, content, and behavior of a document. Markup comes in two types: descriptive and procedural. HTML is a descriptive markup language. A descriptive markup language describes the structure and behavior of a document. This focus allows an author to concentrate more on content and structure, and less on formatting and presentation. Here's an example:

```
<H1>Cooking for One</H1> — display level one header
<OL> — begin ordered (numbered) list
<LI>Take Lean Cuisine out of fridge.
```

```
<LI>Place in microwave.
<LI>Set timer for 5 min.
</OL> — end ordered list
```

The tags H1, OL, and LI describe an object and its components. It's up to a browser to render these properly on your screen. In fact, from browser to browser, each of these objects could be rendered differently. But the important thing is that each browser has a meaningful way to display a first-level header (H1) and a numbered list (OL and LI). From a portability standpoint, this is a good thing.

The other kind of markup language, procedural, describes formatting rather than structure. An example is *troff*, the dinosaur UNIX markup language, which looks like this:

```
.center .12 .Helvetica .bold Table of Contents
```

These *troff* tags tell the output device to render an object as "centered, 12 point Helvetica bold":

Table of Contents

As you can imagine, this type of markup is not very portable and is difficult to maintain.

HTML tags not only govern how a browser displays the contents of an HTML document, but also control how the browser can draw in graphics, video, sound, and so on to create a multimedia experience.

In the same vein, still other HTML tags instruct browsers how to handle and display hypertext links, either within the same HTML file or to other documents or Web-accessible services. The key to building attractive, readable Web pages is knowing how to use HTML markup to highlight and organize your content.

A syntax is not a levy on cigarettes!

When it comes to any kind of formal, computer-readable language, you invariably find a set of rules governing its terms and their order of placement. This set of rules is called the *syntax* of the language. In HTML the syntax describes how a Web browser can recognize and interpret the instructions contained in the markup tags.

What makes HTML particularly interesting is that it's all pure text — in fact, HTML can work completely within the confines of the ASCII 7-bit character set (ISO 646), which contains only 128 distinct viewable characters. Nevertheless, HTML can handle display of so-called higher-order ASCII characters, which normally require eight bits to represent directly and are sometimes called the 8-bit ASCII or Latin-1 character set (ISO 8859/1). Quite a bit of work is under way to make HTML able to handle the Unicode character set, which supports up to 65,535 different characters (of which over 34,000 are defined). The Unicode set includes non-Roman alphabets such as Chinese (Han) ideograms, Hebrew characters, and lots of other interesting stuff.

This diversity lets HTML display things like accents, umlauts, and other diacritical marks often associated with non-English languages (or loan words, like résumé, from those languages), by including instructions on what characters to represent as a part of the markup. In other words, HTML can provide the related instructions to a browser even if you can't always see things in the same format when you're writing the HTML. For example, `<OL>` and `<LI>` don't look like a numbered list inside your text file, but they do when the browser interprets them.

Elements of HTML syntax

The special control characters that separate HTML markup from ordinary text are the left and right angle brackets: < (left bracket) and > (right bracket). These characters indicate that the browser should pay special attention to what they enclose. And here's your big chance to learn another buzzword: *parser.* Inside the browser software, a parser does the work of reading and constructing the display information. A parser reads information in the HTML file and decides which elements are markup and which ones aren't, permitting the browser to take appropriate action.

In HTML, left and right angle brackets can enclose all kinds of special instructions called *tags.* The next six chapters of this book are devoted to introducing, explaining, and demonstrating HTML tags.

In the meantime, here's a general introduction to the way HTML tags look and behave: A tag takes a generic form that looks something like this:

```
<TAG-NAME {ATTRIBUTE{="VALUE"} . . . }>Text{</TAG-NAME>}
```

(By the way, text within the tags is case insensitive, but for readability, we use all caps to make HTML tags stand apart from other text.)

Let's look at the pieces of this generic form:

- `<TAG-NAME>`: All HTML tags have names. For example, `H1` is a level-one header; `OL` is an ordered list. Tags are surrounded by angle brackets that mark their contents for special attention from the parser software.

- `{ATTRIBUTE{="VALUE"}...}`: Some HTML tags require or permit certain named attributes to be associated with them. Here, the notation using curly braces — for example, `{ATTRIBUTE}` — indicates that attributes may be present for some tags, but not for others. In the same vein, some attributes require that values be associated to them, as when supplying the name of an HTML document for a hypertext link; other attributes may not require associated values at all, which is why `{="VALUE"}` is also in curly braces.

  For example, in an `<IMG>` tag used to point to a graphics file, a required attribute is `SRC` (source), to provide a pointer to the file where the graphic resides, as in `<IMG SRC="../gifs/redball.gif."` This syntax proves yet again how important it is to stay close to your source! Finally, the ellipsis (...) indicates that some HTML tags may even include multiple attributes, each of which may take a value or not, depending on the circumstances.

- `Text`: This is the content that's modified by a tag. For example, if the tag were a document title, the HTML string

  ```
  <TITLE>HTML For Dummies Home Page</TITLE>
  ```

  would display the words "HTML For Dummies Home Page" in the title bar at the top of a graphical browser's window. Enclosing this text within `<TITLE>` and `</TITLE>` tags marks it as the title for the document.

- `{</TAG-NAME>}`: The closing tag name is denoted by the left angle bracket (`<`), followed by a forward slash (`/`), the tag name, and finally a closing right angle bracket (`>`). The curly braces indicate that this element does not always occur. However, over 70 percent of the HTML tags require a closing tag as well as an opening tag, so the omission of a closing tag should be considered the exception, rather than the rule. Don't worry; most, if not all, browsers will simply ignore closing tags if they're not necessary.

The majority of HTML tags don't require the assignment of attributes, so don't be too overwhelmed by their full-blown formal syntax. By and large, most tags resemble the `<TAG-NAME>Text</TAG-NAME>` layout like `<TITLE>HTML For Dummies Home Page</TITLE>`.

The ampersand (`&`) is another special HTML control character. It's used to denote a special character for HTML content that might not belong to the 7-bit ASCII character set (like an accent grave or an umlaut), or that might otherwise be interpreted as a markup character (like a left or right angle bracket). Such tagged items are called character entities, and can be expressed in a number of ways. For example, the string `&egrave;` produces a lowercase E with a grave accent mark (è), while the string `&lt;` produces a left angle bracket (<).

Chapter 6 supplies the complete set of HTML character entities. If you work in a language other than English, you might want to consider building macros to replace familiar higher-order ASCII characters in your HTML files. Such macros would let you automate this kind of search-and-replace maneuver as a post-processing step. Then, you could avoid keying seven or eight characters of HTML to produce one output character (this is what computer science nerds like to call *an unfavorable input-output ratio*)! Even better, check out some of the HTML authoring tools in Part VIII: Most of them will automate this kind of thing for you.

In the next section, we'll uncover the roots of HTML, namely SGML, Standard Generalized Markup Language.

Standard Generalized Markup Language (SGML)

Technically speaking, HTML is not a programming language, nor can an HTML document be called a program. Normally, a program is defined as a set of instructions and operations to be applied to external data (usually called the input).

HTML combines instructions within the data to tell a display program, called a *browser,* how to render the data that the document contains. Even though it's not a programming language per se, HTML provides plenty of structuring and layout controls to manage a document's appearance and the linkage mechanisms necessary to provide hypertext capabilities.

Warning: Entering the Acronym Zone

Nearly any writing, speech, or documentation that has to do with computers will be rife with technical jargon and gibberish, no matter what the specific subject might be. To make matters even more confusing, the cognoscenti would much rather abbreviate frequently used technical terms like Hypertext Markup Language as HTML or Standard Generalized Markup Language as SGML, instead of having to say all the words for the concept each time it's mentioned.

The use of strings of first letters for technical terms — such as ROM for read-only memory, RAM for random-access memory, CPU for central processing unit, and so on — happens across the board in the computer world, so you might as well get used to it! Because this kind of shorthand is called an acronym (which literally means *from the point or head of the name* in Greek), we've got to warn you that you've entered a world where acronyms are commonplace. To make your lives a little easier, dear readers, we've tried to include all of the acronyms that we use in this book in the Glossary at the end. That way, if you forget what a particular string of letters means, you'll at least be able to look it up!

Actually, HTML is defined by a particular type of document — called a *Document Type Definition,* or *DTD* — within the context of SGML. Thus, any HTML document is also an SGML document that represents a specific subset of SGML capability.

Generalized Markup Covers Many Sins

SGML originated with work begun at IBM in the 1960s to overcome the problems inherent in moving documents across multiple hardware platforms and operating systems. IBM's efforts were called GML, for General Markup Language. GML was originally targeted for local use at IBM, rather than as a generic way of representing documents. This development was the first publish-once, multiplatform strategy for document preparation — a concept that's become extremely popular today.

GML's originators — Charles Goldfarb, Ed Mosher, and Ray Lorie (the original "GML") — realized by the 1970s that a more general version of markup would make documents portable from one system to another. Their work led ultimately to the definition and birth of SGML in the 1980s, which is today covered by the ISO 8879 standard.

SGML is a powerful and complex tool for representing documents of all kinds. It offers the ability to create document specifications that can then be used to define and build individual documents that conform to those specifications.

Some commercial and government institutions, like the Department of Defense (DoD), have adopted SGML. The DoD mandates that contractors and subcontractors now submit all documentation to the government in SGML. The DoD even mandates the DTDs to which the contractors' documents must conform.

Several quotes from the SGML standard, ISO 8879, should help to illustrate its aims, while underscoring a strong relationship to HTML. First, there's the notion of the markup process:

> Text processing and word processing systems typically require additional information to be interspersed among the natural text of the document being processed. This added information, called "markup," serves two purposes:
>
> a) Separating the logical elements of the document; and
> b) Specifying the processing functions to be performed on those elements.

Charles F. Goldfarb, *The SGML Handbook,* (Clarendon Press, Oxford, 1990, 5).

In stature and in scope, SGML far outstrips HTML; it is used to define complex document types like those used for military standard (Milspec) documents or aircraft maintenance manuals, whose specifications alone can run into thousands of pages.

The notion of *generalized markup* is what makes SGML's document definition system so all-encompassing and powerful. Goldfarb has this to say on that subject:

> ..."generalized markup" [...] does not restrict documents to a single application, formatting style, or processing system. Generalized markup is based on two novel postulates:
>
> a) Markup should describe a document's structure and other attributes rather than specify processing to be performed on it, as descriptive markup need be done only once and will suffice for all future processing.
>
> b) Markup should be rigorous so that the techniques available for process ing rigorously-defined objects like programs and data bases can be used for processing documents as well. (Goldfarb 7-8)

Even though SGML, like HTML, is oriented toward producing documents, the goal is to make those documents behave more like programs, that is, to behave predictably in a computer-oriented world.

Building better pieces and parts

The whole idea behind SGML is to create a formal method for describing the sections, headings, styles, and other components that make up a document so that references to individual items or entries in a document can be described by such definitions. This description lets a document be rendered in a consistent way, no matter what platform displays it. In simplistic terms, SGML is a general-purpose tool for describing documents of just about any conceivable kind.

In its most generic form, an SGML document comes in three parts:

- ✔ A description of the legal character set and the characters used to distin-guish plain text from markup tags
- ✔ A declaration of the document type, including a listing of the legal markup tags it may contain
- ✔ The document itself, which includes actual references to markup tags, mixed with the content for the document

Where HTML fits under the SGML umbrella

All three document parts (see the preceding bulleted list) do not have to be included in the same physical file. In fact, HTML works from the same set of definitions for the first two items so that only the contents and tags that make up an HTML document need to be included with the document itself, as described in the third item.

For HTML, the ISO Latin-1 character set defines character entities for higher-order ASCII characters, along with the angle brackets and forward slash used to indicate markup tags. The declaration of document type comes from a standard DTD for HTML.

Therefore, HTML can be conveyed by pure ASCII text files that conform to the definitions and requirements covered in the first two bulleted items to create instances of documents, the third bulleted item. In other words, all that HTML consists of is content text, character entities, and markup tags.

Welcome to HTML

Despite its more limited nature, HTML shares several important characteristics with its SGML *parent* — namely

- ✔ A character-based method for describing and expressing content
- ✔ A desire to deliver that content equally to multiple platforms
- ✔ A method for linking document components (and documents) together to compose compound documents

Although HTML may be less generalized than SGML, it still leaves plenty of room for unique and powerful expressions, as any quick perusal of Web pages illustrates. Though it may be less than completely generalized, HTML's tags and entities can still do justice to a broad range of content!

Delivering content to a variety of platforms

HTML's tremendous power and appeal come from its capacity to service character-mode and graphical browsers with identical content. The look and feel of any document's content remains the same, subject only to the display limitations of whatever browser you're using.

When you add the capacity to group multiple, related sources of information together — text, graphics, sound, and video — and the capacity to link documents together, the result is *hypertext*. HTML's combination of a simple concise form, powerful controls, and hypertext linkages helps to explain the overwhelming popularity of the Web as an information retrieval and investigation tool.

The four-plus faces of HTML

In a manner of speaking, all there is to HTML besides content is a collection of character entities and markup tags. Some purists insist on remaining within the confines of the SGML DTD for HTML, but the number and kinds of tags and entities used in various Web environments (especially in some of the more advanced browsers) continue to expand with each passing day and each new version of browser software.

Although some browsers may recognize tags and entities unknown to other browsers, HTML includes the convention that all unrecognized markup is ignored. You may lose some of the finer formatting controls with some browsers (like the `<BLINK>` tag, currently recognized only by Netscape), but the content should still be quite accessible.

Today, HTML has several standardization levels, numbered zero through three:

0   The original text-only markup language developed for prototype browsers at CERN prior to HTML's release to the general public. You shouldn't see any tools that remain at this level, except for historical curiosities.

1   The initial public implementation of HTML markup, which included the ability to reference graphical elements in addition to text controls. Many browsers — for example, Lynx and cello — still operate at level 1 HTML.

2   The current implementation of HTML markup, which includes all markup elements for level 1 plus tags for interactive forms. Most graphical browsers — like Mosaic, Netscape, and WinWeb or MacWeb — support level 2 HTML.

3   The name of another HTML level that is no longer under development as such. Throughout the rest of the book, we refer to this level generically as *beyond 2.0,* when we're not referring to some specific HTML standards document.

The group that manages the HTML standards, known as the World Wide Web Consortium or W3C, realized that it took too long for the agglomeration of standards known as HTML 2.0 to make it through the approval process. Thus, it decided to treat the components of what was called HTML 3.0 individually, to get them through the approval process faster. Today, these elements include things like mathematics notation, tables, frames, and more. You'll often hear them called HTML 3.0, but we think it's important for you to recognize that this nomenclature is no longer exact. (In Chapter 12, we cover this information in detail.)

To find out what's current for HTML, you can always go trolling on the Web itself. You should be able to find the current specification, in the form of the HTML DTD, along with online documentation on HTML markup and usage, as well as current information on SGML.

HTML Elements!

Well-structured HTML documents come in three parts, consisting of

- ✔ **A head** that identifies the document as HTML and establishes its title
- ✔ **A body** that contains the content for a Web page. This part holds all displayed text on a page (except for the title), as well as all links to graphics, multimedia information, locations inside the same HTML file, or other Web documents.
- ✔ **A footer** that labels the page by identifying its author, date of creation, and version number (if applicable)

In reality, HTML is very forgiving, so you can sometimes get away with skipping some of these elements. As a matter of good style and practice, however, we strongly recommend that any pages you design begin with the information necessary for all three elements.

Go to the head of the document

An entire HTML document should be bracketed by the identification tags `<HTML>` to open the document and `</HTML>` to close it. These tags identify the DTD for the document to an SGML-sensitive program, to allow it to interpret the document's contents properly. You can get away with omitting this tag for most browsers, but with the increasing convergence of HTML and SGML, doing so may limit the shelf life of your Web pages.

An optional line may sometimes precede your document head. It is called a *document type prolog* and describes, in SGML, that the following HTML document complies to the indicated level of the HTML DTD. Here is an example:

```
<!DOCTYPE HTML PUBLIC "-//IETF//DTD HTML 2.0//EN">
```

By deciphering this line, you can tell that the HTML document conforms to the HTML 2.0 DTD distributed by the Internet Engineering Task Force (IETF). You can also tell that the DTD is PUBLIC and is not system dependent. Finally, you can tell that the HTML tag set is defined by the English language (the EN in the DOCTYPE statement above). Local SGML parsers can also use this DOCTYPE statement to validate the HTML document; that is, the parsers check the document's syntax for conformance and correctness. This prolog will become increasingly important in the future.

A document title is flagged by the HTML tags `<TITLE>`, to open the heading section, and `</TITLE>` to close it. Within this section, you commonly find the actual title and possibly some other document heading tags, which we cover in more detail in Chapters 5 and 7. The important thing about an HTML document heading is that it should identify itself in an informative and catchy way.

HTML also includes a pair of tags, <HEAD> and </HEAD> to physically identify the head of a document. As with the <HTML> and </HTML> tags, many browsers happily let you skip this tag, but for readability and structure, we recommend including it anyway.

The bulk's in the document body

The real content for any HTML document occurs in the body section, which is enclosed within <BODY> and </BODY> tags. The body is where you describe your document's layout and structure by using a variety of tags for text headings, embedded graphics, text paragraphs, lists, and other elements. Not surprisingly, the majority of HTML tags occur within a document's body, simply because that's where all the beef is!

Chapter 5 covers all HTML tags in brief form, and Parts III and IV of this book provide lots of examples. Remember, this is just the overview.

The good stuff's in the graphics and links

You also find all hypertext content within the document's body section. This content can take the form of references to graphics or other files, as indicated by the appropriate use of text tags like <IMG> for in-line graphics. Or, you can have links to other points within the same document or to outside documents by using the *anchor* tags (<A>, </A>) with the appropriate attributes. In fact, because anchors point to generalized URLs (not just other HTML documents), you can also use them to invoke services like FTP to transfer multimedia files from within your Web pages.

Chapters 8, 11, 12, and 14 offer lots of details about using graphics within HTML documents, including good sources for material, appropriate usage, and other sorts of graphical information goodies. By the time you're through with this book, you'll be slinging HTML graphics around with the best WebMasters!

A footer may be optional, but it's a good idea

Technically speaking, HTML doesn't include a separate tag to denote a page footer — that is, there's no <FOOT> and </FOOT> pair to label the information that would typically appear in a footer. Nevertheless, we strongly recommend that you include a footer on every Web page that you create, just for the record.

"What's in a footer?" you ask. Well, it should contain information to describe the page and its author(s). A good footer also helps to identify a document's vintage and contents and lets interested readers contact the owners of the page if they spot errors or want to provide feedback.

For your own sake, it's also smart to include date and version information in each of your HTML files. Doing this enables you to recognize what version you're dealing with whenever you look at a page, plus it provides a great reminder of how stale your pages are getting. As any real Web-head knows, the older the information, the more likely it is to be out-of-date!

Chapter 8 provides lots of details about page footers and includes a particularly fine example of what a good footer should look like. Be sure not to miss it.

Ladies and Gentlemen, Start Your Engines!

Okay, so now you've seen the basic elements of HTML. In the chapters that follow, we introduce you to the details, including more tags than you meet at a Red Tag sale at your local department store. As you come to know and love what HTML can do, you can apply what you're learning to build great Web pages.

Chapter 5

Pigeonholing Page Contents: HTML Categories

In This Chapter

▶ Defining HTML's tag syntax in detail

▶ Categorizing HTML tags

▶ Stepping through HTML, tag-by-tag

*A*t last you've arrived at your first real in-depth look at HTML in this book. In this chapter, we talk some more turkey about HTML syntax, to make sure that you can keep up with all the gory details. We also establish some categories for what HTML can do and group the markup tags into meaningful categories (to make them easier to learn and use). The remainder of the chapter is a reference tool, where we describe all the HTML tags in alphabetical order for easy access.

HTML Syntax Redux

In the preceding chapter, we talk about a general syntax for HTML tags. At this point, here's what we've presented:

✔ Tags are enclosed in left and right angle brackets; for example, `<HEAD>` marks the beginning of the head of an HTML document.

✔ By convention only (HTML itself has no requirement for upper- or lower-case), we present all tags in uppercase for readability. That's why you see `<HEAD>` but not `<Head>` or `<head>` in the rest of this book, even though all three are perfectly legal — and equivalent — HTML tags. We recommend that you follow this practice yourself because it helps you to separate the tags from the real text.

✔ Tags usually come in pairs, so `<HEAD>` marks the beginning of a document heading block, and `</HEAD>` marks the end. All the text that occurs between the opening and closing tags is considered to be the focus of that tag and is handled appropriately. The majority of HTML tags work this way, so we'll be sure to flag all possible exceptions as we introduce them.

✔ Tags can sometimes take on one or more attributes to define data sources or destinations, to specify URLs, or to further specify the characteristics of the text to which a tag is applied. For example, the `<IMG>` tag for placing graphics can use the following attributes to help specify the source and placement of an image on a page:

- `SRC` = source for image, same as URL

- `ALT` = alternate text to display inline if browser isn't graphics-capable or if graphics are turned off

- `ALIGN = (TOP|MIDDLE|BOTTOM)` **and** `(\[WIDTH=number] andr [HEIGHT=number]\)` controls placement of a graphic. We explain this in more detail later, when we tell you what you don't already know!

- `ISMAP` If this attribute is present, it indicates that the graphic is a clickable image map with one or more links to other locations built onto the image. If it's absent, the image is not a map.

Some attributes take on values — in this case, `SRC`, `ALT`, and `ALIGN` all require at least one value — while others, like `ISMAP`, do not. Attributes that do not require values are usually true (turned on) if present and false (turned off) when omitted. Also, tags have default values for required attributes that are omitted, so make sure that you check the HTML specification (if you are unsure).

At this point, you may already know quite a bit about HTML syntax and layout. But there is quite a bit of additional stuff that you need to know, some of which we had to use in our discussion in the preceding bullet item. Discussions of this additional stuff contain some goofy characters that aren't part of HTML itself, but are necessary to explain it formally.

In the sections that follow, we begin with formal syntax conventions and then move on to more interesting properties of HTML itself.

Syntax conventions are no party!

While we're providing formal definitions of the various HTML commands, we use typographical notation in an equally formal way. What this means (in plain language) is that you'd better pay attention to how we write some things down, because we intend for the notation to describe how terms should be combined, constructed, and used.

Metacharacters, anyone?

Describing a formal syntax means using certain characters in a special way to talk about how to treat elements that appear in conjunction with these characters. The descriptions follow the nearly identical HTML notions:

✔ Angle brackets surround a tag (`<HEAD>`)

✔ A forward slash following the left angle bracket denotes a closing tag (`</HEAD>`)

✔ An ampersand leads off a character entity and a semicolon closes it (`andegrave;`)

These special characters clue us (and our browser software) into the need for special handling.

The characters we're going to use for our HTML syntax come from conventions developed for a formal syntax — called a *Backus-Naur Form* (or BNF grammar, for short) — that was developed for programming languages. Because we're forced to deviate somewhat from BNF, we'll lay out all the special characters that we'll use to describe syntax. Table 5-1 contains these characters (which, by the way, are called *metacharacters*), their definitions, and an example for each one.

Table 5-1   The HTML Syntax Metacharacter Set

Char(s)	*Name(s)*	*Definition*	*Example*
|	vertical bar	separates legal choices	ITEM1|ITEM2|ITEM3
( )	parentheses	defines a set of items to treat as a unit	(ITEM1|ITEM2) or (ITEM3|ITEM4)
\\	backslashes	indicates that one or more items can be selected	\ITEM1|ITEM2|ITEM3\
and	logical and	indicates that both items must be selected	(ITEM1|ITEM2) and (ITEM3|ITEM4)
or	logical or	indicates that one or the other item must be selected	ITEM1 or ITEM2
andr	and/or	indicates that one or both items must be selected	ITEM1 andr ITEM2
[ ]	square brackets	indicates nonstandard items, not supported by all browsers	[WIDTH=number]
integer	integer	indicates whole numbers only	1, 2944, -40
. . .	ellipsis	repeats elements as needed	ITEM1|ITEM2|...
{ }	curly braces	contains optional elements, not required	{ITEM1|ITEM2}

Decoding a complex metacharacter example: ALIGN = ?

Nothing beats an example for making sense out of this potential gibberish. Recall our definition of the ALIGN attribute for the <IMG> tag:

```
ALIGN = (TOP|MIDDLE|BOTTOM) and (\[WIDTH=number] andr
    [HEIGHT=number]\)
```

To make sure that you understand what this formalism means, we restate the example as follows:

ALIGN = TOP|MIDDLE|BOTTOM means that ALIGN can take one of the three values, TOP, MIDDLE, or BOTTOM. Basically, you use it to say whether you want an image at the top, middle, or bottom of a display area on-screen.

Also, ALIGN can take a member of the set (TOP|MIDDLE|BOTTOM), and it can sometimes take one or both members of the set (\[WIDTH=number]|[HEIGHT=number]\).

Sometimes, ALIGN can take either or both of a WIDTH and HEIGHT setting. The backslashes (\ \) around the WIDTH and HEIGHT and the logical and/or (andr) entries indicate either or both. Each of those two entries must be assigned some integer value corresponding to a position relative to the current display area, as indicated by the number part. WIDTH and HEIGHT are also supported only on certain browsers, as indicated by the square brackets ([ ]).

As you can see, what we can describe in a single complex line of type takes three paragraphs of details to explain completely. The brevity and compactness of formal syntax makes it appealing to computer nerds; as you review the various tags, we hope that you are able to work your way through this syntax to fully grasp what HTML can do. If not, never fear — we provide plenty of examples for each tag so that you can absorb by osmosis what you can't grasp through formalism! Ouch!

Interesting HTML properties

In addition to the formal syntax for HTML that we use throughout the book, the markup language itself has some interesting general properties that are worth covering before you encounter the tags directly.

No embedded blanks, please!

All HTML tags require that the characters in a name be contiguous. You can't insert extra blanks within a tag or its surrounding markup without causing that tag to be ignored (which is what browsers do with tags they can't recognize).

This means that `</HEAD>` is a valid closing tag for a document heading, but that none of the following are legal:

```
< /HEAD>
</ HEAD>
</H EAD>
</HE AD>
</HEA D>
</HEAD >
```

We hope that you get the idea: Don't use blanks inside tags, except where you're using a blank *deliberately* to separate a tag name from an attribute name (for example, `<IMG SRC="sample.gif">` is legal, but `<IMGSRC="sample.gif">` is not).

When assigning values to attributes, however, spaces are OK. Therefore, all four of the following variants for this `SRC` assignment are legal:

```
<IMG SRC="sample.gif">
<!- Previous line: no spaces before or after = sign -->
<IMG SRC = "sample.gif">
<!- Previous line: spaces before and after = sign -->
<IMG SRC= "sample.gif">
<!- Previous line: no space before, one after = sign -->
<IMG SRC ="sample.gif">
<!- Previous line: one space before, none after = sign -->
```

Where one space is legal, multiple spaces are legal. Don't get carried away with what's legal or not, though — try to make your HTML documents as readable as possible and everything else should flow naturally.

We sneaked some more HTML markup into the preceding example. After each `<IMG>` tag line, we inserted readable HTML comments to describe what occurred on the preceding line. This lets you infer that the HTML markup to open a comment is the string <!- and the string -> closes the comment. As you go through the markup section later on, we cover some style guidelines for using comments effectively and correctly.

What's the default?

If a tag can support an attribute, what does it mean when the attribute isn't present? For `ISMAP` on the `<IMG>` tag, for example, you already know that when the `ISMAP` attribute is present, it means *the image is a clickable map.* If `ISMAP` is absent, this means *the image is not a clickable map.*

This is a way of introducing the concept of a *default,* which is not a way of assigning blame, but rather a way of deciding what to assume when an attribute is not supplied for a particular tag. For `ISMAP`, the default is absent; that is, an image is assumed to be a clickable map only when the `ISMAP` attribute is explicitly supplied.

But how do images get displayed if the ALIGN attribute isn't defined? As a quick bit of experimentation shows you, the default for most graphical browsers is to insert the graphic at the left-hand margin. These kinds of defaults are important, too, and we'll try to tell you what to expect from them.

The nesting instinct

Sometimes it's necessary to insert one set of markup tags within another. You may decide that one word within a heading needs to have special emphasis to make it stand out. For example, it may be more dramatic to have the word *Emergency* stand out in the heading "Emergency Phone Numbers" for a list of numbers you put together.

When you start enclosing one set of markup within another, it's called *nesting*. When the nesting instinct strikes you, the best rule of thumb is to close first what you've opened most recently. For example, the text tags <STRONG> . . . </STRONG> provide a way of bracketing text that requires strong emphasis. If you wanted to emphasize text within a level two heading, <H2> . . . </H2>, the proper way to handle the emphasis is like this:

```
<H2><STRONG>Emergency</STRONG> Phone Numbers</H2>
```

That way, you close the nested <STRONG> tag with its mate, before you close out the <H2> heading. Some browsers may let you violate this rule, but others may behave unpredictably if you don't open and close tags in the right order. Figure 5-1 shows what the <STRONG> emphasis looks like. (Notice that the word *Emergency* appears in heavier type than the rest of the heading.)

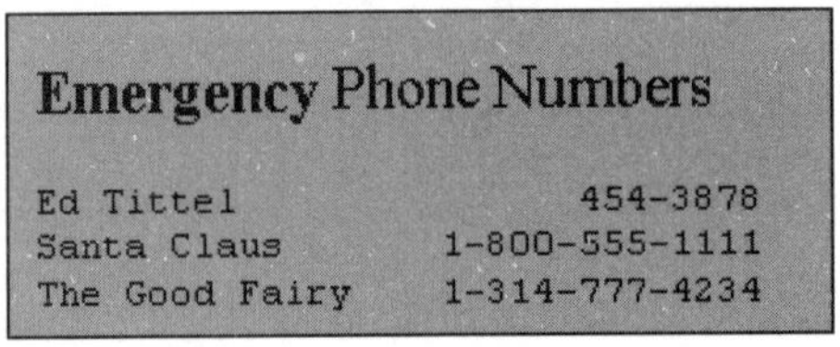

Figure 5-1:
Using
nested tags
for
emphasis
within a
heading.

Emergency Phone Numbers

```
Ed Tittel              454-3878
Santa Claus       1-800-555-1111
The Good Fairy    1-314-777-4234
```

Nesting just doesn't make sense for some tags. For example, within <TITLE> . . . </TITLE>, you're dealing with information that shows up only on a window title, rather than on a particular Web page. Text and layout controls clearly do not apply here (and are cheerfully ignored by some browsers, while making others curl up and die).

Always look back to the left as you start closing tags that you've opened. Close the closest one first, the next one next, and so on. Check the tag details (later on in this chapter) to find out what tags are OK to nest within your outermost open tag. If the tag that you want to use isn't on the OK list, then don't try to nest that tag inside the current open ones. Close out what you've got open and then open the tag that you need.

Keeping your tags in the right nests keeps your readers' browsers from getting confused! It also makes sure that you hatch only good-looking Web pages.

A matter of context

As you discover which tags can appear inside which other tags, you begin to develop an appreciation for the controls and capabilities offered by HTML. In our alphabetical list (later in this chapter), we cover the nesting compatibilities under the heading "Context" to indicate what tags are OK to nest (and by exclusion, what are not).

HTML Categories

Before we take you through the HTML tags in alphabetical order, we'd like to introduce them to you, grouped by category. These categories help to explain how and when the tags are used, and what functions they provide.

We hope that the categories presented in Table 5-2 also help you to organize and understand HTML's numerous tags. (For a complete listing of the HTML character entities, please consult Chapter 6.) Because so many tags come in pairs, we use an ellipsis (. . .) between opening and closing tags to indicate where text and other elements can appear.

Table 5-2	HTML Categories and Their Respective Tags	
Category/ Tags	*Tag Names*	*Category Description/ Brief Explanation*
Comments		To document HTML design, techniques, and so on
<!–. . .–>	Comment	Supports author comments; ignored by browser but digestible by GML parsers or document management systems
Document Structure		Basic document layout and linkage structures
<HTML>. . .</HTML>	HTML	Blocks out an entire HTML document
<HEAD>. . .</HEAD>	Head	Blocks out a document's head
<BODY>. . .</BODY>	Body	Blocks out a document's body
<BASE>	Base	Indicates complete document URL, establishes location context for other URLs referenced

(continued)

Table 5-2 *(continued)*

Category/ Tags	Tag Names	Category Description/ Brief Explanation
<ISINDEX>	Isindex	Indicates that document supports CGI script for searches
<LINK>	Link type	Sets relationship between current document and other documents
<NEXTID>	Next document	Indicates the "next" document that follows current, to permit HTML documents to be chained together
<META>	Structure	Describes aspects of the page's info structure, contents, or relationships to other documents
Document Headings		Supply document title and heading levels, provide important organization and layout elements
<TITLE> ... </TITLE>	Title	Supplies title that labels entire document
<H1> ... </H1>	Level 1 head	First-level heading
<H2> ... </H2>	Level 2 head	Second-level heading
<H3> ... </H3>	Level 3 head	Third-level heading
<H4> ... </H4>	Level 4 head	Fourth-level heading
<H5> ... </H5>	Level 5 head	Fifth-level heading
<H6> ... </H6>	Level 6 head	Sixth-level heading
Links		Create links to anchor or another document, or create anchor point for another link
<A> ... </A>	Anchor or link	Provides fundamental hypertext link capabilities
Layout Elements		Control document appearance, add elements
<ADDRESS> ... </ADDRESS>		Author contact information for document
<BLOCKQUOTE> ... </BLOCKQUOTE>		Use to set off long quotes or citations
 	Line break	Forces a line break into on-screen text flow
<PRE> ... </PRE>	Preformatted text	Preserves spacing and layout of original text in monospaced font
<HR>	Horizontal rule	Draws a horizontal line across the page

Category/ Tags	Tag Names	Category Description/ Brief Explanation
Graphics		References to inline images for documents
<IMG>	Image	Inserts a referenced image into a document with alternate text, clickable map, and placement controls
Forms		Forms-related markup tags
<FORM> . . . </FORM>	Form block	Marks beginning and end of form block
<INPUT>	Input widget	Defines type and appearance for input widgets
<TEXTAREA> . . . </TEXTAREA>	Text area	Multiline text entry widget
<SELECT> . . . </SELECT>	Input pick list	Creates a menu or scrolling list of input items
<OPTION> [. . . </OPTION>]	Selectable item	Assigns a value or default to an input item
Paragraphs		Break up running text into readable chunks
<P>	Paragraph	Breaks up text into spaced regions
Lists		Provide methods to lay out item or element sequences in document content
<DIR> . . . </DIR>	Directory list	Marks unbulleted list of short elements (less than 20 characters in length)
<LI>	List item	Marks a member item within a list of any type
<OL> . . . </OL>	Ordered list	Marks numbered list of elements
<UL> . . . </UL>	Unordered list	Marks bulleted list of elements
<MENU> . . . </MENU>	Menu list	Marks a pickable list of elements
<DL> . . . </DL>	Glossary list	Marks a special format for terms and their definitions
<DT>	Definition term	Marks the term being defined in a glossary list
<DD>	Definition datum	Marks the definition for a term in a glossary list
Text Controls		Character formatting tags
<B> . . . </B>	Boldface	Produces bolded text
<CITE> . . . </CITE>	Short citation	Marks distinctive text for citations
<CODE> . . . </CODE>	Code font	Used for code samples

(continued)

Table 5-2 *(continued)*

Category/ Tags	Tag Names	Category Description/ Brief Explanation
Text Controls *(cont'd)*		Character formatting tags
<DFN>...</DFN>	Defined term	Used to emphasize a term about to be defined in the following text
<EM>...</EM>	Emphasis	Adds emphasis to enclosed text
<I>...</I>	Italic	Produces italicized text
<KBD>...</KBD>	Keyboard text	Marks text to be typed at keyboard
<SAMP>...</SAMP>	Sample text	Marks sample in-line text
<STRONG>...</STRONG>	Strong emphasis	Provides maximum emphasis to enclosed text
<TT>...</TT>	Typewriter text	Produces a typewriter font
<VAR>...</VAR>	Variable	Marks variable or substitution for some other value

Now, let's review the HTML categories that we just introduced, before providing detailed syntax for each tag:

- ✔ **Comments:** Comments give HTML authors a way to annotate their documents, and browsers do not ordinarily display them. Any assumptions, special conditions, or nonstandard elements should be enclosed in comments to help other readers understand what the document is trying to accomplish and to assist with the testing process.

- ✔ **Document Structure:** Numerous tags help to provide structure for HTML documents. They provide an overall HTML label and break up documents into head and body sections. They also provide markup to establish links to other documents and to indicate support for electronic indexing capabilities. While this markup produces little in the way of visible display, it is important to the construction of well-designed Web pages.

- ✔ **Document Headings:** Headings provide structure for a document's content, starting with its title, all the way down to sixth-level headings. They provide meaningful clues for document navigation, and when used in conjunction with a hypertext table of contents, they can permit readers to quickly jump to other sections.

- ✔ **Links:** Links provide the controls to anchor points within a document or to link one document to another. They are the foundation for the Web's hypertext capabilities.

✔ **Layout Elements:** Layout elements introduce specific items within the text of a document, including line breaks, lengthy quotes, and horizontal rules, to divide up distinct text areas and preformatted text to capture spacing and layout exactly from the source, based on a monospaced font (which makes preformatted text kind of ugly). They also include a format for building author information on a page, which is an element that we recommend for all good Web pages.

✔ **Graphics:** Graphics enter an HTML file through the `<IMG>` command, which we've already covered in some detail. Suffice it to say that `<IMG>` points to the graphics source, provides a text alternative for nongraphical browsing, and indicates whether a graphical element is a clickable map.

✔ **Forms:** Forms provide the essential mechanism for soliciting readers, feedback and input on the Web. Forms tags cover how forms are set up, provide a variety of graphical and text widgets for soliciting input, and supply methods to allow readers to select options from various types of pick lists.

✔ **Paragraphs:** The paragraph is the fundamental unit of text for HTML documents as well as ordinary text. The `<P>` tag allows authors to break their content up into easily digestible chunks.

✔ **Lists:** HTML includes numerous styles for building lists, ranging from numbered to bulleted lists, glossary entries complete with definitions, and selectable menu entries. All styles provide useful tools to improve readability by organizing lists of items or elements.

✔ **Text Controls:** HTML also offers numerous inline controls for adding emphasis or special appearance to text. It provides tools for describing user input and for including samples of computer code, computer output, variables, and sample text. You can use text controls to represent different kinds of online text for building materials for online use.

From managing document structure to controlling the look and feel of text on a page, HTML includes tags to make these things happen. In the next section, we examine the nitty-gritty details of all the various HTML 2.0 tags.

HTML Tags

The remainder of this chapter is devoted to an alphabetical listing of a broad range of HTML tags taken from the HTML 2.0 DTD.

Because so many browser-builders are adding extensions to HTML for their own use, and because standards beyond HTML 2.0 have introduced significant changes and enhancements to HTML, you should consider this list neither exhaustive nor complete. We do hope it is informative and useful, however, and we encourage you to skim it over, just to see all the possibilities that HTML offers. For a look at what's beyond HTML 2.0, please check out the disk included with this book (explained in Chapter 12).

The rundown on attributes

In HTML, attributes typically take one of two forms within a tag:

- `ATTRIBUTE="value"`: Where `value` is typically enclosed in quotes (" ") and may be one of the following kinds of elements:

URL	a Uniform Resource Locator
name	a user-supplied name, probably for an input field
number	a user-supplied numeric value
text	user-supplied text
server	server-dependent name (such as page name defaults)
(X|Y|Z)	one member of a set of fixed values

- `ATTRIBUTE`: Where the name itself provides information about how the tag should behave (for example, `ISMAP` in `<IMG>` indicates that the graphic is a clickable map).

For a discussion of attributes for individual tags, look in the "Attributes" section under the tag name. For each one, we provide a definition. We also indicate choices for predefined sets of values or provide an example for open-ended value assignments.

Tag information layout

Before we provide our alphabetical list of tags, you need to understand what information we're presenting and how it's presented. Using the familiar image tag (`<IMG>`), we show you what a typical listing looks like:

<IMG>

Definition: Supplies image source, placement, and behavior information. Used to place in-line graphics on a page.

Attributes:

SRC="URL"

> URL is a standard Uniform Resource Locator and specifies the location for image file, which is usually .GIF or .JPEG format.

ALT="text"

> Supplies an alternate string of text to display (and possibly make clickable) if the browser has no graphics capability or if graphics are turned off.

ALIGN=("TOP" | "MIDDLE" | "BOTTOM") and [WIDTH="number"] andr [HEIGHT="number"]

> Standard use calls for ALIGN to be set to one of the following values: TOP, MIDDLE, or BOTTOM to define placement.
>
> Optional values also permit more precise placement using a pixel-level height and width specification.

ISMAP

> Indicates by its presence that the image (or its text replacement) should be a clickable map. This often invokes special map-handling software through the CGI interface on the Web server handling the request.

Context:

<IMG> is legal within the following markup tags

> <ADDRESS>, <B>, <CITE>, <CODE>, <DD>, <DT>, <EM>, <H*>, <I>, <KBD>, <LI>, <PRE>, <SAMP>, <STRONG>, <TT>, <VAR>
>
> ***Note:*** When referring to heading tags <H1> through <H6> we abbreviate the whole series as <H*> as we did above.

Suggested style/usage: Keep images small and use them judiciously; graphics should add impact and interest to pages without adding too much bulk (or wait time).

Examples:

```
<IMG SRC="images/redball.gif" ALIGN="TOP" WIDTH="50" HEIGHT="50"
ALT="Menu Items">
<IMG SRC="http://www.noplace.com/show-me/pictures/fun.gif"
ALIGN="TOP" ISMAP ALT="Fun places to visit">
```

Tag layout commentary

Notice the use of our HTML syntax notation in the "Attributes" section; you see the syntax here most often. Because <IMG> is a stand-alone tag (that is, there's no closing </IMG>), we don't show a pair of tags here, but we do show tags in pairs whenever appropriate.

The last item for discussion is the "Context" section. In this section, you see where it's legal to put <IMG> tags inside other markup, between <PRE> . . . </PRE> tags, for example. Just because you can use this tag in such a way doesn't mean that you have to do so; as always, use markup judiciously to add impact or value to information. Complex compositions seldom delight anyone other than their makers, so try to keep things simple whenever you can.

The HTML tag team

This section shows an alphabetical listing of the most common and widely used HTML tags, taken from the HTML 1.0 and 2.0 DTDs. Where applicable, we also include information on widely-used extensions to standard tags. See this book's disk and Chapter 12 for an in-depth look at nonstandard tags, other browser-specific extensions to HTML, and a review of a number of tags mentioned in draft standards from *beyond* the HTML 2.0 specification.

<A> ... </A> Anchor

Definition: An anchor marks either the source or the destination of a document link. If it's the destination, it uses the NAME attribute; if it's the source, it uses the HREF attribute.

Attributes:

HREF="URL"

> URL is a standard Uniform Resource Locator specifying the location of another network resource, usually the URL for another HTML file, but it can also be a pointer to services provided by FTP, Telnet, WAIS, e-mail, or Gopher.

NAME="text"

> Supplies a marked location point within the document to act as a destination for a hypertext link; the text supplied for this attribute acts just like an anchor "to hold a place" for a link to attach to.

REL=("next" | "previous" | "parent" | "made")

> The REL attribute specifies the relationship between the current anchor and the destination.

> "next" indicates that the URL points to the next page in a sequence; "previous" indicates that it points to the prior page; and "parent" indicates that the current page is the parent of the destination page. "made" indicates that the destination page contains information about the current anchor page's maker or owner. (***Note:*** This attribute is proposed and not yet supported in an "official" HTML DTD.)

REV=("next" | "previous" | "parent" | "made")

> REV is the reverse of the REL attribute and indicates the destination and the current anchor. All of the attribute values are the same but apply to the page to which URL points. Here, "made" indicates that this document contains information about the maker or owner of the destination page. (***Note:*** This attribute is proposed and not yet supported in an "official" HTML DTD.)

TITLE="text"

> Provides advisory information about the title of the destination document (usually, the same text as enclosed by the <TITLE> . . . </TITLE> tags in that document).

Context:

<A> . . . </A> is legal within

> <ADDRESS>, <B>, <BLOCKQUOTE>, <BODY>, <CITE>, <CODE>, <DD>, <DT>, <EM>, <FORM>, <H*>, <I>, <KBD>, <LI>, <P>, <PRE>, <SAMP>, <STRONG>, <TT>, <VAR>

The following markup can be used within <A> . . . </A>

> <B>, <BR>, <CITE>, <CODE>, <EM>, <H*>, <I>, <IMG>, <KBD>, <SAMP>, <STRONG>, <TT>, <VAR>

Suggested style/usage: Anchors should be innermost when used within nested markup, except when using embedded character controls, font styles, or line breaks. Relative URLs make for more compact references but require more maintenance.

Examples:

```
<A HREF="../../MailRobot/Overview.html">Mail Robot</A>
<A HREF="http://www.w3.org/hypertext/WWW/Archive/
www-announce">archive</A>
```

<ADDRESS> . . . </ADDRESS> Attribution info

Definition: <ADDRESS> . . . </ADDRESS> tags enclose attribution information about an HTML document, which should usually include things like the author's name and address, signature files, contact information, and so on. For more details, please see Chapter 10.

Attributes: None

Context:

<ADDRESS> . . . </ADDRESS> is legal within

> <BLOCKQUOTE>, <BODY>, <FORM>

The following markup can be used within <ADDRESS> . . . <ADDRESS>

> <A>, <B>, <BR>, <CITE>, <CODE>, <EM>, <I>, <IMG>, <KBD>, <P>, <SAMP>, <STRONG>, <TT>, <VAR>

Suggested style/usage: Recommended for inclusion at the end of any document, to supply author contact information for questions or feedback.

Examples:

```
<ADDRESS>Ed Tittel 5810 Lookout Mountain Drive <BR>
Austin, TX 78731-3618<BR>
E-mail: etittel@zilker.net</ADDRESS>
```

<B> . . . </B> Bold style

Definition: Encloses text to be boldfaced.

Attributes: None

Context:

<B> . . . </B> is legal within

> <A>, <ADDRESS>, <B>, <BLOCKQUOTE>, <BODY>, <CITE>, <CODE>, <DD>, <DT>, <EM>, <FORM>, <H*>, <I>, <KBD>, <LI>, <P>, <PRE>, <SAMP>, <STRONG>, <TT>, <VAR>

The following markup can be used within <B> . . . </B>

> <A>, <BR>, <CITE>, <CODE>, <EM>, <I>, <IMG>, <KBD>, <SAMP>, <STRONG>, <TT>, <VAR>

Suggested style/usage: To provide special focus on specific words or phrases in text. For more discussion on effective use of character tags, please consult the following URL:

```
http://www.hal.com/products/sw/olias/Build-html01994-10-17/
   GDgsOXBMCmF84aK.html
```

Examples:

```
<P>The only reason for the trouble, to our way of thinking, is
<B>the complete lack of respect</B> for the older generation.
```

<BASE> Basis for relative addressing

Definition: <BASE> normally occurs within <HEAD> . . . </HEAD> and provides the URL basis for subsequent URL references in <LINK> or anchor statements within the body of the document. This makes URLs quicker and more compact to write, if the <BASE> represents a good starting point for other references (ideally, they should all be within one directory level of this reference).

Attributes:

HREF="URL"

> The fully qualified URL for the current document is required here.

Context:

<BASE> is legal within

> <HEAD>

No additional markup can be used within <BASE>.

Suggested style/usage: Whenever you build complex, multipage collections, it's a good idea to use the <BASE> tag in each page, and to build a directory structure that's easy to use and navigate.

Examples:

```
<HEAD>
<TITLE>Sample Document</TITLE>
<BASE HREF="http://www.w3.org/hypertext/WWW/">
</HEAD>
```

<BLOCKQUOTE>...</BLOCKQUOTE> Quote style

Definition: <BLOCKQUOTE>...</BLOCKQUOTE> is used to set off material quoted from external sources, publications, or other materials.

Attributes: None

Context:

<BLOCKQUOTE>...</BLOCKQUOTE> is legal within

> <BLOCKQUOTE>, <BODY>, <DD>, <FORM>, <LI>

The following markup can be used within <BLOCKQUOTE>...</BLOCKQUOTE>

> <A>, <ADDRESS>, <B>, <BLOCKQUOTE>, <BR>, <CITE>, <CODE>, <DIR>, <DL>, <EM>, <FORM>, <H*>, <HR>, <I>, <IMG>, <ISINDEX>, <KBD>, <MENU>, <OL>, <P>, <PRE>, <SAMP>, <STRONG>, <TT>, <UL>, <VAR>

Suggested style/usage: Whenever you use a quote more than one line long from an external source, it's a good idea to use <BLOCKQUOTE>. Don't forget to attribute your sources (remember to use <CITE> to highlight the actual publication, if applicable).

Examples:

```
<BLOCKQUOTE>A man who knows not how to write may think this no
great feat. But only try to do it yourself and you shall learn how
arduous is the writer's task. It dims your eyes, makes your back
ache, knits your chest and belly together. It is a terrible ordeal
for the whole body.</BLOCKQUOTE>
```

(Anonymous quote taken from Goldfarb's *SGML Handbook*; as true today as it was in the 12th century!)

<BODY> . . . </BODY> Mark off HTML document body

Definition: The <BODY> . . . </BODY> tags delimit the body of an HTML document, and should completely enclose its content.

Attributes: None

Context:

<BODY> . . . </BODY> is legal within

> <HTML>

The following markup can be used within <BODY> . . . </BODY>

> <A>, <ADDRESS>, <B>, <BLOCKQUOTE>, <CITE>, <CODE>, <DIR>, <DL>,
> <EM>, <FORM>, <H*>, <HR>, <I>, <IMG>, <ISINDEX>, <KBD>, <MENU>, <OL>,
> <P>, <PRE>, <SAMP>, <STRONG>, <TT>, <UL>, <VAR>

Suggested style/usage: <BODY> . . . </BODY> has only one use: to set off the body of an HTML document. It is an explicit structure tag that is required for strictly interpreted HTML.

Examples:

```
<HTML>
<HEAD><TITLE>Sample Document</TITLE></HEAD>
<BODY>This document ain't got much body.</BODY>
</HTML>
```

*
 Force line break*

Definition:
 forces a line break in HTML text flow.

Attributes: None

Context:

 is legal within

> <A>, <ADDRESS>, <B>, <BODY>, <CITE>, <CODE>, <DD>, <DT>, <EM>, <FORM>, <H*>, <I>, <KBD>, <LI>, <P>, <PRE>, <SAMP>, <STRONG>, <TT>, <VAR>

No markup can be used within
 (it's a singleton markup element).

Suggested style/usage:
 can force line breaks in text whenever desired. It comes in handy for creating short lines of text.

Examples:

```
There was an old woman<BR>
Who lived in a shoe<BR>
```

<CITE> . . . </CITE> Citation markup

Definition: Use <CITE> . . . </CITE> to highlight document, publication, or other external resource citations.

Attributes: None

Context:

<CITE> . . . </CITE> is legal within

> <A>, <ADDRESS>, <B>, <BLOCKQUOTE>, <BODY>, <CITE>, <CODE>, <DD>, <DT>, <EM>, <FORM>, <H*>, <I>, <KBD>, <LI>, <P>, <PRE>, <SAMP>, <STRONG>, <TT>, <VAR>

The following markup can be used within <CITE> . . . </CITE>

> <A>, <ADDRESS>, <B>, <BLOCKQUOTE>, <BR>, <CITE>, <CODE>, <EM>, <DD>, <DT>, <FORM>, <H*>, <I>, <KBD>, <LI>, <P>, <PRE>, <SAMP>, <STRONG>, <TT>, <VAR>

Suggested style/usage: Use to highlight citations or other references to external data sources.

Examples:

```
<CITE>The Iliad</CITE> is arguably Homer's greatest epic.
```

<CODE>... </CODE> Program code text

Definition: <CODE>... </CODE> is meant to enclose programs or samples of program code to make it easier to read. (See Figure 5-2.)

```
void main () {
crispy rice1, rice2, rice3, rice4;
// rice4 gets the value of rice3 (with i =2):
rice4 = (rice1, rice2, rice3, rice3);
}
```

Attributes: None

Context:

<CODE>... </CODE> is legal within

> <A>, <ADDRESS>, <B>, <BLOCKQUOTE>, <BODY>, <CITE>, <CODE>, <DD>, <DT>, <EM>, <FORM>, <H*>, <I>, <KBD>, <LI>, <P>, <PRE>, <SAMP>, <STRONG>, <TT>, <VAR>

The following markup can be used within <CODE>... </CODE>

> <A>, <B>, <BR>, <CITE>, <CODE>, <EM>, <I>, <IMG>, <KBD>, <SAMP>, <STRONG>, <TT>, <VAR>

Suggested style/usage: To set off samples of program code or other computer-based information within a document body.

Examples:

```
<CODE>
void main and#40;and#41; and#123;<BR>
crispy rice1, rice2, rice3, rice4;<BR>
and#47;and#47; rice4 gets the value of rice3 and#40;with i
=2and#41;:<BR>
rice4 = and#40;rice1, rice2, rice3, rice3and#41;;<BR>
and#125;
</CODE>
```

<DD> Definition description

Definition: The descriptive part of a definition list element.

Attributes: None

Context:

<DD> is legal within

<DL>

The following markup can be used within <DD>

<A>, <B>, <BLOCKQUOTE>, <BR>, <CITE>, <CODE>, <DIR>, <DL>, <EM>, <FORM>, <I>, <IMG>, <ISINDEX>, <KBD>, <MENU>, <OL>, <P>, <PRE>, <SAMP>, <STRONG>, <TT>, <UL>, <VAR>

Suggested style/usage: For glossaries or other kinds of lists where a single term or line needs to be associated with a block of indented text. (See Figure 5-3.)

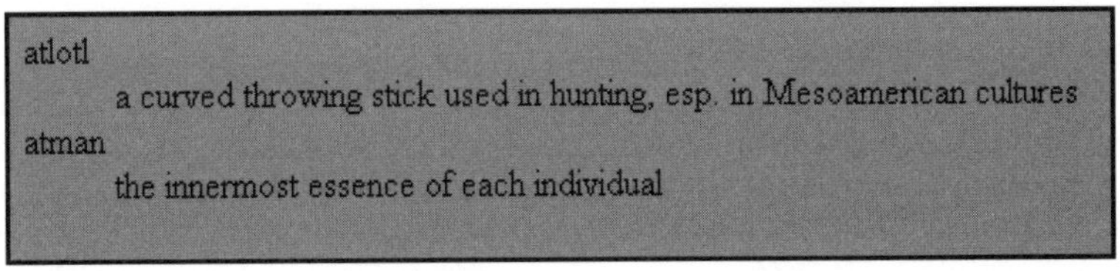

Figure 5-3:
The browser view of the "atlotl/atman" definition list.

atlotl
        a curved throwing stick used in hunting, esp. in Mesoamerican cultures
atman
        the innermost essence of each individual

Examples:

```
<DL>
<DT>atlotl
<DD>a curved throwing stick used in hunting, esp. in esoamerican
 cultures
<DT>atman
<DD>the innermost essence of each individual
</DL>
```

<DIR>... </DIR> Directory list

Definition: List style typically used for lists composed of short elements, like filenames. (See Figure 5-4.)

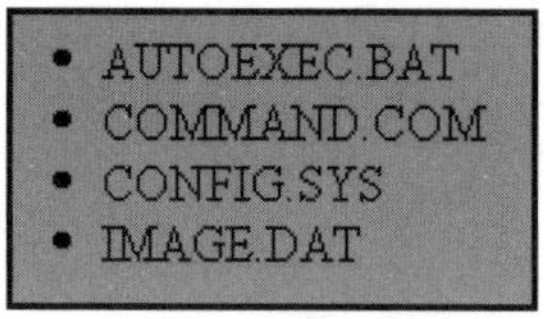

Figure 5-4:
A sample
<DIR> . . .
</DIR>
listing.

- AUTOEXEC.BAT
- COMMAND.COM
- CONFIG.SYS
- IMAGE.DAT

Attributes:

COMPACT

> Renders the directory style list more compactly than usual. ***Warning:*** This attribute is currently not supported by all browsers.

Context:

<DIR> . . . </DIR> is legal within

> <BLOCKQUOTE>, <BODY>, <DD>, <FORM>, <LI>

The following markup can be used within <DIR> . . . </DIR>

> <LI>

Suggested style/usage: Use <DIR> . . . </DIR> to build lists of short elements (usually, less than 20 characters).

Examples:

Here are some files you'll commonly find in a top-level DOS directory:

```
<DIR>
<LI>AUTOEXEC.BAT
<LI>COMMAND.COM
<LI>CONFIG.SYS
<LI>IMAGE.DAT
</DIR>
```

<DL> . . . </DL> Definition list

Definition: <DL> . . . </DL> encloses a collection of definition items <DD> in a definition list, usually used for glossaries or other situations where short, left-justified terms are followed by longer blocks of indented text. Definition lists are usually rendered with the term (<DT>) in the left margin and the definition (<DD>) on one or more lines indented slightly from the term.

Attributes:

COMPACT

> Indicates that line leading (white space between lines) should be reduced (see example). ***Warning:*** This attribute is currently not supported by all browsers.

Context:

<DL> . . . </DL> is legal within

> <BLOCKQUOTE>, <BODY>, <DD>, <FORM>, <LI>

The following markup can be used within <DL> . . . </DL>

> <DT>, <DD>

Suggested style/usage: For lists of terms and definitions, like glossaries or a dictionary or other situations where left-justified elements are followed by longer indented blocks of text. (See Figure 5-5.)

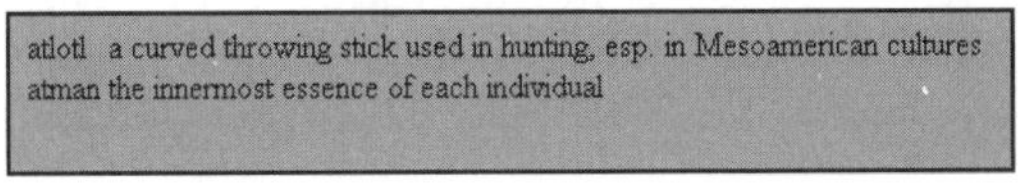

Figure 5-5:
COMPACT
version of
definition
listing from
Figure 5-3.

atlotl a curved throwing stick used in hunting, esp. in Mesoamerican cultures
atman the innermost essence of each individual

Examples:

```
<DL COMPACT>
<DT>atlotl
<DD>a curved throwing stick used in hunting, esp. in Mesoamerican
cultures
<DT>atman
<DD>the innermost essence of each individual
</DL>
```

<DT> Definition term
Definition: The descriptive part of a definition entry.

Attributes: None

Context:

<DT> is legal within

> <DL>

The following markup can be used within <DT>

> <A>, <B>, <BR>, <CITE>, <CODE>, <EM>, <I>, <IMG>, <KBD>, <SAMP>,
> <STRONG>, <TT>, <VAR>

Suggested style/usage: For glossaries, definition lists, or other situations where left-justified short entries pair up with longer blocks of indented text.

Examples:

See definitions for <DL> and <DD>.

<EM> . . . </EM> Emphasis

Definition: The <EM> tag provides typographic emphasis, usually rendered as italics. While <EM> and <I> often give the same effect, use <EM> except when referring to formatting in the text, as in "The italic parts are mandatory." This improves consistency between documents from various sources if, for example, a reader prefers to use color instead of italics for emphasis. (See Figure 5-6.)

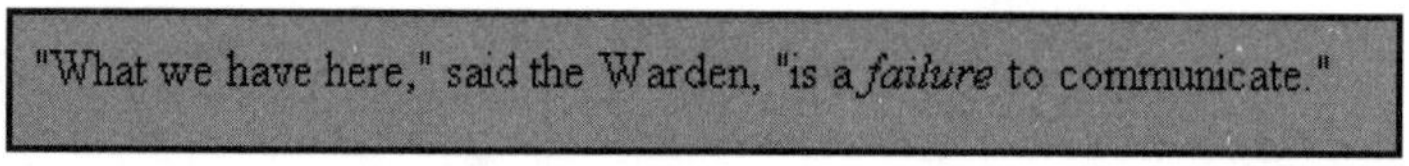

Figure 5-6:
Use of
simple text
emphasis
inline.

"What we have here," said the Warden, "is a *failure* to communicate."

Attributes: None

Context:

<EM> . . . </EM> is legal within

> <A>, <ADDRESS>, <B>, <BLOCKQUOTE>, <BODY>, <CITE>, <CODE>, <DD>,
> <DT>, <EM>, <FORM>, <H*>, <I>, <KBD>, <LI>, <P>, <PRE>, <SAMP>,
> <STRONG>, <TT>, <VAR>

The following markup can be used within <EM> . . . </EM>

<A>, <B>, <BR>, <CITE>, <CODE>, <EM>, <I>, <IMG>, <KBD>, <SAMP>, <STRONG>, <TT>, <VAR>

Suggested style/usage: Wherever mild emphasis in text is needed, but be sure to keep usage to a minimum, both in terms of the number of words emphasized and how often text emphasis occurs.

Examples:

```
"What we have here," said the Warden, "is a <EM>failure</EM> to
communicate."
```

<FORM> . . . </FORM> User input form

Definition: For defining an area that contains objects to solicit user input, ranging from selecting buttons or checkboxes, to areas for text input.

Attributes:

ACTION="URL"

URL is a standard Uniform Resource Locator. ACTION specifies the name of a resource for the browser to execute as an action in response to clicking on an on-screen Submit or Reset button.

The URL typically points to a CGI script or other executable service on a Web server that performs an action in response to being accessed. (*Note:* CGI stands for Common Gateway Interface, and defines how browsers can communicate with servers on the Web; for more details on CGI, please consult Chapter 12.)

METHOD=("GET" I "POST")

The METHOD attribute tells the browser how to interact with the service designated by the ACTION's URL. If no method is specified, GET is the default.

If GET is selected, the browser constructs a query URL that consists of the URL of the current page that contains the form, followed by a question mark, followed by the values of the form's input areas and other objects. The browser sends this query URL to the target URL specified by ACTION. The WWW server in the specified target URL uses the information supplied in the incoming URL to perform a search, process a query, or provide whatever services it has been programmed to deliver.

If POST is selected, the browser sends a copy of the form's contents to the recipient URL as a data block to the standard input service (stdin( ) or STDIN in the UNIX world). This makes it easy to grab and process form data. POST is the preferred method for most HTML programmers because with POST you can pass much more information in a cleaner fashion to the server than with the GET method.

Anything the recipient program writes to output returns to the sender as a new HTML document for further display or interaction. The recipient program can also save form data to a file on the local WWW server.

ENCTYPE="MIME type"

This attribute specifies the format of the submitted data in case the protocol does not impose a format itself. With the POST method, this attribute is a MIME type specifying the format of the posted data. The default value is "application/x-www-form-urlencoded" (for a discussion of URL encoding, see Chapter 16).

Context:

<FORM> . . . </FORM> is legal within

    <BLOCKQUOTE>, <BODY>, <DD>, <LI>

The following markup can be used within <FORM> . . . </FORM>

    <A>, <ADDRESS>, <B>, <BLOCKQUOTE>, <CITE>, <CODE>, <DIR>, <DL>, <EM>, <H*>, <HR>, <I>, <IMG>, <INPUT>, <ISINDEX>, <KBD>, <MENU>, <OL>, <P>, <PRE>, <SAMP>, <SELECT>, <STRONG>, <TEXTAREA>, <TT>, <UL>, <VAR>

Suggested style/usage: Use <FORM> . . . </FORM> whenever you want to solicit input from your readers, or to provide additional back-end services through your Web pages.

Not all browsers are equally adept with forms, so it's often a good idea to include an FTP URL that offers plain text for the form, with instructions about how to submit the information via e-mail. This method is not as convenient or straightforward as processing the form within the browser, but it enables readers with nonadept browsers to submit their input or queries anyway.

Examples:

Because forms are so complex, we refer you to Chapter 12 instead of providing one here.

<H>...</H*> Header levels 1 through 6*

Definition: Headers come in different styles and weights to help you organize your content for better readability.

Attributes: None

Context:

<H*>...</H*> is legal within

> <A>, <BLOCKQUOTE>, <BODY>, <FORM>

The following markup can be used within <H*>...</H*>

> <A>, <B>, <BR>, <CITE>, <CODE>, <EM>, <I>, <IMG>, <KBD>, <SAMP>, <STRONG>, <TT>, <VAR>

Suggested style/usage: Use headings regularly and consistently to help add structure and provide guideposts to your documents. Some experts don't recommend using a sub-header level unless you plan on using at least two of them beneath a parent level. In other words, they recommend that you don't use a single <H3>...</H3> beneath an <H2>...</H2> pair. This follows the old principle of outlining, where you don't indent unless you have at least two sub-topics to put beneath a topic. We think that the occasional exception is OK, but this remains a pretty good guideline.

Notes:

- One of our examples below violates this guideline, to better squeeze all 6 levels into a single screen shot. (See Figure 5-7.)

- Heading levels should be used in increments or decrements of one (when transitioning up or down in document hierarchy).

Examples:

```
Good Style:
<H1>Level One First</H1>
<H2>Level Two A</H2>
<H2>Level Two B</H2>
<H3>Level Three AA</H3>
<H3>Level Three BB</H3>
<H1>Level One Second</H1>
```

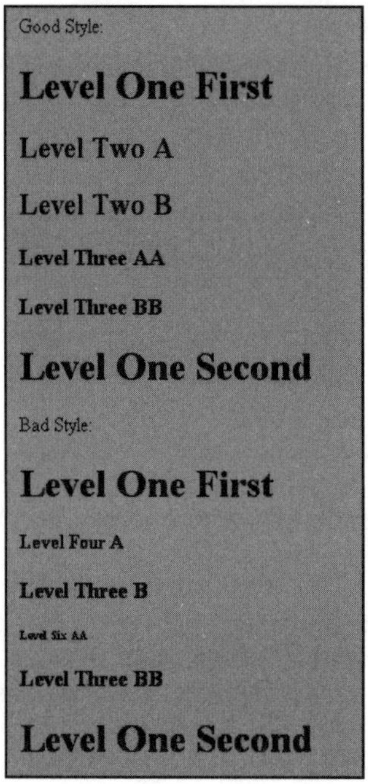

Good Style:

Level One First

Level Two A

Level Two B

Level Three AA

Level Three BB

Level One Second

Bad Style:

Level One First

Level Four A

Level Three B

Level Six AA

Level Three BB

Level One Second

Figure 5-7:
All six
header
levels on
one screen!

```
Bad Style:
<H1>Level One First</H1>
<H4>Level Four A</H4>
<H3>Level Three B</H3>
<H6>Level Six AA</H6>
<H3>Level Three BB</H3>
<H1>Level One Second</H1>
```

<HEAD> . . . </HEAD> Document head block

Definition: Defines page-level information about an HTML document, including its title, Base URL, index information, next page pointer, and possible links to other HTML documents.

Attributes: None

Context:

<HEAD> . . . </HEAD> is legal within

    <HTML>

The following markup can be used within <HEAD> . . . </HEAD>

<BASE>, <ISINDEX>, <LINK>, <META>, <NEXTID>, <TITLE>

Suggested style/usage: For strictly interpreted HTML, <HEAD> . . . </HEAD> is required at the head of an HTML document. Even though many browsers will render documents that lack a <HEAD> . . . </HEAD> block at the beginning, it's still good practice to include one, especially if you want to establish a Base URL when you have numerous graphics or local document links in your page.

Note: Although the <HEAD> . . . </HEAD> block produces no browser output other than a document title, it remains an important component of proper HTML page design.

Examples:

```
<HTML>
<HEAD>
<TITLE>A Nearly Pointless HTML Page</TITLE>
<BASE HREF="http://www.bigcorp.com/index.html">
</HEAD>
<BODY>
  . . .
</BODY>
</HTML>
```

<HR> Horizonal rule

Definition: Draws a horizontal rule across the page, usually one or two pixels wide.

Attributes:

None standard. Netscape offers attributes to control the width, length, thickness, and shading of horizontal rules (see Chapter 14 for more information on current extensions).

Context:

<HR> is legal within

<BLOCKQUOTE>, <BODY>, <FORM>, <PRE>

No markup can be used within <HR> because it is a singleton tag that takes no attributes.

Suggested style/usage: Wherever good design can benefit from placement of a horizontal rule — typically to emphasize natural divisions between text items or topics, or to separate a page header and footer from the body — the <HR> tag can add a lot to page design. (See Figure 5-8.)

Figure 5-8:
A short demon-stration of horizontal rules.

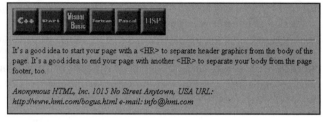

It's a good idea to start your page with a <HR> to separate header graphics from the body of the page. It's a good idea to end your page with another <HR> to separate your body from the page footer, too.

Anonymous HTML, Inc. 1015 No Street Anytown, USA URL:
http://www.hmi.com/bogus.html e-mail: info@hmi.com

Examples:

```
<HTML>
<HEAD>
<TITLE> The Horizontal Rule Rule </TITLE>
</HEAD>
<BODY>


<IMG SRC="bogusb.gif" ALIGN="MIDDLE">
<!— This image is a bogus button bar plucked from another applica-
tion —>
<HR>
It's a good idea to start your page with a andlt;HRandgt; to
separate header graphics from the body of the page. It's a good
idea to end your page with another andlt;HRandgt; to separate your
body from the page footer, too.
<HR>
<ADDRESS>
Anonymous HTML, Inc. 1015 No Street Anytown, USA
URL: http://www.hmi.com/bogus.html e-mail: info@hmi.com
</ADDRESS>


</BODY>
</HTML>
```

<HTML> . . . </HTML> Main document head

Definition: These tags should enclose an entire HTML document, as the outermost layer of document structure. For most browsers in use today, this tag is optional, but movements toward more rigorous interpretation of SGML DTDs for HTML indicate that this may not remain true for much longer.

Attributes:

VERSION="version information"

> This reports the DTD version to an application. To date, the default value is "-//IETF//DTD HTML//EN//2.0".

Context:

<HTML> ... </HTML> is not legal within any other markup tags.

The following markup can be used within <HTML> ... </HTML>

> <BODY>, <HEAD>

Suggested style/usage: Use <HTML> ... </HTML> to enclose all HTML documents.

<I> ... </I> Italicize text

Definition: Italicizes all enclosed text.

Attributes: None

Context:

<I> ... </I> is legal within

> <A>, <ADDRESS>, <B>, <BLOCKQUOTE>, <BODY>, <CITE>, <CODE>, <DD>, <DT>, <EM>, <FORM>, <H*>, <I>, <KBD>, <LI>, <P>, <PRE>, <SAMP>, <STRONG>, <TT>, <VAR>

The following markup can be used within <I> ... </I>

> <A>, <B>, <BR>, <CITE>, <CODE>, <EM>, <IMG>, <KBD>, <SAMP>, <STRONG>, <TT>, <VAR>

Suggested style/usage: Use italics sparingly for emphasis or effect, remembering that its distinctiveness fades quickly with overuse. (See Figure 5-9.)

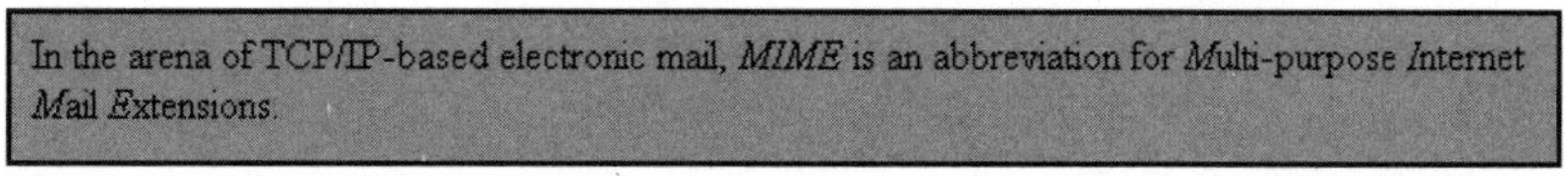

Figure 5-9:
Use italics
sparingly for
emphasis.

In the arena of TCP/IP-based electronic mail, *MIME* is an abbreviation for *Multi-purpose Internet Mail Extensions*.

Examples:

```
In the arena of TCPand#47;IP-based electronic mail, <I>MIME</I> is
an abbreviation for <I>M</I>ulti-purpose <I>I</I>nternet <I>M</
I>ail <I>E</I>xtensions.
```

<IMG>

Definition: Supplies image source, placement, and behavior information. Used to place in-line graphics on a page.

Attributes:

SRC="URL"

> URL is a standard Uniform Resource Locator specifying the location of the image file which will usually be .GIF or .JPEG format.

ALT="text"

> Supplies an alternate string of text to display (and possibly make clickable) if the browser has no graphics capability, or graphics are turned off.

ALIGN=("TOP" | "MIDDLE" | "BOTTOM") <u>and</u> \WIDTH="number" <u>andr</u>
HEIGHT="number"\

> Standard use calls for ALIGN to be set to one of the following values: TOP, MIDDLE, or BOTTOM to define placement of graphic.

> Optional values for HEIGHT and/or WIDTH also permit more precise placement using a pixel-level height and width specification.

ISMAP

> Indicates by its presence that the image (or its text replacement) should be a clickable map. This often invokes special map-handling software through the CGI interface on the Web server handling the request.

Context:

<IMG> is legal within

> <A>, <ADDRESS>, <B>, <BLOCKQUOTE>, <CITE>, <CODE>, <DD>, <DT>, <EM>, <FORM>, <H*>, <I>, <KBD>, <LI>, <P>, <PRE>, <SAMP>, <STRONG>, <TT>, <VAR>

Suggested style/usage: Keep images small and use them judiciously; graphics should add impact and interest to pages without adding too much bulk (or wait time).

Examples:

```
<IMG SRC="images/redball.gif" ALIGN="TOP" ALT="Menu Items">
<IMG SRC="http://www.noplace.com/show-me/pictures/fun.gif"
ALIGN="TOP" ISMAP ALT="Fun places to visit">
```

<INPUT> Input object

Definition: <INPUT> defines an input object within an HTML form; these objects come in several different types, and also include several different ways to name and specify the data they contain.

Attributes:

TYPE =
("TEXT" | "PASSWORD" | "CHECKBOX" | "HIDDEN" | "RADIO" | "SUBMIT" | "RESET")

> Defines the type of input object being described. TEXT, CHECKBOX, and RADIO define how data entry areas appear on-screen; use PASSWORD to prompt for a password; HIDDEN allows the form to pass data to the Web server that users can't see; SUBMIT and RESET provide methods to ship the information on a form to the server, or to clear the data from the form.

NAME="text"

> The name of the input item, as passed to the CGI script for the form as part of a name, value pair (this is how the script identifies values with their corresponding form fields).

VALUE="text"

> The value for the input item, as passed to the CGI script for the form as part of a name, value pair.

SIZE="number"

> The size of a TEXT type input item, as measured by the number of characters it contains.

MAXLENGTH="number"

> The maximum number of characters allowed in a TEXT type input item.

CHECKED

> For checkboxes or radio buttons, inclusion of this attribute indicates that the box was checked or the button selected, usually as a default.

ALIGN=("TOP" | "MIDDLE" | "BOTTOM")

> Determines how text and images in a form will align, for forms that contain images. Otherwise, these settings behave the same as for <IMG>.

Context:

<INPUT> is legal within

> <FORM>

As a singleton tag, <INPUT> doesn't permit other markup to be used within its operation.

Suggested style/usage: <INPUT> is an essential ingredient for HTML forms of all kinds, since it provides the mechanism to solicit input from readers, and deliver it to the underlying forms-handling services supplied by the related CGI script or other forms-handling program.

Examples:

Since HTML forms are pretty complex, we refer you to Chapter 10 for a number of informative and interesting examples.

<ISINDEX> Document is indexed

Definition: <ISINDEX> indicates that a searchable index for the document is available on the server, typically in the form of a CGI script that allows searches (normally supplied by a "SEARCH" button somewhere in the document).

Attributes: None

Context:

<ISINDEX> is legal within

> <BLOCKQUOTE>, <BODY>, <DD>, <FORM>, <HEAD>, <LI>

No markup can be used within <ISINDEX>.

Suggested style/usage: Long, complex documents typically benefit from being searchable, but any kind of document with large numbers of terms or details (for example, the HTML specifications or the IETF's RFCs) can benefit from <ISINDEX> support. With <ISINDEX>, you can query documents with a keyword search mechanism by adding a question mark to the end of the URL followed by a list of keywords separated by a plus sign (which, not coincidentally, happens to be called URL encoding). For example:

```
http://www.biggus.com/rome/gov/index.html?empire+fall+europe
```

Examples:

Please consult Chapter 14 for a detailed discussion of search engines, for more information on URL encoding, and for how to use <ISINDEX> in your documents.

<KBD> . . . </KBD> Keyboard text style

Definition: Indicates that text should be typed in at a computer keyboard. <KBD> . . . </KBD> changes the type style for all the text it contains (typically, into a Courier font, or some other font like those typically used in character-mode computer terminal displays). (See Figure 5-10.)

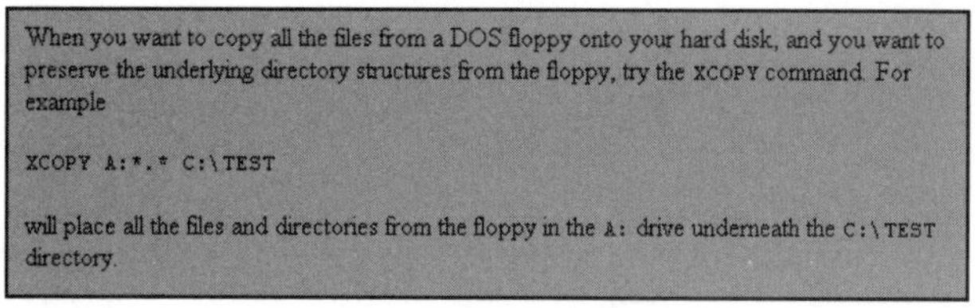

Figure 5-10:
Using
keyboard
text style.

> When you want to copy all the files from a DOS floppy onto your hard disk, and you want to preserve the underlying directory structures from the floppy, try the XCOPY command. For example
>
> XCOPY A:*.* C:\TEST
>
> will place all the files and directories from the floppy in the A: drive underneath the C:\TEST directory.

Attributes: None

Context:

<KBD> . . . </KBD> is legal within

> <A>, <ADDRESS>, <B>, <BLOCKQUOTE>, <BODY>, <CITE>, <CODE>, <DD>, <DT>, <EM>, <FORM>, <H*>, <I>, <LI>, <P>, <PRE>, <SAMP>, <STRONG>, <TT>, <VAR>

The following markup can be used within <KBD> . . . </KBD>

> <A>, <B>, <BR>, <CITE>, <CODE>, <EM>, <I>, <IMG>, <SAMP>, <STRONG>, <TT>, <VAR>

Suggested style/usage: Whenever you want to illustrate text to be typed in on a computer, please use <KBD> . . . </KBD> to set it off from the body text.

Examples:

```
When you want to copy all the files from a DOS floppy onto your
hard disk, and you want to preserve the underlying directory
structures from the floppy, try the <TT>XCOPY</TT> command. For
example<BR>
<BR>
<KBD>XCOPY A:*.* C:\TEST</KBD><BR>
<BR>
will place all the files and directories from the floppy in the
<TT>A:</TT> drive underneath the <TT>C:\TEST</TT>
directory.
```

<LI> List item

Definition: An element belonging to one of the various HTML list styles.

Attributes: None

Context:

<LI> is legal within

> <DIR>, <MENU>, <OL>, <UL>

The following markup can be used within <LI>...</LI> (the end tag is optional)

> <A>, <B>, <BLOCKQUOTE>, <BR>, <CITE>, <CODE>, <DIR>, <DL>, <EM>,
> <FORM>, <I>, <IMG>, <ISINDEX>, <KBD>, <MENU>, <OL>, <P>, <PRE>,
> <SAMP>, <STRONG>, <TT>, <UL>, <VAR>"

Suggested style/usage: Use to set off elements within lists. (See Figure 5-11.)

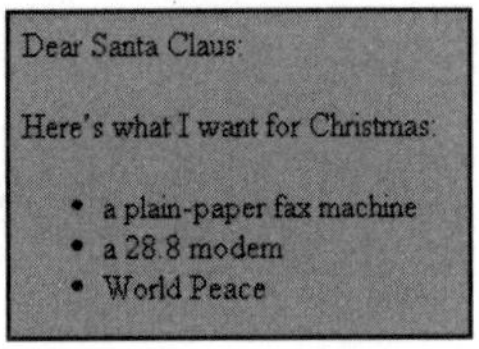

Figure 5-11:
A seasonal
sample
of list
elements.

> Dear Santa Claus:
>
> Here's what I want for Christmas:
>
> - a plain-paper fax machine
> - a 28.8 modem
> - World Peace

Examples:

```
Dear Santa Claus:
<P>Here's what I want for Christmas:
<UL>
<LI>a plain-paper fax machine
<LI>a 28.8 modem
<LI>World Peace
</UL>
```

<LINK>

Definition: Provides information that links the current document to other documents or URL resources.

Attributes:

HREF="URL"

> The address of the current link destination, accessible through normal Web linkage mechanisms. Works the same as the anchor tag <A>...</A>.

URN="permanent name"

> A Uniform Resource Name provides a permanent address for a Web-based resource; unlike a URL, which can move or disappear over time, a URN is meant to be a permanent fixture on the Web landscape. This may be a text field with an FTP address, or provide contact information requiring human (not browser) action to follow.

REL=("next" | "previous" | "parent" | "made")

> The REL attribute specifies the relationship between the current anchor and the destination (also known as a *forward relationship type*). "next" indicates that the URL points to the next page in a sequence, "previous" indicates that it points to the prior page, while "parent" indicates that the current page is the parent of the destination page. "made" indicates that the destination page contains information about the maker or owner of the current anchor page.

REV=("next" | "previous" | "parent" | "made")

> REV is the reverse of the REL attribute, and indicates the destination and the current anchor. All of the attribute values are the same, but apply to the page that the URL points to. Here, "made" indicates that this document contains information about the maker or owner of the destination page.

TITLE="text"

> Provides advisory information about the title of the destination document (usually the same text as enclosed by the <TITLE> . . . </TITLE> tags in that document).

METHODS="method1,method2,method3,..."

> Provides a comma-separated list of HTTP methods for accessing the object or objects on the other side of the link (e.g., http, FTP, GOPHER, WAIS, news, and so on). This helps to instruct the browser as to the best methods to access the information from the destination (that is, like the TITLE attribute, METHODS supplies advisory information to guide the browser's action).

Context:

<LINK> is legal only within the <HEAD> . . . </HEAD> tags.

As a singleton tag, <LINK> permits no enclosed markup.

Suggested style/usage: Typical uses include authorship attributions, access to glossaries or tutorials, and information about prior (outdated) or newer (more current) versions of the document in which the <LINK> occurs.

Examples:

See Chapter 9 for an example of this tag in use.

<MENU> . . . </MENU>

Definition: Encloses a menu list, where each element is typically a word or a short phrase that fits on a single line, rendered more compactly than most other list types.

Attributes:

COMPACT

> Renders the list as compactly as possible (not currently supported by all browsers).

Context:

<MENU> . . . </MENU> is legal within

> <BLOCKQUOTE>, <BODY>, <DD>, <FORM>, <LI>

The following markup can be used within <MENU> . . . </MENU>

    <LI>

Suggested style/usage: For short, simple lists, the <MENU> list style provides the most compact way to display such information. Use the COMPACT attribute to really squeeze things down, if you must. (See Figure 5-12.)

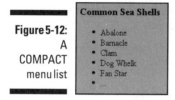

Figure 5-12:
A
COMPACT
menu list

Common Sea Shells
- Abalone
- Barnacle
- Clam
- Dog Whelk
- Fan Star
- ...

Examples:

```
<H3>Common Sea Shells</H3>
<MENU COMPACT>
<LI>Abalone
<LI>Barnacle
<LI>Clam
<LI>Dog Whelk
<LI>Fan Star
<LI>. . .
</MENU>
```

<META>

Definition: The META element is used within the HEAD element to embed document meta-information (or "information about information") not defined by other HTML elements. Servers/clients can extract such information for use in identifying, indexing, and cataloging specialized document meta-information. Although it's preferable to use named elements that have well-defined semantics for each type of meta-information, such as title, this element is provided for situations where strict SGML parsing is necessary and the local DTD is not extensible.

Attributes:

NAME

    Used to name a property such as author, publication date, and so on. If absent, you can assume that the name is the same as the value of HTTP-EQUIV.

CONTENT

Used to supply a value for a named property.

HTTP-EQUIV

This attribute binds the element to an HTTP response header. If the semantics of the HTTP response header named by this attribute is known, then the contents can be processed based on a well defined syntactic mapping, whether or not the DTD includes anything about it. HTTP header names are not case sensitive. If absent, the NAME attribute should be used to identify this meta-information and it should not be used within an HTPP response header.

Context:

<META> is legal within

<HEAD>

No markup can be used within <META>.

Suggested style/usage: When your documents are governed by a specific SGML DTD, or if you want to advertise aspects of its content (see examples below), meta information can make your information more accessible to spiders and robots for automatic indexing, and more accessible to other programs that you might use to help you manage an HTML document collection.

Examples:

```
<META HTTP-EQUIV=Expires CONTENT="Mon, 04 Dec 1996 23:00:00 GMT">
<META HTTP-EQUIV="Keywords" CONTENT="SGML, HTML, markup">
<META HTTP-EQUIV="Reply-to" CONTENT="etittel@zilker.net">
```

<NEXTID>

Definition: Indicates the next document to follow the current one, in a logical series.

Attributes:

N="URL"

The Uniform Resource Locator for the next document in the series.

Context:

<NEXTID> is legal only within the <HEAD> ... </HEAD> tags.

As a singleton tag, <NEXTID> permits no enclosed markup.

Suggested style/usage: <NEXTID> is usually placed by HTML authoring tools, but you can add one manually to tell a robot (or an attentive human reader) what document comes next in this series, if any.

<OL> ... </OL> Ordered list

Definition: An ordered list numbers the elements by order of occurrence.

Attributes:

COMPACT

> Renders the list as compactly as possible (not currently supported by all browsers).

Context:

<OL> ... </OL> is legal within

> <BLOCKQUOTE>, <BODY>, <DD>, <FORM>, <LI>

The following markup can be used within <OL> ... </OL>

> <LI>

Suggested style/usage: Ordered lists work well for step-by-step instructions or other information where the order of presentation is important. (See Figure 5-13.)

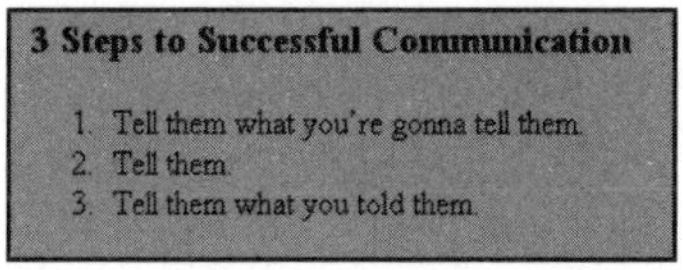

Figure 5-13:
A short
ordered list!

3 Steps to Successful Communication

1. Tell them what you're gonna tell them.
2. Tell them.
3. Tell them what you told them.

Examples:

```
<H3>3 Steps to Successful Communication</H3>
<OL COMPACT>
<LI>Tell them what you're gonna tell them.
<LI>Tell them.
<LI>Tell them what you told them.
</OL>
```

<OPTION>

Definition: Defines the various options available within a <SELECT> ... </SELECT> tag pair for a forms definition, where users must select a value from a predefined list of options. Also provides a mechanism for selecting a default value if the user chooses no value explicitly.

Attributes:

VALUE="text"

> Defines the value for a specific <SELECT> option, which equals the text string assigned to VALUE.

SELECTED

> Defines a default value for a <SELECT> field within a form, should the user choose no value explicitly.

Context:

<OPTION> is legal only within the <SELECT> ... </SELECT> tag pair.

As a singleton tag <OPTION> cannot include any markup inside it.

Suggested style/usage: For defining a set of scalar values for a <SELECT> field, and for supplying a default for such sets where appropriate.

Examples:

Because forms are so complex, we can't fit a good example here; please examine the contents of Chapter 10 to find all the information you need.

<P>

Definition: <P> defines paragraph boundaries for normal HTML text, where the break occurs immediately before the text that follows the tag.

Attributes: None

Context:

<P> is legal within

> <ADDRESS>, <BLOCKQUOTE>, <BODY>, <DD>, <FORM>, <LI>

As a singleton tag, no markup is valid within <P>.

Suggested style/usage: Paragraphs are a fundamental unit of text, used to break the flow of ideas or information into related chunks. Good writing style calls for regular use of paragraphs, and for treating each idea or concept separately in its own paragraph. (See Figure 5-14.)

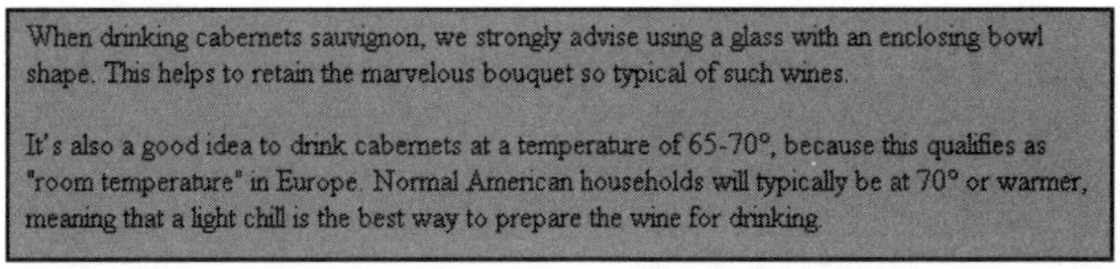

Figure 5-14:
Using the
<P> tag to
break up
text.

> When drinking cabernets sauvignon, we strongly advise using a glass with an enclosing bowl shape. This helps to retain the marvelous bouquet so typical of such wines.
>
> It's also a good idea to drink cabernets at a temperature of 65-70°, because this qualifies as "room temperature" in Europe. Normal American households will typically be at 70° or warmer, meaning that a light chill is the best way to prepare the wine for drinking.

Examples:

```
<P>When drinking cabernets sauvignon, we strongly advise using a
glass with an enclosing bowl shape. This helps to retain the
marvelous bouquet so typical of such wines.
<P>It's also a good idea to drink cabernets at a temperature of
65-70and#176;, because this qualifies as "room temperature" in
Europe. Normal American households will typically be at 70and#176;
or warmer, meaning that a light chill is the best way to prepare
the wine for drinking.
```

<PRE> ... </PRE> Preformatted style

Definition: <PRE> ... </PRE> provides a way of inserting preformatted text into HTML files. This can be valuable for reproducing formatted tables or other text where you want to preserve its original layout, like code listings where you want to be able to preserve exact formatting, indentation, and so on. (See Figure 5-15.)

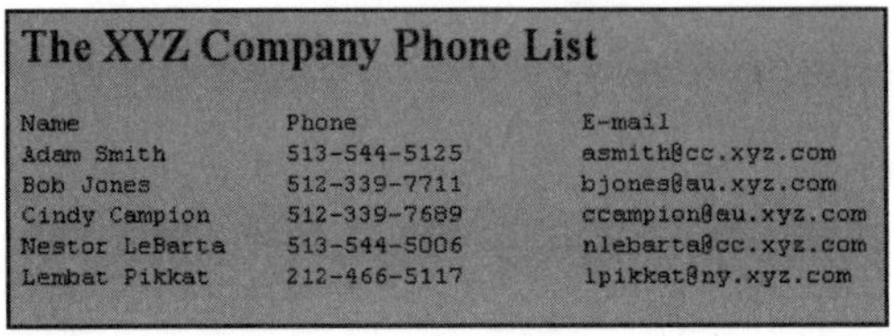

Figure 5-15:
<PRE>
makes it
easy to
enclose
preformatted
text.

The XYZ Company Phone List

```
Name                Phone               E-mail
Adam Smith          513-544-5125        asmith@cc.xyz.com
Bob Jones           512-339-7711        bjones@au.xyz.com
Cindy Campion       512-339-7689        ccampion@au.xyz.com
Nestor LeBarta      513-544-5006        nlebarta@cc.xyz.com
Lembat Pikkat       212-466-5117        lpikkat@ny.xyz.com
```

Attributes:

WIDTH="number"

> This specifies the maximum number of characters for a line and allows the browser to select an appropriate font and indentation setting.

Context:

<PRE> . . . </PRE> is legal within

> <BLOCKQUOTE>, <BODY>, <DD>, <FORM>, <LI>

The following markup can be used within <PRE> . . . </PRE>

> <A>, <B>, <BR>, <CITE>, <CODE>, <EM>, <HR>, <I>, <KBD>, <SAMP>,
> <STRONG>, <TT>, <VAR>

Suggested style/usage: When assembling text to use within a <PRE> . . . </PRE> block, it's OK to use link tags and text controls. You can obtain line breaks just by using the return key, but because <PRE> text is typically set in a monospaced font (like Courier), try to keep line lengths at 80 columns or less. This tag is great for presenting text-only information, like .sig files or other e-mail information, or USENET news articles.

Examples:

```
<H2>The XYZ Company Phone List</H2>
<PRE>
Name            Phone           E-mail
Adam Smith      513-544-5125    asmith@cc.xyz.com
Bob Jones       512-339-7711    bjones@au.xyz.com
Cindy Campion   512-339-7689    ccampion@au.xyz.com
Nestor LeBarta  513-544-5006    nlebarta@cc.xyz.com
Lembat Pikkat   212-466-5117    lpikkat@ny.xyz.com
</PRE>
```

<SAMP>...</SAMP> Sample text

Definition: <SAMP...</SAMP> should be used for sequences of literal characters, or to represent output from a program or other data source. (See Figure 5-16.)

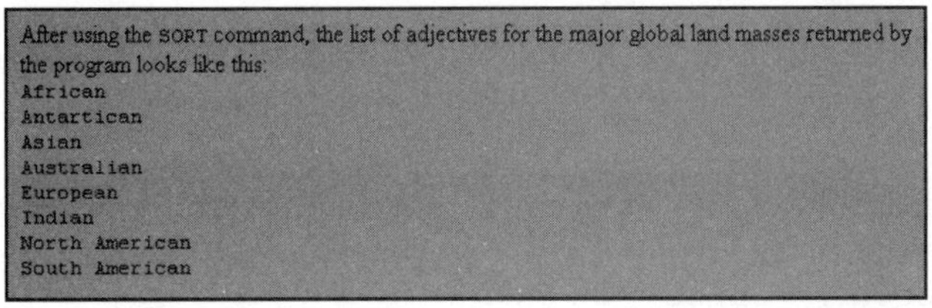

Figure 5-16: A listing of sample SORT output.

After using the SORT command, the list of adjectives for the major global land masses returned by the program looks like this:
African
Antartican
Asian
Australian
European
Indian
North American
South American

Attributes: None

Context:

<SAMP>...</SAMP> is legal within

> <A>, <ADDRESS>, <B>, <BLOCKQUOTE>, <BODY>, <CITE>, <CODE>, <DD>, <DT>, <EM>, <FORM>, <H*>, <I>, <KBD>, <LI>, <P>, <PRE>, <SAMP>, <STRONG>, <TT>, <VAR>

The following markup can be used within <SAMP>...</SAMP>

> <A>, <B>, <BR>, <CITE>, <CODE>, <EM>, <I>, <IMG>, <KBD>, <SAMP>, <STRONG>, <TT>, <VAR>

Suggested style/usage: Whenever you want to reproduce output from a program, script, or other data source, use <SAMP>...</SAMP>.

Examples:

```
After using the <CODE>SORT</CODE> command, the list of adjectives
for the major global land masses returned by the program looks like
this:
<SAMP>
African<BR>
Antartican<BR>
Asian<BR>
Australian<BR>
European<BR>
Indian<BR>
North American<BR>
South American<BR>
</SAMP>
```

<SELECT> . . . </SELECT> Select input object

Definition: The SELECT tags allow users to pick one or more options out of a list of possible values supplied in an input form, where each alternative is represented by an <OPTION> element.

Attributes:

MULTIPLE

> This attribute appears when users are allowed to select more than one element from the set of <OPTION> values supplied within a <SELECT> . . . </SELECT> tag pair.

Context:

<SELECT> . . . </SELECT> is legal only within the <FORM> tag.

The following markup can be used within <SELECT> . . . </SELECT>

> <OPTION>

Suggested style/usage: Use to provide pickable lists of scalar values within HTML forms whenever users can pick only from a predetermined set of possible values.

Examples:

Because HTML forms are so complex, please refer to Chapter 10, which covers them in considerable detail.

<STRONG> . . . </STRONG> Strong emphasis

Definition: A text control for providing strong emphasis on key words or phrases within normal body text, lists, and so on. (See Figure 5-17.)

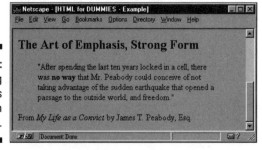

Figure 5-17:
Using strong
emphasis
for high
impact.

Attributes: None

Context:

<STRONG> ... </STRONG> is legal within

>   <A>, <ADDRESS>, <B>, <BLOCKQUOTE>, <BODY>, <CITE>, <CODE>, <DD>, <DT>, <EM>, <FORM>, <H*>, <I>, <KBD>, <LI>, <P>, <PRE>, <SAMP>, <STRONG>, <TT>, <VAR>

The following markup can be used within <STRONG> ... </STRONG>

>   <A>, <B>, <BR>, <CITE>, <CODE>, <EM>, <I>, <IMG>, <KBD>, <SAMP>, <STRONG>, <TT>, <VAR>

Suggested style/usage: Use within running text to provide the strongest degree of in-line emphasis available in HTML. Remember, overuse blunts the effect, so use emphatic text controls sparingly in your documents.

Examples:

```
<H2>The Art of Emphasis, Strong Form</H2>
<BLOCKQUOTE>"After spending the last ten years
locked in a cell, there was <STRONG>no way
</STRONG> that Mr. Peabody could conceive of
not taking advantage of the sudden earthquake
that opened a passage to the outside world, and
freedom."
</BLOCKQUOTE>
<P>
From <CITE>My Life as a Convict</CITE> by James T. Peabody, Esq.
```

<TEXTAREA> ... </TEXTAREA> Text input area

Definition: Used to define a text input area for an HTML input form, typically for multiple lines of text.

Attributes:

NAME="text"

>   Supplies a name for the form field, which will be paired with the value that's ultimately entered for submission to the underlying CGI script or other service program that processes the form. This is a required attribute for which no reasonable default is possible.

ROWS="number"

"number" defines the number of lines of text that the field can accommodate. Typical values for nonnarrative forms range from 2 to 6, but HTML
allows large text areas if needed. (Prudence dictates that page-long input
is better handled by allowing users to upload text files from the editor of
their choice, rather than typing into a text field on a form.) This is a
required attribute, but takes a default of 1.

COLS="number"

"number" defines the number of columns for any given line of text in the
TEXTAREA field. Common practice is to limit the number of columns to 72
or less, that being a common limitation for the number of characters a line
can hold within the outside page frame of a browser program on-screen
(80 is the typical maximum for normal character-mode displays). This is a
required attribute but takes a default of 80.

Context:

<TEXTAREA> ... </TEXTAREA> is legal within

<FORM>

No markup is allowed in the <TEXTAREA> tag.

Suggested style/usage: The end tag marks the end of the string used to initialize
the field (which can include a default string supplied by the form's author).
Thus, even if the field is empty — meaning that <TEXTAREA> and </TEXTAREA>
are adjacent to one another — the end tag is essential to indicate a null value
for the field.

Use TEXTAREA whenever you have a multiline input field in a form.

Examples:

Forms are fairly complex HTML structures that require nearly all of the possible
forms-related tags to create a working example. We therefore refer you to
Chapter 10, which covers forms in great detail and includes several useful
examples.

<TITLE> ... </TITLE> Document title

Definition: Encloses the title for an HTML document, which commonly appears
in the title bar in the browser's window. If a title is not supplied, the default title
is the HTML filename.

Attributes: None

Context:

<TITLE> . . . </TITLE> is legal only with <HEAD> . . . </HEAD>

No markup can be used within <TITLE> . . . </TITLE> because it does not normally display within an HTML document, but rather on the title bar of the window in which the document appears.

Suggested style/usage: We strongly recommend that you define a useful title for each and every HTML document you write. Because many Webcrawlers and other automated search tools use titles to help locate information for users, an accurate, descriptive title helps them find your content.

Examples:

See any of the figures in this section: We've tried to entitle all of them to be informative about the example at hand. A title about titles is a bit much, even for us!

<TT> . . . </TT> Teletype text

Definition: Encloses text to be displayed in a monospaced (teletype) font; typically, some variety of Courier is used in most browsers. (See Figure 5-18.)

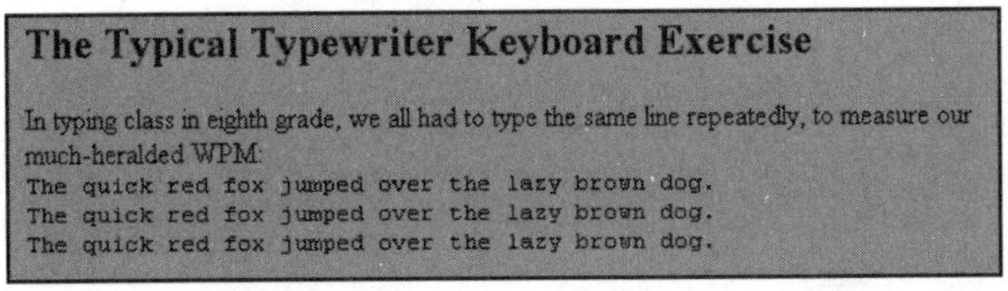

Figure 5-18:
The
archetypal
<TT>
example.

> **The Typical Typewriter Keyboard Exercise**
>
> In typing class in eighth grade, we all had to type the same line repeatedly, to measure our much-heralded WPM:
> ```
> The quick red fox jumped over the lazy brown dog.
> The quick red fox jumped over the lazy brown dog.
> The quick red fox jumped over the lazy brown dog.
> ```

Attributes: None

Context:

<TT> . . . </TT> is legal within

<A>, <ADDRESS>, <B>, <BLOCKQUOTE>, <BODY>, <CITE>, <CODE>, <DD>, <DT>, <EM>, <FORM>, <H*>, <I>, <KBD>, <LI>, <P>, <PRE>, <SAMP>, <STRONG>, <TT>, <VAR>

The following markup can be used within <TT> ... </TT>

<A>, <B>, <BR>, <CITE>, <CODE>, <EM>, <I>, <IMG>, <KBD>, <SAMP>, <STRONG>, <TT>, <VAR>

Suggested style/usage: Use for monospaced text, where character position is important, or when trying to imitate the look of line-printer or typewriter output.

Examples:

```
<H2>The Typical Typewriter Keyboard Exercise</H2>
In typing class in eighth grade, we all had to type the
same line repeatedly, to measure our much-heralded WPM:
<BR><TT>
The quick red fox jumped over the lazy brown dog.<BR>
The quick red fox jumped over the lazy brown dog.<BR>
The quick red fox jumped over the lazy brown dog.<BR>
</TT>
```

<UL> ... </UL> Unordered list style

Definition: An HTML list style that produces bulleted lists of items. (See Figure 5-19.)

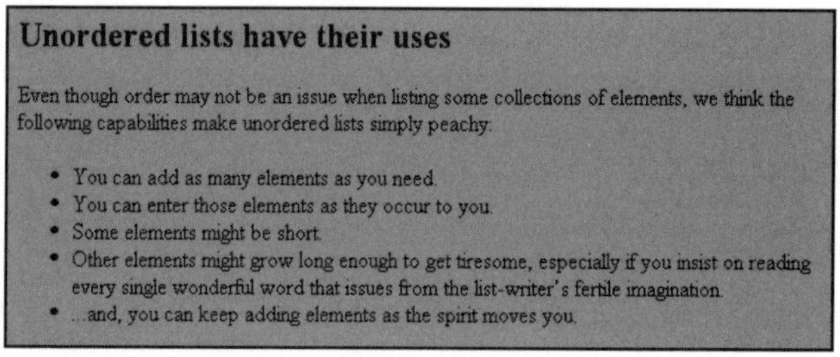

Figure 5-19:
A typical
unordered
list.

Unordered lists have their uses

Even though order may not be an issue when listing some collections of elements, we think the following capabilities make unordered lists simply peachy.

- You can add as many elements as you need.
- You can enter those elements as they occur to you.
- Some elements might be short.
- Other elements might grow long enough to get tiresome, especially if you insist on reading every single wonderful word that issues from the list-writer's fertile imagination.
- ...and, you can keep adding elements as the spirit moves you.

Attributes:

COMPACT

If present, COMPACT instructs the browser to render this list with only a minimal amount of leading between the lines (this reduces the amount of white space, and makes the listing more compact).

Context:

<UL> ... </UL> is legal within

    <BLOCKQUOTE>, <BODY>, <DD>, <FORM>, <LI>

The only markup that can be used within <UL> ... </UL> is <LI>.

Suggested style/usage: To create bulleted lists of items where their order is not important, or where sequence does not apply.

Examples:

```
<HTML>
<HEAD>
<TITLE>Unordered List</TITLE>
</HEAD>
<BODY>
<H2>Unordered lists have their uses</H2>
Even though order may not be an issue when listing some
collections of elements, we think the following capabilities make
unordered lists simply peachy:
<UL>
<LI> You can add as many elements as you need.
<LI> You can enter those elements as they occur to you.
<LI> Some elements might be short.
<LI> Other elements might grow long enough to get tiresome,
especially if you insist on reading every single wonderful word
that issues from the list-writer's fertile imagination.
<LI> . . .and, you can keep adding elements as the spirit moves
you.
</UL>
</BODY>
</HTML>
```

<VAR> ... </VAR> Variable text style

Definition: This text control tag pair is used to highlight variable names in HTML text, to indicate to users that they will be supplying this information when they input text at the keyboard. (See Figure 5-20.)

Variable text means "user-supplied"

Sometimes, you need a way to set off text that's generic when you explain it, but will be particular when a user actually substitutes a real value:

When you use the DOS COPY command the syntax is
COPY *filename*

Thus, if you wanted to copy the file named "FOO.BAR" you would enter the string:
COPY FOO.BAR

Attributes: None

Context:

<VAR> ... </VAR> is legal within

> <A>, <ADDRESS>, <B>, <BLOCKQUOTE>, <BODY>, <CITE>, <CODE>, <DD>, <DT>, <EM>, <FORM>, <H*>, <I>, <KBD>, <LI>, <P>, <PRE>, <SAMP>, <STRONG>, <TT>, <VAR>

The following markup can be used within <VAR> ... </VAR>

> <A>, <B>, <BR>, <CITE>, <CODE>, <EM>, <I>, <IMG>, <KBD>, <SAMP>, <STRONG>, <TT>, <VAR>

Suggested style/usage: Use to indicate a placeholder for a value that the user will supply when entering text at the keyboard (see example).

Examples:

```
<H2>Variable text means "user-supplied"</H2>
Sometimes, you need a way to set off text that's generic when you
explain it, but will be particular when a user actually substi-
tutes a real value:
<P>
When you use the DOS <CODE>COPY</CODE> command the syntax is <BR>
<CODE>COPY</CODE>, <VAR>filename</VAR><BR>
<P>
Thus, if you wanted to copy the file named <CODE>"FOO.BAR"</CODE>
 you would enter the string:<BR>
<CODE>COPY FOO.BAR</CODE>
```

Whew! That's the facts, Jack. Time for a break or a deep breath and then take another giant step forward in your budding career as WebMaster. Join us in Chapter 6 where you get the rest of the HTML puzzle pieces with an in-depth discussion of entities.

Chapter 6

Introducing the Unrepresentable: HTML Entities

• •

In This Chapter

▶ Coloring outside the character boundaries

▶ Producing special characters

▶ Inspecting the ISO-Latin-1 character set

• •

*N*ow you've seen the panoply of HTML tags and have gone through examples in Chapter 5 that included strange notations like < or °. These odd locutions aren't as cryptic as they first appear — they're simply a way to instruct the browser to look up these symbols and replace them with equivalent characters, while it renders a document. The symbol < produces the less-than sign < on your computer screen, and the symbol ° produces the degree symbol °.

Entities Don't Have to Be an Alien Concept

Why are these contortions necessary? We know three important reasons:

✔ To let browsers represent characters that might otherwise be interpreted as markup.

✔ To let browsers represent higher-order ASCII characters (those with codes over 127) without having to fully support higher-order ASCII or non-ASCII character types. Also, these codes support some characters that are even outside the ASCII character set altogether (as is the case with non-Roman alphabet character sets and some widely used diacritical marks).

✔ To increase portability of SGML documents. Entities are placeholders in the SGML document instance and can be rendered on the fly according to a particular site's requirements. An example is the &COMPANY; entity. One subcontractor could define this entity as *ACME Software,* another as *Alternative Solutions.*

Okay, so now you know what character and numeric entities are for. They let browsers display symbols and not interpret them as markup tags. They also let browsers represent a larger range of characters than might otherwise be possible, while keeping the actual character set as minimal as possible.

As you travel into the land of HTML character and numeric entities, you encounter strange characters and symbols that you may never use. On the other hand, if your native language isn't English, you can probably find lots of diacritical marks, accents, and other kinds of character modifications that let you express yourself much more effectively!

Producing Special Characters

Three characters can act as special signals to the browser to let it know that it should look up a string in a character table instead of just displaying the string on-screen:

✔ **Ampersand (&):** If a string starts with &, it flags the browser that what follows is a character code instead of an ordinary string of characters.

✔ **Pound sign (#):** If the next character after a & is a #, this tells the browser that what follows next is a string of numbers that corresponds to the character code for the symbol to be produced on-screen. This kind of code is called a *numeric entity*.

If the next character is anything other than the pound sign, this tells the browser that the string that follows is a symbol's name, which must be looked up in a built-in table of equivalent character symbols. This is called a *character entity*.

✔ **Semicolon (;):** When the browser sees a ;, this signals the end of the string that represents a character code. The browser then uses whatever characters or numbers follow either the ampersand or the pound sign to perform the right kind of lookup operation and display the requested character symbol. If the browser doesn't recognize the information supplied, most browsers display a question mark (?) instead.

A couple of things about character and numeric entities might differ from your expectations, based on what you've learned about HTML tags so far and what you might know about computer character sets:

✔ When reproducing the string of characters for an entity, HTML is case sensitive. Because this means that < is different from <, you need to reproduce character entities exactly as they're stated in Table 6-1. That's one reason why we prefer using numeric entities — it's harder to make a mistake. The following code sample and browser display (in Figure 6-1) make this point rather nicely:

```
<HEAD>
<TITLE>Checking character codes</TITLE>
</HEAD>
<BODY>
<H2>Copy character entities exactly...or else!</H2>
<P>
<TT>
<!- semicolon has a numeric code of 59      ->
<!- space has a numeric code of 32          ->
<!- ampersand has a character code of &amp; ->
<!- less-than has a character code of &lt;  ->
Less-than lowercase&#32;:&#32;&amp;lt&#59;&#32; = &lt;<BR>
Less-than uppercase&#32;:&#32;&amp;LT&#59;&#32; = &#32;&LT;<BR>
Less-than mixed-case:&#32;&amp;Lt&#59;&#32; = &#32;&Lt;<BR>
Less-than mixed-rev&#32;:&#32;&amp;lT&#59;&#32; = &#32;&lT;<BR>
</TT></BODY></HTML>
```

✔ The numeric codes for reproducing characters within HTML do not
come from the ASCII collating sequence; they come from the ISO-Latin-1
character set codes, shown later in this chapter in Table 6-1.

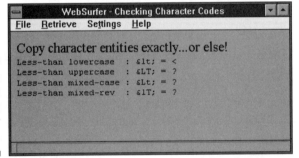

Figure 6-1:
Using and
misusing
character
entities.

If you concentrate on reproducing characters exactly as they appear in Table 6-1
or copying the numbers that correspond to the ISO-Latin-1 scheme, you can
produce exactly the right effects on your readers' screens.

Nothing Ancient about the ISO-Latin-1 HTML

The name of the character set that HTML uses is ISO-Latin-1. The *ISO* part
means that it's taken from the International Standards Organization's body of
official international standards — in fact, all ISO standards have corresponding
numeric tags, so ISO-Latin-1 is also referred to as ISO8859-1. The *Latin* part

means that it's derived from the Roman alphabet commonly used worldwide to represent text in many different languages. The number *1* refers to the version number for this standard (in other words, this is the first version of this character set definition).

ISO-Latin-1 distinguishes between two types of entities used to represent characters:

- **Character entities:** Strings of characters that represent other characters; for example, < and È show a string of characters (lt and Egrave) that stand for others (< and È).

- **Numeric entities:** Strings of numbers that represent characters. These are identified by a pound sign (#) that follows the ampersand (&). For example, < and È show a string of numbers (60 and 232) that stand for characters (< and È).

Table 6-1 illustrates that there are many more numeric entities than character entities. In fact, every character in the ISO-Latin-1 set has a corresponding numeric entity, but this is not true of the character entities.

Table 6-1		The ISO-Latin-1 Character Set	
Character	*Character Entity*	*Numeric Entity*	*Description*
			Em space - not collapsed
			En space
			Nonbreaking space
		&#00; – &#08;	Unused
		&#09;	Horizontal tab
		&#10;	Line feed or new line
		&#11; – &#31;	Unused
		&#32;	Space
!		&#33;	Exclamation mark
"	&quot;	&#34;	Quote
#		&#35;	Number sign
$		&#36;	Dollar sign
%		&#37;	Percent sign
&	&amp;	&#38;	Ampersand
'		&#39;	Apostrophe

Character	Character Entity	Numeric Entity	Description
(		(	Left parenthesis
)		)	Right parenthesis
*		*	Asterisk
+		+	Plus sign
,		,	Comma
-		-	Hyphen
.		.	Period (full stop)
/		/	Solidus (slash)
0–9		0 – 9	Digits 0–9
:		:	Colon
;		;	Semicolon
<	<	<	Less than
=		=	Equal sign
>	>	>	Greater than
?		?	Question mark
@		@	Commercial at
A–Z		A – Z	Letters A–Z (uppercase)
[		[	Left square bracket
\		\	Reverse solidus (backslash)
]		]	Right square bracket
^		^	Caret
_		_	Underscore
`		`	Grave accent
a–z		a – z	Letters a–z (lowercase)
{		{	Left curly brace
|		|	Vertical bar
}		}	Right curly brace
~		~	Tilde
		&#127; –	Unused

(continued)

Table 6-1 (continued)

Character	Character Entity	Numeric Entity	Description
¡		&#161;	Inverted exclamation
¢		&#162;	Cent sign
£		&#163;	Pound sterling
¤		&#164;	General currency sign
¥		&#165;	Yen sign
¦		&#166;	Broken vertical bar
§		&#167;	Section sign
¨		&#168;	Umlaut (diaeresis)
©		&#169;	Copyright
ª		&#170;	Feminine ordinal
<<		&#171;	Left angle quote, guillemet left
¬		&#172;	Not sign
-		&#173;	Soft hyphen
®		&#174;	Registered trademark
—		&#175;	Macron accent
°		&#176;	Degree sign
±		&#177;	Plus or minus
^{2}		&#178;	Superscript two
^{3}		&#179;	Superscript three
´		&#180;	Acute accent
µ		&#181;	Micro sign
¶		&#182;	Paragraph sign
·		&#183;	Middle dot
ç		&#184;	Cedilla
^{1}		&#185;	Superscript one
º		&#186;	Masculine ordinal
>>		&#187;	Right angle quote, guillemet right

Character	Character Entity	Numeric Entity	Description
1/4		&#188;	Fraction one-fourth
1/2		&#189;	Fraction one-half
3/4		&#190;	Fraction three-fourths
¿		&#191;	Inverted question mark
À	&Agrave;	&#192;	Uppercase A, grave accent
Á	&Aacute;	&#193;	Uppercase A, acute accent
Â	&Acirc;	&#194;	Uppercase A, circumflex accent
Ã	&Atilde;	&#195;	Uppercase A, tilde
Ä	&Auml;	&#196;	Uppercase A, diaeresis or umlaut mark
Å	&Aring;	&#197;	Uppercase A, ring
Æ	&AElig;	&#198;	Uppercase AE diphthong (ligature)
Ç	&Ccedil;	&#199;	Uppercase C, cedilla
1	&Egrave;	&#200;	Uppercase E, grave accent
É	&Eacute;	&#201;	Uppercase E, acute accent
Ê	&Ecirc;	&#202;	Uppercase E, circumflex accent
Ë	&Euml;	&#203;	Uppercase E, diaeresis or umlaut mark
Ì	&Igrave;	&#204;	Uppercase I, grave accent
Í	&Iacute;	&#205;	Uppercase I, acute accent
Î	&Icirc;	&#206;	Uppercase I, circumflex accent
Ï	&Iuml;	&#207;	Uppercase I, diaeresis or umlaut mark
Ð	&ETH;	&#208;	Capital Eth, Icelandic
Ñ	&Ntilde;	&#209;	Uppercase N, tilde
Ò	&Ograve;	&#210;	Uppercase O, grave accent
Ó	&Oacute;	&#211;	Uppercase O, acute accent
Ô	&Ocirc;	&#212;	Uppercase O, circumflex accent

(continued)

Table 6-1 *(continued)*

Character	Character Entity	Numeric Entity	Description
Õ	Õ	Õ	Uppercase O, tilde
Ö	Ö	Ö	Uppercase O, diaeresis or umlaut mark
x		×	Multiply sign
Ø	Ø	Ø	Uppercase O, slash
Ù	Ù	Ù	Uppercase U, grave accent
Ú	Ú	Ú	Uppercase U, acute accent
Û	Û	Û	Uppercase U, circumflex accent
Ü	Ü	Ü	Uppercase U, diaeresis or umlaut mark
Ý	Ý	Ý	Capital Y, acute accent
Þ	Þ	Þ	Capital THORN, Icelandic
ß	ß	ß	Lowercase sharp s, German (sz ligature)
à	à	à	Lowercase a, grave accent
á	á	á	Lowercase a, acute accent
â	â	â	Lowercase a, circumflex accent
ã	ã	ã	Lowercase a, tilde
ä	ä	ä	Lowercase a, diaeresis or umlaut mark
å	å	å	Lowercase a, ring
æ	æ	æ	Lowercase ae diphthong (ligature)
ç	ç	ç	Lowercase c, cedilla
è	è	è	Lowercase e, grave accent
é	é	é	Lowercase e, acute accent
ê	ê	ê	Lowercase e, circumflex accent
ë	ë	ë	Lowercase e, diaeresis or umlaut mark

Character	Character Entity	Numeric Entity	Description
ì	&igrave;	&#236;	Lowercase i, grave accent
í	&iacute;	&#237;	Lowercase i, acute accent
î	&icirc;	&#238;	Lowercase i, circumflex accent
ï	&iuml;	&#239;	Lowercase i, diaeresis or umlaut mark
∂	&eth;	&#240;	Lowercase eth, Icelandic
ñ	&ntilde;	&#241;	Lowercase n, tilde
ò	&ograve;	&#242;	Lowercase o, grave accent
ó	&oacute;	&#243;	Lowercase o, acute accent
ô	&ocirc;	&#244;	Lowercase o, circumflex accent
õ	&otilde;	&#245;	Lowercase o, tilde
ö	&ouml;	&#246;	Lowercase o, diaeresis or umlaut mark
÷		&#247;	Division sign
ø	&oslash;	&#248;	Lowercase o, slash
ù	&ugrave;	&#249;	Lowercase u, grave accent
ú	&uacute;	&#250;	Lowercase u, acute accent
û	&ucirc;	&#251;	Lowercase u, circumflex accent
ü	&uuml;	&#252;	Lowercase u, diaeresis or umlaut mark
ý	&yacute;	&#253;	Lowercase y, acute accent
þ	&thorn;	&#254;	Lowercase thorn, Icelandic
ÿ	&yuml;	&#255;	Lowercase y, diaeresis or umlaut mark

One thing to note about using this information: If you frequently need to work with character or numeric entities in your documents, it's easier to use some kind of HTML editing tool to handle character replacements automatically. Or, look for a file-oriented search-and-replace utility that you can use as a post-processing step on your files. For Windows users, point your browser at

```
ftp://oak.oakland.edu/fdrepl.zip
```

This file is a ZIP archive that contains a utility named *Find-Replace* that works under Windows 3.*x*.

Part VII of this book (Chapters 20–22) covers HTML and related tools for a variety of platforms. If you're a serious Web developer or often need to use character codes in your pages, please check out the tools available on your favorite platform. These tools can save you time and effort and make you a happier, more productive WebMaster.

Chapter 7

Building Basic HTML Documents

*B*uilding your first Web page is exciting if you keep this thought firmly in mind: You can change anything at any time. Good Web pages are always evolving. Nothing is cast in concrete — change is just a keystroke away.

Now that the pressure is off, you can start building your own simple, but complete, home page. Think of it as a prototype for future pages. Later you can add all sorts of bells and whistles to change your home page into any kind of page you want — be it for a business, an academic institution, or a government agency.

The layout, or the way the page looks to the user, creates the first impression of your whole Web site. If that first impression isn't pleasing, the first time may also be the last time that the user visits your page. Not to worry, though: Your home page can be pleasing to the eye if you follow the *KISS* (Keep it Simple, Stupid) approach.

The Web itself is a confusing concept to many users. Everything that you do to keep your page *intuitively obvious* makes your viewers happy and keeps them coming back for more.

Chapter 3 presented the basic concepts of a good Web page. It emphasizes the form and content over the HTML controls and presents the elements of page layout and information flow. You might want to review Chapter 3 before continuing here.

The basics are content, layout, first impression, and KISS. Okay, now get on with it.

The Template's the Thing!

Well-constructed Web pages contain the following four sections: Title, Heading, Body, and Footer.

If you look at a number of Web pages, you'll undoubtedly see that most contain these sections in one form or another. You may also notice, with some amount of frustration, that the pages that don't contain all these elements either aren't pleasing to your eye or aren't intuitive in their presentation. Plus, you can't easily find what you're looking for. We're not going to let that happen to your pages because you are going to use the following basic template for each HTML document you produce:

```
<HTML>
<HEAD><TITLE>Your Title</TITLE>
</HEAD>
<BODY>
<P>
Your headings and wonderful text and graphics go here.
<P>
<ADDRESS>
Your Name<BR>
Phone number<BR>
Standard Mail Address<BR>
E-Mail Address
</ADDRESS>
<P>
Copyright &copy; 1995.  Your Name <BR>
Revised — Revision Date <BR>
URL: <A HREF = "http://this.page's.url.here">
http://this.page's.url.here</A>
</BODY>
</HTML>
```

Getting started on the correct path is really that simple. This template actually works. Figure 7-1 shows what it looks like when viewed with Netscape.

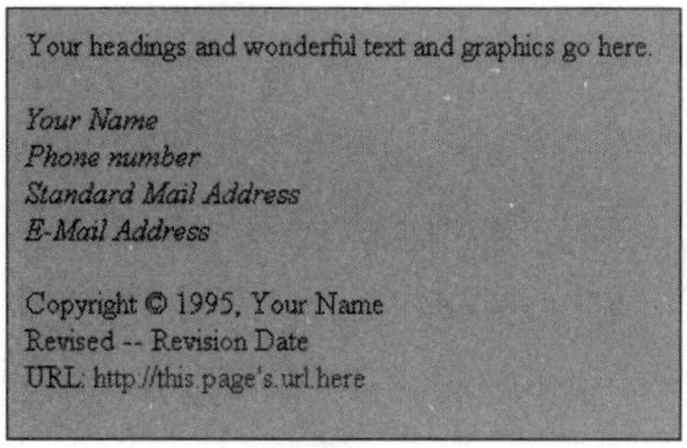

Figure 7-1:
The basic
Web page
template
viewed with
Netscape.

Your headings and wonderful text and graphics go here.

Your Name
Phone number
Standard Mail Address
E-Mail Address

Copyright © 1995, Your Name
Revised -- Revision Date
URL: http://this.page's.url.here

✔ Use your browser to open your Web page HTML document file from your local hard disk.

✔ If you're using Netscape, remember to set the memory and disk caches to zero so that Netscape reloads each new version of your file from the disk, instead of loading the one in its cache. Other browsers cache pages, too, so make sure that you're reading what you just edited — not some older version!

As you can see, your home page is currently plain and simple. That's not going to have folks flocking to see it, is it? That's because you need to add your own wonderful text and graphics. Even though a growing number of Internet surfers use GUI browsers, please follow our advice (from Chapter 2) and put your energy into providing high-quality content and important links. Don't worry; in the next chapter, you'll add some graphics, too.

Page Layout: Top to Bottom

Now that you have a basic template, you can start changing it. To begin the fun, your first home page shouldn't occupy more than a single screen; this limit makes the page much easier to edit and test. You can get more than enough information on a single screen and help your audience avoid unnecessary scrolling.

A *single screen* seems like an easy concept, but is it? A single screen is the amount of information that a browser can display on the monitor without scrolling. This amount varies depending upon the readers' browsers and their monitor resolutions. You may not want to design for the lowest common denominator for both elements, but please understand the following: If you assume that the user can see your page the same way that you see it in *your* browser, you're making a bad assumption. No easy answer to this problem exists, but testing your pages on a relatively low-resolution monitor with several different browsers can help you see your pages through your reader's eyes. Getting this view is well worth taking the extra time!

Also, you may find it helpful to sketch your design ideas on paper first or to use a drawing program to create a model of your layout and components. (Figure 7-2 shows an example.) This model shows the spatial relationships on the page and the amounts and locations of the ever-important breathing room that page designers call *white space*. Although you can leave too much white space on a page, most designers err in the other direction and wind up with far too little.

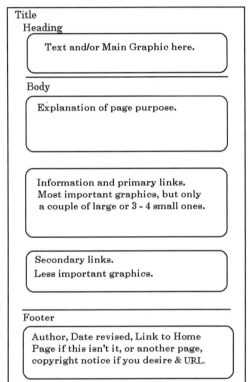

Figure 7-2:
A sketch of
basic Web
page layout.

It's essential to organize your page logically so that viewers can scan it easily. Because everyone is always in a hurry, put the most important information near the top, in larger type, and with plenty of white space surrounding it. Place the remaining items below as you work your way through the content.

Remember, you're not trying to stuff as much as possible on a single page — you're trying to cover what's important for the topic at hand. If you have lots of material to cover, or more topics to deal with, you can easily make more pages and link them to this one. A good rule of thumb comes from professional presenters, who say that a single slide should try to convey no more than three to five pieces of related information. We think that the same is true of a single HTML-based screenful of information, too!

What's in a Name? Thinking Up Good Titles and Headings

In HTML files, the title provides the most important basis for indexing a document. That's because titles are more readily available to casual surfers than are the contents inside a page.

On the other hand, a document's headings provide an important visual contrast within any page. This happens because the user's browser settings determine the font and page size, and also control the line length. If you use appropriate content and layout, you can make the headings on your home page both attractive and informative, without making everybody read the fine print.

Titles

The title of your page is important. It is used by many Web indexing crawlers — the software robots that relentlessly cruise the Web, looking for information — to create index records in *their* databases for *your* pages. Also, the title is used for the name field in the *bookmark* or *hotlist* sections of most browsers, which collect URLs that users intend to revisit. That is, they use your title to figure out what's on your page.

Because you want people to find and read your pages, you need to make titles as descriptive as possible. Try to limit the length of a title so that it fits on a single line. Think of the title as the key words that describe the contents of your page. Understanding how titles get used should help you build titles that work — we hope you get the idea!

One way to arrive at a truly descriptive title is to type a list of the keywords that best describe your page. Then, use them in a sentence. Next, delete the conjunctions, adverbs, and unnecessary adjectives. With a little rearranging, what's left should be a pretty good title.

Here's an example of constructing a title:

- ✔ **Words:** George, classical guitar player, bicycle racing
- ✔ **Sentence:** George is a classical guitarist who races bicycles.
- ✔ **Title:** George's classical guitar and bike racing page

This title should fit on one line when viewed by most browsers. Test it with your favorite browser to see how it looks.

Headings

Discussing headings can get somewhat confusing because each Web page should have a heading after the title and various headings in the body of the text. In the print world, for example in this book, headings are the emphasized text placed before paragraphs. Because often there are many headings on a given page, we'll strive to tell you what kind of heading we mean, and where on a page it is located, when we discuss this topic.

Headings may be the most important text in your Web page. They are the first text that the viewer scans. If the headings aren't attractive and instantly informative, the viewer may be off to another page with a single click. If they can hook your audience and make them want to learn more, then you've written good headings.

You are primarily concerned with the content of your headings and the consistency of their meaning and usage throughout your Web pages. Your headings should arise naturally when you analyze your text. They should paraphrase an important concept that you are about to present. If you remove all text from your document (except for the headings), you should be left with a good outline or a detailed table of contents.

Welcome to my parlor . . .

The vastness of the Web has spawned the development of lots of search tools to find and catalog what's out there. These tools are basically programs that traverse the Web, simply looking at everything they encounter and following every link they can find, to see where it takes them. That's why these software robots are called Web crawlers or Web spiders. They live on the Web, picking up all the tasty tidbits they can find. For more information on such exotic but helpful beasts, please consult Chapter 14.

If the situation permits, headings may even be humorous. Headings could contain a common theme to help catch the viewer's eye and interest. The best approach to writing headings is to use your imagination and keep your audience in mind. We used this approach with the headings in this book; it is a hallmark of the whole . . .*For Dummies* series.

As a quick example, Table 7-1 shows some of the headings from this book in their "plain" and "humorous/theme" forms.

Table 7-1	Headings: Plain versus Extra-Spicy
Plain	*More Interesting*
Building Better Documents	Building Better Document Bodies
Building Good Paragraphs	Good Bones: Building Strong Paragraphs
Logos and Icons	Eye-Catchers: Logos, Icons, and Other Gems

In your Web page, you have only a few headings per screen or page; make the most of them. Keep the size of like headings consistent throughout your pages to help the viewer understand the level of importance of the information.

Although most browsers recognize at least four levels of headings and the HTML *Document Type Definition* (DTD) goes as deep as six levels, viewers can have difficulty distinguishing beyond the fourth level. Most well-constructed Web pages use no more than three levels of headings, even for very long documents.

Your home page will probably be more like the one in Figure 7-3 at this stage. It has one large heading line at the top and a medium-sized heading line toward the bottom. We removed all graphics from this page to show you that you can still achieve a pleasing layout by using just a few well-worded headings and text links on a full Web page.

> **Welcome to HTML for Dummies**
>
> FILES | CONTENTS | SEARCH | CONTACT | NEW
> HOW TO NAVIGATE
>
> Click here for a non-imagemap version
>
> ═══════════════════════════════
>
> You have reached the *HTML for Dummies* Web Pages, a charming, and hopefully helpful, addition to the WWW universe. These pages are designed to aid you in three key areas:
>
> To help you find current information on the Web about HTML
> To provide working examples and code for all the Web tricks in the book
> To introduce *HTML for Dummies* - your friendliest resource for HTML material offline!
>
> To get on with your exploration of these pages, you can use the MENU or NEXT buttons. MENU will send you to the master ordered list of available pages. NEXT will take you page by page through all the information here.
>
> Please spend some time exploring, and be sure to e-mail us your comments, if you feel so inclined. Enjoy!
>
> ═══════════════════════════════
>
> E-Mail: *HTML for Dummies* at html4dum@outer.net
>
> Text - Copyright © 1995, 1996 Ed Tittel & Steve James.
> Dummies Design and Art - Copyright © 1995, 1996 IDG Books Worldwide, Inc.
> Web Layout - Copyright © 1995, 1996 LANWrights & IMPACT Online.
> Revised -- January 15th, 1996 [JMS - IMPACT Online]

Figure 7-3: HTML document with headings and links viewed with Netscape.

The following HTML file, which your HTML files should resemble by the end of the next chapter, creates a Web page similar to the one shown in Figure 7-3.

The ⟨H1⟩ . . . ⟨/H1⟩ tags produce the larger type font of the header line. You should use the standard heading tags, ⟨H1⟩ through ⟨H4⟩, only for paragraph headings, hyperlinks, and other places where you want the text on a line by itself with white space above and below. Do not use header tags to merely increase the font size in your text. Doing so can cause trouble for you, as we explain later.

```
<HTML>
<HEAD>
<TITLE> HTML for DUMMIES HomePage - IDG Books</TITLE>
<!-Turn a BASE HREF on if you have any problems with the
 way this page behaves (e.g. unresolved graphics). Also
 be sure to provide an absolute URL that points to the
 home page on your Web server, e.g.
BASE HREF="http://www.outer.net/html4dum/html4dum.htm"
This is the proper BASE reference for our own HTML for Dummies
           server. ->
</HEAD>
<BODY>
<A NAME="top"></A>
<IMG ALIGN=MIDDLE WIDTH=60 HEIGHT=0
```

```
    SRC=graphics/space.gif ALT=" ">
<A HREF="http://outer.net/cgi-bin/ht4menum.map">
<IMG BORDER=0 ALIGN=TOP SRC="graphics/ht4menum.gif"
 ALT="Navigation Bar" ISMAP></A><BR>
<IMG ALIGN=MIDDLE WIDTH=130 HEIGHT=0
    SRC=graphics/space.gif ALT=" ">
<B><A HREF="ftpstuff.htm">FILES</A> &#32;&#124;
<A HREF="contents.htm">CONTENTS</A> &#32;&#124;
<A HREF="search4d.htm">SEARCH</A> &#32;&#124;
<A HREF="contact.htm">CONTACT</A> &#32;&#124;
<A HREF="whatsnew.htm">NEW</A><BR>
<IMG ALIGN=MIDDLE WIDTH=240 HEIGHT=0
    SRC=graphics/space.gif ALT=" ">
<A HREF="navigate.htm">HOW TO NAVIGATE</A></B><P>
<A HREF="html4du2.htm">Click here for a non-imagemap
 version</A>
<IMG ALIGN=MIDDLE WIDTH=160 HEIGHT=0
    SRC=graphics/space.gif ALT=" ">
<A HREF="registrn.htm">Click here to register online!</A>
<P>
<IMG WIDTH=100% SRC="graphics/line.gif"
    ALT="-==-==-==-==-==-"><P>
You have reached the <I> HTML for Dummies</I> Web Pages,
 a charming, and hopefully helpful, addition to the WWW
 universe. These pages are designed to aid you in three
 key areas:
<UL>
<LI> To help you find current information on the Web
 about HTML
<LI> To provide working examples and code for all the Web
 tricks in the book
<LI> To introduce <I> HTML for Dummies</I> - your
 friendliest resource for HTML material offline!
</UL>
<P>
To get on with your exploration of these pages, you can use the MENU
or NEXT buttons. MENU will send you to the master ordered list of
available pages. NEXT will take you page by page through all the
information here.<P>
Please spend some time exploring, and be sure to e-mail
 us your comments, if you feel so inclined. Enjoy!<P>
<IMG WIDTH=100% SRC="graphics/line.gif"
    ALT="-==-==-==-==-==-"><BR>
```

```
<P>
<IMG HEIGHT=1 WIDTH=130 SRC="graphics/space.gif"
   ALT=" _ ">
Be sure to visit the new <A HREF="http://www.idgbooks.com">IDG Books
            Web site</A>!
<IMG ALIGN=TOP SRC="graphics/new.gif"><P>
<P>
<IMG WIDTH=100% SRC="graphics/line.gif"
   ALT="-==-==-==-==-==-"><BR>
<A HREF="contents.htm"><IMG SRC="graphics/next.gif"
   ALT="NEXT " BORDER=0></A>
<A HREF="search4d.htm#menu"><IMG SRC="graphics/menu.gif"
   ALT="MENU " BORDER=0></A><BR>
<ADDRESS>
E-Mail: <A HREF="mailto:html4dum@outer.net">
HTML for Dummies at html4dum@outer.net</A><BR>
</ADDRESS>
URL: <A HREF =
 "http://www.outer.net/html4dum/html4dum.htm">
http://www.outer.net/html4dum/html4dum.htm</A>
<BR>
Text - Copyright &copy; 1995, 1996 Ed Tittel &amp;
 Steve James.<BR>
Dummies Design and Art - Copyright &copy; 1995, 1996
 IDG Books Worldwide, Inc.<BR>
Web Layout - Copyright &copy; 1995, 1996 <A HREF="http://www.io.com/
            ~mcintyre/lanwrght/lanwrght.htm">
LANWrights</A> &amp;
<A HREF="http://impactonline.com"> IMPACT Online.</A><BR>
Revised — January 15th, 1996 [JMS - IMPACT Online]<BR>
</BODY>
</HTML>
```

Two schools of thought exist regarding the use of heading sizes. The *information school* says, "Heading tags should be used in increments or decrements of one and always start with <H1>." This approach definitely provides for an ordered, standardized structure to your content and makes it easy for Web crawlers to pick out the headings for their indexes.

The *design school* screams, "BORING!" when the information school mentions its incremental approach. Instead, the design school states, "Use headings to draw attention to content. Putting an <H1> next to an <H3> or an <H4> creates more visual interest." As with most HTML design decisions, the choice is yours.

Experiment with heading tags to see what you think looks best. Remember, too much emphasized text diminishes the overall effect. Use it sparingly — emphasis works better when it remains exceptional. If you're a fan of fairy tales, it's kind of like crying "Wolf!"

Building Better Document Bodies

The body of your Web document lies at the heart of your page, between the header and the footer. Body content depends on the type and amount of information that you want to put online and the kind of audience that you're trying to reach.

Personal Web pages are generally quite different from business, academic, and government ones in the content and form of their bodies, although the layout for each type may be strikingly similar. The bodies of personal home pages (perhaps more accurately called *"Welcome"* pages, but who are we to quibble?) tend to contain a brief textual introduction followed by numerous links to local pages and to pages at other Web sites. The primary differences in the layout and content of well-designed Web page bodies occur when the information that they contain also differs significantly.

The bodies of most personal Web pages contain text for, or pointers to, the following elements:

- **Résumé:** mostly dense text with a picture
- **Personal History:** mostly plain text
- **Favorite Sports or Hobbies:** text with an occasional picture and links to sports or hobby sites
- **Favorite Web Sites:** lists of links to Web sites

The body of a commercial artist's Web pages might contain

- **Pictures, Pictures, Pictures:** usually small thumbnail-size pictures that are links to the much larger versions
- **Credentials:** a page containing a résumé, a list of shows, exhibits, and awards, and other professional activities
- **Professional References:** links to online samples of his or her work on other pages around the Net

The bodies of many government agency pages contain large amounts of boring text (No! I don't believe it. . .) that *should be* revised into hypertext pages using HTML. In the meantime, many are friendly enough to provide a brief description of the text and an FTP hyperlink so you can easily download these monsters.

So, how much text is enough but not too much in the body of a Web page? The answer lies in the minds of your viewers. May we suggest, however, that large amounts of scrolling almost always causes them to think, "Enough already!"

Textual sound bites — NOT!

When Web surfers want to read pages and pages of dense text, they buy the book or download the file and print it. For online reading, a large quantity of text isn't much fun and is viewed as a waste of bandwidth by many users (especially those who dial in with slower connections).

This view doesn't imply that your Web pages should be the textual equivalent of 30-second video bites on TV. It simply indicates that, at the current level of WWW development, most users are looking for fast ways to find the information that they want. They aren't going to dig deeply into a sea of text to find it. Your job is to make the good information easily available to your readers by using an appropriate page layout and providing good indexes with hypermedia links within the body of your pages.

Balanced composition

The body on personal Web pages should contain three to five short, well-written paragraphs. If these paragraphs are interspersed with moderately sized headings, enough white space, and small graphics to add visual interest, readers will probably scan them in their entirety.

Good use of separators and numerous links to additional pages are also very much in vogue. Using these techniques should result in a page that's between one and three screens long. Avoid making pages longer than three full screens. Hardly anybody has a 33-inch, high-resolution monitor . . . yet.

Controlling long pages

Web pages composed of over five screens of text or five screens of URL link lists usually should be split into multiple pages. If your content insists on being served in long pages, you can greatly increase its readability by linking a table of contents (TOC) to each section and providing a link back to the beginning. This linking structure has an effect similar to splitting the page into multiple page files but still lets your readers capture the entire document as a single file. Also, this structure makes it easier for you to edit the HTML file. You'll want to balance your convenience against the penalty of moving a single large chunk of data — moving it takes a long time! Just make sure that you aren't overdoing the links.

Speaking of chunks, a concept called *chunking* exists in writing. This concept deals with how to separate a long document. The basic chunking rule of thumb says, "Chunk the document at the idea or concept level." Large chunks take time to render, scroll, and search. Little-bitty chunks can make a concept fuzzy because waiting to download each separate page interrupts the reader's concentration. This is a good time for you to take the middle ground and chunk only as much as your users can easily catch.

It looks like we've drifted out of the content stream and into the control stream. The two components tend to blur when we discuss the layout of long Web page bodies. Nevertheless, content remains your most important concern, but when you have a lot of content, you can make it more approachable with effective use of controls.

The bottom line on bodies

The basic rules for creating great Web page bodies are

- ✔ Keep the layout consistent between pages to provide continuity for the reader.
- ✔ Provide plenty of white space and headings for easy visual scanning.
- ✔ Write short paragraphs and use them sparingly.
- ✔ Use meaningful graphics but use them only when absolutely necessary.
- ✔ Make liberal use of hypertext links to additional pages, instead of making your audience scroll, scroll, scroll.
- ✔ Vary the placement of the hyperlink words to provide more visual contrast to the page.
- ✔ Choose meaningful hyperlink words, NOT "Click Here."

Good Bones: Building Strong Paragraphs

"Omit needless words!" cried William Strunk, Jr. He also propounds Rule 17 in *The Elements of Style* (cowritten with E.B. White), which states:

"Vigorous writing is concise. A sentence should contain no unnecessary words, a paragraph no unnecessary sentences, for the same reason that a drawing should have no unnecessary lines and a machine no unnecessary parts. This requires not that the writer make all his sentences short, or that he avoid all detail and treat his objects only in outline, but that every word tell."

Combine Rule 17 with Rule 13 from the same work; it reads: "Make the paragraph the unit of composition." Together, these two principles inform the essence of writing clear, accurate prose.

WWW users demand the clearest and most concise text you can muster. But alas, not everyone on the Web is an English professor. Many have never heard of, (much less, read), Strunk and White. Nevertheless, all WWW surfers are readers of some language, so regardless of the language, clarity promotes accurate communication in your writing. To this end, follow these steps to writing better paragraphs:

1. **Create an outline for your information.**

2. **Write one paragraph for each significant point, keeping the sentences short, direct, and to the point.**

3. **Edit your text mercilessly, omitting all needless words and sentences.**

4. **Proofread and spellcheck.**

5. **Ask a few volunteers to evaluate your work.**

6. **Revise your text and edit it again as you revise it.**

7. **Solicit comments when you publish online.**

Listward Ho: Choosing List Structures

Chapters 4 and 5 presented the different types of HTML lists. Now we can show you when, why, and how to use each type.

Generally speaking, lists are used to distinguish lines of text from paragraphs via special formatting, usually some form of indentation. Some list types precede each line with a bullet character or a number. The following three lists are the most common types in use, although HTML 2.0 and Netscape extensions may provide more list types in the future.

The unordered list

The *unordered* or *bulleted* list is handy for emphasizing several short lines of information. The following shows HTML markup for an unordered list (displayed with Netscape in Figure 7-4).

```
<UL>
<LI> This is noticed.
<LI> So is this.
<LI> And so is this.
</UL>
```

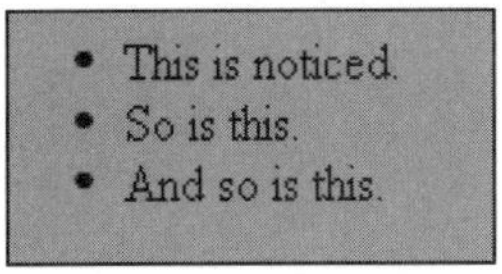

Figure 7-4:
An unordered list viewed with Netscape.

- This is noticed.
- So is this.
- And so is this.

The ordered list

Use the *ordered* or *numbered* list when the listed items have an obvious sequence. Here's the HTML markup for an ordered list (displayed with Netscape in Figure 7-5):

```
<OL>
<LI> First do A.
<LI> Then do B.
<LI> Lastly do C.
</OL>
```

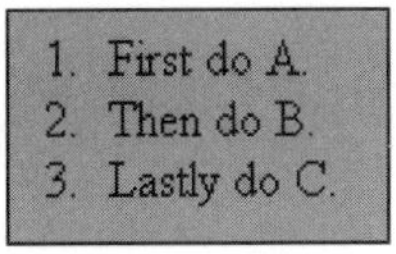

Figure 7-5:
An ordered list viewed with Netscape.

1. First do A.
2. Then do B.
3. Lastly do C.

The definition list

The *definition* or *glossary* list combines items in pairs. The first item is the term, and the second item is the definition. Here's the markup; see the display shown in Figure 7-6.

```
<DL>
<DT> Term A
<DD> Definition of Term A.
<DT> Term B
<DD> Definition of Term B.
</DL>
```

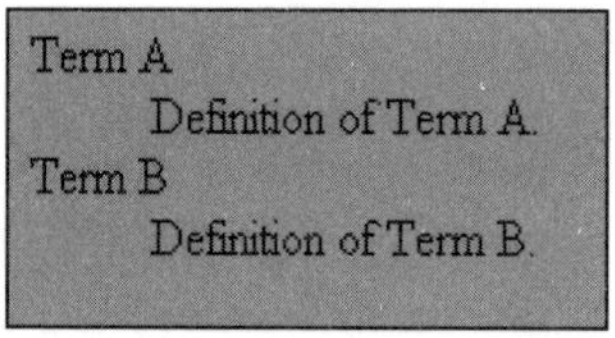

Figure 7-6:
A definition
list viewed
with
Netscape.

Term A
    Definition of Term A.
Term B
    Definition of Term B.

Although you should keep your page layout simple, lists and even nested lists (to produce outline formatting, as explained in Chapter 9) can be necessary to optimally display your specific information. However, use them intelligently and sparingly.

The following HTML document section shows the tags for an unordered list in the Web page body. The list serves to emphasize and separate the text lines.

```
-==-==-==-==-==-==-==-==-==-==-==-==-==-==-==-==-==-<BR>
You have reached the <I> HTML for Dummies</I> Web Pages, a charming,
            and hopefully helpful, addition to the WWW universe.
            These pages are designed to aid you in three key areas:

<UL>
<LI> To help you find current information on the Web about HTML
<LI> To provide working examples and code for all the Web tricks in
     the book
<LI> To introduce <I> HTML for Dummies</I> - your friendliest re-
     source for HTML material offline!
</UL>
<P>
```

```
To get on with your exploration of these pages, you can use the MENU
or NEXT buttons. MENU will send you to the master ordered list of
available pages. NEXT will take you page by page through all the
information here.<P>
Please spend some time exploring, and be sure to e-mail us your
comments, if you feel so inclined. Enjoy!<BR>
-==-==-==-==-==-==-==-==-==-==-==-==-==-==-==-==-==-<BR>
```

Figure 7-7 shows how this displays in Netscape. The bulleted list definitely emphasizes the body lines and adds to the visual richness of the page.

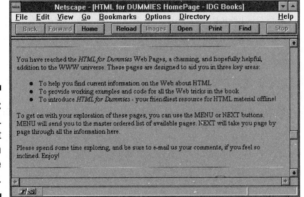

Figure 7-7:
An HTML document section showing the bulleted list.

Hooking Up: Linking Your Pages

Hypermedia links within the body of your pages bring out the power of the Web. To many users, surfing the Web is the ultimate video game. Following links just to see where they go can be interesting and informative.

As a Web page designer and Web weaver, you obviously want your users to like your pages well enough to tell others, who tell others, and so on. Therefore, you must provide good links within your own Web pages and to other Internet resources.

Links to pages within your Web are relative

From previous discussions, you know that links come in two flavors: relative and full. You can use a relative link, such as this one from the preceding *HTML for Dummies* page,

```
<A HREF="ftpstuff.htm">Click here to jump straight to the FTP page!</A>
```

only within your own Web, because the URL referenced is relative to the directory containing the Web page that calls the reference. In this case, the reference is to a file (ftpstuff.htm) in the same directory as the current HTML file (the current URL). The reference is relative to the server's document root plus the path in the file system where the current URL is stored. Got that? Don't worry, you'll understand it better later.

When you create links to HTML documents, you can use the `.html` or the `.htm` extension as long as you are consistent. Some platforms, servers, and browsers are forgiving when the "l" is left off the extension while others are not, so be warned. In the past, Web servers required the full four letter extension for both the filenames and the links that call them. Today, as long as your naming scheme is consistent, you can use either a four- or three- letter extension. But before you take our word for it, ask your Webmaster or system administrator about how your server really works; believe us, they know more about your server than we do!

A bit of advice regarding overuse of links: Use them only when they convey needed information and then use each specific link only once per page. Users can get very irritated when you make a link out of each occurrence of a commonly used word or phrase on a single page.

Links to the world outside of your Web are physical

A physical or full link, such as

```
<A HREF = "http://www.outer.net/html4dum/html4dum.htm">
```

gives the entire `http` URL address. You may use physical URLs for all of your links without any noticeable difference in speed, even on your local server. However, relative links are much shorter to type into your HTML file, and may improve your overall productivity.

When including physical URLs for links, we strongly recommend that you link to the resource first and capture the URL using your browser. Then, you can paste this URL right into your HTML file with little or no chance of introducing a typing error.

Whether it is better to use relative or physical links is a debate for the newsgroups or your local UNIX user's group. You are primarily concerned with the content of the links within your Web, their relationships to each other, and their contribution to your overall Web. Chapter 9 contains more advanced information on using Web links.

Choose your hyperlinks with care

Your home page may have links similar to those in the *HTML for Dummies* home page, shown all the way back in Figure 7-3. Notice which words in the list are included in the hyperlink text (highlighted and/or underlined). You must click on these words to open the link.

Choose your link text and images very carefully. Keep the text short and the graphics small. And never, never, never use the phrase *click here* by itself as the link text. "Why?" you ask. Because your readers may think that you didn't care enough to write appropriate text with a meaningful word or phrase for the link.

Well-chosen hyperlinks let your users quickly scan hyperlink text and choose links without reading the surrounding nonhighlighted text. The surrounding text is usually included only to provide readers with clarification of the link text anyway. Remember, users are in a hurry to scan your page and quickly pick out the important links by their unique wording or graphics. Make this task easy for them by using meaningful hyperlinks.

The next chapter goes beyond the Web building that you saw in this chapter. Move "onward, through the fog" to put the finishing touches on your first fantastic home page!

Chapter 8

Beyond Basics: Adding Flair and Impact to Your Pages

● ●

In This Chapter

▶ Adding logos, icons, and other little gems

▶ Building high-impact graphic pages

▶ Putting your best footer forward

▶ Copyrighting your copy

▶ Including version information

▶ Pointing to the author

▶ Using comments in HTML documents

● ●

*W*hen you see a Web page with a layout that you especially like, view its source to examine the formatting techniques employed. You can use your browser's Save As feature to save the HTML source to your own hard disk for later study, or you can print it.

At the same time, you can add the page to your bookmark file so that you can find it again to look at its images. Some browsers also let you save the images associated with a page to files on your hard disk. However, before you publish somebody else's work on your pages, be aware of copyright laws. (If you're in doubt whether it's okay to reuse something, the safest course of action is, "Don't do it!")

Borrowing Can Lead to Sorrow

Imitation may be the sincerest form of flattery, but stealing other authors' work and including it on your Web pages (as if it were your own) is against the law in most countries. However, learning new techniques from the work of others is the way most Web weavers expand their horizons.

Use the techniques that you learn to build your Web pages, with your information, in your own unique manner. You can always e-mail another Web author and request permission to use something of theirs in your page. Most Web authors are happy to help you because they, too, have been helped by others in their quest for new Web tools and techniques.

Eye-Catchers: Logos, Icons, and Other Little Gems

Graphics add impact and interest to your Web pages for users with GUI browsers. Unless the primary focus of your Web pages is computer graphics, you should use small graphics and only where they add extra value to your pages. Again, keep in mind that the only acceptable speed for computer users is instantaneous. The larger the graphic, the slower it loads.

Speaking of small, fast-loading graphics, it's time for you to add some sparkle to your plain-Jane home page. So far, it has nice-looking headings and simple black bullets next to the list lines (Figure 7-7). Because the basic layout of the page is well-established, all you need is a few splashes of color in appropriate locations to really spice things up.

Adding an image to your HTML document is as simple as inserting a line using the <IMG> tag:

```
<IMG SRC="graphics/redball.gif">
```

This line contains the mandatory source reference (URL) to a GIF file named *redball*. It is a relative reference to the file that the WWW server program expects to find in the same directory as the current page (that is, the page from which the link is called). For example, if the URL that calls for the red ball image is

```
graphics/redball.gif
```

using the relative URL (as shown) for the red ball would cause the server to look for

```
http://www.outer.net/html4dum/graphics/redball.gif
```

Alternatively, you may use the following image tag with the full URL for the red ball:

```
<IMG SRC="http://www.outer.net/html4dum/graphics/redball.gif">
```

If you want to link to an image file of a red ball (`redball.gif`) located in some other Web site, you must use a full URL (sometimes called an absolute URL) in the `<IMG>` tag like this:

```
<IMG SRC="http://www.someothersite.net/icons/redball.gif">
```

Using a full URL as a link means that each time the user's browser loads the icon, it actually links to the remote location. This increases the time needed for the browser to load the file. If the remote location is not online, the browser can't load the image. Therefore, having your graphic files on your own WWW server usually works better.

Two exceptions to this occur when you want to include, from another location, an image that changes over time (weather map, clock, and so on) or when you want an extremely large image. In the first case, the remote site maintains the changing image and your users see it directly from their site, but included in your page. In the second case, you save your server's disk space by pointing to the remote location for the 10MB picture.

The rest of this section discusses several small graphic elements as they are used in the following HTML document and displayed in Figure 8-1. The document used only two different small graphic elements — a red ball (`redball.gif`) and a rainbow line (`linerbo.gif`) — a total of six times. Both the `redball.gif` and the `linerbo.gif` are only 1K in size. They download and display quickly.

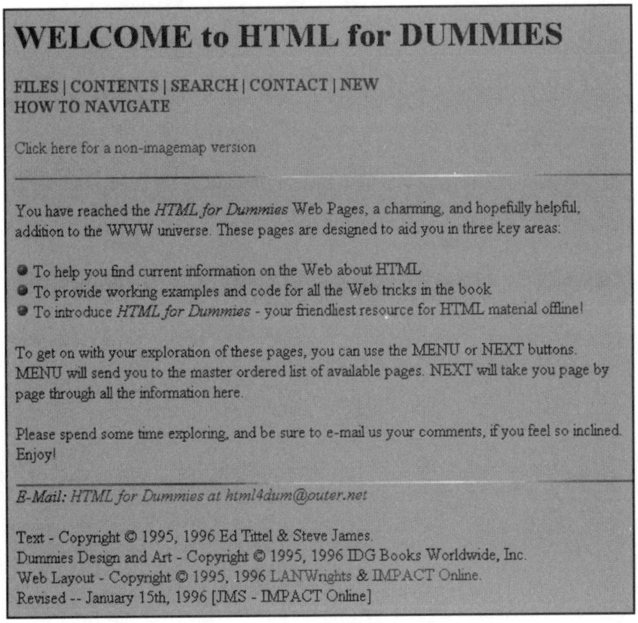

WELCOME to HTML for DUMMIES

FILES | CONTENTS | SEARCH | CONTACT | NEW
HOW TO NAVIGATE

Click here for a non-imagemap version

You have reached the *HTML for Dummies* Web Pages, a charming, and hopefully helpful, addition to the WWW universe. These pages are designed to aid you in three key areas:

● To help you find current information on the Web about HTML
● To provide working examples and code for all the Web tricks in the book
● To introduce *HTML for Dummies* - your friendliest resource for HTML material offline!

To get on with your exploration of these pages, you can use the MENU or NEXT buttons. MENU will send you to the master ordered list of available pages. NEXT will take you page by page through all the information here.

Please spend some time exploring, and be sure to e-mail us your comments, if you feel so inclined. Enjoy!

E-Mail: HTML for Dummies at html4dum@outer.net

Text - Copyright © 1995, 1996 Ed Tittel & Steve James.
Dummies Design and Art - Copyright © 1995, 1996 IDG Books Worldwide, Inc.
Web Layout - Copyright © 1995, 1996 LANWrights & IMPACT Online.
Revised -- January 15th, 1996 [JMS - IMPACT Online]

Figure 8-1: The Netscape view of headers, links, and graphics.

Reusing the same graphic on a single Web page adds no time or disk storage requirements when caching is activated in the user's browser. Therefore, using the rainbow line and the red ball three times each helps keep load and display times for these images to a minimum. Recycling images makes as much sense for Web pages as it does for the environment!

```
<HTML>
<HEAD>
<TITLE> HTML For Dummies HomePage - IDG Books</TITLE>
</HEAD>
<BODY>
<H1>WELCOME to HTML for DUMMIES</H1>
<IMG SRC="LINERBO.GIF">
<BR>
<A HREF="ftpstuff.htm">Click here for a non-imagemap version!</A><P>
<IMG SRC="LINERBO.GIF"><BR>
You have reached the <I> HTML For Dummies</I> Web Pages, a charming,
          and hopefully helpful, addition to the WWW universe.
          These pages are designed to aid you in three key areas:
<P>
<IMG SRC="REDBALL.GIF"> To help you find current information on the
          Web about HTML<BR>
<IMG SRC="REDBALL.GIF"> To provide working examples and code for all
          the Web tricks in the book<BR>
<IMG SRC="REDBALL.GIF"> To introduce <I> HTML For Dummies</I> - your
          friendliest resource for HTML material offline!
<P>
To get on with your exploration of these pages, you can use the MENU
          or NEXT buttons. MENU will send you to the master
          ordered list of available pages. NEXT will take you
          page by page through all the information here.<P>
Please spend some time exploring, and be sure to e-mail us your
          comments, if you feel so inclined. Enjoy!
<P>
<IMG SRC="LINERBO.GIF"><BR>
<ADDRESS>
E-Mail: <A HREF="mailto:html4dum@outer.net">
HTML For Dummies at html4dum@outer.net</A><BR>
</ADDRESS>
URL: <A HREF = "http://www.outer.net/html4dum/html4dum.htm">
http://www.outer.net/html4dum/html4dum.htm</A>
<BR>
Text - Copyright &copy; 1995, 1996 Ed Tittel &amp; Steve James.<BR>
Dummies Design and Art - Copyright &copy; 1995, 1996 IDG Books
          Worldwide, Inc.<BR>
Web Layout - Copyright &copy; 1995, 1996
<A HREF="http://www.io.com/~mcintyre/lanwrght/
          lanwrght.htm">LANWrights</A> &amp;
<A HREF="http://www.io.com/~mcintyre/homepage.htm"> IMPACT Online.</
          A><BR>
Revised — January 15th, 1996 [JMS - IMPACT Online]<BR>
</BODY>
</HTML>
```

Horizontal rules — but rainbow lines bring smiles

Separating the large "WELCOME to HTML for DUMMIES" heading from the text section with the rainbow line graphic adds the first touch of color to our page. We could accomplish this separation with a simple HTML horizontal rule tag <HR>. However, because <HR>'s only display is as a 3-D line (gray, black, and white to give the 3-D effect), you don't get the same visual impact that the brightly colored rainbow line provides. This baby changes from red, to violet, blue, green, yellow, orange, and back to red for a much nicer look.

Using the rainbow line to bracket the announcements at the start of the page and again just above the footer information sets them apart from the surrounding text, thereby drawing the user's attention. When used this way, colored ruler lines are perfect for segmenting your pages into eye-pleasing information blocks. You can make these lines with most paint programs in any length, thickness, and color combination imaginable. You can also find many on public access, graphic Web sites where they are available for your use, generally with no strings attached. In fact, feel free to use ours any way you like!

Rather than list any of the more than 7,000 sites with GIFs and JPEGs available for download here, we suggest that you search for "GIF" or "JPEG" on one of the many Web search engines such as

```
http://www.yahoo.com
http://www.webcrawler.com
http://www.excite.com
http://www.lycos.com
```

You'll find more information about search engines in Chapter 14, including an even more comprehensive list of URLs.

Just a couple of thoughts about using colored line images in place of <HR>: It may be quicker and easier to click the HTML editor button that inserts the <HR> into your document than to type the link to the colored line image, especially if you have more than a few of them over many pages. Also, some Web searching spiders or agents use the <HR> to distinguish breaks in text for their indexes. They won't necessarily recognize the colored line image as a replacement for the <HR> tag.

Colored balls beat list dots

The unordered list structure, used in the previous version of the page to provide black dots (bullets) to the left of the link lines, has been replaced by red ball graphics. These graphics are not just colored dots. They contain highlights and shadows that make them resemble three-dimensional balls. If you want to alternate them in red, white, and blue or some other colors, it increases their eye-catching effect and differentiates each line.

One word of caution about replacing lists with colored balls: The HTML 2.0 standard includes the unordered or bulleted list for a reason — that is, to list items in a nonsequential order and set them off by preceding each one with a symbol. Every browser renders these bullets in a standard fashion. Some browsers can even display 3-D colored balls instead of black dots. We can't say this about individual images of little colored balls. Thus, if you use your own images to create snappy lists, the standard HTML 2.0 list structure is not reflected in your document.

Just as with `<HR>` versus colored lines, an active spider or agent looking at your page can deduce that an object following an `<LI>` tag is part of the list it just entered and could organize this information accordingly, but they cannot recognize an imitation list with colored balls. If you're presenting a true list of items, you may want to use the actual HTML list tags. If you want to add some life to your page with colored balls next to some lines, go for it.

Using colored balls and other small icons within lines of text is as simple as inserting the tagged URL in the text at the point that you want it displayed. In the line below, the red ball is created by `<IMG SRC="graphics/redball.gif">` and displayed before `To help you. . . .` Notice the space between the `>` and the `To`. Although browsers generally ignore spaces, Netscape, Mosaic, and others may recognize a single space before or after text to help you format sentences properly and keep images from crowding text.

```
<IMG SRC="graphics/redball.gif"> To help you find current information
on the Web about HTML<BR>
```

Also notice that there is a space after `information`, but there is no space before `on`. Browsers usually ignore multiple spaces when they render text anyway, but when you're working in and around HTML tags, careful placement of spaces while writing the code can prevent painstaking reformatting work later on.

Icons

The term *icon* is used here to describe any small graphic image that can be substituted for a unit of text. A few well-designed and carefully located icons can help your users quickly find their way around your Web pages.

Icons stored as GIF files are usually small and load quickly. In most instances, an icon is simply added as a standard image-tagged URL in the position where you want it displayed.

Most icons are so small that you don't need to align text next to them, but for larger images, we discuss alignment later in this chapter. The default for most browsers is to align the text to the bottom of the image.

The *book title* icon that you can see on most of the *HTML For Dummies* Web pages resides in a file named ht4menum.gif. This lets you know at a glance that you're on a ...*For Dummies* page. We added this icon to the HTML document in the line shown below:

```
<H1><IMG ALIGN=TOP SRC="graphics/ht4menum.gif"> HTML For Dummies
Contents</H1><P>
```

Graphics as hyperlinks

The HTML 2.0 Checked icon at the bottom of the *HTML For Dummies* home page illustrates the use of a graphic as the hyperlink. Netscape displays a colored border around the icon to indicate that it's a link, if you turn on the border option. The following line from the HTML document shows how the image icon tag is nested within the link reference tags to make the icon act as a hyperlink:

```
<A HREF="http://www.webtechs.com/html-val-svc/">
<IMG SRC="http://www.webtechs.com/html-val-svc/images/valid_html.gif"
ALT="HTML 2.0 Checked!"></A>
```

Notice also the use of the alternate text attribute, ALT="HTML 2.0 Checked!", in the image tag. Text-only browsers display "HTML 2.0 Checked!" as the hyperlink instead of the icon. Some graphic browsers display an image holder icon and the alternate text when their image display function is turned off.

The creative use of the HTML Checked icon as the hyperlink to HALsoft's HTML checking page adds visual interest to the home page as well as giving a link to another useful site. If you use a few well-selected icons in this manner, your Web pages stand out and are remembered.

Logos

Logos are special-use graphics. They vary from icon size to much larger, sometimes too large. Remember KISS? Complex logos that take too long to load are nugatory on any Web page.

Use logos to identify your business or institution in a pleasing, eye-catching manner. Don't use them to overpower the page or to irritate the users. A moderately sized logo at the top of the home page is generally acceptable. Using icon-sized logos in the footer of each Web page is equally acceptable. Remember that text-only browsers and GUI browsers with image loading turned off (for faster page loading) won't display your fantastic logos, anyway.

Figures 8-2 and 8-3 illustrate the visual effects of a moderately sized GIF and logo at the top of a page. The *HTML For Dummies* logo file is only 14,000 bytes, so it loads in only a few seconds. The secondary logo is only 5,000 bytes or so. Both images are small and therefore fit easily on display screens with resolution as low as 640 × 480 pixels. Figure 8-2 also illustrates the view with the image loading turned off in Netscape.

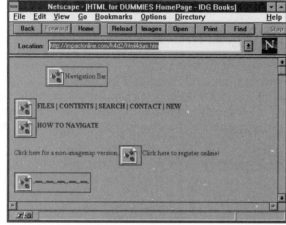

Figure 8-2:
HTML
document
logo viewed
with
Netscape
and image
display
turned off.

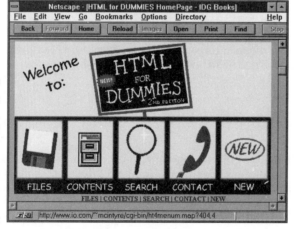

Figure 8-3:
HTML
document
logo viewed
with
Netscape
and images
displayed.

Here's the HTML code that produced these two views:

```
<HTML>
<HEAD>
<TITLE> HTML for DUMMIES HomePage - IDG Books</TITLE>
```

```
<!-Turn a BASE HREF on if you have any problems with the
 way this page behaves (e.g. unresolved graphics). Also
 be sure to provide an absolute URL that points to the
 home page on your Web server, e.g.
BASE HREF="http://www.outer.net/html4dum/html4dum.htm"
This is the proper BASE reference for our own HTML for Dummies
server. ->
</HEAD>
<BODY>
<A NAME="top"></A>
<IMG ALIGN=MIDDLE WIDTH=60 HEIGHT=0
   SRC=graphics/space.gif ALT=" ">
<A HREF="http://outer.net/cgi-bin/ht4menum.map">
<IMG BORDER=0 ALIGN=TOP SRC="graphics/ht4menum.gif"
 ALT="Navigation Bar" ISMAP></A><BR>
<IMG ALIGN=MIDDLE WIDTH=130 HEIGHT=0
   SRC=graphics/space.gif ALT=" ">
<B><A HREF="ftpstuff.htm">FILES</A> &#32;&#124;
<A HREF="contents.htm">CONTENTS</A> &#32;&#124;
<A HREF="search4d.htm">SEARCH</A> &#32;&#124;
<A HREF="contact.htm">CONTACT</A> &#32;&#124;
<A HREF="whatsnew.htm">NEW</A><BR>
<IMG ALIGN=MIDDLE WIDTH=240 HEIGHT=0
   SRC=graphics/space.gif ALT=" ">
<A HREF="navigate.htm">HOW TO NAVIGATE</A></B><P>
<A HREF="html4du2.htm">Click here for a non-imagemap
 version</A>
<IMG ALIGN=MIDDLE WIDTH=160 HEIGHT=0
   SRC=graphics/space.gif ALT=" ">
<A HREF="registrn.htm">Click here to register online!</A>
<P>
<IMG WIDTH=100% SRC="graphics/line.gif"
   ALT="-==-==-==-==-==-"><P>
You have reached the <I> HTML for Dummies</I> Web Pages,
 a charming, and hopefully helpful, addition to the WWW
 universe. These pages are designed to aid you in three
 key areas:
<UL>
<LI> To help you find current information on the Web
 about HTML
<LI> To provide working examples and code for all the Web
 tricks in the book
<LI> To introduce <I> HTML for Dummies</I> - your
 friendliest resource for HTML material offline!
```

(continued)

```
</UL>
<P>
To get on with your exploration of these pages, you can use the MENU
or NEXT buttons. MENU will send you to the master ordered list of
available pages. NEXT will take you page by page through all the
information here.<P>
Please spend some time exploring, and be sure to e-mail
 us your comments, if you feel so inclined. Enjoy!<P>
<IMG WIDTH=100% SRC="graphics/line.gif"
   ALT="-==-==-==-==-==-"><BR>
<P>
<IMG HEIGHT=1 WIDTH=130 SRC="graphics/space.gif"
   ALT=" _ ">
Be sure to visit the new <A HREF="http://www.idgbooks.com">IDG
Books Web site</A>!
<IMG ALIGN=TOP SRC="graphics/new.gif"><P>
<P>
<IMG WIDTH=100% SRC="graphics/line.gif"
   ALT="-==-==-==-==-==-"><BR>
<A HREF="contents.htm"><IMG SRC="graphics/next.gif"
   ALT="NEXT " BORDER=0></A>
<A HREF="search4d.htm#menu"><IMG SRC="graphics/menu.gif"
   ALT="MENU " BORDER=0></A><BR>
<ADDRESS>
E-Mail: <A HREF="mailto:html4dum@outer.net">
HTML for Dummies at html4dum@outer.net</A><BR>
</ADDRESS>
URL: <A HREF =
 "http://www.outer.net/html4dum/html4dum.htm">
http://www.outer.net/html4dum/html4dum.htm</A>
<BR>
Text - Copyright &copy; 1995, 1996 Ed Tittel &amp;
 Steve James.<BR>
Dummies Design and Art - Copyright &copy; 1995, 1996
 IDG Books Worldwide, Inc.<BR>
Web Layout - Copyright &copy; 1995, 1996 <A HREF="http://www.io.com/
~mcintyre/lanwrght/lanwrght.htm">
LANWrights</A> &amp;
<A HREF="http://impactonline.com"> IMPACT Online.</A><BR>
Revised — January 15th, 1996 [JMS - IMPACT Online]<BR>
</BODY>
</HTML>
```

Building Graphic Page Layouts

As you should now thoroughly understand, the graphic layout of the Web pages you see in this chapter did not occur by accident. These page layouts were drawn with the best locations for graphics noted. The graphics were carefully chosen and sized to fit the layout and purpose of each page.

As you can see in Figure 8-1, the graphics were added sparingly to brighten and enhance the visual contrast within the page. Upon first viewing the page, the user sees the large name. This is good because the primary purpose of the page is to focus on the *HTML For Dummies* book.

As the user scans down the page, the rainbow lines, red balls, and highlighted hyperlinks focus the attention on the important parts of the page. The overall layout is very conservative, yet, more interesting than without the graphics.

The top portion of the page, shown in Figures 8-2 and 8-3, illustrates the additional thought that must go into the design and layout of pages that use larger graphics. The page works well for non-GUI browsers yet show the much more interesting graphic and logo on GUI browsers. If you experiment with the various formatting tags available in HTML and follow the suggestions in this book, you can do the same and much more on your Web pages.

Working with graphics files

You must work with graphics on two distinct levels to arrive at a good page layout and optimum functionality. You must consider not only the graphics' size and complexity, but also the size of the image files and length of time required to download them.

The original file for the logo in Figure 8-3 was a 1MB file that covered the entire screen. Careful cropping, resizing, and resampling (using fewer pixels per inch) resulted in the current file size of only 14,000 bytes. This change results in a dramatic improvement in load time — it's not unusual for a megabyte of data to require minutes to load over a slow link, but a 14,000-byte file moves in seconds, even over slow telephone lines.

You don't have to become an expert at using graphics manipulation programs such as Paint Shop Pro, Photo Styler, Graphics WorkShop, Wingif, or Lview Pro to produce high-quality images for your Web pages. However, if you are going to do a lot of work with images, you probably should become fairly adept at one of these shareware programs or a commercial equivalent.

GIF and JPEG file formats

Although you can use many different types of graphic files on the Web, most browsers have internal display capabilities for only GIF and JPEG. Browsers use external helper applications to display the other file types. Also, compressed GIF and JPEG files are the smallest, and therefore the fastest to load, of all the commonly used file types.

Most good shareware image manipulation programs, such as those mentioned above, can load and save both GIF and JPEG format files. These programs also support the GIF87a and interlaced GIF89a formats. If you're using a Macintosh, the program to use for interlaced GIFs is *GifConverter*.

Whenever you build GIF89a graphics, be sure to test any interlaced graphics on multiple browsers. Some color depths lend themselves better to interlacing (and transparency, too, for that matter) than others. Unfortunately, this is a trial-and-error process and not an exact science; that's why testing your images across multiple browsers on multiple platforms is a must!

Seeing through the graphic to the background

The GIF89a format also introduced the *transparent background* feature. This feature turns off one of the colors of the image — when displayed by a browser — allowing whatever is behind the image to show through at every point where the color is "turned off" or transparent. Usually, this is the background color, but images can be laid over other images or text as well. To the user, your image appears to float on the browser's background, rather than appearing as a square of some other color surrounding the image.

Programs such as *giftrans* for UNIX and DOS and *Transparency* for the Macintosh create images with transparent backgrounds for browsers that support the GIF89a format. For Windows users, *LView for Windows* is also worth checking out in this capacity. This capability really adds to the impact and drama on a Web page.

A new pic's resolution . . .

One last technical aspect of dealing with images involves the number of bits per pixel stored in the file. Although reducing the bits per pixel reduces the resolution (and therefore, the quality) of the image as seen by the browser, try storing your image with 7 or even 5 bits per pixel if you really need to show a large image as quickly as possible. Check your graphics program for more information on this technique. Alternatively, you can reduce the number of colors in the picture to lower its overall image size. Check your graphics program for more information on these techniques.

A standard GIF image requires 8 bits per pixel, which results in 256 colors. Seven bits of information per pixel produces 128 colors, 5 bits gives 32 colors, and so on. Some programs, such as *Paint Shop Pro* (shareware) and *Photoshop*

(commercial) even allow you to set a specific number of colors. For example, setting the number of colors to 43 results in 7 bits per pixel, but the remaining 85 empty color definitions are set at 0,0,0 (or undefined) which results in a smaller (and faster) graphic than one set to 7 bits per pixel alone. Most of these programs also tell you how many unique colors appear in an image and let you manipulate the number of colors until you can achieve the best compromise between size and fidelity.

Rules for graphical thumbs

Keep these rules of thumb firmly in mind while you design your Web pages:

✔ Sketch your layout with and without the graphics.

✔ Focus on overall page look and content.

✔ KISS your images . . . small and simple.

✔ Use compressed interlaced GIFs or JPEGs.

✔ Link a thumbnail version of an image to the larger file instead of dumping a megabyte-sized file on your unsuspecting users.

✔ Include the size of the image file in the text that describes a large image.

✔ Use graphics sparingly for maximum effect.

✔ Images or graphics should enhance the text information.

Footers Complete Your Page

The *Yale C/AIM WWW Style Manual: Interface Design* provides a wonderful rationale for using footers on your Web pages as a matter of course:

> State the title, the author, the date, and provide at least one link to a local home page in every WWW page in your system, and you will have gone 90% of the way toward providing your readers with an understandable WWW interface. (`http://info.med.yale.edu/caim/StyleManual_Top.HTML`)

All elements mentioned, except the title, are contained in the footer of each Web page. Unlike the HTML header and body, the footer is not a marked element of an HTML document. By convention, it is the bottom portion of the page body.

Footers contribute greatly to your Web pages by providing the authorship, contact information, legal status, version/revision information, and a link to your home page. The footer should contain some or all elements listed in Table 8-1.

Slice up your graphics for better response time!

"What is an *interlaced GIF?*" you ask. It is a method of storing the GIF file so that the browser can load a low-resolution image on the first of multiple passes and then fill in to the normal resolution on the subsequent passes. This gives the image a "Venetian blind" look as it is drawn.

The total load time for a given image remains the same, but some browsers, such as Netscape, load the text of the page with the first pass of the images. This lets the user begin scrolling and reading while the other three image passes are completed. Therefore, the user gets to your information much faster, which generally results in a happier user.

Table 8-1	Footer Elements
Author's name	
Author's institution or company	
Author's phone number	
Author's e-mail address	
Author's postal mailing address	
Page owner's name	
Page owner's phone number	
Page owner's e-mail address	
Page owner's postal mailing address	
Legal disclaimer or language designating the page as the official communication of the company or institution	
Date of page's last revision	
Official company or institutional seal, logo, or other graphic mark	
Copyright notice	
URL of the page	
Hypertext link(s) to home page or to other pages	
Hypertext link(s) to other sections of this page	

Your basic home page HTML document already contains the minimum suggested footer information for a home page:

```
<ADDRESS>
Your Name<BR>
Phone number<BR>
Standard Mail Address<BR>
E-Mail Address
</ADDRESS><P>
Copyright &copy; 1996, Your Name <BR>
Revised — Revision Date <BR>
URL: <A HREF = "http://this.page's.url.here"> http://
this.page's.url.here</A>
```

Even though it is a home page, it contains a link to itself in the URL line. All other local pages in your Web should also contain a link in the footer to your full home page URL, like the example just shown. Why? If a user saves your page as an HTML file and later wants to know its address, there it is on the bottom of the page, both visible and as a link. Nifty, huh? Don't you wish everyone did this?

The name of your home page file depends on your WWW server's requirements. Some servers require a specific name and extension, such as `index.html` where the extension includes all four letters: html. It's a UNIX thing. Don't worry though; it's easy to do. On an NCSA WWW server with a default configuration, the default HTML page filename is `index.html`; therefore, these URLs are equivalent:

```
<A HREF="http://www.foo.net/goo"> <!— least desirable —>
<A HREF="http://www.foo.net/goo/"> <!— better —>
<A HREF="http://www.foo.net/goo/index.html"> <!— most desirable —>
```

Businesses and institutions may have special requirements regarding credits, addresses, logos, and other footer information. Frequently, the author or person in charge of maintaining the page may not be the owner of the page. The owner may be a business and the author an employee. Depending on the purposes of the page, contact information for both may be required in the footer.

Government agencies and other public institutions frequently want to put what seems like their entire staff directory and departmental history in their footers. At least they're at the bottom of the page. However, if you are going to have a long footer, place a link back to the home page above it so the user doesn't have to scroll as far to find it.

Figure 8-4 illustrates a well-balanced footer for a business-style home page, from the *HTML For Dummies* home page, of course. It contains all important footer elements in a visually pleasing layout. It doesn't contain a phone number or snail-mail address, but you may not want folks calling you or writing letters to you at home, either. Anyway, on the Net — e-mail rules!

Figure 8-4:
Footer of the
HTML For
Dummies
home page
viewed with
Netscape.

E-Mail: *HTML for Dummies at html4dum@outer.net*
URL: http://www.outer.net/html4dum/html4dum.htm
Text - Copyright © 1995, 1996 Ed Tittel & Steve James.
Dummies Design and Art - Copyright © 1995, 1996 IDG Books Worldwide, Inc.
Web Layout - Copyright © 1995, 1996 LANWrights & IMPACT Online.
Revised -- January 15th, 1996 [JMS - IMPACT Online]

Use a URL line as part of your page

Notice that the URL is visible in the footer. It's a good idea to put the URL for each page in the footer in small type. This helps viewers who print your page, but don't add it to their browser's hotlist, to find it again on the Web. And it's a nice finishing touch that tells users that you really do care about them.

Instead of placing all the footer information directly in each page, you may want to put some of it on a page of its own and include a link to that information in the footer instead. This works especially well if your information requires a long legal disclaimer or other complex language. Please check with your legal representative concerning the fine points of using disclaimers on the Web.

Copyright

Copyright law hasn't quite caught up with the explosion in electronic publishing on the Web. However, it won't hurt you or your organization to put your copyright notice at the bottom of any Web page that you don't want freely copied without being attributed to you or without your permission.

The copyright notice shown in Figure 8-4 is simply standard text except for the copyright symbol. Most browsers can display the copyright symbol © if you use the character entity © in the file. Otherwise, you can simulate it with (C) or (c) if your lawyer approves.

Counting coup: versions, dates, and times

Why should you even bother to note when you change your pages? One of the greatest values of publishing on the Web is your ability to change your pages quickly as your content changes. Not only do your users need to know when this occurs, but you also need to know which version you're providing so that you can be certain to change old stuff when newer versions are ready.

Version numbering

If it's appropriate to your information, you may want to use version numbers in addition to a revision date. This allows you to refer to a particular page as version 12B, for example, rather than the second revision from December. It's less ambiguous, more direct, and shorter, too!

Revision date

Placing the revision date in the footer of each page keeps track of its chronology. The format for the date should be January 02, 1996 to avoid confusion. In the USA, this date would be abbreviated 01/02/96. In Europe, this abbreviation would be read as the 1st of February, 1996. The international ISO 8601 standard date notation is YYYY-MM-DD (year, month, day), which would result in 1996-01-02. Use that format for dates if you want to be really up-to-date!

If for some reason you don't want to show the revision date on the page, you'll be much happier in the long run if you use the HTML comment tags and hide the revision date inside them. We discuss using HTML comments later in this chapter.

Time stamp

The time may be added to the date for sensitive information. Because users from all over the world can view your information at any time, 24-hour UTC (Universal Time, which used to be called GMT — Greenwich Mean Time) is the most appropriate format. The proper format is hh:mm:ss (hour:minute:second). Make sure that you note the time as UTC (that is, 18:30:00 UTC or 18:30:00Z for 6:30 p.m.). The *Z* stands for *Zulu* in the NATO radio alphabet and refers to the Zulu or Zero meridian of longitude where UTC is measured. Now aren't you so happy to know that little tidbit of information for the next time you're on *Jeopardy!*?

New

If some of the information on your pages changes frequently, but at irregular intervals, you can alert your users with a small graphic or *** NEW *** notice followed by the revision date. You should remove this marker after the information is no longer considered new (usually a few days to a month, at the longest). New notices that hang around for months are worthless and clutter your page.

Pointers to the Author or Owner

You can choose between an e-mail link or a form as your method for obtaining feedback. Your choice may depend upon which of these options your Web service provider makes available to you. Of the two, e-mail is the simplest and most generally used for personal home pages. Businesses tend to use custom forms in their attempts to obtain more specific information about their users (and to try to turn them into paying customers).

The e-mail link for feedback

The `mailto:` link is a special link that starts an e-mail program on some servers so that the user can send e-mail to the page owner. Every well-constructed home page has some way for the user to give feedback to the developer or owner of the page. The most general approach is to provide your e-mail address in text inside the HTML `<ADDRESS>` . . . `</ADDRESS>` tags. Although it isn't supported by all Web server software or even all browsers, the `mailto:` link is another frequently used method. If you want to use it despite its less-than-universal availability, here's how:

```
E-Mail: <A HREF="mailto:html4dum@outer.net"> HTML For Dummies at
    html4dum@outer.net</A>
```

In this example, the actual hyperlink is `mailto:html4dum@outer.net` and the second instance of the e-mail address in `HTML For Dummies at html4 dum@outer.net` has been added so that something is highlighted on the page and for readers who can't use the `mailto:` URL. You can customize the wording to your heart's content, outside the actual address portion (`<A HREF = "mailto:html4dum@outer.net">.</A>`). You can also put text in front of it as shown by the `E-Mail:` in the example taken from our own *HTML For Dummies* Web pages. (The preceding e-mail lines are displayed in the *HTML For Dummies* page footer, Figure 8-4.)

Forms for feedback

Instead of using e-mail, some home page authors set up a form that generally requests the user's name, address, and other information and gives the user space to type a message to the page owner. Forms are an advanced HTML feature that provide an area on the screen for direct user input. They rely upon underlying UNIX-based CGI (Common Gateway Interface) scripts on the Web server. Creating forms for feedback and other uses is discussed in more detail in Chapter 10.

Comment Your HTML Documents for Posterity

Do yourself a big favor and annotate your HTML documents liberally with comments. You will thank yourself many times over in the future if you add comments that explain links or lists more fully or state when information needs to be updated.

Comment lines are formatted like this:

```
<!- comment text ->
```

The comment line starts with $<!-$ and ends with $->$. Comments inside the HTML document are ignored by most newer browsers. As a general rule, place comments on a line separate from other HTML text. This won't interrupt your HTML text because browsers also ignore white space between HTML tags. To be on the safe side, don't use any special characters (<, >, &, !) within comments, either.

If you've made it this far, congratulations, you are no longer a complete HTML ignoramus. You've already discovered enough to design and create well-balanced, attractive, and user-friendly Web pages. You're on a roll, so keep right on going to find out even more fun things to add to your Web pages.

Part III
Advanced HTML

The 5th Wave   By Rich Tennant

IN THE AFTERMATH OF ANOTHER FAILED BID TO CAPTURE THE HOME PC MARKET, "KLEIN'S DEPARTMENT STORE" ATTEMPTS TO UNLOAD ITS INVENTORY OF CHIA-PET PCs.

CHIA-PETS
JUST ADD WATER
AND WATCH THEM
GROW

MikroWave
SlowCooker
cooks all day—
in an instant!

BY POPULAR
DEMAND!

FINALLY!

SALE

THE
Chia-Pet
PC

In this part . . .

Once you master the basics of HTML markup, you really begin to appreciate the wonderful things your documents can do for the Web (and that the Web can do for your documents). In this part of the book, you tackle the composition of complex pages, plus you find out how to use HTML's advanced features to solicit user input and to use graphics for navigation.

Along the way, we hope you start to develop an appreciation for readable page styles and begin to apply some of the ideas, tools, and techniques we provide along the way. This is your first real exposure to all the capabilities that make Web pages beautiful and exciting, so we hope you take advantage of what you learn.

On the other hand, none of these bells and whistles should diminish your fixation on content. Users may wander by your pages and be sucked in by sexy graphics or compelling layouts, but what will keep them in your thrall is the quality and readability of your content. So don't let all the wonderful formats, layouts, and other bells and whistles you read about in this part of the book get in the way — the idea is to *enhance* your content, not obliterate it!

Chapter 9

Going High-Rise: Building Complex Pages

· ·

In This Chapter

▶ Expanding your home page into a Web

▶ Moving around inside your documents and local Web

▶ Jumping to remote sites

▶ Sampling and analyzing sophisticated Web pages

▶ 3-D and beyond

· ·

*Y*ou're probably not satisfied with your nice, simple, single-screen home page. Because of all the wonderful stuff you've seen out there, you really want to make a Web of pages with all sorts of great material in them, right? That's pretty natural, and it doesn't compromise the KISS principle either.

If you recall, we suggested that you'd want to make more pages as you expanded your Web. But the more pages you add, the more difficulty your users will have in finding their way around. While you're growing your own Web, your most important job is to make your users' journey through it as enjoyable as possible. In fact, you've already discovered the necessary methods and techniques in previous chapters. Now it's time to put them to use.

This chapter covers important aspects of creating complex Webs. After this discussion, we show you examples of more advanced Web pages with comments about their elements and layout.

There's No Place Like Home

Home isn't only your home page; it's your own Web, the local constellation of planets orbiting your home page. It's your local turf in cyberspace, where Web surfers can find the information that you think is important. But even if your site is fantastic and beautiful, users can be put off if they have trouble navigating your Web. That's why you need a clear mental picture of its fully developed organization before you start expanding things.

Organization

If you listen closely to your content, it can tell you the organizational style that it needs — or rather, demands. Hierarchical style, linear style, and randomly interlinked combinations of these two styles are the standard organizational structures used in most Webs. These structures — which we'll call *Web structure* — are illustrated in Figures 9-1, 9-2, and 9-3.

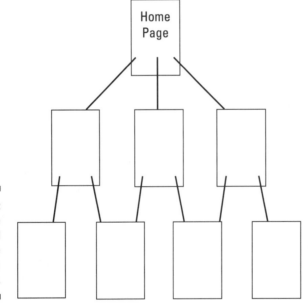

Figure 9-1:
The
hierarchical
structure
looks like a
family tree.

It's straightforward to "Web-ify" a linear document, but the converse is not true: Organizing a random collection of ideas and concepts into a linear document is very difficult, if not impossible. When designing and using links within or among Web documents, you need to be clear about the organization and interconnectedness of their content.

The hierarchical, or tree, structure is used most often in Web designs. It's logical and has a familiar look to most computer users (hints: hard disk file trees and GUI help systems). This kind of organization is easy for users to navigate, especially when you include links back to the home page on each page.

When using a hierarchy, your information should progress from the most general (trunk) level, or a table of contents on your home page, to the most detailed content in the outermost leaves. Your content dictates the divisions in the tree, but you can include interesting links between seemingly unrelated branches to better inform your users. Also, try providing multiple links to individual pages. In this way, the structure includes aspects of the index of a book, as well as its table of contents.

Keep in mind that readers can enter your Web space from somewhere other than your home page, so make sure that you give navigational clues to *jumped-in* users. You want them to find your home page or other relevant pages easily. It's frustrating to land on a page whose URL you obtained by e-mail from some cohort who says, "Check out this page," only to be forced to blunder around because you can't tell where home is!

Also, remember your readers experience the *lost in hyperspace* problem quite often. That's one excellent reason to provide navigational clues at the top and bottom of each Web page that you create. For an example of good style (even if we do say so ourselves), check out this URL:

```
http://www.outer.net/html4dum/
```

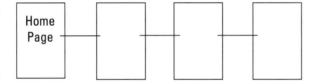

Figure 9-2:
Linear
structure.

Simple, booklike, but also *rigid and confining* are common descriptions of the linear structure. If your information presents a series of steps or follows a process from start to finish, linear structure is a fitting choice for your document organization. It keeps users on track and out of trouble. Here, you can make good use of links to "next page," "previous page," and "top or start page."

Be sure to put links to your home page (or the starting point) on each page in a linear structure. Without such links, users dropped into the middle of your Web have only the browser's controls to get out. If you trap them this way, they'll talk about you and your Web on the Net, but the talk won't be flattering!

The WWW itself is a Web structure. It's a great example of the fantastic freedom of movement and free-flowing design that are implicit in this kind of loosely linked environment. Also, Web structure can quickly demonstrate how easy it is to get lost.

Being lost on the Web isn't quite the same as being lost in a big city. Users can always use the browser's controls to go back to the previous URL or go to another URL. If you want users to get the most out of your Web, you need to provide obvious hyperlinks from each of your pages to other appropriate pages within your own Web or to other locations on the WWW.

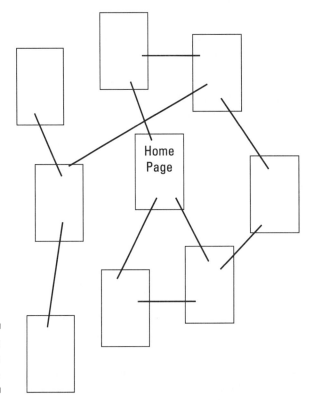

Figure 9-3:
Web
structure.

Home
Page

Providing structure without constraining users' freedom to explore your space is the goal of any well-designed Web structure. If your information on related subjects is extensive, put hyperlinks within the text to specific paragraphs in other pages where the user can see more detailed information about the content. Be careful how you do this, though — as we mentioned in Chapter 7, too much linkage can be just as detrimental as not enough!

Hypertext linking is the most time-consuming part of HTML document development. Do it well, and your users will love you forever. We discuss this issue in more detail later in this chapter.

When you build a complex Web structure, always, always, always put a link to your home page on each page. It's also a great idea to reproduce the URL for each page in its footer in small type. If you provide this information, users can return to any specific page in your Web by using that URL later on, even if they didn't add it to their bookmark lists.

It's story (board) time, boys and girls!

Remember doing the sketch of your home page along with Chapter 7? It's time for you to find your pencil and paper again. This time, you'll be drawing your Web structure. For a personal Web, pencil and paper will probably do nicely.

First Things First: List 'Em Out

Make a list of the major pieces of information that you want to include in your Web. These major points will probably be the links on your home page and may be similar to the following:

- ✔ Who you are
- ✔ What you do
- ✔ Personal history
- ✔ Your family
- ✔ Hobbies
- ✔ Sports
- ✔ WWW land (jump list)

Sketch the Web

In the preceding example, there are no other topics to consider, so a simple hierarchical structure looks appropriate. The simple sketch of this structure (shown in Figure 9-4) should look familiar.

Using this sketch to analyze your home page, you can see some links that aren't readily apparent from looking at the HTML document. These links exist among the "Who you are" page and the "What you do," "Personal history," and "Sports" pages as well as among the "Your family" and the "Hobbies" and "Sports" pages. All these secondary pages are therefore linked to the "Home page."

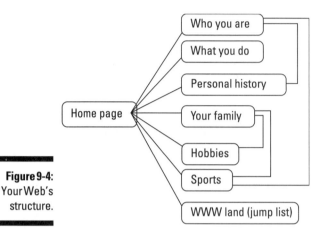

Board the whole story

This simple sketch doesn't provide enough information for you to fully visualize your Web. What you really need to do now is to prepare a storyboard for these pages — that is, unless you can mentally picture the elements and links on each of the eight separate pages.

Every movie, TV show, and comic book gets storyboarded before any production takes place. Producing a set of Web pages is a lot like making a TV show, especially if you think of each Web page as a separate scene. Over time, though, an entire collection of Web documents and associated materials will evolve from your work, making it resemble a whole season's worth of TV episodes instead of a single show.

To prepare a storyboard, simply prepare a sketch of the layout of each Web page with the URLs for links written on each one. For small Webs, some Web authors use a white marker board with colored pens. The colors are handy for showing different types of links, forms, or other HTML elements.

For more complex Webs, many authors use a sheet of paper for each Web page, some string, some push pins, and a large bulletin board (cork type, not BBS). This allows for complex arrangements that can be easily changed. Also, the storyboard method is invaluable for identifying potential hypertext links if you attach the text of each Web page to its layout sheet. Whenever you're creating a Web of more than a handful of pages, create a storyboard. Doing this saves you much more time than it takes initially, and after you're finished, you'll appreciate its value.

Anchors Away: Jumping Around Your Documents

We did say that it wasn't too terrible to create Web pages spanning up to three screens if your information demands the extra room. You may even expand your home page to more than one screen if you carefully drop your anchors and don't go overboard on the images.

You can use two different anchor tag attributes for movement within your pages. To provide viewers with links to specific parts within a Web page (called intradocument linking), use the `NAME="text"` anchor to provide the destination of an `HREF="#label"` tag. Use the standard `HREF="URL"` (called interdocument linking) to let users jump from page to page. Or to jump to a specific location within another page, you can combine both approaches and use `HREF="URL#label"`.

There's an important distinction to note when talking about following links inside a browser program. With interdocument linking (between documents), most browsers land the reader at the first line of the target document. On the other hand, intradocument linking (within the same document) takes you to a place other than the default top of the page, unless there's a named anchor at the top of the page and the URL calls this anchor out.

Here's another interesting quirk about browsers — namely, their behavior with named anchors that occur near the bottom of a document. If an anchor appears near the bottom, most browsers do NOT bring the named anchor to the first line on the screen. This is because the browser usually renders a full screen of text; thus, if the anchor is near the bottom of a document, the link may take you to a point toward the bottom of the screen rather than to the absolute bottom of the document itself.

Linking to text in another page

The *HTML For Dummies* home page provides a good example of how you should use the `NAME="text"` attribute in an anchor tag. The HTML line in the home page document

```
<A HREF="search4d.htm#menu"><IMG SRC="graphics/menu.gif" ALT="MENU "
      BORDER=0></A>
```

specifies a hypertext relationship between the `menu.gif` graphic (the yellow button with the blue square inside) in the current document and the named anchor `menu` in the target document that is in the `search4d.htm` file. The pound sign (#) indicates that the browser should position the reader not at the top of the page, but at the named anchor in the target document, menu in this case. If the anchor isn't found, you'd get the default instead, which is the top of the document.

The browser displays the information at that location in the file, starting with the heading, "Menu and Order of Pages." This may seem unduly abstract, but you'll catch on if you remember this: The anchor with the NAME="text" attribute is the destination for some link. As the author, you have control over how your information is displayed. If you think users will find a nugget of information within a specific page relevant and important, then give it a name with the NAME attribute and create a link to it.

Linking to text within a page: table of contents links

You can use the NAME="text" attribute to create a really jumping table of contents (TOC) for long text documents. Providing a linked TOC takes a little more time, but it's a great way to impress your users. Remember to provide a link back to the TOC after each block of text in the destination document.

The following HTML code illustrates how to use the TOC links within a large document:

```
<!- Make this an anchor for return jumps.->
<A NAME="TOC">Table of Contents</A>
<P>
<!- This is the link to the section 1. below.->
<A HREF="#SEC1">Section 1.</A><BR>
<A HREF="#SEC2">Section 2.</A><BR>
<A HREF="#SEC3">Section 3.</A><BR>

<!- This is a named anchor called "SEC1".->
<A NAME="SEC1"><H2> CFR Section 1.</H2></A>
<P> Text of section 1 is here.
<BR>
<!- This is a link back to the TOC at the top of the page->
<A HREF="#TOC">(TOC)</A>
<P>
<A NAME="SEC2"><H2> CFR Section 2.</H2></A>
<P> Text of section 2 is here.
<BR>
<A HREF="#TOC">(TOC)</A>
<P>
<A NAME="SEC3"><H2> CFR Section 3.</H2></A>
<P> Text of section 3 is here.
<BR>
<A HREF="#TOC">(TOC)</A>
<P>
```

Seeing the (TOC) after each text section may seem strange at first, but your users quickly become accustomed to this method of intradocument linking. We'd recommend using this approach for longer, more complex documents or for a collection of related documents, but not for shorter pieces. An omnipresent TOC in a short document might seem obtrusive to your readers. (See Figure 9-5.)

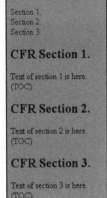

Figure 9-5:
Table of
Contents
and text
links.

You can use this same general method for links to anything within a single HTML document. It may look strange in the HTML document, but this is the way you create hypertext links within a text paragraph. Only use the "text" in each NAME="text" once per document, though, to keep the browser from becoming terminally confused. Otherwise, you never know where your users might wind up!

Named anchors should be named with text starting with a character from the set {a–z, A–Z}. They should never be exclusively numeric, like <A NAME="12">blah</A>. Anchors should also be uniquely named within the same document. These names are case sensitive, so that NAME="foo" and NAME="FOO" are different. So are these: NAME="Three Stooges" is not the same as NAME="ThreeStooges" is not the same as NAME="THREESTOOGES". You get the idea. . . .

Jumping to Remote Pages

Hypermedia links from text in your pages directly to other Web sites amazes and amuses your users. Although you can't create NAME="text" anchors in text at remote sites, you may be able to use anchors already in place there. If you find a linked TOC at another site, you can reference the same links that it uses.

Remember, if you can link to it by using your browser, you can copy the link into the text of your Web pages. Just make sure that you include the full URL in the `HREF="URL"`.

Hypertext links to outside resources

Links to Web sites outside of your own Web require fully qualified URLs, such as

```
URL: <A HREF = "http://www.outer.net/html4dum/html4dum.htm">
http://www.outer.net/html4dum/html4dum.htm</A><BR>
Text - Copyright &copy; 1995, 1996 Ed Tittel &amp; Steve James.<BR>
Dummies Design and Art - Copyright &copy; 1995, 1996 IDG Books
          Worldwide, Inc.<BR>
Web Layout - Copyright &copy; 1995, 1996
<A HREF="http://www.io.com/~mcintyre/lanwrght/
          lanwrght.htm">LANWrights</A> &amp;
<A HREF="http://impactonline.com"> IMPACT Online.</A><BR>
Revised — January 15th, 1996 [JMS - IMPACT Online]<BR>
```

The three links (`HREF`) connect the *HTML For Dummies* home page to itself, to the LANWrights Web site, and to the IMPACT Online Web site. Why include the page's own URL as a link? It not only shows the user the URL, but it also allows direct linking if the user has saved the HTML source for this page to his or her own computer.

All these tags and links make for difficult reading unless you view them through a browser, as shown in Figure 9-6. Through the browser, hypertext words are shown in a different color, underlined, or both, depending on your browser's preference settings.

Figure 9-6:
External
links.

> *E-Mail: HTML for Dummies at html4dum@outer.net*
> URL: http://www.outer.net/html4dum/html4dum.htm
> Text - Copyright © 1995, 1996 Ed Tittel & Steve James.
> Dummies Design and Art - Copyright © 1995, 1996 IDG Books Worldwide, Inc.
> Web Layout - Copyright © 1995, 1996 LANWrights & IMPACT Online.
> Revised -- January 15th, 1996 [JMS - IMPACT Online]

Jump pages

The term *jump page* refers to a Web page that contains a list of URLs to other Web pages, usually remote sites. You'll find that HTML list tags are invaluable tools that enable you to create visually pleasing and easily understood lists of links. Jump pages differ from basic Web pages only because the viewer primarily sees highlighted hyperlinks. This is appropriate for quick scanning, but not for general reading.

You can use icon images and spacer lines to visually separate sections of your list. You should carefully choose those words you use for each hyperlink; keep the main point of the information to which the link refers in mind. Figure 9-7 illustrates a portion of a jump page.

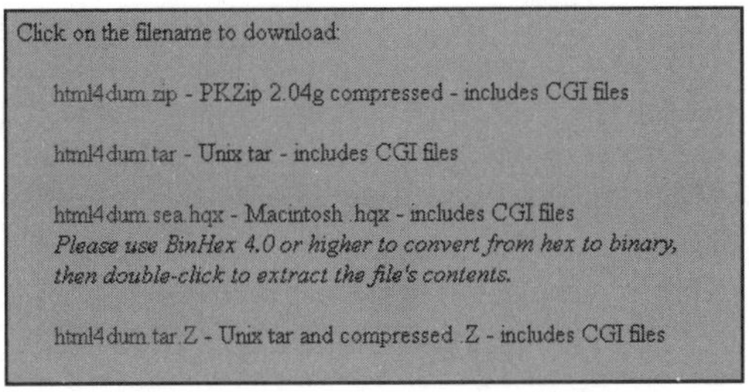

Figure 9-7:
A portion of the *HTML For Dummies* jump page.

Click on the filename to download:

html4dum.zip - PKZip 2.04g compressed - includes CGI files

html4dum.tar - Unix tar - includes CGI files

html4dum.sea.hqx - Macintosh .hqx - includes CGI files
Please use BinHex 4.0 or higher to convert from hex to binary, then double-click to extract the file's contents.

html4dum.tar.Z - Unix tar and compressed .Z - includes CGI files

When typing URLs for links, we strongly recommend that you first link to the destination and capture those URLs by using your browser. Then paste these URLs directly into your HTML file to cut down on typos and syntax errors.

A special <LINK>

The <LINK> tag provides information that links the current Web page to other Web pages or to other URL resources. When you want to be sure that your Web pages tell browsers and other WWW software about themselves, put a <LINK> in the <HEAD>...</HEAD> section. Chapter 5 shows several attributes that you may use in the <LINK> tag. If you start using one of the advanced HTML-generating programs, it may insert several <LINK> tags of various types within the head section of each page. The programs use these links to keep track of the pages themselves.

Perhaps NAME="text" is the most commonly used tag. It is used to provide an anchor from other locations. This named anchor is used for reference access from other locations or documents. Your HTML code should look like this:

```
<HTML>
<HEAD>
<TITLE> The Title of Your Page </TITLE>
<LINK NAME="My Home Page">
</HEAD>
<BODY>
<H1> The Heading of Your Page That Users See </H1>
and so on...
</BODY></HTML>
```

The Nesting Instinct: Lists Within Lists

When you create longer Web pages, you want to keep visual diversity high by using text formatting. However, because you are working with text, you have only headings, emphasized text (bold, strong, font size), and indented lists as tools. Lists within lists create the old, familiar outline form when displayed by most browsers.

The browser display in Figure 9-8 was created by the following HTML code. As you look through this HTML markup, remember that you're seeing only a fragment, not the whole thing:

U.S. Federal Government

- Agency for Toxic Substances and Disease Registry
- Blue Goose The National Wildlife Refuge System
- Bureau of Indian Affairs Main Server and also BIA Division of Energy and Mineral Resources
- Bureau of Land Management
- Bureau of Mines
- Bureau of Reclamation
- Department of Defense
    - □ DoD Environmental Restoration Bulletin Board
- Department of Energy
    - □ Design for Environment Project (DfE)
    - □ Department of Energy Information Page
    - □ EREN, Energy Efficiency and Renewable Energy Network
    - □ EREC, Energy Efficiency & Renewable Energy Clearinghouse
    - □ Home Page
    - □ Lessons Learned Program
- Department of the Interior
    - □ National Biological Service-Southeastern Biological Science Center

Figure 9-8:
Nested list
example.

```
<p><h2>U.S. Federal Government</h2>
<ul>
<li><a href="http://atsdr1.atsdr.cdc.gov:8080/atsdrhome.html">Agency
            for
Toxic Substances and Disease Registry</a>
<li><A HREF="http://bluegoose.arw.r9.fws.gov/">Blue Goose</A> The
            National Wildlife Refuge System
<li><A HREF="http://info.er.usgs.gov/doi/bureau-indian-
            affairs.html">Bureau
of Indian Affairs</a> Main Server and also BIA <A
HREF="http://snake2.cr.usgs.gov/">Division of Energy and Mineral
Resources</a>
<li><A
HREF="http://info.er.usgs.gov/doi/bureau-land-management.html">Bureau
            of
Land Management</a>
<li><A HREF="http://www.usbm.gov/">Bureau of Mines</a>
<li><A HREF="http://info.er.usgs.gov/doi/bureau-of-
            reclamation.html">Bureau
of Reclamation</a>
```

```
<li>Department of Defense
<ul>
<li><a href="http://www.dtic.dla.mil/envirodod/envirodod.html">DoD
 Environmental Restoration Bulletin Board</a>
</ul>
<li>Department of Energy
<ul>
<li><a href=http://w3.pnl.gov:2080/DFE/home.html>Design for Environ-
             ment
Project</a> (DfE)
<li><A HREF="http://web.fie.com/web/fed/doe/">Department of Energy</
             A>
Information Page
<li><a href="http://www.eren.doe.gov/ee/ee.html">EREN</a>, Energy
Efficiency and Renewable Energy Network
<li><a href="http://www.nciinc.com/~erec">EREC</a>, Energy Efficiency
             &
Renewable Energy Clearinghouse
<li><a href="http://www.doe.gov">Home Page</a>
<li><a href=http://venus.hyperk.com/trl/ll/ll.html>Lessons Learned
Program</a>
</ul>
<li>Department of the Interior
<ul>
<li><a href="http://www.nfrcg.gov/">National Biological Service-
             Southeastern
Biological Science Center</a>
</ul>
</ul>
```

Carefully track the list start (`<UL>`) and end (`</UL>`) tags. Directly under the U.S. Federal Government heading you see a start tag, and at the bottom of the listing you see its end tag. This placement of the tags indents and bullets all items that fall between them and are marked with the `<LI>` tags. This is a normal unordered list. What about all items that are indented a second time and preceded by a box rather than a bullet, you ask?

Each of these sections is contained within another pair of list tags. For example, immediately under the Department of Defense heading is the second level list start tag, and its end tag is immediately before the Department of Energy heading. The text between them, "DoD Environmental Restoration Bulletin Board," is marked with the `<LI>` tag, which causes the browser to indent it farther and place the box in front of it (in Netscape).

Some browsers keep track of the number of nests you use and change the bullets of each successive nesting to blocks or other symbols. It may be easier to visualize nested lists without the `<LI>` lines:

```
<UL> Start level 1.
     <UL> Start level 2.
        <UL> Start level 3.
        </UL> End level 3.
     </UL> End level 2.
</UL> End level 1.
```

Nested lists are a good way to instruct a browser to indent certain lines of text without using the `<PRE>` . . . `</PRE>` or `<BLOCKQUOTE>` . . . `</BLOCKQUOTE>` tags. Along with the indentations, your readers will have to cope with either bullets or numbers, but that's fine for lists, as shown in the earlier example.

Browser developers are already working on giving browsers the ability to respond to HTML tag attributes for various types of symbols instead of bullets and blocks in lists. Who knows what they'll think of next?

Sampling Sophisticated Pages

Now it's time for a quick look at a couple of complex Web pages. We also encourage you to surf the Web for pages that strike your fancy. When you find one, view its source to see how the author worked the underlying magic. The Web is one of the few places where you can easily look behind the curtain to see how the illusion is created, so be sure to take full advantage of this opportunity.

The two following Web pages illustrate what you can accomplish if you use these tools and your imagination. You'll see a Web page screen (or two) viewed through Netscape, followed by the HTML markup for those screens. After each figure and HTML example, you'll see our comments on the techniques and coding used.

HTML For Dummies home page

Our own *HTML For Dummies* home page shows what you can do with HTML 2.0. It's eye-catching but not overdone (see Figure 9-9). The information is arranged nicely and gives the user multiple avenues of access. The image map and commands at the top and the buttons near the bottom make it easy to navigate quickly through the site. Users who want to "turn the pages" can use the arrow buttons to move linearly through the site. The "menu" page acts as a table of contents from which users can jump anywhere in the site. The "search" function lets users find anything contained in the site and jump directly there.

The entire home page is less than two screens long. It makes liberal use of color and blank space to keep the text readable. The image map graphic loads quickly because it's been designed with only a few colors and simple graphics components. The image map's functionality is repeated in the text immediately beneath it for users who don't have GUI browsers. The line "Click here for a non-imagemap version" displays an alternate home page (see Figure 9-10) for browsers that can't display image maps.

The footer contains all the requisite information including the page's own URL, which users will find handy should they capture the HTML source and later need to return to the online version. It's just a click away with the URL included as a hyperlink.

Welcome to:
HTML FOR DUMMIES
NEW!
NEW
FILES CONTENTS SEARCH CONTACT NEW
FILES | CONTENTS | SEARCH | CONTACT | NEW
HOW TO NAVIGATE
Click here for a non-imagemap version

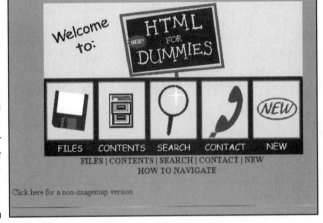

Figure 9-9: *HTML For Dummies* home page using a CGI image map.

You have reached the *HTML for Dummies* Web Pages, a charming, and hopefully helpful, addition to the WWW universe. These pages are designed to aid you in three key areas:
• To help you find current information on the Web about HTML
• To provide working examples and code for all the Web tricks in the book
• To introduce *HTML for Dummies* - your friendliest resource for HTML material offline!
To get on with your exploration of these pages, you can use the MENU or NEXT buttons. MENU will send you to the master ordered list of available pages. NEXT will take you page by page through all the information here.
Please spend some time exploring, and be sure to e-mail us your comments, if you feel so inclined. Enjoy!
Be sure to visit the new IDG Books Web site! NEW
E-Mail: HTML for Dummies at html4dum@outer.net
URL: http://www.outer.net/html4dum/html4dum.htm
Text - Copyright © 1995, 1996 Ed Tittel & Steve James.
Dummies Design and Art - Copyright © 1995, 1996 IDG Books Worldwide, Inc.
Web Layout - Copyright © 1995, 1996 LANWrights & IMPACT Online.
Revised -- January 15th, 1996 [JMS - IMPACT Online]

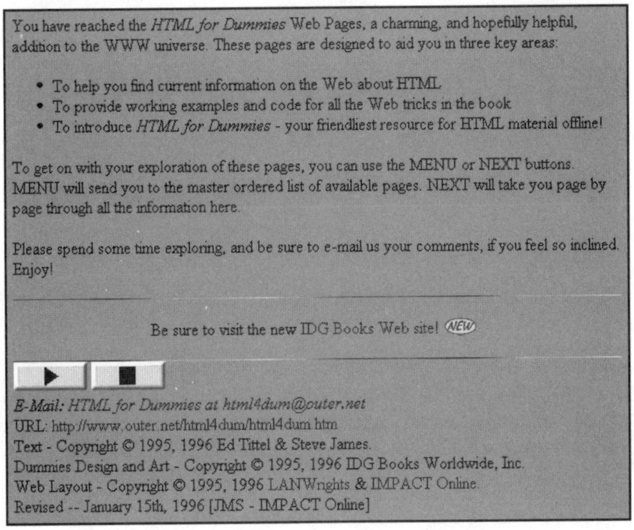

Figure 9-10: *HTML For Dummies* home page without the image map.

The HTML code for the *HTML For Dummies* home pages is HTML 2.0-compliant. It shows some interesting tricks that you may find useful. The use of the ALT line after the "line.gif" shows a divider even when the browser doesn't load images automatically. Using "WIDTH=100%" in the "line.gif" tag displays the rainbow separator line across the whole width of the browser's page, regardless of the monitor type or window size. To get the equivalent of a "tab" in HTML, the "space.gif" file is used in several places. This is merely an image with either the same color as the background or a transparent background GIF file. When used with the appropriate width and height parameters, it holds the space to the left of either text or an image, simulating the Tab key. It provides indentations without bullets like those produced by list tags.

```
<HTML>
<HEAD>
<TITLE> HTML For DUMMIES HomePage - IDG Books</TITLE>
<!-Turn a BASE HREF on if you have any problems with the way this
 page behaves (e.g. unresolved graphics). Also be sure to provide
 an absolute URL that points to the home page on your Web server,
 e.g. BASE HREF="http://www.outer.net/html4dum/html4dum.htm"
This is the proper BASE reference for our own HTML For Dummies
 server. ->
<BODY>
<A NAME="top"></A>
<IMG ALIGN=MIDDLE WIDTH=60 HEIGHT=0 SRC=graphics/space.gif
 ALT=" ">
<A HREF="http://www.io.com/~mcintyre/cgi-bin/ht4menum.map">
<IMG BORDER=0 ALIGN=TOP SRC="graphics/ht4menum.gif"
 ALT="Navigation Bar" ISMAP></A><P>
<IMG ALIGN=MIDDLE WIDTH=130 HEIGHT=0 SRC=graphics/space.gif
 ALT=" ">
<B><A HREF="ftpstuff.htm">FILES</A> &#32;&#124;
<A HREF="contents.htm">CONTENTS</A> &#32;&#124;
<A HREF="search4d.htm">SEARCH</A> &#32;&#124;
<A HREF="contact.htm">CONTACT</A> &#32;&#124;
<A HREF="whatsnew.htm">NEW</A><BR>
<IMG ALIGN=MIDDLE WIDTH=240 HEIGHT=0 SRC=graphics/space.gif
 ALT=" ">
<A HREF="navigate.htm">HOW TO NAVIGATE</A></B><P>
<A HREF="html4du2.htm">Click here for a non-imagemap version
</A><P>
<IMG WIDTH=100% SRC="graphics/line.gif"
 ALT="-==-==-==-==-==-==-==-==-==-==-==-==-=="><P>
You have reached the <I> HTML For Dummies</I> Web Pages, a
 charming, and hopefully helpful, addition to the WWW universe.
 These pages are designed to aid you in three key areas:
<UL>
```

```
<LI> To help you find current information on the Web about HTML
<LI> To provide working examples and code for all the Web tricks
 in the book
<LI> To introduce <I> HTML For Dummies</I> - your friendliest
 resource for HTML material offline!
</UL>
<P>
To get on with your exploration of these pages, you can use the
 MENU or NEXT buttons. MENU will send you to the master ordered
 list of available pages. NEXT will take you page by page through
 all the information here.<P>
Please spend some time exploring, and be sure to e-mail us your
 comments, if you feel so inclined. Enjoy!<P>
<IMG WIDTH=100% SRC="graphics/line.gif"
 ALT="-==-==-==-==-==-==-==-==-==-==-==-==-==-==-">< BR>
<P>
<IMG HEIGHT=1 WIDTH=130 SRC="graphics/space.gif" ALT=" _ ">
Be sure to visit the new <A HREF="http://www.idgbooks.com">IDG
 Books Web site</A>!
<IMG ALIGN=TOP SRC="graphics/new.gif"><P>
<P>
<IMG WIDTH=100% SRC="graphics/line.gif"
 ALT="==-==-==-==-==-==-==-==-==-==-==-==-==-==-=="><BR>
<A HREF="contents.htm"><IMG SRC="graphics/next.gif" ALT="NEXT "
 BORDER=0></A>
<A HREF="search4d.htm#menu"><IMG SRC="graphics/menu.gif"
 ALT="MENU " BORDER=0></A><BR>
<ADDRESS>
E-Mail: <A HREF="mailto:html4dum@outer.net">
HTML For Dummies at html4dum@outer.net</A><BR>
</ADDRESS>
URL: <A HREF = "http://www.outer.net/html4dum/html4dum.htm">
http://www.outer.net/html4dum/html4dum.htm</A><BR>
Text - Copyright &copy; 1995, 1996 Ed Tittel &amp; Steve James.
 <BR>
Dummies Design and Art - Copyright &copy; 1995, 1996 IDG Books
 Worldwide, Inc.<BR>
Web Layout - Copyright &copy; 1995, 1996
<A HREF="http://www.io.com/~mcintyre/lanwrght/lanwrght.htm">
LANWrights</A> &amp;
<A HREF="http://impactonline.com"> IMPACT Online.</A><BR>
Revised — January 15th, 1996 [JMS - IMPACT Online]<BR>
</BODY>
</HTML>
```

As you can see in Figure 9-11, you don't have to use an image map to provide your users with nicely arranged, clickable images. This page differs only slightly in appearance from the primary home page and provides the same functionality.

Figure 9-11:
Another view of the *HTML For Dummies.*

The following HTML code shows the lines necessary to display the "Welcome to HTML For Dummies" graphic and the Files, Contents, Search, Contact, and New graphics below it as clickable links to files. If you don't want to deal with image maps and don't mind the separation between the images, this kind of presentation is easy to achieve.

```
<IMG ALIGN=MIDDLE WIDTH=60 HEIGHT=0
 SRC=graphics/space.gif ALT=" ">
<A HREF="contents.htm"><IMG SRC=graphics/ht4logoi.gif
 BORDER=0 ALT="HTML For Dummies Logo"></A><BR>
<IMG ALIGN=MIDDLE WIDTH=60 HEIGHT=0
 SRC=graphics/space.gif ALT=" ">
<A HREF="ftpstuff.htm"><IMG SRC="graphics/ht4filei.gif"
 BORDER=0  ALT="FILES"></A>
<A HREF="contents.htm"><IMG SRC="graphics/ht4conti.gif"
 BORDER=0 ALT="CONTENTS"></A>
<A HREF="search4d.htm"><IMG SRC="graphics/ht4seari.gif"
 BORDER=0 ALT="SEARCH"></A>
<A HREF="contact.htm"><IMG SRC="graphics/ht4tacti.gif"
 BORDER=0 ALT="CONTACT"></A>
          <A HREF="wahtsnew.htm"><IMG SRC="graphics/ht4newi.gif"
<B><A HREF="ftpstuff.htm">FILES</A> &#32;&#124;

<IMG ALIGN=MIDDLE WIDTH=130 HEIGHT=0
 SRC=graphics/space.gif ALT=" ">
```

```
<A HREF="contents.htm">CONTENTS</A> &#32;&#124;
<A HREF="search4d.htm">SEARCH</A> &#32;&#124;
<A HREF="contact.htm">CONTACT</A> &#32;&#124;
<A HREF="whatsnew.htm">NEW</A><BR>
<IMG ALIGN=MIDDLE WIDTH=240 HEIGHT=0 SRC=graphics/space.gif ALT=" ">
<A HREF="navigate.htm">HOW TO NAVIGATE</A></B><P>
<IMG WIDTH=100% SRC="graphics/line.gif"
   ALT="-==-==-==-==-==-"><P>
```

Shockwave Productions HTML page

The *Shockwave Productions* HTML page featured in Figure 9-12 shows the magic that can be performed on the Web by using currently available, leading-edge tools. This page illustrates the use of HTML 3.0, Netscape extensions, Java applets, and more. It should give you an idea of the nearly limitless possibilities for your own Web site.

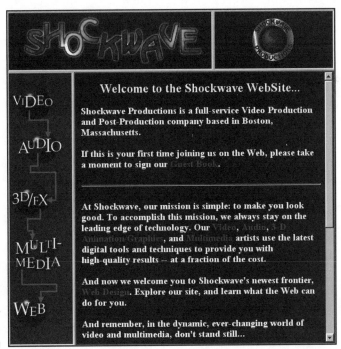

Figure 9-12:
Shockwave Productions HTML page.

The view shown below was captured using Netscape 2.0b4 for Windows 95 (the 32-bit version), which allows the Java applet that controls the Shockwave logo in the upper-right frame to flip like a tossed coin. As you'll see, the page also makes use of Netscape's frames, with four of them on the same page. You can go to different sections of the Web site by clicking on the word in the left frame (Video, Audio, 3D/FX, Multimedia, or Web). Doing so displays the section's pages in the main frame (bottom right). Both of the bottom frames contain scroll bars that move only the information within the frame. This allows the SHOCKWAVE name in the upper-left frame and the flipping logo in the upper-right frame to remain visible while you browse the site.

The following HTML code shown for this page isn't as complex as you may think. However, the work that went into creating the images was considerable. Although it looks like one large graphic, the lower left frame is composed of separate GIF files for each "button," created to join seamlessly with one another.

The call to the Java applet is simple in the following code, but the applet itself is much more complicated. We hope that you have a 32-bit Java-enabled browser to view the flipping Shockwave logo. Although it isn't shown in Figure 9-12, the page also includes an e-mail address and `mailto:` line at the bottom.

This page shows how frames, tables, borders, and background colors can enhance your Web page, if you know how to artistically intertwine them. However, as the warning goes, "Don't try this at home without proper training and practice." If you're dying to try this stuff out, be prepared to spend some serious time researching and learning these topics and technologies!

```
<HTML>
<HEAD>
<TITLE>Shockwave Productions</TITLE>
<FRAMESET ROWS="115,*">
<FRAMESET COLS="400,*" SCROLLING="no">
<FRAME SRC="htitle.html" NAME="title" SCROLLING="no" MARGINHEIGHT="0"
            NORESIZE>
<FRAME SRC="javaplanet.html" NAME="java" SCROLLING="no"
            MARGINHEIGHT="0" NORESIZE>
</FRAMESET>
<FRAMESET COLS="130,*">
<FRAME SRC="hoptions.html" NAME="options" MARGINWIDTH="1"
 NORESIZE>
<FRAME SRC="hmain.html" NAME="main">
</FRAMESET>
</FRAMESET>
<NOFRAMES>
</HEAD>
<BODY BACKGROUND="images/background.gif" TEXT="#FFFFFF"
 LINK="#9F0F9F"
ALINK="#FF0000" VLINK="#FF0000">
<IMG SRC="images/SWtitle.gif" BORDER=0 ALT="[SHOCKWAVE]">
<TABLE BORDER=0 CELLPADDING=0 CELLSPACING=0>
<TR>
```

```
<TD ALIGN=LEFT VALIGN=TOP WIDTH=128>
<IMG SRC="images/buffer.gif" border=0 width=128 height = 1>
<A HREF = "N1/video/videowelN1.html"><IMG border=0 width=100
height=100 SRC="images/videobutt.gif" ALT="[VIDEO]"></A>
<A HREF = "N1/audio/audiowelN1.html"><IMG border=0 width=100
height=100 SRC="images/audiobutt.gif" ALT="[AUDIO]"></A>
<A HREF = "N1/grx/grxwelN1.html"><IMG border=0 width=100
height=100 SRC="images/3dfxbutt.gif" ALT="[3DFX]"></A>
<A HREF = "N1/media/mediawelN1.html"><IMG border=0 width=100
height=100 SRC="images/mmbutt.gif" ALT="[MULTI-MEDIA]"></A>
<A HREF = "N1/web/webwelN1.html"><IMG border=0 width=100
height=100 SRC="images/webbutt.gif" ALT="[WEB]"></A>
<IMG SRC="images/buffer.gif" BORDER=0 WIDTH=128 HEIGHT=1>
</TD ALIGN=CENTER>
<TD VALIGN=TOP>
<HR>
<P>
<CENTER>
<H2>Welcome to the Shockwave WebSite...</H2>
<H4><P></CENTER><FONT SIZE=4>
Shockwave Productions is a full-service Video Production and Post-
Production company based in Boston, Massachusetts.<P>If this is
 your first time joining us on the Web, please take a moment to
 sign our <A HREF="guest/guestN1.html">Guest Book</A>.<P><HR><P>
At Shockwave, our mission is simple: to make you look good.
To accomplish this mission, we always stay on the leading edge of
technology.  Our <A HREF="N1/video/videowelN1.html">Video</A>, <A
HREF="N1/audio/audiowelN1.html">Audio</A>,
 <A HREF="N1/grx/grxwelN1.html">3-D Animation/Graphics</A>, and
 <A HREF="N1/media/mediawelN1.html">Multimedia</A> artists use the
 latest digital tools and techniques to provide you with high-
quality results — at a fraction of the cost.<P>
And now we welcome you to Shockwave's newest frontier, <A HREF="N1/
          web/webwelN1.html">Web Design</A>.  Explore our site,
 and learn what the Web can do for you.<P>
And remember, in the dynamic, ever-changing world of video and
 multimedia, don't stand still...<BR><P>
<CENTER><IMG SRC="images/catch.gif"
 ALT="[Catch the Wave!]"><P></CENTER>
<HR><P>
Coming soon!  Visit our <A HREF="../vrml/vrmlwel.shtml">VRML</A>
 site!<P>
Check here for more innovations as our new web site becomes fully
 active in the next few weeks.  Special thanks to all who gave us
 suggestions, and the many, many people who visited our old site.
```

```
<P>
Enjoy your visit with Shockwave!<P><HR><P>
<CENTER><A HREF="mailto:info@swave.com">
<IMG SRC="images/address.gif" BORDER=0 ALT="[info@swave.com]">
</A></CENTER>
</TD>
</H4>
</TR>
</TABLE>
</CENTER>
</BODY>
</NOFRAMES>
</HTML>
```

Really Cool: Java, VRML, Shockwave

Okay! Okay! Stop throwing things. You're not alone. Everyone wants their Web pages to be as magical as the Shockwave Productions page. Take your time, learn the basics of HTML, and then progress to using the really cool tools, and your pages can look great, too!

So what are these really cool tools? Because you twisted our arms (ouch!), we'll give you a hint here, even though it's beyond the scope of this book. Keep in mind that, although these tools are available now, you'll be on the cutting edge of technology if you start using them. That's a position similar to Wile E. Coyote after he runs off the mesa top after the Roadrunner. He's hanging in midair but not falling (yet). So if you run right out and try to grab these futuristic tools . . . don't look down.

Java

According to Sun Microsystems, Java is "a simple, object-oriented, distributed, interpreted, robust, secure, architecture-neutral, portable, high-performance, multithreaded, and dynamic language." Yeah, right??

Well, it's a programming language that's somewhat based on C++ but is supposed to be much easier to use. It's used to produce small programs, called *applets,* that are distributed on the Web along with HTML documents. Your browser quickly downloads applets to your computer, where they run to produce sound, video, special effects, or just about anything that your computer and browser are capable of doing. In the near future, many Java applets will be available for you to use in your Web pages in a manner similar to the way you use GIFs and JPEGs now, except applets actually do things. Check out Java's Web site for more information. (WARNING: Java's not expected to be commercially released until mid-1996!)

```
http://www.javasoft.com/
```

VRML

The Virtual Reality Modeling Language (VRML) is a language for describing multiparticipant interactive simulations — virtual worlds networked via the global Internet and hyperlinked with the World Wide Web. What it will be in the future depends on the limits of your imagination. In real-world terms, it provides a way to add 3-D data to the Web. VRML browsers are already available, and a few Web sites contain VRML files. How fast it grows will depend primarily on the cost of the hardware that replaces your 2-D monitor with 3-D goggles. They're available now, but they are costly and aren't quite ready for prime-time use. Everything that you ever wanted to know about VRML and more can be found at

```
http://www.vrml.org/
```

Shockwave

Shockwave for Director is the name of the Macromedia product and technology that was designed to deliver Macromedia Director files over the Internet. Shockwave for Director includes the following elements:

- The Shockwave plug-in for Web browsers, like Netscape Navigator 2.0, allows movies to be played seamlessly within the same window as the browser page.

- Afterburner is a post-processor program for Director movie source files. Multimedia developers use it to prepare content for Internet distribution. Afterburner compresses movies and makes them ready to upload to an HTTP server, where they can be accessed by Internet users with Shockwave-enabled Web browsers.

These are both rather complicated programming systems, primarily useful to professionals in the multimedia field. Undoubtedly, Shockwave files will be showing up on the commercial Web sites in the near future. They may even be available at sites, much as GIF and JPEG files are currently available. Only time and the market will tell. Check out Shockwave for Director at

```
http://www.macromedia.com/Tools/Shockwave/index.html
```

Congratulations! You've now gone far enough (or too far?) into HTML to know where home is and how to get back there from the North Forty. Now that you really know your way around a Web site, you're ready to link to the realm of HTML forms. This is where you invite your users talk back to you and give them an easy way to do so.

Chapter 10

Strictly Pro Forma: Using Forms for Feedback

● ●

In This Chapter

▶ Learning what forms are for

▶ Dealing with browser and server limitations

▶ Learning about form tags

▶ Using form tags

▶ Forming good attitudes

▶ Formulating good layouts

● ●

*W*hen all the pieces come together properly, it's easy to see how the Web brings people or organizations together. At first glance, the Web might look pretty much like a one-way street — that is, an environment where WebMasters communicate aplenty with Web users, with not much interaction between the two. But it doesn't have to be that way.

What HTML Forms Are For

The essence of serving up useful information is relevancy and immediacy. But the best judge of the quality of your information is your audience. Wouldn't it be wonderful if your readers could give you feedback on your Web pages? Then they could tell you what parts they like, what they don't like, and what other things they'd like to see included in your site.

This is where HTML forms come into the picture. Up to this point in the book, we've talked about all of the basics — and even a few advanced techniques — for communicating with your audience. In this chapter, you'll learn how to turn the tables and create HTML text that lets your audience communicate with you!

As it turns out, HTML supports a rich variety of input capabilities to let you solicit feedback. In the pages that follow, you find out about the tags to use, the controls and inputs they enable, and some layout considerations for building forms. You also see some interesting example forms that can help you understand what HTML forms look like and how they behave.

Living within Your Forms Limitations

By the time you read this, forms support in HTML, which you recall from Chapter 4 is a hallmark of HTML 2.0, is final and more or less finished in its current form. This means that the underlying HTML markup for forms will only change if the underlying standard changes. But because forms have been supported for only about a year, they still qualify as *new-and-untried* instead of *old-and-familiar* for many Web users. Nevertheless, we think that working with forms is becoming totally commonplace, so you should become familiar with them and their capabilities to see if you can use them within your Web pages.

Beware of browser!

Although most of the "hot" browsers — Mosaic and its variants, Netscape, Internet Explorer, and the like — already include forms support, other browsers may not. In fact, you won't know how well your favorite browser handles forms until you start testing your forms tags against it. If you follow our suggestions and test your pages against multiple browsers, you can immediately observe different levels of robustness and capability when it comes to forms implementations.

The bottom line is that not all browsers support forms equally, but that support is pretty commonplace. By the time you read this, support should no longer be a problem — at least for users with current browser versions. But for older browsers, don't be surprised if forms don't work that well, or if they don't work at all.

Assuming that the information your form solicits is important to you, consider adding an FTP URL to your page to let users download a file containing a text-only version of the form's content. Then they can download the file and complete it by using any text editor. If you include an e-mail address inside the file, they can send it back to you, and you'll get feedback (even from users who can't view your forms). That way nobody gets left out!

Sorry, servers...

Because the Web is a client/server environment, you should also be aware that just because your browser supports forms doesn't automatically imply that the server installed at your site can handle them. Unfortunately, keeping up with HTML advancements means that Web servers have to change right along with the clients. In other words, your server may not support the input-handling programs necessary to process a form's input when it gets delivered.

However, there is a silver lining in this potentially dark cloud: The most common implementations of the *httpd* server come from NCSA and CERN and run in the UNIX environment. Both of these groups have standardized their forms-handling technology and offer useful, robust forms-handling capability.

These implementations are so common, in fact, that we assume that your Web server works the way that they do. This means that you may have to alter some of the approaches to CGI scripting and other programming that you might use to handle forms on your server. If you're not using UNIX and the NCSA or CERN implementations of *httpd,* you should investigate the particulars that your server's implementation requires and alter our instructions accordingly.

What's in a Form?

When adding forms support to a Web page, you include special tags that let you solicit input from users. You surround these tags with text that prompts user responses. You also include tags that gather the input and ship it to your Web server or to other servers that may offer services — like Gopher or Archie — that your form knows how to query. Here's how the process works:

- ✔ On a particular Web page, you include tags to set up a form and to solicit input from users. Some of your users will work their way through this material and provide the information that you want. This essentially amounts to filling out the form that you've supplied.

- ✔ After a form has been filled out, users can then direct their input to a program running on the Web server that delivered the form. In most cases, they need to select a particular control, called SUBMIT, that gathers the information and sends it to the proper destination on your Web server.

- ✔ Assuming that the program is available for use (installed and running properly, that is), it accepts the input information. Then the program decodes and interprets the contents for further action.

✔ After the input is received and interpreted, the program can do pretty much anything it wants. In practice, this boils down to recognizing key elements in a form's content and custom-building an HTML document in response. Building a document isn't required, but it is a pretty common-place capability within forms-handling programs.

✔ The custom-built document is then delivered to the user in response to the form's content. At this point, additional interaction can occur (if the "return page" includes another form), requested information can be delivered (in response to requests on the form), and so on.

The information collected from a form can be 1) written to a file, 2) submitted to a database such as Informix or Oracle, or 3) e-mailed to someone in particular. Forms also allow a user to participate in building a Web document such as on one Web site that allows users to dictate how a story is played out; in this case, the users collectively determine the outcome.

Thus, forms not only provide communication from users to servers, but also provide for ongoing interaction between users and servers. This is pretty powerful stuff and adds a lot of value to your Web pages.

Forms involve two-way communication

The input-catching programs on your server rely on an interface between Web browsers and servers called the *Common Gateway Interface* (CGI). This interface codifies how browsers can send information back to servers. It sets up the formatting for the user-supplied input information, so that forms-handling programs know what to expect and how to deal with what they receive.

The ACTION attribute in the <FORM> tag specifies a URL that indicates a specific CGI script or program that collects and munges the form data that users enter. Likewise, the METHOD tag describes the way in which input data is delivered to a forms-handling program.

In this chapter, we concentrate on the input side of HTML forms — that is, you find out how to build forms. This is a pure exercise in building the front end of a form — that is, the part the users see. You won't learn how to build the back end — that is, how to build CGI or equivalent programs so that your server can deal with forms input — until Chapter 13. Not to worry, however — there's plenty of interesting front-end material to master here!

Tag! You're a form . . .

HTML includes several different classes of forms tags (for the details on syntax and usage, please consult Chapter 5). To begin with, all HTML forms occur within the <FORM> . . . </FORM> tags. The <FORM> tag also includes attributes that specify where and how to deliver input to the appropriate Web server.

Within the <FORM> . . . </FORM> tags, all other forms-related tags and text must appear. These tags include methods for

- ✔ specifying input (the <INPUT> tag and its many attributes).
- ✔ setting up text input areas (the <TEXTAREA> . . . </TEXTAREA> tags).
- ✔ selecting values from a predefined set of possible inputs (the <SELECT> . . . </SELECT> tags).
- ✔ managing the form's content (using the SUBMIT attribute for INPUT to deliver the content to the server, or the RESET attribute to clear its contents, and start over).

Forms input tags support multiple ways to interact with users, including

- ✔ creating text input fields, where users can type in whatever they want.
- ✔ generating pull-down menus, often called "pick lists" because they require making one or more selections from a set of predefined choices.
- ✔ creating labeled check boxes or radio buttons on-screen, which users can select to indicate choices. Check boxes allow multiple selections, and radio buttons allow just one selection.

This may not sound like much, but when you combine it with the ability to prompt users for input with surrounding text, it provides a surprisingly powerful way to ask for information right on a Web page. Thus, the real answer to the question at the head of this section: "What's in a Form?" has to be: "Almost anything you want to put there!"

The remainder of this chapter steps you through all the details of building a form, so you can use the capabilities that we just described.

Using Form Tags

To start out, you should set up your <FORM> environment to build a form within a Web page. It's okay to add a form to an existing HTML file or to build a separate one just to contain your form. We recommend that you add shorter forms (half a screen or less) to existing files but that you create new files for forms that are longer than half a screen.

Setting the <FORM> environment

The two key attributes within the <FORM> tag are METHOD and ACTION. Together, these attributes control how information is sent to the Web server and determine which input-handling program will receive the form's contents.

There's no rhythm to METHOD

The METHOD indicates how the information is sent to the server when the form is submitted. METHOD can take one of two possible values: POST or GET.

Of these two methods, we prefer POST because it causes a form's contents to be parsed one element at a time. GET, on the other hand, it concatenates all the field names and their associated values into one long string. Because UNIX (and most systems) has a limit on how long a single string can be (for UNIX it's 255 characters), it's not hard to imagine that some of the information might get lost when its contents are truncated.

That's why you see us use POST as our only METHOD for submitting forms in this book. That's also why you should do the same, unless you're dead certain that the number of characters in a form will never, ever exceed 255.

Lights, camera ... ACTION

ACTION supplies the URL for the CGI script or other input-handling program on the server that will receive a form's input. The URL can be a full specification or simply a relative reference. Either way, you need to make sure that it points at the right program, in the right location, to do the job that's expected. You also need to make sure that the CGI script or program is executable and that it behaves properly. You'll hear a lot more about this in Chapter 15, which gets into the ins and outs of testing your HTML documents and their related CGI programs.

Let's make an assumption ...

Because you won't have to worry about handling input until Chapter 13, we follow two conventions for all the syntax in this chapter:

- ✓ In every <FORM> tag, METHOD="POST".

- ✓ For every ACTION, URL="/cgi/*form-name*" where we replace the placeholder *form-name* with the actual name of the form under discussion (that is, for the form named get-inf.html, URL="/cgi-bin/get-inf").

These conventions make it easy to create sample HTML files to implement the forms in this chapter (you can also find these examples on the disk that comes with this book).

Knowing what's (in)coming: the <INPUT> tags

The <INPUT> tag defines a basic form element. It takes at least two attributes, namely TYPE and NAME. TYPE indicates what kind of element should be displayed on the form. NAME assigns a name to go with the input field or value that corresponds to the <INPUT> tag.

NAME is used to identify the contents of a field in the form information that ultimately uploads to the input-handling Web server. In fact, what the server receives is a series of name-value pairs. The name that identifies the value is the string supplied in the NAME="string" attribute, and the value is what the user enters or selects for that particular field. Read on — you'll see an example in the next section that should make all this clear!

TYPE-casting still works!

The TYPE attribute can take any of the following values:

- CHECKBOX: Produces an on-screen check box for users to make multiple selections.

- HIDDEN: Produces no visible input area; use this to pass data needed for other uses through the form. For example, this might be an ongoing series of forms based on an earlier interaction during which the user identifies him- or herself — a HIDDEN field contains the name-value pair for that data, but it doesn't show it on the current form. (Some browsers display these fields, but at the *bottom* of a form, and each field has no accompanying label, as with NetManage's WebSurfer browser.)

- IMAGE: Lets you designate a graphic as a selectable item in a form. You can use this to include icons or other graphical symbols.

- RADIO: Creates a radio button for a range of selections, from which the user may select only one.

- RESET: Creates a button labeled "reset" in your form. Include this so that users can clear a form's contents and start over. Be sure to place it well away from other controls — you don't want them to clear the form by accident!

- SUBMIT: Creates a button labeled "submit" (by default, or whatever value you supply for the VALUE attribute for SUBMIT) in your form. The type SUBMIT tells the browser to bundle the form data and pass it all to the CGI script indicated by the ACTION attribute. In plain English (remember that?) SUBMIT is the button used to send in the filled-out form, so a form is useless without an <INPUT> field of type SUBMIT.

✔ TEXT : Provides a one-line area for text entry. Use this for short fields only (as in the example that follows). For longer text fields, use the `<TEXTAREA> . . . </TEXTAREA>` tags instead.

These TYPE attribute values provide a wide range of input displays and data types for form input. As you look at HTML forms on the Web and in this book with a new (and more trained) eye, you can see how effectively these types can be used.

Other <INPUT> attributes

Most of the remaining attributes exist to modify or qualify the `<INPUT>` attribute with TEXT type as the default. Following is a quick review to remind you of what we covered in Chapter 5:

✔ VALUE="value" : Supplies a default value for a TEXT or HIDDEN element or supplies the corresponding value for a radio button or check box selection. This can be used to determine the label of a submit or a reset button, like VALUE="Submit to Admin" for a submit or VALUE="Clear Form" for a reset.

✔ SRC="URL" : Provides a pointer to the graphic for an IMAGE.

✔ CHECKED : Makes sure that a certain radio button or check box is checked when the form is either visited for the first time or when it is reset. You can control default settings with the CHECKED attribute of <INPUT>.

✔ SIZE="number" : Indicates the number of characters that a TEXT element can display without scrolling.

✔ MAXLENGTH="number" : Sets the maximum number of characters that a value in a TEXT element can contain.

✔ ALIGN=(TOP|MIDDLE|BOTTOM) : For IMAGE elements, determines how the graphic is aligned on the form, vis-à-vis the accompanying text.

A TEXT-oriented <INPUT> example

That's it for the `<INPUT>` tag. Following is a look at a relatively simple example of a survey form:

```
<HTML>
<HEAD>
<TITLE>Reader Contact Information</TITLE>
<!— the name of this form is usr-inf.html —>
</HEAD>
<BODY>
<H3>Reader Contact Information</H3>
```

```
<P>Please fill out this form, so we'll know how to get in
touch with you. Thanks!
<FORM METHOD="POST" ACTION="/cgi/usr-inf">
<P>Please enter your name:
<P>First name: <INPUT NAME="first" TYPE="TEXT" SIZE="12"
   MAXLENGTH="20">
MI: <INPUT NAME ="MI" TYPE="TEXT" SIZE="3" MAXLENGTH="3">
Surname: <INPUT NAME="surname" TYPE="TEXT" SIZE="15"
   MAXLENGTH="25">
<P>
<P>Please give us your mailing address:
<P>Address 1: <INPUT NAME="adr1" TYPE="TEXT" SIZE="30"
   MAXLENGTH="45">
<P>Address 2: <INPUT NAME="adr2" TYPE="TEXT" SIZE="30"
   MAXLENGTH="45">
<P>City: <INPUT NAME="city" TYPE="TEXT" SIZE="15"
   MAXLENGTH="30">
<P>State: <INPUT NAME="state" TYPE="TEXT" SIZE="15" MAXLENGTH="15">
   ZIP&#47;Postal Code: <INPUT NAME="zip" TYPE="TEXT" SIZE="10"
   MAXLENGTH="10">
<P>Country: <INPUT NAME="country" TYPE="TEXT" SIZE="15"
   MAXLENGTH="15">
<P>
<P>Thank you! <INPUT TYPE="SUBMIT"> <INPUT TYPE="RESET">
</FORM>
<ADDRESS>
Sample form for <I>HTML For Dummies</I> Version 2.2
1//05/96 http://www.noplace.com/HTML4D/usr-inf.html
</ADDRESS>
</BODY></HTML>
```

Figure 10-1 shows this HTML form on Netscape. Note the positions of the one-line text boxes immediately after the field names, and note the ability to set these boxes on individual lines (as with Address1 and Address2) or together (as with First name, middle initial (MI), and last name (Surname)). These options make it easy to build simple, usable forms.

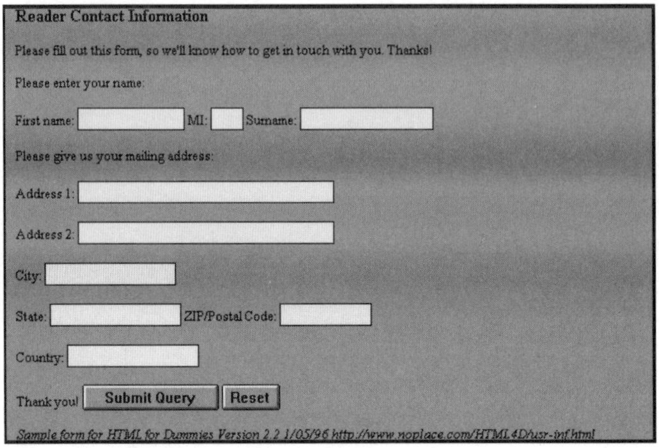

Figure 10-1:
The Reader
Contact
Information
form
on-screen.

Being <SELECT>ive

The `<SELECT> . . . </SELECT>` pair works much like a list style, except that it builds a pickable list of `<OPTION>` elements instead of the `<LI>` list items. Within the `<SELECT>` tag, the following attributes can occur:

- ✓ `NAME="text"`: Provides the name that is passed to the server as the identifying portion of the `name-value` pair for this element.

- ✓ `SIZE="number"`: Controls the number of elements that the pick list displays; although you can still define more than this many elements, it keeps the size of the list more manageable on-screen.

- ✓ `MULTIPLE`: Indicates that multiple selections from a list are possible; if this flag isn't present in a `<SELECT>` statement, your users can select only a single element from the pick list.

There's really not that much work involved in building a `<SELECT>` field for your form. In the following example, you see how easy it is to construct a list of spices from which a user can select and order:

```
<HTML>
<HEAD>
<TITLE>&lt;SELECT&gt; Spices</TITLE>
   <!- the name of this form is sel-spi.html ->
   </HEAD>
   <BODY>
   <H3>This Month's Spicy Selections!</H3>
```

```
<P>Spice up your life.  Order from this
   month's special selections.<BR> All items
   include 2 oz. of the finest condiments,
   packed in tinted glass bottles for best
   storage.


<HR>
   <FORM METHOD="POST" ACTION="/cgi/sel-spi">

<P>Pepper Selections:
   <SELECT NAME="pepper" SIZE="4" MULTIPLE>
   <OPTION>Plain-black
   <OPTION>Malabar
   <OPTION>Telicherry
   <OPTION>Green-dried
   <OPTION>Green-pickled
   <OPTION>Red
   <OPTION>White
   </SELECT>
   <P>
   Please pick a button to indicate how the pepper<BR>
   should be delivered:<BR>
   Ground <INPUT TYPE="RADIO" NAME="grind" VALUE="ground"> <BR>
   Whole <INPUT TYPE="RADIO" NAME="grind" VALUE="whole"> <BR>
   <P>
   <HR>
   <P>Imported and Domestic Oregano:
   <SELECT NAME="oregano" SIZE="4" MULTIPLE>
   <OPTION> Italian-whole
   <OPTION> Italian-crumbled
   <OPTION> Greek-whole
   <OPTION> Indian
   <OPTION> Mexican
   <OPTION> Organic-California
   </SELECT>
   <P>Thanks for your order! <INPUT TYPE="SUBMIT" VALUE="Send Order">
<INPUT TYPE="RESET">
   </FORM>
   <ADDRESS>
   Sample form for <I>HTML For Dummies</I> Version 2.2
   1/5/96 http://www.noplace.com/HTML4D/usr-inf.html</ADDRESS></
            BODY></HTML>
```

Figure 10-2 shows what nice results you can get from using `<SELECT>` elements to provide options for your users to pick from. Notice also the radio buttons that enable users to specify whether they want whole or ground pepper. By giving both radio buttons the same `NAME`, we indicate that only one option can be chosen.

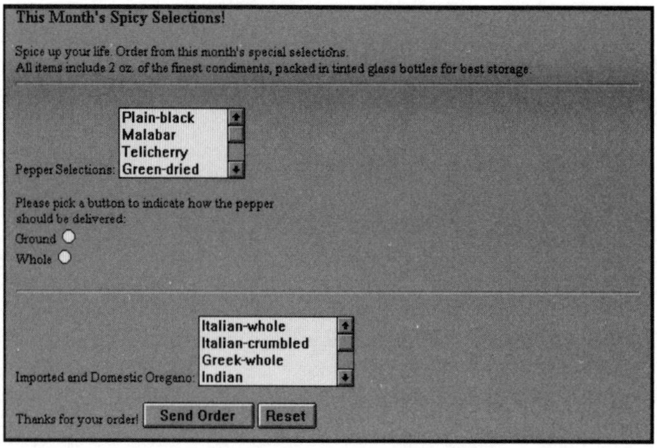

Figure 10-2:
The
`<SELECT>`
tag creates
scrolling
pick lists of
choices for
users to
select.

<TEXTAREA> lets users wax eloquent . . . or profane!

The `<TEXTAREA>` . . . `</TEXTAREA>` tags let you create input elements of more or less arbitrary size on a form. Any text that appears between the opening and closing tags will be displayed within the text area on-screen (and if left unaltered, supplies the default value delivered by the form).

`<TEXTAREA>` takes three important attributes:

- ✔ `NAME="text"`: Provides the identifier part of the all-important `name-value` pair delivered to the server.
- ✔ `ROWS="number"`: Specifies the number of lines of text that the text area will contain.
- ✔ `COLS="number"`: Specifies the number of characters that can fit onto any one row of the text area; this value also sets the width of the text area on-screen.

The example that follows shows how a text area is used to provide space for free-form feedback or information as part of a survey-style form:

```
<HTML>
<HEAD>
<TITLE>&lt;TEXTAREA&gt; On Display</TITLE>
   <!-- the name of this form is txt-ara.html -->
</HEAD>
   <BODY>
   <H3>The Widget Waffle Iron Survey</H3>
<P>Please fill out the following information so that we
   can register your new Widget Waffle Iron.
<HR>
   <FORM METHOD="POST" ACTION="/cgi/txt-ara">
<P>Model Number
   <SELECT NAME="mod-num" SIZE="3">
   <OPTION>102 (Single Belgian)
   <OPTION>103 (Double Belgian)
   <OPTION>104 (Single Heart-shaped)
   <OPTION>105 (Double Heart-shaped)
   <OPTION>204 (Restaurant Waffler)
   <OPTION>297 (Cone Waffler)
   </SELECT>
   <HR>
   <B>Please complete the following purchase information:</B><BR>
<P>Serial number: <INPUT NAME="snum" TYPE="TEXT" SIZE="10"
   MAXLENGTH="10">
   <P>Purchase Price: <INPUT NAME="price" TYPE="TEXT" SIZE="6"
   MAXLENGTH="10">
   <P>Location: <INPUT NAME="location" TYPE="TEXT" SIZE="15"
   MAXLENGTH="30">
   <HR>
   <B>Please tell us about yourself:</B>

<P>Male <INPUT NAME="sex" TYPE="CHECKBOX" VALUE="male">
   Female <INPUT NAME="sex" TYPE="CHECKBOX" VALUE="female">
   <P>Age:
   under 25 <INPUT NAME="age" TYPE="CHECKBOX" VALUE="lo">
   25-50 <INPUT NAME="age" TYPE="CHECKBOX" VALUE="med">
   over 50 <INPUT NAME="age" TYPE="CHECKBOX" VALUE="hi">
<P>
<HR>
   Please share your favorite waffle recipe with us. If we like
   it, we'll include it in our next Widget Waffler cookbook!
   Here's an example to inspire you.
```

(continued)

```
<P><TEXTAREA NAME="recipe" ROWS="10" COLS="65">
   Banana Waffles
   Ingredients:
   2 c. waffle batter (see Widget Waffler cookbook for recipe)
   2 ripe bananas, peeled, sliced 1/4" thick
   1 tsp. cinnamon
   Preparation:
   Mix ingredients together.
   Preheat Widget Waffler (wait 'til light goes off).
   Pour 1/2 c. batter in Waffler (wait 'til light goes off).
   Keep browned waffles warm in oven until ready to serve.
   </TEXTAREA>
<P>Thank you! <INPUT TYPE="SUBMIT" VALUE="Register now">
<INPUT TYPE="RESET">
</FORM>
<ADDRESS>
   Sample form for <I>HTML For Dummies</I> Version 2.2
   1/05/96 http://www.noplace.com/HTML4D/usr-inf.html</ADDRESS>
</BODY></HTML>
```

The screen that results from this HTML document is shown in part in Figure 10-3. Notice the use of check boxes for survey information, coupled with the text input area for recipes. Makes us wonder: "What time's breakfast?"

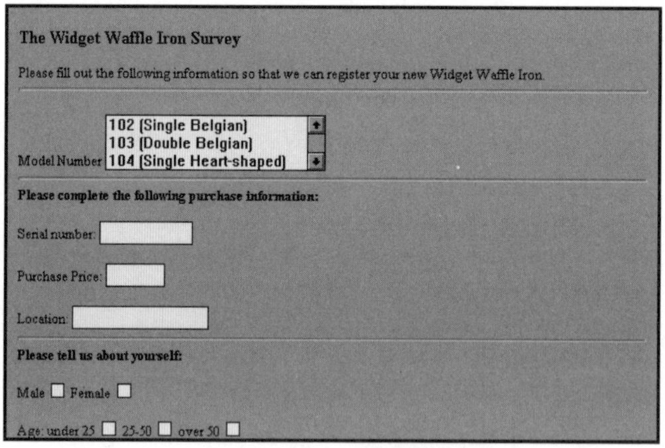

Figure 10-3:
Notice how
you can
supply
example
information
for the text
area in a
form.

At this point, you've seen about all the nifty little tricks — we like to call them *widgets* — that work within forms, but you can't really appreciate what forms can do until you've browsed the Web to look at the many examples out there. Our examples barely scratch the surface, so there's a lot more to see!

Formulating Good Attitudes

Whenever you create an HTML form, it's especially important to test it against as many browsers as you possibly can. Don't forget to work with character-mode browsers, such as Lynx, as well as more exciting graphical browsers. Remember also that, although some browsers support some pretty keen extensions, the effort that it takes to use them is wasted on those readers who pass through in other browsers that don't support them.

Ultimately, the HTML rules regarding layout versus content apply to forms: If you can create a clear, readable layout and make the form interesting to your users, you'll probably be a lot happier with the information returned than if you spend extra hours tuning and tweaking graphics elements and precise placement of type, widgets, and fields. Remember, too, that the form's just the front end for your user interaction or data collection. In Chapter 13, you pick up the back end of the forms business as you tackle the demanding but rewarding task of building CGI scripts and other input-handling programs for your server. If you need more details on this subject, don't forget to check out our other book: *Foundations of WWW Programming with HTML and CGI* by Ed Tittel, Mark Gaither, Sebastian Hassinger, and Mike Erwin (IDG Books Worldwide, Inc.). It even includes an analysis of the HTML and CGI code for the *HTML For Dummies* registration form!

In the next chapter, you find out how to turn graphics into addressable on-screen selectors called clickable maps. These add zest to forms and other HTML documents, because they let users select links at different points within a graphic.

Chapter 11

The Map's the Thing!

● ●

In This Chapter

▶ Using clickable maps

▶ Finding out what it takes to present maps

▶ Carving up maps for use

▶ Knowing the limitations to map use

▶ Mapping your way to perfection

● ●

*Y*ou've already found out how to insert graphics into your HTML documents by using the <IMG> tag. You've even seen examples of using graphics as hypertext links within anchor tags (<A HREF=. . .> <IMG SRC=. . .> </A>). In this chapter, we show you how to take the next logical step and treat a graphic as a collection of selectable regions, each of which points to some kind of hypertext link or resource.

Where Are You? (Using Clickable Maps)

Geographically speaking, a map takes a land mass and divides it up along boundary lines into named regions: typically, these might be countries, counties, or other kinds of territories. When it comes to using graphics in this way on the Web, the boundaries are obvious in the graphic that's displayed, and users simply select the portion of the graphic that attracts their interest. Users familiar with graphical interfaces have no trouble interacting with on-screen buttons, icons, and other kinds of interface controls. Graphical maps add this kind of capability to a single image displayed on a Web page.

In Web-speak such graphical maps are usually called *image maps* or *clickable maps*. We prefer the latter term because it emphasizes the important aspects of this graphical element:

✔ It breaks a graphic into discrete regions that function as a map of individual hyperlinks.

✔ Regions are selected by putting the cursor inside them and clicking the mouse.

You should already have a clue about the fundamental limitation inherent in a clickable map: It absolutely requires a graphical browser. The image that represents the map and drives the selection process doesn't appear in a character-mode browser, period. Therefore, if you use clickable map elements, you must implement alternate methods for users with text-only browsers.

An example of a clickable map should lend some reality to this concept. Figure 11-1 shows the *HTML For Dummies* home page main graphic (named HT4MENUM.GIF in the /GRAPHICS subdirectory). This graphic features a set of buttons at the bottom, where each button contains a major access category for the *HTML For Dummies* pages. As part of a set of Web pages for this book, it acts as the gateway to a page, or set of pages, for each category or topic mentioned.

Figure 11-1:
The *HTML For Dummies* home page (server version) includes a row of buttons on the bottom.

In this chapter, you see how to set up an image as a clickable map and how to use it to drive page navigation. Please note: The approach that we used to build the identical graphic for the pages on the diskette (the one that comes with this book) breaks the image up into pieces. The top part of the graphic represents one piece (HT4LOGOI.GIF) and each button has its own associated icon file. We did this because a local HTML file cannot use an image map; such a restriction exists because there's no server in the background to map the user's selection coordinates into a corresponding URL. Instead, each button's icon is directly linked to a URL, and clicking on a graphical element automatically selects the right link.

Cosmic Cartography: What It Takes to Present Maps on the Web

Building a clickable map requires three ingredients:

✔ **Creating (or selecting) a usable image:** This can be an existing graphic or a custom-built one. Our *HTML For Dummies* button bar uses five custom-built icons, one for each button.

✔ **Creating the *map file*:** Requires a step-by-step investigation of the image file inside a graphics program that can give you the pixel addresses (coordinates) of each point on the boundary of the regions you want to create (or use of a map-building utility, like the one we mention later in the chapter).

Our icons are all about the same size, so working through this process is very easy: The image starts in the upper-left corner of the button bar (at vertical location 142, or about the middle of this 285-pixel-high image), and is consistently 143 pixels high. The individual buttons vary slightly in width, producing the following set of coordinates:

```
( 0,142)- -( 99,142)- - - (199,142)- - - (299,142)- - - (399,142)- (499,142)
|              |              |              |              |              |
|   button 1   |   button 2   |   button 3   |   button 4   |   button 5   |
|              |              |              |              |              |
( 0,285)- -( 99,285)- - - (199,285)- - - (299,285)- - - (399,285)- (499,285)
```

Unfortunately, the only way to produce this collection of numbers is to view the graphic from within a graphics program (We used PaintShop Pro 3.0, a widely-available shareware program for Windows.) or to use an image-map construction program. If you do it by hand with a graphics program, you must position the cursor on each boundary point and write down the corresponding x and y values. That's what our preceding diagram represents: It's the map information for our button bar.

If you use a tool, it can generate the map for you, after you tell it what kind of shapes you're outlining. One example is Tom Boutell's excellent program called *mapedit,* which builds map files for you on command. It's available for lots of computer types including Macintosh, DOS/Windows, Windows NT, and UNIX. To find a suitable version, use "mapedit" as the search string in your favorite Web search engine. (A quick jump to Yahoo! turned up over 40 sites that offer one or more versions of this program.)

✔ **Establishing the right HTML information in your page:** You need to link the image, the map file, and a CGI script to handle decoding map coordinates and use that information to select the appropriate link to follow.

Here, we take you through the generalities of making this work in your HTML document. Later on, we show you how to build a complete back-end CGI script to translate the pixel coordinates for a user's map selection into a corresponding HTML link. In this chapter, we only cover the techniques and generalities needed to construct the image map and to create links between map regions and hypertext documents or resources.

By obtaining the information for the images and map files and establishing a convention to call the script that handles coordinate-to-link translation, you have most of what you need to know to set up a clickable map.

Just as we did in Chapter 10, we suggest that you use the name of the image map as the name for its corresponding script file: Thus, if the image is named HT4MENUM.GIF, the script would be called HT4MENUM.MAP, or simply HT4MENUM. If your scripts are in a CGI directory, one level down from your HTML files, the corresponding URL for this script would then be `/cgi-bin/ht4menum.map`.

Warning: different maps for different servers

Unfortunately, clickable maps are a topic where the two most popular *httpd* servers — NCSA and CERN — differ from one another. You find format differences in defining image maps for one kind of server versus the other. You also find Web servers that don't support either format, especially if they're not running UNIX. (Windows NT currently supports about 15 different Web servers, many of which use their own proprietary image map formats; the leading Macintosh Web server — WebSTAR — supports NCSA format.)

In order to get your clickable map to work, you must work within the requirements of the server where the map resides. If you don't know what those requirements are, we strongly suggest that you contact your local WebMaster — or at least, the system administrator for your Web server. He or she should be able to set you straight right away and can probably help you find some useful information about how to build clickable maps for your system, above and beyond what we tell you here.

Throughout the chapter, where differences between the CERN and NCSA requirements exist, we fill you in. If you're not using an *httpd* server of either variety, you'll want to investigate your server's requirements immediately and adjust our examples and recommendations to meet those requirements!

Dealing with shapes in maps

You can use various ways to identify boundaries when assembling coordinates to build a clickable map. Both CERN and NCSA image map definitions recognize the following regions:

- **Circle:** (Specified by the coordinates for a point at the center and the number of pixels for the radius.) Use this to select a circular (or nearly circular) region within an image.

- **Rectangle:** (Specified by the coordinates for the upper-left and lower-right corners.) Use this to select a square or rectangular region in your image. (This is the one we use in our button bar map.)

- **Polygon:** (Specified by the coordinates for the point at the vertex of each edge.) Use this to outline the boundaries of regularly or irregularly shaped regions that aren't circular or rectangular. Although it takes more effort, the more points you pick to define the outline, the more the region behaves as the user expects it to when they click it.

✔ **Point:** (Specified by its x and y coordinates.) Use this only when a specific point is easy for a user to select. (A point is usually too small a region on-screen and requires exact control to select — we recommend surrounding a point with a small circle or square to give users a little room to be sloppy.) We've never actually used a point reference in an image map, except as the vertices for a polygon or rectangle or as the center of a circle.

Selecting boundaries for map regions is what determines the selection of the corresponding links. Even though users see a nicely shaped graphic to click on, what really drives the selection process are the areas that you outline on top of that graphic.

The better the map regions fit the figure layout, the more the map behaves like users expect it to! The moral of the story is: Take your time and, when in doubt, pick more points to outline something, rather than less. (Even better, use a tool that follows your cursor movement to build the image map for you.)

We mentioned Tom Boutell's mapedit program earlier; you can find alternatives galore on the Web. For example, an interactive, Web-based image map tool called *MapMaker* is available at

```
http://www.tns.lcs.mit/cgi-bin/mapmaker
```

If you provide the program with a URL for the graphics file that you want to build a map for, it guides you through the rest of the process using your very own Web browser!

Building and Linking to CERN Map Files

Map files for CERN *httpd* servers take a general form that looks something like this:

```
default URL
circle (x,y) r URL
rectangle (x1,y1) (x2,y2) URL
polygon (x1,y1) (x2, y2) (x3,y3) ... (xn,yn) URL
point (x,y) URL
```

The shapes are pretty much self-evident, except for the polygon, which represents an attempt to trace a region's outline by connecting a series of points. If this sounds like "connect-the-dots" you've definitely got the underlying concept!

Don't forget to close your polygons; make sure that the last segment fills the gap between your last point and your first.

The other entry that might seem mysterious is the `default` URL: Define the default so that if a user clicks on a location that's not defined in the map, a fail-safe connection can still be chosen. This can be a script that sends a message back to the user, saying, "Click within the lines!" or "You have selected an area of the image that is not defined. Please try again."

The menu bar map file

Thus, for our menu bar example, the CERN map would be

```
rectangle (0,142) (98,285) http://www.outer.net/html4dum/ftpstuff.htm
rectangle (99,142) (198,285) http://www.outer.net/html4dum/contents.htm
rectangle (199,142) (298,285) http://www.outer.net/html4dum/search4d.htm
rectangle (299,142) (398,285) http://www.outer.net/html4dum/contact.htm
rectangle (399,142) (499,285) http://www.outer.net/html4dum/whatsnew.htm
default http://www.outer.net/html4dum/contents.htm
```

Because the button bar is a collection of rectangles, filling in the coordinates is easy. (Why do you think we picked this example?) Then, we provide a default link to the `contents` page if somebody insists on staying outside the nice little boxes that we gave them to play in! Notice, too, that we use URLs here that are relative to where the current document is in the file system of the server. Absolute URLs are easier to debug and to relocate, but relative ones are less work to enter. You plays your keystrokes, and you takes your chances!

Creating and storing map files

You can create the map file with any plain text editor, but you should store it on the server in a special directory for your map definition files. For this example, we call the file HT4MENUM.MAP and store it in the `http://www.outer.net/cgi-bin/` directory, along with all our other scripts.

With either CERN or NCSA servers, image maps need to be placed in a certain part of the file system. Contact your system administrator or your WebMaster to find out where this is and if you have *write* permissions. If you don't, you'll need to enlist their help in getting those files installed. (Normally, you can e-mail them to the administrator with an explanation of what they are, what they should be named, and where you assume they'll be installed; if you don't know those things yet, ask your administrator to supply those details before you mail him or her anything!)

Using map files

To use a map file with the CERN *httpd*, your system must already have a program that handles image maps. The name of this program, which is included with the CERN distribution *httpd* materials, is *htimage*. If it's not installed, you must arrange for that to happen in order to use image maps on your system. After it's available, you must also know how to invoke it on the server. For the purposes of this example, we assume it lives on the directory path /CGI-BIN/.

Defining a clickable map in your HTML document

After the map's defined and stored in the right location, it's time to bring all three elements together in your HTML file. Here's how you do it:

```
<A HREF="http://www.outer.net/cgi-bin/ht4menum.map">
<IMG SRC="graphics/ht4menum.gif" ISMAP>
</A>
```

Here's what's going on in this series of statements:

✔ The opening anchor tag combines the *htimage* location, which handles the coordinate-to-URL translation, with the full specification for the map file. Even though there's no space between the name of the program (*htimage*) and the map file specification, the server still knows what to do.

✔ The IMG tag points to the button bar graphic, but adds the ISMAP attribute to indicate that it's a clickable map.

✔ The closing anchor tag </A> indicates that the graphic specified by IMG is the target for the map file specified in the opening anchor tag.

There you are! Once you've made sure that all the right pieces are in place on your CERN server, you can try this, too.

Building and Linking to NCSA Map Files

Map files for NCSA *httpd* servers look an awful lot like those for CERN servers, but there are some differences. They take a general form that looks something like this:

```
default URL
circle URL x,y r
rect URL x1,y1 x2,y2
poly URL x1,y1 x2,y2 x3,y3 ... xn,yn
point URL x,y
```

The shapes are the same as the CERN variety and are defined by the same kinds of coordinates, but the names are shorter, and the URLs come first in the list of attributes. Here again, defaults work the same way: to provide a handler for people who click outside the image frame.

The button bar map file

For the *HTML For Dummies* home page main graphic, for example, the NCSA map would be

```
rect http://www.outer.net/html4dum/ftpstuff.htm (0,142) (98,285)
rect http://www.outer.net/html4dum/contents.htm (99,142) (198,285)
rect http://www.outer.net/html4dum/search4d.htm (199,142) (298,285)
rect http://www.outer.net/html4dum/contact.htm (299,142) (398,285)
rect http://www.outer.net/html4dum/whatsnew.htm (399,142) (499,285)
default http://www.outer.net/html4dum/contents.htm
```

Except for a slight change in the shape's name (rect instead of rectangle) and a reordering of the arguments (URL first, then coordinates), the map is pretty much identical to the CERN variety.

Creating and storing map files

You can create the NCSA map file with any plain text editor, just like the CERN variant. It should also be stored on the server in a special directory for your map definition files. For this example, we use the same name, HT4MENUM.MAP, and store it in the same http://www.outer.net/cg-bin/ directory, along with all our other scripts.

Using map files

Like CERN, in order to use a map file with the NCSA *httpd*, your system must already have a program that handles image maps. The name of this program, which is included with the NCSA distribution *httpd* materials, is *imagemap*. If it's not installed, you must arrange for that to happen in order to use image maps on your system. You also want to check that you have the latest version; check that information in

```
http://hoohoo.ncsa.uiuc.edu/docs/setup/admin/imagemap.txt
```

against what's installed on your server. If the date is more recent at the NCSA server, download the file, rename it to `imagemap.c`, and recompile it. Throw the old version away and use your new one instead.

After you have *imagemap* available, you must also know how to invoke it on the server. For the purposes of this example, we assume it lives on the directory path /CGI-BIN/.

Defining a clickable map in your HTML document

After the map's defined and stored in the right location, again it is time to bring all three elements together in your HTML file, but this time the NCSA way. Here's how you do it:

```
<A HREF=" http://www.outer.net/html4dum/ht4menum.map">
<IMG SRC="graphics/ht4menum.gif" ISMAP>
</A>
```

Here's what's going on in this series of statements:

- ✔ The opening anchor tag combines the *imagemap* location, which handles the coordinate-to-URL translation, with the full specification for the map file. Even though there's no space between the name of the program (*imagemap*) and the map file specification, the server still knows what to do.

- ✔ The IMG tag points to the button bar graphic, but adds the ISMAP attribute to indicate that it's a clickable map.

- ✔ The closing anchor tag </A> indicates that the graphic specified by IMG is the target for the map file specified in the opening anchor tag.

There you are! After you've made sure that all the right pieces are in place on your NCSA server, you can try this, too.

Even though the differences between the two flavors of *httpd* may seem trivial — and we think they are, too — they're still essential to creating clickable images that actually work. When it comes to computers in general, and the Web in particular, the devil is in the details. If you don't get your details straight, you get bedeviled instead! That's why you need to get the details straight before you try anything too exotic.

"The Map Is Not the Territory"

Although Alfred Korzybski wasn't thinking of clickable images when he uttered the title of this section, it's still a point worth pondering. Because not all users can see an image map, you need to be prepared to give them the same set of selections that your graphically-able users get in visual form. How might you go about doing this?

Because what you're providing in the image map is an array of choices, you could also add an equivalent set of text-based links right below the image. Here's what the HTML for this would look like:

```
<HTML>
<HEAD>
<TITLE> HTML For DUMMIES HomePage - IDG Books</TITLE>
<!—Turn a BASE HREF on if you have any problems with the way
  this page behaves (e.g. unresolved graphics). Also be sure to
  provide an absolute URL that points to the home page on your Web
  server, e.g.
  BASE HREF="http://www.outer.net/html4dum/html4dum.htm"
This is the proper BASE reference for our own HTML For Dummies
server. —>
<BODY>
<A NAME="top"></A>
<IMG ALIGN=MIDDLE WIDTH=60 HEIGHT=0 SRC=graphics/space.gif
  ALT=" ">
<A HREF="http://www.outer.net/cgi-bin/html4dum.map">
<IMG BORDER=0 ALIGN=TOP SRC="graphics/ht4menum.gif"
  ALT="Navigation Bar" ISMAP></A><P>
<IMG ALIGN=MIDDLE WIDTH=130 HEIGHT=0 SRC=graphics/space.gif
  ALT=" ">
<B><A HREF="ftpstuff.htm">FILES</A> &#32;&#124;
<A HREF="contents.htm">CONTENTS</A> &#32;&#124;
<A HREF="search4d.htm">SEARCH</A> &#32;&#124;
<A HREF="contact.htm">CONTACT</A> &#32;&#124;
<A HREF="whatsnew.htm">NEW</A><BR>
<IMG ALIGN=MIDDLE WIDTH=240 HEIGHT=0 SRC=graphics/space.gif
  ALT=" ">
<A HREF="navigate.htm">HOW TO NAVIGATE</A></B><P>
<A HREF="html4du2.htm">Click here for a non-imagemap version</A>
<P>
<IMG WIDTH=100% SRC="graphics/line.gif"
ALT="-==-==-==-==-==-==-==-==-==-==-==-=="><P>
You have reached the <I> HTML For Dummies</I> Web Pages, a
  charming, and hopefully helpful, addition to the WWW universe.
```

```
These pages are designed to aid you in three key areas:
<UL>
<LI> To help you find current information on the Web about HTML
<LI> To provide working examples and code for all the Web tricks
in the book
<LI> To introduce <I> HTML For Dummies</I> - your friendliest
resource for HTML material offline!
</UL>
<!- rest of file continues here, but this is all we include ->
```

As shown in Figure 11-2, this results in a text bar (right underneath the graphic) that offers the same choices that the graphic does. Users with graphical browsers won't be discommoded by this redundancy, and character-mode browsers will see a reasonable facsimile of what their graphically advantaged brethren see in living color. We call this *mastering the art of compromise!*

Figure 11-2:
A text-based alternative combined with the button bar keeps everybody in the know.

Of Clickable Maps and URLs

Image links can sometimes play hob with relative URL specifications within HTML documents. One unforeseen side effect of following the links through a map-reading script — to the map and back to the target page — can be a complete mangling of the context within which URLs are addressed. In English, this means it's a really, really, really good idea to use full URLs, instead of relative references, in HTML documents that also include clickable maps.

Another solution is to include a <BASE> tag inside the <HEAD>...</HEAD> tags, with the URL for the document in which it's included. This forces the server to treat the directory where the current document resides as the default context for relative references, even if clickable map references are used.

Either way, it's smart to be cagey when using relative URL references in documents with clickable maps. You should test this practice thoroughly to make sure that everything works as it should or use the <BASE> tag. Avoiding trouble is, in general, the best way to cure the URL "relative reference blues"!

Get ready for some real action in the next chapter, as you finally roll up your sleeves and get down and dirty on the back-end side of the Web environment. Here, you'll get the lowdown on what happens with CGI scripts, input-handling programs for forms, search engines, and other tools that extend what the Web can do for your users. Better buckle up!

Chapter 12

Stick Out Your Neck!
HTML Extensions

• •

In This Chapter

▶ Understanding what's ineffective

▶ Adding on through the standards process

▶ Coming HTML attractions

▶ Going proprietary: the Netscape extensions

▶ Extending proprietary: Microsoft's Internet Explorer extensions

▶ Playing HTML by the rules . . . or not?

• •

B y now, you may have seen or written enough HTML to know that it's easy to make an occasional mistake. In case you haven't noticed, most browsers are pretty forgiving about such things. Maybe you think it's just a case of open-minded software, but it's really part of the way that HTML processing works: The specifications require that any HTML tags that can't be recognized are simply ignored.

Of course, many browsers take that even further. The newer ones make all kinds of assumptions regarding the fallibility of the all-too-human authors who write HTML documents. Among other things, this means that some browsers make educated guesses about where missing closing tags should go — for example, that the closing anchor tag </A> belongs at the end of the next word or line break after the opening <A. . .> anchor tag.

In fact, not all browsers are the same — some recognize markup tags that others don't. In some cases, one browser tracks recent additions to an HTML specification more closely than another. In other cases — which you find out more about later in this chapter — a browser recognizes both standard markup and its own unique enhancements to HTML.

If Your Browser Can't See It, Is It Really There?

When it comes to HTML markup, either your browser recognizes it and renders it on-screen, or it doesn't recognize it and skips the tags altogether. This raises the interesting question that is the title of this section. It also helps to explain why some browsers are more popular than others. The bottom line, though, remains the same: If your browser can't recognize the markup, it behaves as if it weren't there.

This behavior allows browsers to render content in their own way rather than just skipping what's *inside* nonstandard tags. But it also causes some inconsistencies among browsers, so you never know what a page is going to look like until you see it drawn on the screen. These differences among browsers can sometimes be subtle — for example, Netscape puts more white space on pages than Mosaic. In case we haven't said it enough, test your Web pages with as many browsers as possible and always include a character-mode browser in your test.

The State of the HTML Art

HTML is governed by a standard specification for any given version: We discuss these specifications in Chapter 4 as the Document Type Definitions (DTDs) for HTML versions 1.0, 2.0, and 3.0. At this point, though, you need to understand how the standards-making process works so that you see the perfectly good reasons why browsers differ, even though they claim to support the same HTML standard(s).

A "simple explanation" for browser diversity

The simple explanation for browser differences is that they all track and interpret standards differently. The upshot of working with evolving standards leads to the following assumptions within computer programs like Web browsers:

- ✔ You can usually assume that any new implementation completely replaces the current official (frozen) standard.

- ✔ Developers adopt features and functions already present in developing standards. This is true for a variety of reasons, ranging from personal taste to a firm belief that certain features are more or less guaranteed to be in the "emerging standard" when it finally becomes official.

> ✔ Some developers even add features and capabilities outside the standard. These additions can range from behaviors that modify parts of an existing standard (like Netscape's addition of the "HEIGHT" and "WIDTH" attributes to the <IMG> tag) or that add new functionality or controls that were never part of any standard (like Netscape's <CENTER> . . . </CENTER> tags).

The use of evolving standards is a common pattern for software in many industries, from networking protocols (such as TCP/IP that the Web uses for networking communications) to compiler implementations (for standards-governed programming languages like FORTRAN and C). The process can get confusing, but it reflects the living, breathing nature of the state-of-the-art in computer activity.

Viva la difference: adding value . . . or adding confusion?

Some cynics in the room even think that vendors add "enhancements" to standards to try to shape the future direction that standards will take. For their part, most vendors defend such things as ways of adding value to a standard and making their products more attractive to users. In simple terms, this means that they purposely make their browsers different to create unique capabilities that people will pay extra to buy.

It's tough to say whether difference is an attempt to anticipate new standards or to deliberately try to appeal to users. We'd like to sidestep this burning issue and take the opportunity to warn you that standards are like Scripture or the Law — that is, they are subject to interpretation around a core of commonly held beliefs (or an *official standard*) and tend to differ, even though they all start with the same foundation.

What's in Store for HTML?

In general, what's in store for future versions of HTML is

> ✔ the addition of new markup tags to support sophisticated layout and formatting capabilities
> ✔ the obsolescence of simpler, less useful markup

HTML 2.0 Rules!

For HTML 2.0, this means adding forms support and getting rid of formatting commands that were never used very much — such as obsolete tags like `<XMP>`, `<PLAINTEXT>`, and `<LISTING>` — all of which have now been superseded by the `<PRE>` tag. Version 2.0 also introduces the character highlighting elements — `<I>` (italic), `<B>` (bold), and `<STRONG>` (extra dark) — to replace the older HPx (highlighted phrase, type x) markup. These new elements are routinely supported in most browsers (the 2.0 specification was finally "frozen" in December, 1995).

HTML 3.0 is still developing . . . but it's already passé!

HTML 3.0 is a concept that you still hear many people talk about, but it's actually something that never appears by that name. The stewards of HTML at the W3C and the IETF decided that one of the main reasons it took over a year to get HTML 2.0 approved was because it contained so many different aspects, some of which were controversial. Because the whole package of enhancements and changes had to be approved en masse, the less controversial stuff languished while waiting on other components.

When HTML 3.0 was introduced, the standards writers and their champions were sanguine about a speedy approval for HTML 2.0. The lesson of history has been that the more elements there are in a standard, the longer it takes to get approved. Thus, what used to be called "HTML 3.0" is now a collection of standards and draft standards for things like mathematics notation, frames, embedded applications, tables, and a whole slew of other nifty HTML bells and whistles.

This time, the standards groups and workers have decided to tackle the elements one at a time, so that each can proceed in parallel, and the less controversial ones can be approved as quickly as possible, without having to wait for their more controversial counterparts. As this chapter's being written, the standards groups appear confident that the standard extensions for mathematics notation, tables, and frames will all be approved soon (perhaps by the time you read this). That's why we give them solid coverage later in this chapter!

You might be wondering who decides the future of HTML. It's in the hands of the *HTML working group,* a group of researchers involved in discussing and developing HTML standards and overseen by the staff at the W3C and the IETF, through a mailing list at `html-wg@oclc.org`. (To subscribe, send a message with subject `SUBSCRIBE HTML-WG "<your name here>"` to `listproc@oclc.org`.)

Evolving HTML standards

Even though the features we previously mention appear to have priority in the development and standards communities, HTML is like a RonCO product: "But wait, there's more...." Here are some other elements under consideration for future HTML standards, many of which represent major increases in capability and functionality:

- ✔ Document divisions
- ✔ Style sheets
- ✔ Footnotes (and other embedded text elements)
- ✔ Text flow around graphics
- ✔ Object-oriented text and formatting variables

Actually, quite a few more features are under development for the future HTML DTDs. (And they are probably still in flux as you read this!)

The only way to check out the state of HTML standards is to go out and look at what's happening. You can start with the following URLs:

HTML 2.0 DTD and terminology

```
http://www.w3.org/hypertext/WWW/MarkUp/html-spec/
http://www.hpl.hp.co.uk/people/dsr/html/terms.html
```

Future HTML standard DTD working drafts

```
http://www.w3.org/hypertext/WWW/MarkUp/html3/CoverPage.html
```

If you start looking at the URLs mentioned in Chapter 9, you can probably find links to new specifications and other HTML works-in-progress there, too!

Proposed Standard HTML Extensions

On the diskette that accompanies this book, we include information about a wide variety of standard HTML extensions. If you jump into that set of pages, and pick the Tag Index entry on the Contents (contents.htm) page or the Menu and Search page (search4d.htm), you see that we use more or less the same notation as in Chapter 5 to introduce tags for HTML that are covered in standards beyond the HTML 2.0 DTD and specification.

As you try out these tags, don't be surprised if some browsers don't support them; not all browser vendors keep up with the latest and greatest versions of the draft HTML standards. See Table 12-1 for a listing of extended tags. We include only those tags that have been under discussion and development for some time that should, therefore, also have the greatest chance of working in your browsers. (As of our last test, most of them work in both Netscape and Internet Explorer, among others, except for some of the MATH notation.) That is not the same thing as a guarantee of support, however! The best way to figure out what's usable is to try out new tags, and then test them thoroughly with the browsers you expect your audience to be using.

Common new HTML tag attributes

Many new Post-2.0 HTML tags share some of the same attributes. Instead of listing these dozens of times, we put them in this sidebar for your personal enjoyment (but also to lower the page count for what would otherwise be an unbearably long section in this chapter).

In the **Attributes** section for a tag, you often see the following attribute names show up under the heading *Standard Attributes*; if you want the details, please check back here! In the meantime, here's our standard set of attribute definitions, which you find in a majority of the new HTML tags:

CLASS: This attribute is used to subclass tag names, and is also a space separated list of SGML NAME tokens. Class names are normally interpreted hierarchically: the most general class is on the left; the most specific class is on the right; and they are separated by a period. Although it's common to use the CLASS attribute to attach a different style to some element, it's advisable to choose class names on the basis of the element's semantics, because this allows other uses, such as restricting searches through documents by matching on element class names.

CLEAR: This attribute is common to all block-like elements. It is useful when you have text flowing around a table or figure in the margin and you want to start the address element below the figure rather than alongside it. It allows you to move unconditionally:

- **clear=left**: move down until left margin is clear
- **clear=right**: move down until right margin is clear
- **clear=all**: move down until both margins are clear

Your browser defaults or style sheets may provide minimum widths for each class of block-like elements. However, if it doesn't and you decide to place the address alongside the figure, you need minimum widths specified as

- **clear="40 en"**: move down until there are at least 40 en units free
- **clear="100 pixels"**: move down until there are at least 100 pixels free

ID: ID is an SGML identifier. You can use it as the target for hypertext links or to name specific elements in associated style sheets. Because identifiers are NAME tokens, they have to be unique within the scope of the current document, an attribute which overrules the NAME attribute described next.

LANG: One of the ISO standard language abbreviations that can be used by parsers to select language-specific choices for hyphenation rules, ligatures, quotation marks, and so on. The two-letter language code from ISO 639 is what composes the language attribute, which can optionally be followed by a period and a two-letter country code from ISO 3166.

MD: MD specifies a cryptographic checksum or message digest for the associated graphic (specified by the SRC attribute). Use it when you want to make sure that a linked object is the one intended by the document's author, and that the object hasn't been modified at all. Elements which support URI-based links generally allow the MD attribute.

SRC: SRC specifies the graphical content of a figure, while the image is specified as a URI. You may see this attribute together with the MD attribute.

Table 12-1   HTML Categories and Their Extended Tags

Category / Tag	Tag Name	Category Description / Brief Explanation
Comments		To document HTML design, techniques, and so on
<!——!>	Comment	Supports author comments; ignored by browser
Document Structure		Basic document layout and linkage structures
<BANNER>	Document Banner*	Defines a nonscrolling banner
<BASE>	Document Base	Indicates complete document URL, establishes location context for other URLs referenced
<BGSOUND>	Background Sound E	Links a background sound to a document
<BODY>	Document Body EI	Blocks out a document's body
<BODY>, <BODYTEXT>	Body Text*	Encloses the main body text
<DIV>	Document Divisions*	Defines multiple document sections or divisions
<FN>	Footnotes*	Defines footnotes
<HEAD>	Heading	Blocks out a document head

(continued)

Table 12-1 *(continued)*

Category/ Tag	Tag Name	Category Description/ Brief Explanation
<HTML>	Main document head	Blocks out an entire HTML document
<ISINDEX>	Is Indexed [NI]	Indicates that a document supports CGI script for searches
<LANG>	Language*	Sets the language for text rendering
<LINK>	Document Link	Sets relationship between current document and other documents
<META>	Meta	Imbeds document meta-information
<NEXTID>	Next Document	Indicates the "next" document that follows current, to permit HTML documents to be chained together
<RANGE>	Range of a Document*	Defines a documents range
<SPOT>	Spot ID*	Defines a location to be used in a <RANGE> tag
<STYLE>	Style Notation*	Defines alternate display styles
Document Headings		Supply document title and heading levels, provide important organization & layout elements
<H*>	Document Headings	Indicates first-through-sixth level headings
<TITLE>	Title	Supplies title that labels entire document
Links		Create links to anchor or another document, or create anchor point for another link
<A>	Anchor	Provides fundamental hypertext link capabilities

Category/ Tag	Tag Name	Category Description/ Brief Explanation
Layout Elements		Control document appearance, add elements
<ABBREV>	Abbrev*	Identifies abbreviations
<ACRONYM>	Acronym*	Identifies acronyms
<ADDRESS>	Address	Supplies author contact information for document
<AU>	Author*	Identifies the author
<BQ>	Blockquote*	Sets off long quotes or citations
 	Line Break [NI]	Forces a line break into on-screen text flow
<CENTER>	Center [N]	Centers text or images
<CREDIT>	Credit*	Identifies the source of a figure or quote
<DEL>	Deleted Text*	Identifies deleted text
<HR>	Horizontal Rule [NI]	Draws a horizontal line across the page
<INS>	Inserted Text*	Identifies inserted text
<MARQUEE>	Marquee [E]	Defines a scrolling marquee
<NOBR>	No Break [N]	Prevents a text line break
<NOTE>	Admonishments*	Identifies an admonishment
<PERSON>	Person*	Identifies people to be associated with the document, similar to <AUTHOR>
<Q>	Quotation*	Identifies a short quotation
<TAB>	Horizontal Tab*	Inserts a tab space
<WBR>	Word Break [N]	Forces a text line break within <NOBR>
Graphics		References to inline images for documents
<AREA>	Image Map Area [E]	Defines the clickable area of a client side imagemap

(continued)

Table 12-1 *(continued)*

Category/ Tag	Tag Name	Category Description/ Brief Explanation
<IMG>	Image [EI, NI]	Inserts a referenced image into a document, with alternate text, clickable map & placement controls
<MAP>	Client Side Image Map [E]	Defines a client side imagemap
Forms		Forms-related markup tags
<FORM>	Form	Marks beginning & end of form block
<INPUT>	Form Input	Defines type & appearance for input widgets
<OPTION>	Form Select Option	A way of assigning a value or default to an input item
<SELECT>	Form Select	Creates a menu or scrolling list of input items
<TEXTAREA>	Form Textarea	Multiline text entry widget
Paragraphs		Break up running text into readable chunks
<P>	Paragraph	Breaks up text into spaced regions; according to HTML 2.0 DTD closing tag </P> is optional
Lists		Provide methods to lay out item or element sequences in document content
<DD>	Definition List Definition	Marks the definition for a term in a glossary list
<DIR>	Directory List	Indicates an unbulleted list of short elements (less than 20 characters in length)
<DL>	Definition Lists	Marks a special format for terms and their definitions

Category/ Tag	Tag Name	Category Description/ Brief Explanation
<DT>	Definition List Term	Marks the term being defined in a glossary list
<LH>	List Heading*	Defines a heading for a list
<LI>	List Item [NI]	Within a list of any type, <LI> marks a member item
<MENU>	Menu List	Indicates a pickable list of elements
<OL>	Ordered Numbered List [NI]	Indicates a numbered list of elements
<UL>	Unordered Bulleted List [NI]	Indicates a bulleted list of elements
Text Controls		Character formatting tags
<B>	Bold	Produces bolded text
<BASEFONT>	Basefont [N]	Sets the base font size
<BIG>	Big Print*	Displays text in a large font
<BT>	Bold Upright*	Renders text in bold and upright
<CITE>	Citation	Marks distinctive text for citations (usually in italics)
<CODE>	Code	Use for code samples (usually Courier font)
<DFN>	Definition	Use to emphasize (usually in italics) a term about to be defined in the following text
<EM>	Emphasis	Adds emphasis to enclosed text (usually underline)
<FONT>	Font Size [N, EI]	Alters the font size from the base size
<I>	Italics	Produces italicized text
<KBD>	Keyboard Text	Marks text to be typed at keyboard (usually Courier font)
<PRE>	Preformatted Text	Preserves spacing and layout of original text in monospaced font
<S>	Strikethrough*	Renders text with a strikethrough mark

(continued)

Table 12-1 *(continued)*

Category/ Tag	Tag Name	Category Description/ Brief Explanation
<SAMP>	Sample	Marks sample inline text (usually Courier font)
<SMALL>	Small Print*	Displays text in a small font
<STRONG>	Strong	Maximum emphasis to enclosed test (usually bold)
<SUB>	Subscript*	Renders text in subscript
<SUP>	Superscript*	Renders text in superscript
<T>	Upright*	Renders text in upright
<TT>	Teletype	Produces a typewriter font (usually Courier)
<U>	Underline*	Renders text with an underline
<VAR>	Variables	Variable or substitution for some other value
Math Elements		Special math tags
<ABOVE>	Math Line Above*	Draws a line or symbol above text
<ARRAY>	Math Array*	Defines a math array
<ATOP>	Math Box Atop*	Places one section of text above another
<BAR>	Math Vector: Bar*	Draws a bar above a letter
<BELOW>	Math Line Below*	Draws a line or symbol below text
<BOX>	Math Box*	Defines a math box
<CHOOSE>	Math Box Choose*	Similar to <ATOP>, places one expression over another, encloses both in brackets
<DDOT>	Math Vector: Double Dot*	Draws a double dot or *umlaut* above a letter
<DOT>	Math Vector: Dot*	Draws a single dot above a letter
<HAT>	Math Vector: Hat/Caret*	Draws a hat or caret above a letter

Category/ Tag	Tag Name	Category Description/ Brief Explanation
<ITEM>	Math Array Item*	Defines an item of an array
<LEFT>	Math Box Left*	Defines the delimiter which appears on an expression's left side
<MATH>	Mathematics*	Defines math expressions; allows for special math related rendering elements
<OF>	Math Root Of*	Separates the radix from the radicand in a root expression
<OVER>	Math Box Over*	Places one section above another within a math box
<RIGHT>	Math Box Right*	Defines the delimiter which appears on an expression's right side
<ROOT>	Math Root*	Defines a root
<ROW>	Math Array Row*	Defines a row of an array
<SQRT>	Math Square Root*	Draws a square root symbol
<TEXT>	Math Text*	Identifies inserted math text
<TILDE>	Math Vector: Tilde*	Draws a tilde above a letter
<VEC>	Math Vector: Right Arrow*	Draws a right arrow above a letter
Figures		Figure tags
<CAPTION>	Caption*, Table Caption [EI]	Adds a caption to a figure or table
<FIG>	Figures*	Similar to <IMG>; inserts a figure and allows text wrapping
<FIGTEXT>	Figure Text*	Similar to <CAPTION>; adds textual information to a figure
<OVERLAY>	Overlay*	Overlays an image over a base figure

(continued)

Table 12-1 *(continued)*

Category/ Tag	Tag Name	Category Description/ Brief Explanation
Table		Table tags
<TABLE>	Table*, [E!]	Defines a table
<TD>	Table Data Cell*, [E!]	Defines a table data cell
<TH>	Table Header Cell*, [E!]	Defines a table header cell
<TR>	Table Rows *, [E!]	Defines a table row

Legend:
+ - Altered, changed or updated from 2.0 DTD
* - New tag
N - Netscape extension, tag listed in Netscape section
E - Microsoft Internet Explorer extension, tag listed in Microsoft section
N! - Netscape alterations to a tag, tag additions and alterations listed in Netscape section
E! - Microsoft Internet Explorer alterations to a tag, tag additions and alterations listed in Microsoft section

Accessing Tag Information on the Diskette

To provide you with an easy lookup tool for any HTML tag related to this chapter, we reproduce the information from Table 12-1 in HTML form on the diskette in a file named `tagindex.htm`. In this file, each tag's name is turned into a hyperlink that you can use to look up whatever information is available about that tag. There are three categories of information that may apply to any tag, as follows:

1. The standard HTML definition is available through a hyperlink on the tag's name, if applicable (if not, it appears as plain text, rather than as a hyperlink).

2. If a Netscape extension is defined for the tag, a Capital N (N) appears as a hyperlink in column 2 of the table.

3. If an Internet Explorer extension is defined for the tag, a Capital IE (IE) appears as a hyperlink in column 2.

Otherwise, the same legend information appears in the HTML version of the table, to indicate new or changed tags and the presence or absence of Netscape and Internet Explorer extensions.

You also have the option of exploring the three tag sets — standard "beyond HTML 2.0" tags, Netscape 2.X extensions, and Internet Explorer extensions — in alphabetical order from the tag index page. Simply select the appropriate "Guided Tour" options at the head of the page to go through the tags from each set in order.

In the sections that follow, we explain the background information on HTML extensions in general, and provide some specific information on Netscape and Internet Explorer extensions. Here again, though, the really useful information is on the diskette. Don't forget to visit our Website, at

```
http://www.outer.net/html4dum/tagindex.htm
```

for links to the most current available information about HTML standards, and the various flavors of HTML extensions.

Nonstandard HTML Extensions

The folks at Netscape Communications are the developers of Netscape, a highly functional, graphically oriented Web browser. Today, Netscape is widely regarded as the most popular browser in use on the Net. Netscape also pioneered the idea of adding capabilities to HTML on its own, whenever it wants to provide features or functionality for their browser that would otherwise be unavailable. These added capabilities are called *extensions,* and when it comes to such things, Netscape's work has received serious attention.

Today, Netscape is no longer the only browser development company that adds capabilities to HTML outside the standards effort. While these extensions make for more attractive pages if you're using Netscape, they don't do anything for many other browsers (but there's a trend among other browser vendors to adopt Netscape extensions, if only to protect their smaller marketshares). Can this possibly help to explain Netscape's burgeoning popularity? Well, we don't think HTML extensions are the only reason for Netscape's success, but we do know that lots of browsers out there in daily use can't understand and render these exotic features.

Netscape's changes to HTML markup

Netscape has introduced numerous new elements to its implementation of HTML markup including the tag information from the diskette, and the entities listed below. While you're out surfing the Web, you may notice some sites advertising themselves as "Netscape-friendly," while others may state a bit more forcefully, "Don't visit this site unless you're using Netscape!" As you read through the next section, and browse the Netscape extensions from the diskette, you'll probably get the idea that interesting things are going on in HTML documents that use Netscape's extensions. Whether they make it worth keeping non-Netscapers away from your pages is something only you can decide!

New Entities:

Entity	Description	Display
®	Registered Trademark	®
©	Copyright	©

By the time you read about these Netscape extensions, the information from the diskette may very well be out-of-date. HTML is nothing, if not a moving target! For the latest news on the subject, please check the following URL:

```
http://www.netscape.com/assis/net_sites/html_extensions_3.html
```

In the ever-changing world of the Web, the only way to get the freshest information is to go out and pick it up yourself! For the latest version of the Netscape browser, please check the following URL:

```
http://home.mcom.com/comprod/mirror/index.html
```

Microsoft's Internet Explorer

Not to be outdone by Netscape (or anybody else in the software industry), Microsoft's new 32-bit Web browser is called Internet Explorer. Microsoft Internet Explorer has added some useful and inane elements or attributes for existing elements which it supports uniquely. For the latest information about the Internet Explorer Extensions, please visit the following URL:

```
http://www.microsoft.com/windows/ie/IE20HTML.htm
```

Some Cool Colors

Internet Explorer recognizes a number of predefined Color names in the `<BODY BACKGROUND="colorname">` tag. These include: Black, Maroon, Green, Olive, Navy, Purple, Teal, Gray, Silver, Red, Lime, Yellow, Blue, Fuchsia, Aqua, White.

For an idea of what these look like, you can build yourself a simple HTML template page that includes only the necessary header information and a `<BODY>` tag that calls the color of your choice. If you name each one after the color, you can use them as a form of "color chart" forever afterwards!

For Tag Info, See "tagindex.htm"

To view the information about what Microsoft has done to HTML, take the Internet Explorer guided tour from the head of the tag index page. It guides you through an alphabetized list of all the new tags, and enhancements to existing tags, that Microsoft has seen fit to support in its browser. We're told that even though the only version that's available today runs on Windows 95, that Microsoft will be releasing versions of Internet Explorer for Windows 3.*X* and Windows NT sometime in 1996. If one of these platforms interests you, keep your eyes peeled on the Microsoft Web site for late breaking news!

That's it for the Microsoft Explorer extensions. If that's your browser of choice, we recommend that you play with these tags, and look for examples at Microsoft's (and other people's) sites to help you incorporate them into your pages. Or do we? Read on for a discussion of the dangers in using proprietary HTML tags. . . .

The Perils of (In) Compatibility

Some people argue passionately that extensions to any standard, whether proprietary to one vendor or generally adopted, are a good thing. They give users a chance to try out new and (hopefully) interesting capabilities and provide a platform for informed consensus about what should be included in the next standard. "This helps make things better in the long run," runs the argument.

We view proprietary extensions as more of a mixed blessing: True, they help advance the state of the art, but they also create *haves* and *have-nots* on the Web. That is, those who have the right browser can partake of this bounty, but others who do not have the right software cannot. Even though this division is as inevitable on the Web as it is anywhere else in the world, that doesn't mean we have to like it!

The only truly rational argument we can find against using proprietary extensions is that it complicates page testing. Because some browsers can't render what other browsers can, it becomes important to test your pages in both environments, to make sure they work equally well on both sides of the tracks. If properly approached, this means more work for you. But because you can do anything you want with HTML anyway, we'll let *you* decide!

This concludes our discussion of the innards of HTML. While the topic is never far away from our minds, in the following chapters we move on to the back end, server-side of the Web world. We think you'll agree that understanding both sides of the Web equation helps you to build better pages and to take full advantage of the services that the Web can offer. So please read on!

Part IV

Beyond HTML?
CGI Programs and
"Real" Applications

In this part . . .

*O*ne of the Web's most fascinating but least understood capabilities is its management of interaction between users running browsers and the programs and protocols on Web servers that make things happen. This capability stands behind the forms-handling and clickable maps we discuss in Chapters 10 and 11, and it opens the door for online search engines, query processing, and many other customized interactions you may encounter on the Web.

The cornerstone that holds up most Web-based interaction is the Common Gateway Interface (CGI), which specifies how browsers can request services from properly-equipped Web servers. In Chapter 13, you have a chance to get acquainted with CGI and with the kinds of programs and services it supports. These truly open up the Web to all kinds of interesting functionality by providing a way to communicate information from just about any kind of computer-based program and service to Web users.

Chapter 14 discusses interesting tools and technologies to make your Web documents more usable, especially through a variety of programs and services available with CGI programs. It also addresses some of the ways in which you can deal with long or complex documents and how to avoid the pitfalls of perfectionism. It's especially informative about how to make your content more accessible to the many robots and spiders that prowl the Web, looking for information to acquire on behalf of the wide variety search engines that will index this material and serve it up to savvy Web users upon request.

You should find this part of the book an eye-opening discussion of how to extend your Web pages to encompass whatever services you think your users need. We also try to point you at important repositories for CGI programs and other useful gizmos so you won't have to reinvent the wheel!

Chapter 13

The Common Gateway Interface (CGI)

●●●

In This Chapter

▶ Getting acquainted — a quick CGI overview

▶ Specifying CGI

▶ Making smart programming choices

▶ Forming connections — handling forms data

▶ Sampling the capabilities

●●●

*B*uilding HTML forms and handling user interaction through Web pages require action on both sides of the client/server connection. So far, this book has concentrated mainly on the client-side, except for the clickable image map files that we described in Chapter 11.

In this chapter, we move across the network connection from the client to the server-side and describe the Common Gateway Interface (CGI). The CGI lets Web pages communicate with programs on the server to provide customized information or to build interactive exchanges between clients and servers.

Along the way, we show you the history and foundations of CGI and cover the basic details of its design and use. We also introduce you to the issues surrounding your choice of a *scripting,* or programming, language for CGI, and give you the chance to read through some interesting example programs. Because you're getting these programs — and the code to run them — as part of this book (the code is on the diskette), we hope that you end up using them as part of your own Web pages!

If you've been reading carefully, you've already noticed one important thing about CGI programs: They run on the Web server, not on the client-side (where you run your browser to access Web-based information). This means that you can't use our CGI programs on your own machine, unless it can run Web server software (usually called an *HTTP daemon,* or more simply, *httpd*) at the same time that it runs your browser.

On Windows NT, Macs, and UNIX machines, running both a Web server and a browser is quite doable; on Windows 3.*x* and Windows 95 computers, it's a bit trickier. For the latter machines, Quarterdeck's $99 WebServer software package fits the bill quite nicely: It supports the latest version of CGI (1.1) and lets you work both sides of the client/server street with ease. For more information on this product, visit Quarterdeck's Web site at

```
http://www.qdeck.com
```

The "Common Gateway" Is NOT a Revolving Door!

Gateway *scripts,* or programs, add the capability for true interaction between browsers and servers across the Web. This is a powerful capability that's limited only by your imagination and the tools at hand. Gateway scripts supply the underlying functions that let you perform searches on Web documents or databases that provide the capacity to accept and process forms data, and that deliver the intelligence necessary to customize Web pages based on user input.

If you build Web pages, you must manage this interaction across the Web: That is, you must build the front-end information that users see and interact with, as well as the back-end programming that accepts, interprets, and responds to user input and information. This does require some effort and some programming, but if you're willing to take the time to learn CGI, you are limited only by the amount of time and energy you have for programming your Web pages.

Describing CGI programs

It doesn't really matter whether you call your server-side work a program or a script — in fact, this distinction is often used to describe the tools you'd use to build one. That is, scripts get built with scripting tools or languages; programs get built with programming languages. Like a script read by an actor, a scripting language creates a set of actions and activities that must be performed in the prescribed order each time a script is executed; that's why scripts are often said to be *interpreted.* Programming languages, on the other hand, must usually be transformed into a special executable form by a special program called a *compiler* that takes the programming language statements and turns them into equivalent computer instructions; that's why programs are often said to be *executed.* Because both approaches work equally well with the Web's Common Gateway Interface, for convenience, we simply refer to them as *CGI programs.* You can call them whatever you want!

CGI is the method that UNIX-based CERN and NCSA Web servers use to mediate interaction between servers and programs. Because UNIX was the original Web platform, it sets the model (yet again) for how the Web handles user interaction. Although you might find other platforms that support Web servers—like Windows NT and the Macintosh—they, too, must follow the standard set for the CERN and NCSA implementations of *httpd*. Whether or not they conform to the CERN or NCSA models, Web servers must provide CGI capabilities, or a similar set of functions to match what CGI can do.

What's going on in a CGI program?

You can think of a CGI program as an extension to the core WWW server services. In fact, CGI programs are like worker bees that do the dirty work on behalf of the server. The server is an intermediary between the client and the CGI program. It's good to be the queen bee, and to make all those workers do their things at your behest!

The server invokes CGI programs, based on information provided by the browser (as in the `<FORM>` tag, where the `ACTION` attribute supplies a URL for the particular program that services the form). The browser request sets the stage for a series of information hand-offs and exchanges:

- The browser makes a request to a server for a URL, which actually contains the name of a CGI program for the server to run.

- The server fields the URL request, figures out that it points to a CGI program (usually by *parsing* the filename and its extension or through the directory where the file resides), and fires off the CGI program.

- The CGI program performs whatever actions it's been built to supply, based on input from the browser request. These actions could include obtaining the date and time from the server's underlying system, accumulating a counter for each visit to a Web page, searching a database, and so on.

- The CGI program takes the results of its actions and returns the proper data back to the server; often the program formats these results as a Web page for delivery back to the server (if the Content-Type is `text/html`).

- The server accepts the results from the CGI program and passes them to the browser, which renders them for display to the user.

- If this exchange is part of an ongoing, interactive Web session, these results could include additional form tags to accept further user input, along with a URL for this or another CGI program. Thus, the cycle begins anew.

This is a kind of disjointed way to have a *"conversation"* over the Web, but it does allow information to move both ways. The real beauty of CGI programs is that they extend a simple WWW server in every conceivable direction and make that server's services more valuable.

What's in CGI Input?

A request for a CGI program is encoded in HTML in a basic form as shown in this example:

```
<A HREF="http://www.hal.com/hal-bin/silly_quote.pl">Silly Quote</A>
```

The URL declaration says to execute the `silly_quote.pl` CGI program on the `www.hal.com` WWW server from the `hal-bin` directory. This request has no additional input data to pass to the CGI program. (The clue is that no "?" is appended to the URL — see the explanation of the question mark argument later in this chapter.) The result of the CGI program is a Web page created on-the-fly and returned to the browser.

The information gathered by an HTML form or requested by a user (with a search request or other information query), passes to CGI programs in one of two ways:

- As an appendage to a CGI program's URL (most commonly, for WAIS requests or other short information searches). This way uses the `METHOD="GET"` option.

- As a stream of bytes through the UNIX default standard input device (*stdin*) in response to the `ACTION` setting for an HTML `<FORM>` tag. This way is best used with the `METHOD="POST"` option.

In the next section, you see how forms create special formats for information that is intended for use in CGI programs. Also, you see how that information is delivered and used in those programs.

Short and sweet: the "extended URL" approach

Most search engines use what's called a *document-based query* to obtain information from users. This query consists of nothing more than special characters appended to the end of the search engine's URL. Document-based queries are intended to solicit search terms or key words from a browser and then deliver them to a CGI program that uses them to search a database or a collection of files. Their simplicity is what makes document-based queries so good for soliciting small amounts of input from users and why you see them in so many Web pages.

Document-based queries depend on three ingredients for their successful operation:

- ✔ The `<ISINDEX>` tag within the `<HEAD>` section of an HTML document enables the browser to search the document.
- ✔ A special URL format is generated by adding the contents of a query to the URL, with the search terms added at the end and denoted by question marks.
- ✔ Special arguments in your underlying CGI program.

Here's how the process actually works:

- ✔ The `<ISINDEX>` tag in the `<HEAD>` of the document causes the browser to supply a SEARCH *widget* that allows the user to enter keywords (a widget is a bit of software that performs a particular task; in this case, it handles packages and sending search requests). These keywords are then bundled into an HTTP request and are passed to the corresponding CGI program. If the CGI program finds that no arguments are appended to the URL, it returns a default page that includes the search widget to the browser. This sometimes happens the first time a search is requested because the complete search widget may not be included on every Web page.
- ✔ At the prompt, the reader enters a string to search for, and presses Enter (or otherwise causes the string to be shipped to the CGI program for handling).
- ✔ The browser calls the same URL as before, except it appends the search string following a question mark. So, if the search engine program's URL is

```
http://www.HTML4d.com/cgi-bin/searchit
```

and the string to be searched for is "tether," the new URL then becomes

```
http://www.HTML4d.com/cgi-bin/searchit?tether
```

- ✔ The server receives the URL exactly as formatted and passes it to the searchit program, with the string after the question mark passed as an argument to searchit.
- ✔ This time, the program performs an actual search and returns the results as another HTML page (instead of the default prompt page that was sent the first time).

Every part of this operation depends on the others: The browser activates the `<ISINDEX>` tag that allows the query to be requested and entered; then the browser also appends the query string to the URL and passes on the query as an argument to the search program. The search program uses the query value as the focus of its search operation and returns the search results to the browser, via another custom-built HTML document.

Long-winded and thorough: the input-stream approach

As you build an HTML form, you have important definitions to make, including the assignment of names and associated values to your variables or selections. When users fill out HTML forms, they're actually instructing the browser to build a list of associated `name=value` pairs for each selection made or for each field that's filled in.

Name=value pairs take the following form:

```
name=value&
```

The equal sign (=) separates the name of the field from its associated value. The ampersand (&) separates the end of the value's string from the next item of text information in a completed form. For `<SELECT>` statements where `MULTIPLE` choices are allowed, the resulting list has multiple `name=value` pairs where the name remains the same, but the value assignment changes for each value chosen.

Reading through forms information delivered to a CGI program's standard input device *(stdin)* is a matter of checking certain key environment variables (covered in the next section), and then parsing (separating into individual words or units of information) the input data. This reading consists of separating name=value pairs, and using the names, with their associated values, to guide subsequent processing. The easiest way to do this, from a programming perspective, is to first parse and split out name=value pairs by looking for the ending ampersand (&), and then divide the pairs into the name and value parts by looking for the equal sign (=).

Here are some Perl code fragments that you can use to parse your forms' input data. (It assumes that, in keeping with our recommendation, you use `METHOD="POST"` for passing data.)

```perl
# this reads the input stream from the Standard Input
# device (stdin) into the buffer variable $buffer, using
# the environment variable CONTENT_LENGTH to know how
# much data to read
read(stdin, $buffer, $ENV{'CONTENT_LENGTH'});

#Split the name=value pairs on '&'
@pairs = split (/&/, $buffer);

# Go through pairs and determine the name and value for
# each named form field
```

```
for each $pair (@pairs) {
# Split name from value on "="
  ($name, $value) = split(/=/,$pair);
# Translate URL syntax of + for blanks
  $value =~ tr/+/ /;
# Substitute hexadecimal characters with their normal
  equivalents
  $value =~ s/%([a-fA-F0-9][a-fA-F0-9])/pack("C",hex($1))/eg;
# Deposit the value in the FORMS array, associated to name
  $FORM($name) = $value;
```

Handling environment variables

As part of the CGI environment, the *httpd* server's software version and configuration are of interest, as are the multiple variables associated with the server. You can use the following shell program to produce a complete listing of such information; it is a valuable testing tool when installing or modifying a Web server.

```
#!/bin/sh

echo Content-type: text/plain
echo

echo CGI/1.1 test script report:
echo

echo argc is $#. argv is "$*".
echo

echo SERVER_SOFTWARE = $SERVER_SOFTWARE
echo SERVER_NAME = $SERVER_NAME
echo GATEWAY_INTERFACE = $GATEWAY_INTERFACE
echo SERVER_PROTOCOL = $SERVER_PROTOCOL
echo SERVER_PORT = $SERVER_PORT
echo REQUEST_METHOD = $REQUEST_METHOD
echo HTTP_ACCEPT = $HTTP_ACCEPT

echo PATH_INFO = $PATH_INFO
echo PATH_TRANSLATED = $PATH_TRANSLATED
echo SCRIPT_NAME = $SCRIPT_NAME
echo QUERY_STRING = $QUERY_STRING
echo REMOTE_HOST = $REMOTE_HOST
echo REMOTE_ADDR = $REMOTE_ADDR
echo REMOTE_USER = $REMOTE_USER
echo CONTENT_TYPE = $CONTENT_TYPE
echo CONTENT_LENGTH = $CONTENT_LENGTH
```

This UNIX shell script is widely distributed around the Net. We found this version in the NCSA hoohoo collection at

```
http://hoohoo.ncsa.uiuc.edu/cgi-bin/test-cgi
```

Running this script on a Web server (in this case, the NCSA Web server hoohoo) produces the following output:

```
CGI/1.1 test script report:

argc is 0. argv is .

SERVER_SOFTWARE = NCSA/1.4b2
SERVER_NAME = hoohoo.ncsa.uiuc.edu
GATEWAY_INTERFACE = CGI/1.1
SERVER_PROTOCOL = HTTP/1.0
SERVER_PORT = 80
REQUEST_METHOD = GET
HTTP_ACCEPT = */*, image/gif, image/x-xbitmap, image/jpeg
PATH_INFO =
PATH_TRANSLATED =
SCRIPT_NAME = /cgi-bin/test-cgi
QUERY_STRING =
REMOTE_HOST = etittel.zilker.net
REMOTE_ADDR = 198.252.182.167
REMOTE_USER =
AUTH_TYPE =
CONTENT_TYPE =
CONTENT_LENGTH = n
```

Each capitalized variable name (on the left-hand side of the equal sign) and its associated output are environment variables set by CGI. These are always available for use in your programs.

Two environment variables are especially worthy to note:

✔ The QUERY_STRING variable is associated with the GET method of information-passing (as is common with search commands) and must be parsed for such queries or information requests.

✔ The CONTENT_LENGTH variable is associated with the POST method of information-passing (as is recommended for forms or other lengthier types of input data). The browser accumulates the variable while assembling the forms data to deliver to the server; the variable then tells the CGI program how much input data it has to read from the standard input device.

The environment variables also identify other items of potential interest, including the name of the remote host and its corresponding IP address, the request method used, and the types of data that the server can accept. As you become more proficient in building CGI programs, you find further uses for many of these values.

Forming Up: Input-Handling Programs

When you create a form in HTML, each input field has an associated unique NAME. Filling out the form usually associates one or more values with each name. As shipped from the browser to the Web server (and on to the CGI program targeted by the URL), the form data is a stream of bytes, consisting of name=value pairs separated by ampersand characters (&).

Each of these name=value pairs is URL-encoded, which means that spaces are changed into plus signs (+) and some characters are encoded into hexadecimal. Decoding these URL encodings is what caused the interesting translation contortions in our Perl code sample in the preceding section.

If you visit the NCSA CGI archive, you can find links to a number of input-handling code libraries that can help you build forms. You can find all this information at

```
ftp://ftp.ncsa.uiuc.edu/Web/httpd/Unix/ncsa_httpd/cgi/
```

- ✔ **Bourne Shell:** The AA Archie Gateway, which contains calls to *sed* and *awk* to convert a GET form data string into separate environmental variables (AA-1.2.tar.Z)

- ✔ **C:** The default scripts for NCSA *httpd*, including C routines and example programs for translating the query string into various structures (ncsa-default.tar.Z)

- ✔ **Perl:** The Perl CGI Library contains a group of useful Perl routines to decode and manage forms data (cgi-lib.pl.Z)

- ✔ **TCL:** The TCL argument processor includes a set of TCL routines to retrieve forms data and insert it into associated TCL variables (tcl-proc-args.tar.Z)

What this means to you, gentle reader, is that most of the work of reading and organizing forms information is already widely and publicly available in one form or fashion. This simplifies your programming efforts because you can concentrate on writing the code that interprets the input and builds the appropriate HTML document that's returned to your reader as a response.

Coding CGI

We conclude this chapter by examining three different CGI programs. We've also included their code and a great deal of associated information on the diskette that comes with this book. Each of these programs is available in three versions: AppleScript (for use on an Apple *httpd* server), Perl (for use on any system that supports a Perl interpreter/compiler), and C (for use on any system that supports a C compiler).

Ladies and gentlemen: Choose your weapons!

Before we launch you into these excellent examples, we'd like to encourage you to use them in your own HTML documents and CGI programs (we're giving the license to this code away, so you can use it without restrictions). We want to conclude the discussion portion of this chapter with an investigation of why we chose to implement each of these programs in three forms, and how you can choose a suitable language for writing your CGI programs.

It's quite true that you can build your CGI programs with just about any programming or scripting language that your Web server supports. Nothing can stop you from ignoring all of the options that we cover here and use something completely different.

Nevertheless, we can think of some good reasons why you should consider using these options and equally good reasons why you should ignore other options. We cheerfully concede that there are probably as many opinions on this subject as there are CGI programmers, but we'd like you to consider carefully before deciding on a CGI language that you're likely to spend considerable time and effort learning and using.

For example, we included the NCSA test-cgi script earlier in this chapter. It's written in the basic C shell, a command language that is common on many UNIX systems and makes an adequate scripting language for many uses. Nevertheless, we don't think that UNIX shells are suitable for heavy-duty CGI programming, because they mix UNIX system commands freely within their own syntax.

The problem with CGI programming under UNIX is that it depends on the standard input *(stdin)* and standard output *(stdout)* devices as the methods for moving data between Web servers and browsers. Each new UNIX process automatically creates its own *stdin* and *stdout;* sometimes UNIX shells can get confused regarding where its input is coming from and where its output is going to. This confusion can be a side effect of *spawning* tasks (or having one running program start another program up to perform a specific task and report its results back to the original program when its finished) or running system commands, but whatever the cause, it can lose the input or output for CGI programs. That's the main reason why we don't recommend shell scripts of any kind for heavier-duty CGI applications (for example, forms-processing versus query-handling).

On the plus side, Perl offers straightforward access to UNIX system calls and capabilities within a tightly structured environment. It includes the positive features of languages like C, Pascal, *awk*, *sed*, and even Basic, and offers power-ful string-handling and output-management functions. Perl is emerging as the favorite of many Web programmers (and is certainly our favorite CGI gurus' language of choice). Best of all, Perl implementations are already available for UNIX, DOS, Windows NT, the Macintosh OS, and the Amiga, with numerous other implementations under way. We've had excellent luck moving Perl from one platform to another, with only small changes.

We include C because it's a powerful programming language and remains a tool of choice in the UNIX environment. What features and functions it doesn't offer as built-ins are readily available in the form of system *APIs* (Application Pro-gramming Interfaces, or the set of routines used to invoke system functions and other kinds of prepackaged functionality within a program) and code libraries. C is also very portable (barring the use of system APIs, which changes from one system to another); one version of C is available for just about every plat-form, and, with multiple implementations, are available for popular platforms and operating systems. We're especially fond of the GNU C and the related GNU Tools from the Free Software Foundation pioneered by Richard Stallman.

If you use the Macintosh as a Web server, AppleScript is pretty much your only option. Even so, it has proven to be a worthwhile tool for building CGI programs and is widely used in the Macintosh Web community. Be sure to consult Chapter 21 for some excellent pointers on Macintosh tools and technologies for the Web, if you're a real Mac-o-phile!

Whatever language you choose for your CGI programs, be sure that it provides good string-handling capabilities and offers reasonable output controls. Because you'll be reading and interpreting byte stream input and creating HTML docu-ments galore, look for these important capabilities. Also, we recommend that you pick a language that is already widely used in the Web community; you'll likely find lots of related modules, libraries, and code widgets that may save you programming time and make your job easier. But hey—it's your choice!

In this chapter, we just barely scratch the surface of CGI as a topic. For more information, consult your favorite search engine and use "CGI" or "CGI script" as your search string. It turns up tons of useful references. Also, one of the authors of this book has cowritten two other books that are largely devoted to CGI programming. They are *The Foundations of WWW Programming with HTML and CGI* and *World Wide Web Programming Secrets with Perl and CGI* both by Ed Tittel, Mark Gaither, Sebastian Hassinger, and Mike Erwin. (The former book was published in 1995, the latter in 1996. Both books were published by IDG Books Worldwide, Inc., Programmers Press, and both have list prices of $39.99 in the U.S.). Although you can also find other books on this subject, you won't find any others that your authors like more!

Example 1: What time is it?

This short Perl program accesses the system time on the server and writes an HTML page with the current time to the user's screen.

```
#!/usr/local/bin/perl
#
# time-cgi.pl
#
# CGI to return the time on the server
# v 1.0  -  2/14/95
# singe@outer.net <Sebastian Hassinger>
#
# called from simple anchor
# (i.e. <A HREF="http://www.outer.net/cgi-bin/time.pl">)
# the first line tells the UNIX shell that this script should be run
#            # using Perl in the /usr/local/bin directory
#
#


$| = 1;        # output *not* buffered - This is a switchused by
               # Perl internally. It tells Perl not to buffer
               # the text the script sends back to the Web client.
               # All data will be output immediately to the client
               # thereby avoiding any data loss when the connection
               # to the client is broken.

print "Content-Type: text/html\n\n\n";
               # This is the first line the CGI
               # must return to signal the Web client that the data
               # to follow should be interpreted as HTML.
               # The line states the MIME type of the document to
               # follow, and the carriage returns after the
               # 'Content-Type:' line (\n) are required.
```

```
chop ( $time = '/bin/date '+%r'' );
           # Sets the $time variable to the current time
           # using the UNIX 'date' command and the %r format
           # built-in to that command to return the time in
           # AM/PM 12-hour format. The ' ' (back-ticks) tell
           # Perl to use the text in between as input to the
           # Bourne shell and to return the results. The 'chop'
           # command wrapping variable assignment deletes the
           # trailing carriage return from the shell output
           # (i.e., the raw data returned to the variable will
           # be '11:15:30 AM\n' and the chop command takes away
           # the \n).

print "<HTML><HEAD><TITLE>Current Time on this Web Server
       </TITLE>","</HEAD><BODY>\n";
           # Set up the top of the page for the client. From
           # here on out, everything we output is going to be
           # HTML-formatted - in essence, we are creating an
           # HTML document on-the-fly.
           # the print command can be broken up over several
           # lines using comma-separated chunks of double-
           # quoted text.

print "<H2>The time on the server is now:<BR><STRONG>$time
       </STRONG><BR></H2>";

           # We just outputted our variable using HTML tag to
           # pretty up our text. Note that \n carriage returns
           # do not affect a carriage return on the client -
           # only <BR> tags do.

print "<HR><ADDRESS>This page generated by time-cgi.pl<P>",
   "Contact: singe@outer.net</ADDRESS></BODY></HTML>";
           # Finish off the page with contact info.

# The script will now complete its execution, the shell opened by
# the httpd server to run the CGI script will close, and the
# connection between the server and the client will be broken.
```

Example 2: Counting page visits

This AppleScript program establishes a counter that tracks the number of times a page is visited. This kind of tool can provide useful statistics for individuals or organizations curious about how much traffic their pages actually receive.

```
- counter.acgi (AppleScript CGI to return the number of times
- the CGI has been accessed )
-
- singe@outer.net <Sebastian Hassinger>
- 2/15/95
- simple example of AppleScript CGI for running on a Mac
- equipped with MacHTTP 2.0.1

- First, set up variables as properties so that they will
- persist inside the object that is called when the client
- accesses the CGI. Regular variables in AppleScript
- don't need to be declared as properties before use, but
- they would lack the scope to be used inside event handling
- objects. Also, the counter and access_date properties will
- retain their values even if you quit and launch the script
- again, so long as it isn't edited.

property crlf : (ASCII character 13) & (ASCII character 10)
- Set up a UNIX-style carriage return/line feed to make sure
- the lines break properly on the Web client.

property http_10_header : "HTTP/1.0 200 OK" & crlf & "Server:
         MacHTTP" & crlf & "MIME-Version: 1.0" & crlf &
            "Content-type: text/html" & crlf & crlf
- This is a standard http header, we're constructing it for
- use later in the script, to signal the client what type of
- data we're returning. MacHTTP is unlike the NCSA UNIX-based
- httpd server in that it does not supply any missing http
- headers for the CGI's output, so in addition to the usual
- 'Content-type:' header we used in the UNIX CGIs, we supply
- the HTTP version, the server name, MIME version and result
- code (200, in this case, signalling the client that we're
- returning a complete HTML document).

property html_footer : "</BODY><HR><ADDRESS>This page generated
by counter.acgi.<P>" & "Example AppleScript CGI<P>Contact
singe@outer.net with questions." &
"</ADDRESS>"
- This is a boilerplate for the bottom of the page we'll
- return to the client.

property access_time : current date
- Create the variable used to return the current time to
- the client, initialize to date and time.
```

```
- Properties persist from one running of the script to another,
- so this should tell us how long the script has been running,
- too.

property counter : 0
- Initialize counter variable to zero.

on event WWWsdoc
- This is the event trigger for the message MacHTTP will send
- to the CGI.

  set counter to counter + 1
  - increment counter

  try -wrap the whole script in an error handler
    return http_10_header & "<TITLE>AppleScript Counter
         CGI</TITLE>" &
    "<H2>Counter CGI</H2><P>" &
    "<P>This script has been run " &
    counter & " times since " & access_time & html_footer
- Spit back at the client our http document header, the body
- of the HTML document, our counter and access_time variables,
- and the HTML footer boilerplate.

  on error msg number num
- report the error message and number to the WWW client
    return http_10_header & "Error " & num & ", " & msg
  end try
end event WWWsdoc
```

Example 3: Decoding clickable map coordinates

This C program can distinguish whether the right or left side of a graphic is selected (as well as define a default to handle when the graphic isn't selected at all). It shows how a script handles the definitions inside an image map file.

```
/*
 * Copyright (c) 1995 Mike W. Erwin
 * mikee@outer.net
 * All rights reserved.
 *
 * Redistribution and use in source and binary forms, with or
 * without modification, are permitted provided that: (1) source
 * code distributions retain the above copyright notice and this
 * paragraph in its entirety, (2) distributions including binary
 * code include the above copyright notice and this paragraph in
```

```
* its entirety in the documentation or other materials provided
* with the distribution, and (3) all advertising materials
* mentioning features or use of this software display the following
* acknowledgement:
* THIS SOFTWARE IS PROVIDED "AS IS" AND WITHOUT ANY EXPRESS OR
* IMPLIED WARRANTIES, INCLUDING, WITHOUT LIMITATION,
                 THE IMPLIED
* WARRANTIES OF MERCHANTABILITY AND FITNESS FOR A PARTICULAR
* PURPOSE.
*
* x and y coordinates are passed by the Web client on the command
* line, and this program will store them in the argv variable.
* The 'hot spots' will be read from the configuration file
* '/www/conf/ismapper.conf,' which should be in the form:
* <top left coordinates>,<bottom right coordinates> <url>
* with one line for each rectangle, and one line in the form:
* default <url> in case the click does not fall into any of the
* hot spots. Note that there is no space between the comma and
* the coordinates, and whitespace between the coordinates and the
* URL.
*/
/*
*    C CGI used to return a URL to hot spots being clicked on
*    Version 1.0.0
*    2/28/95
*/
/*
*    To compile: "cc -o ismapper ismapper.c"
*/


/*
*    Standard UNIX include files
*/

#include <stdio.h>
#include <ctype.h>

/*
*    Globals
*/

#define MAX_LINE_SIZE  255
#define true           1
#define false          0
```

```c
char *author = "mikee@outer.net";
char *config_file = "/www/conf/ismapper.conf";

char URL [ MAX_LINE_SIZE ];
char default_URL [ MAX_LINE_SIZE ];
char global_error [ MAX_LINE_SIZE ];


/******************************************************************
 * main()
 *
 * This function takes the x and y mouse down as its arguments and
 * will return a pointer to the start of the URL in the file
 * that matches the boundaries of the rectangle specified in the
 * file.
 *
 * The format of the config file is:
 *
 * 6,6:73,144      http://www.outer.net/ismap.test/left.html
 *
 ********************************************************************/

char *read_config_file (int x, int y)

{
  FILE *config;
  char *line, new_line[MAX_LINE_SIZE];
  char *url = NULL;
  short found = false;

  if ((config = fopen(config_file, "r")) == NULL) {
    strcpy(global_error,"Configuration file not found");
    return (NULL);
  }

  do {
    int top, left, bottom, right;

    line = fgets(new_line, MAX_LINE_SIZE, config);

    sscanf(new_line,"default%*[\t ]%s", default_URL);
    sscanf(new_line,"%d,%d:%d,%d%*[\t ]%s",&top, &left,
    &bottom, &right, URL);
```

```
    if ((x >= top) && (x <= bottom) && (y >= left) &&
    (y <= right))
       found = true;
  }
    while (line && !found);

  if (found)
    url = URL;
  else
    url = default_URL;

  fclose(config);
  return(url);
}


*****************************************************************
* main()
*
* This is the official start of the C program.  It makes a single
* call to our "get_time" function above then formats the output for
* HTML on the standard output
*
******************************************************************/

main (int argc, char **argv)
{
      int x_coordinate = 0 , y_coordinate = 0;
    char *destination_url;

    if (argc != 3) {
     printf("Content-Type: text/html\n\n\n");
     printf("<HTML><HEAD><TITLE>CGI Error</TITLE>< HEAD><BODY>\n");
     printf("<H2>Invalid number of arguments</H2>");exit (1);
    }

    x_coordinate = (int) atoi(argv[1]);
    y_coordinate = (int) atoi(argv[2]);

    destination_url = read_config_file(x_coordinate, y_coordinate);

    if (destination_url != NULL) {
     printf("Location:\t%s\n",destination_url);
    }
    else {
```

```
    printf("Content-Type: text/html\n\n\n");
    printf("<HTML><HEAD><TITLE>Ismapper ERROR");
    printf("</TITLE></HEAD><BODY>\n");
    printf("<H1>No area matched and no default URL is defined.");
    printf("%s</H1>\n",global_error);
    printf("<HR>Contact %s for help.\n",author);
    }
  exit(1);
}
```

Installing and Using CGIs

Most Web servers are configured to look for CGI programs in a particular directory that's under the server's control. Normal users (including you) probably
won't be able to copy CGI scripts into this directory without obtaining help
from their friendly neighborhood systems administrator or WebMaster. Before
you can install and use any CGI program on a particular server, you want to talk
to these individuals (if not both), tell them what you're trying to do, and ask for
their help and advice in making it happen.

Don't be hurt or surprised if this process takes some time: Systems administrators and WebMasters tend to be chronically busy people. You may have to wait
a while to get their attention, and then discuss your needs with them. Make
your initial approach by e-mail or a phone call, and briefly explain what you
want to do. (For example: "I want to include a counter CGI on my home page to
track visitors.") Among other things, you may discover that they already have a
CGI available for that very purpose on your server, and they'll simply tell you
how to include its reference in your CGI invocation of your home page. (You
may not have to use our code at all!)

Also, most such individuals are responsible for the safe and proper operation of
the server and/or the Web site where you want to run a CGI program. Don't be
offended if you hear them say, "Well, I need to look it over first to make sure that
it's okay before you can use it." That's because they're only trying to make sure
that you're not planning on introducing software that could cripple or compromise
their system. So, please, don't take it personally when this happens — these
people are just doing their jobs, and asking for a review shows you that they
care about what happens on their (and your) server. This is actually a good thing!

Finally, the systems administrator or WebMaster can show you how to install
and use CGIs more quickly and efficiently than if you try to figure it out for
yourself. So, be ready to wait your turn to get some time and be ready to listen
and learn when your turn comes. You won't be disappointed!

As the sample CGI programs in this chapter should illustrate, there are as many ways to skin the proverbial CGI as there are ideas and approaches about how to implement them. We sincerely hope that you can use the paltry tools we include with this chapter, and that you investigate the contents of the diskette that comes with the book. On the disk, you can find C, Perl, and AppleScript versions for all three programs. In the next chapter, we extend our coverage of server-side Web activities, as we investigate search engines, Webcrawlers, and other interesting server-side services.

Chapter 14

Help Them Find Their Way: Aids to Web Navigation

• •

In This Chapter

▶ Searching for Web satisfaction

▶ Staying out of the maze

▶ Providing added document structure

▶ Doing things the database way

▶ Avoiding diminished returns

▶ Where's the search leading us?

• •

*I*f you think that forms are where the fun is in HTML, be prepared to enjoy yourself further. In this chapter, you find out about additional widgets and techniques that you can use to make your documents searchable so that users can find things with a topic or keyword search. This is probably overkill for basic home pages, but it's a wonderful thing for larger, more complex documents. (In fact, without a searchable version of the HTML 2.0 DTD, we probably couldn't have written this book.)

You need to help your potential readers find your Web site and then help them move around easily within your site after they arrive. Fortunately, you have a lot of help from an unsavory-sounding source, the Web spider.

There's a Spider on the Web

If you think of the Web as a vast, gossamer skein of interconnected documents all over the world, you're pretty close to understanding the basic topology. But knowing how the strands of the Web are arranged is only half the picture. You also need to understand a little about the denizens inhabiting the Internet cyberspace realm.

Webcrawlers and Search Engines

In addition to the vast multitude (to be redundant) of users, happily browsing their way through the myriad links on the Web, cyberbeasts are frolicking through these documents as well. Some of them are computer programs, sometimes called *robots* or *spiders*, that do nothing but follow links around the Web (to see where they lead), and catalog and categorize what they find along the way.

The best known cyberbeasts lurk behind the scenes of popular search engine sites at

Yahoo: Guide to the WWW

```
http://www.Yahoo.com
```

Infoseek Net Search

```
http://www2.infoseek.com
```

The Internet Yellow Pages

```
http://www.mcp.com
```

Lycos Search Engine

```
http://lycos.cs.cmu.edu
```

Webcrawler Searching

```
http://www.webcrawler.com
```

Harvest Search Engine

```
http://harvest.cs.colorado.edu
```

WebAnts

```
http://thule.mt.cs.cmu.edu:8001/webants
```

We already mentioned search engines a time or two — like in Chapter 7 when we talked about the importance of using informative titles on your HTML documents. Well, call them spiders, robots, Webcrawlers, or "Hey, you!," these tireless, automatic searchers use document titles, headings, and the first paragraph of text to help them catalog and report on what they find. The search engines compile and manage the information that the spiders report to them.

Then, humans use this information when running a variety of Web search programs, like the ones previously listed, to help locate Web sites of interest to them.

If your Web site is listed in all of the major Web search sites, you are much more likely to attract a large number of users to view your work. Because the number of Web sites surpassed 1.5 million in 1995, users have a lot of variety to choose from! Just having yours listed at a search site greatly increases the number of visitations (hits), because it makes your site more visible to the public. Therefore, including the following information in your home page is of the utmost importance:

- ✔ **A title:** (with informative words that spiders can use as search words)
- ✔ **An introductory paragraph:** (again, with informative words used several times)
- ✔ **Anchors:** (links with URLs) to your other main pages with descriptive text

Placing these features in your home page, and in each of your Web pages, increases the chances that the spiders index your pages and give them a high relevance number (100 or 1,000 being the highest). Just being listed is helpful, but if a search retrieves 4,000 pages, only the first 10 to 25 are listed on the screen. The user must click a button to see the next batch. If your page isn't on the first screen, users are less likely to see it and, therefore, less likely to visit.

Spiders use a variety of complex methods to determine their relevance indexes, but all rely on the words in the title and first paragraph to a large extent. Some even use the number of times certain words occur in one page and not on other pages. So put each of the page's important words in the first paragraph a couple of times; that way, you're more likely to get a higher relevance ranking.

Don't wait for the spider to catch your site — register it

Each of the Web search sites listed earlier in this chapter provides a method for registering your site or at least telling them its URL. Make sure that you register or list your site at all possible locations. Such listings shouldn't cost you anything, and they don't take much time or effort, either. Also, you can pay to be listed at numerous online *malls* if you like their exposure and can afford their charges. These malls aren't used nearly as much as the free search engines, but if you're in a specialized industry, one or more of them may be right up your alley (find them by doing a search for **mall** or **market place** on one of the free search sites).

Searching Your Documents for Details . . .

The latest versions of these Web robots and crawlers don't delve deeply into the contents of all of the documents that they find. In computer lingo, they search broadly (go everywhere and grab one or a few pages from each site) but not deeply (they don't catalog the entire contents of every site). They'll probably find your site, but you're lucky if you get more than your home page indexed and listed in their search engine. If your site contains large, complex documents, you may need to support a different kind of search tool locally to make it easier for serious researchers to find exactly what they want.

The functionality that's required is something like the electronic equivalent of an index for a book: a list of keywords, topics, or phrases that provides pointers to their locations within the documents at your site. Fortunately for users, this kind of technology is easy to employ because the documents are already in electronic formats, and merely require a bit of extra massaging to accommodate this kind of use.

As a budding Web author, you may be wondering what you have to do to add this kind of capability to your documents. We can give you two different kinds of answers to this question. (And you can also see our discussion of CGI programs in Chapter 13.)

- ✔ **In nontechnical terms:** You have to create an index to your document and then figure out how to link that index to the actual content.

- ✔ **In technical terms:** You must do the following:

    - • Add the `<ISINDEX>` tag to your document's `<HEAD>` . . . `</HEAD>` section.

    - • Use a database or some similar program to build an index of keywords and phrases for your document.

    - • Identify all the index words as anchors for hypertext links in your document (so that the index can take you to those words and phrases).

    - • Establish the anchors in your document.

    - • Create a CGI program to handle user requests for keywords or phrases; the program should build a list of links for each corresponding instance in the document.

Basically, the way this sort of thing works is that you turn on the search capability in the user's browser (if available) by including the `<ISINDEX>` tag in your document's head section. Then, you provide a URL for the input-handling CGI program that builds search responses for users with specific requests. This program uses the electronic equivalent of an index — a list of keywords and phrases with pointers to their locations in the document's text — to respond to queries. These responses consist of HTML documents, with links to the locations in your document set where the requested keywords or phrases reside.

As programming problems go, this one is not too difficult. You do have to locate or build an indexing tool to prepare the data files that you can search in response to user queries. These data files usually consist of alphabetized (or ASCII-collated) lists of the keywords and phrases that your index recognizes. If you build your program so that it returns information for unsuccessful searches (`String not found` is good; a list of near-matches is even better), you are able to field some of the weird non sequiturs that bored users are sometimes tempted to try on your indexing program.

Then you can use the CGI program that searches the list to build an HTML document that lists the *hits* in order of occurrence, with links to the various locations in your document where matches were found. This creates a hotlist of these locations that your users can select to find the information they seek.

We also suggest pulling some surrounding text from each part of the document where a hit occurs and writing that to your *return page* with your CGI program as well. Including surrounding text lets users understand some of the context in which a hit occurs, and helps them to decide which links they really want to follow.

For an outstanding example of what a well-organized index can offer, please investigate the searchable version of the HTML 2.0 specification available at the following URL:

```
http://hopf.math.nwu.edu:80/html2.0/dosearch.html
```

This document is the work of the HTML working group, an Internet Engineering Task Force (IETF) group focused on making HTML into an Internet RFC-level specification.

The Bigger Things Get, The Easier It Is to Get Lost!

You're wondering why such indexing tools are worthwhile. It's because finding your way around complex collections of information — like the HTML 2.0 specification and its related DTD — can get kind of hairy without computer-aided assistance. A good rule of thumb for deciding whether you need indexing is to print out all the pages in your Web creation: If the pile of pages gets more than $1/4$ to $1/2$ inch thick, it's time to start thinking about indexing!

Indexing is also extremely valuable for sites that contain large documents that cover government rules or regulations. By their nature, these documents are best displayed in a single file, even though they may be 100 screens long. Readers of large documents greatly appreciate a searchable index for these documents.

If you're worried about how much work is involved, don't be. If your question is "Do I have to get into heavy database programming and implement all of the functionality mentioned in the preceding section just to make my document searchable?" — the answer is (fortunately) "No."

In fact, using the first type of search engine we mentioned at the beginning of this chapter — the kind that looks for documents based on titles — we were able to come up with a number of pointers to help you get started on this kind of effort for your own materials. Using the following search query to Yahoo!'s search engine

```
http://search.yahoo.com/bin/search?p=indexing
```

we came up with a number of tools and locations that we can recommend for further investigation:

- Indexmaker is a Perl script whose function is to produce an index for a virtual document consisting of a number of HTML files in a single directory. (This is the tool used to build the searchable HTML 2.0 Specification that helped us write this book.)

  ```
  http://hopf.math.nwu.edu/docs/utility.html#indexmaker
  ```

- For inclusion in an online searchable index at the MIT Artificial Intelligence Laboratory, try this URL:

  ```
  http://www.cs.indiana.edu/item-index/intro.html
  ```

- For local indexing and related services, please consult

  ```
  http://www.ai.mit.edu/tools/site-index.html
  ```

- Harvest is an integrated set of tools to gather, extract, organize, search, cache, and replicate relevant information on the Internet. (Harvest may be a bit too formal for documents not in need of wide distribution.)

  ```
  http://rd.cs.colorado.edu/harvest/
  ```

- Finally, here's the URL for a whole page of information about indexing and related tools:

  ```
  http://union.ncsa.uiuc.edu/HyperNews/get/www/indexing.html
  ```

Rest assured that somewhere in the haystack of information we just shared with you is the needle you may very well be seeking. Plus, it's no accident that the tool we admire most shows up first on the list! Yahoo!'s search engine is a great magnet for finding that needling program in the cyberhaystack!

Documentary Integuments: Indexes, Jump Tables, and Internal Links

You may have already heard this in several chapters, but we feel compelled to remind you that as documents get bigger and more complicated, more structure is needed. That's one reason why we think that indexes are a great idea. But it's also why you should make liberal and extensive use of internal links in your documents to help your readers navigate without their having to scroll, scroll, scroll.

Starting off a long document with a hyperlinked table of contents is a really good idea; it can act like a "jump table" to provide an immediate way to take your readers from the list of topics to the real thing with a click of the mouse. Also breaking longer blocks of text into regular screenfuls of information, coupled with navigation controls (which range from *navigation bars* to full-blown clickable *image maps* with nice-looking 3-D buttons) really helps your users keep from getting lost in your Web. Explicit document navigation controls should never be more than one screenful of information away. (Even better is always having a control in sight when you need it.)

Searchable indexes can greatly help readers in search of specific information, which is why they're a natural complement to our recommended frequency of navigation controls. Searchable indexes may be more difficult to implement, but if your content is appropriate, so be it. Your users will show their appreciation by returning time and again to your Web site, and they will bring their friends.

Doing Things the Database Way

For really long and complex documents (read "governmental regulations, tax code, how to build your own aircraft carrier, and so on"), the only good way to manage the information is with a database. Whether you decide to operate within the confines of a document-management program or use Paradox to build your own set of HTML document controls, when the number of files you have to manage exceeds 100, you'll appreciate getting some mechanical help and organization. Plus, the ability to search files on keywords or specific text makes finding things surprisingly easier. (We won't even mention the other nice things a good database can do for you, such as search and replace, automatic update propagation....)

This added level of structure and control will cost you, to be sure, but it's worth considering because of the time and effort that it can save you and your users. If you don't believe us, try managing a huge, intertwined collection of files without computer assistance for even a brief time. You'll be singing a different tune after dealing with changes and changes and changes....

Stay Away from Diminishing Returns

On the other hand, you can go overboard in organizing your materials. The temptation may be nearly overwhelming to break your documents into perfectly formatted single screens of beautifully laid-out information, for your user's enjoyment. Before you succumb to this impulse, remember the following "home truths" about the Web:

- ✔ All your beautiful graphics and on-screen controls aren't visible with character-mode browsers.

- ✔ What looks wonderful to you through your Super-Geewhiz 3-D VR Metaverse goggles looks pretty drab to the guy down the hall running the third version back of cello or Mosaic on a plain VGA monitor.

- ✔ When aiming for perfection, the "last 10 percent" usually costs as much — and takes as much time to achieve — as the first 90 percent. Don't waste your time making the excellent look sublime; you have better ways of filling your days (we hope)! Concentrate on content if you really want to better your site.

As thrilling as the quest for the perfect page may be, it's usually not worth the effort. And, if the people who pay the bills (and your salary) find out about your costly quest for the "holy WWW grail," even being penitent may not help you escape their buzz saw wrath. Remember the words of the mystic sage upon seeing the infinite majesty of the Universe: "Enough already!"

Where's the Search Leading Us?

As the Web becomes more commonplace and its publishing model better understood, you should expect to see more tools to help you add structure to your creations. Today, proper decorum suggests indexing larger, more complex documents, either with a linked table of contents or a searchable index.

By the time you read this, you'll be able to use some of the extensions to HTML via browsers like Netscape to simultaneously show graphical road maps of your documents' overall structure and relationships in one frame and the actual text in another. You will be able to orient your users with animated tutorials and other amazing feats of technology. The trend is clear, though: more and better communications based on a shared model of what Web pages can deliver, along with shared toolsets to help realize those models.

With this metaphorical view through the cyberportal of tomorrow, however, we leave the tools and advanced capabilities of HTML and CGI behind, and dive back into the reality of Web publishing, as you move on to tackle the nitty-gritty details of testing your work. Allez!

Part V

Call the Exterminator! Debugging Web Pages

The 5th Wave   By Rich Tennant

FROM THE DEPARTMENT OF DEFENSE COMES...

THE STEALTH PC   THE STEALTH LAN

THE STEALTH MAINFRAME   THE STEALTH LAPTOP

NO SMOKING

In this part . . .

We've tried to repeatedly stress the idea that once you think you've finished your HTML documents, only then does the real work begin. None of the subsequent effort is as important, demanding, and persnickety as the focus for this part of the book — namely, checking your work and testing your pages to make sure they behave the way you want them to.

Testing involves everything from spell-checking your content to tracing each and every link on each individual page to make sure that all the pieces hook together properly. In Chapter 15, we take you through a semi-formal approach to testing that should prepare you to thoroughly check your work.

In Chapter 16, the really crucial side of testing comes into play — that is, once you've checked your work to make sure it's mechanically correct and accurate, you need to make sure that your content is being properly communicated. This means interacting with prospective users, soliciting their feedback, and then acting on what they have to say. Then, because you need to recheck your work each time you make a change to one of your pages, you get to start all over again before you can proceed any further.

You may ask yourself, "What's the point of testing, if it means more work and rework?" The answer, in a word, is *quality*: In this part of the book, in addition to explaining the mechanics and methods of testing and working with feedback, we also justify the effort involved by the results produced. If you want quality Web pages that create a positive impression of you or your organization, testing is a crucial ingredient. By the time you work through the next two chapters, we sincerely hope you agree!

Chapter 15

Testing, Testing, 1-2-3

● ●

In This Chapter

▶ Learning why to test your Web pages

▶ Finding out whose opinions count

▶ Investigating what to test

▶ Testing your own Web pages

▶ Writing a test plan

● ●

*O*f course you want to get your wonderful Web creations on the Web ASAP. But — "You only get one chance to make a good first impression." Nobody has time to get it right the first time, but they can always make the time to fix it later. So why not take that little bit of time while you're creating your Web pages and run them through a few tests to validate their HTML syntax and to judge their acceptance by your audience?

Why Test Your Pages?

Do you want to read this on the `comp.infosystems.www.authoring.html` newsgroup and realize that you're the "Spacecadet"?

> "Did you see that mess of a home page Spacecadet put up yesterday?"

> "Yeah. What a rookie! He forgot to close a heading tag and I got inch-high text for a zillion screens."

> "That was a bummer. Did you run into the missing links, too? I guess he's never heard of testing before publishing."

Get the picture?

The rest of this chapter discusses how you can effectively test your own Web pages, along with HTML testing and validation procedures. Chapter 16 discusses how to get others to help you with your testing, how to obtain user feedback, and what to do with it.

What You Think Doesn't Count

It doesn't matter what you think of your Web pages. Of course you like your Web pages; you created them. They look great on your browser and your monitor and you're proud of them. So you can keep'm on your computer for only you to view, you can print'm, frame'm, and hang'm on your wall, or you can publish'm on the WWW. The choice is always yours.

You wanna publish'm, do ya? You want to share them with the WWW community, and show them your creations? You want them to visit your Web frequently and applaud your work? Now the tables have turned. No matter how much you like your Web pages, your users' likes and dislikes determine your Web's future.

The rest of this chapter assumes that, regardless of the content in your Web pages and regardless of your desired user audience, you want to provide Web pages that please your users and keep them coming back for more. The testing procedures discussed in the following paragraphsbelow are aimed at helping you create and maintain an enjoyable and informative site for your audience.

Rule number 1: Users Rule.

Rule number 2: When in doubt, refer to Rule number 1.

These rules do not mean that you must do everything every user asks of you. If your Web page is about earthquakes, you certainly don't want to include information on kite flying just because somebody requests it. However, if some of your users request a different arrangement of earthquake information so that they can review more easily, you would be well advised to accommodate their wishes. Change for the sake of change is upsetting to most folks, but change for the better, with valid reasons and advanced user education, can be beneficial to everyone involved.

Expect (and Test for) the Unexpected

"I should test for WHAT?" You should test for every possible, impossible, logical, illogical, expected, and unexpected occurrence. "But I want to publish my pages this century." Okay, then make sure that you plan for the *somewhat* unexpected.

In particular, you want to test in the following three areas:

✔ **Predicted ranges and values:** Everything that you intentionally put into your Web pages and expect users to access. This includes all links, images, `ALT="wording"`, forms input sections and expected values, clickable map areas, and so on.

✔ **Boundaries:** The edges of the envelope of the expected. More problems occur at the edges than in the middle of most computer programs, which is what your HTML-coded Web page strongly resembles. Many programs work perfectly with expected values and correctly ignore values outside their boundaries, but then fail on those values at the exact boundaries between the expected and the unexpected.

For example, making the expected range from 1 to 100 and putting in an error-checking routine for values less than 0 and more than 101 may work fine until someone puts in 0 or 101. Make sure you try the boundary values, too!

✔ **Outside the boundaries:** Everything not included in the two preceding bullets. Of course you can't click on every pixel on every page any more than you can enter every out-of-range value on every form. You can try a few out-of-bounds values and clicks to make sure you haven't missed the somewhat obvious. Many a mistake has been found in a program when the programmer sneezed, causing him to click his mouse button with the cursor on a place where "no user in his right mind would ever click."

Don't lose sleep over testing absolutely everything. Do approach testing as something that definitely benefits your Web pages if done logically, methodically, and repeatedly during your Web page development and maintenance.

In Vitro Vitrification: Alpha Testing Methods

Testing your Web pages is very much like testing any computer program. A certain amount of testing occurs while you are in the midst of creating the page because you have to look at it with a browser or your HTML editor's browser view. If you are using a completely WYSIWYG HTML authoring environment, most of the developmental HTML syntax testing is done for you by the authoring program.

As you proceed with your development of a page, you tag and view, tag and view, and so on, until you decide that you like what you see. When you have coded all features that you want into the page, it's ready for more stringent testing.

The following steps generally guide you through what is called the *alpha* testing phase. You and only a few trusted assistants Accomplish this phase. Most of the big, ugly, and obvious problems should be removed by the end of alpha testing. If you're developing your own home page and personal Web, you should still go through the steps because you're developing a Web site to show it off to the WWW community.

1. **Run it through a spell-checker.**

   And while you're at it, correct the spelling.

2. **Test the page by itself on your own computer with local files and relative URLs.**

   Fix the problems and test again.

3. **Test the page in the Web of other pages on your own computer.**

   Fix the problems and test again.

4. **Test the page by itself on the Web server in your private area with relative or full URLs.**

   Fix the problems and test again.

5. **Submit the page's URL to an online HTML validation form for syntax checking.**

   Fix the problems and resubmit until it's clean. Hey, nobody produces perfect code the first time.

6. **Test the page with the other pages in your private Web on the Web server.**

   Fix the problems and test again.

7. **Enlist a few work associates or close friends to critique the page.**

   Otherwise, keep it private and get them to keep quiet about it. Fix the problems and test again.

After iterations of comments and revisions until your alpha testers abandon you — or until they don't find anything else to nitpick — your page(s) may be ready for honest-to-goodness beta testing (where you actually ask other people to pick your page apart and tell you about it). That's discussed in the next chapter. The rest of this chapter explains some details of your alpha testing.

WebBuilder, test thy HTML thyself

The two strongest reasons for testing your Web pages with an HTML testing and validation program prior to making them available to the WWW community are

✔ Your Web pages may contain HTML tag errors or nonstandard tags that would cause them to display improperly on some browsers.

✔ Your Web pages may not contain either required or optional HTML tags that are important to Web crawlers or spiders in the future. Without proper usage of the tags that crawlers search on, your pages may not be listed in future indexes and jump pages; therefore, it won't be easy for users to find your Web.

If you haven't created your page on a strict HTML syntax-checking, authoring system, submit it to one of the following online HTML syntax validation systems.

Weblint is a Perl script that checks your HTML for errors over the Web through an HTML form, or you can ftp it, as follows:

```
http://www.khoros.unm.edu/staff/neilb/weblint/lintform.html
ftp.khoros.unm.edu/pub/perl/www
```

Htmlchek version 4.1 is an HTML syntax and cross-reference checker that checks HTML documents for errors, creates a cross-reference, automatically expands entities (such as European characters) to their proper HTML form, and performs other useful services. It is available via the Web or by anonymous ftp, as follows:

```
http://uts.cc.utexas.edu/~churchh/htmlchek.html
ftp.cs.buffalo.edu/pub/htmlchek
```

Lvrfy is a simple, UNIX-based link-checking program that checks your pages for broken links. It's available from

```
http://www.cs.dartmouth.edu/~crow/lvrfy.html
```

Checker is a broken-link finder. Versions of this program are available for numerous systems at:

```
http://www.ugrad.cs.ubc.ca/spider/q7f192/branch/checker.html
```

Georgia Tech College of Computing HTML Validation Service at

```
http://www.cc.gatech.edu/grads/j/Kipp.Jones/HaLidation/validation-
            form.html
```

Web Techs HTML Validation Service validates HTML 2.0, 3.0, the Mozilla DTD from Netscape, and HotJava DTD from Sun Microsystems at

```
http://www.webtechs.com/html-val-svc/index.html
```

HTML Form-Testing Home Page at

```
http://www.research.digital.com/nsl/formtest/
```

Or you can download a stand-alone UNIX HTML syntax checker from

```
http://www.webtechs.com/html-tk/
```

After you get the report from one of the syntax checkers, revise your Web page if necessary. Most of these syntax checkers adhere to the HTML 2.0 DTD, so any tags that you use that don't conform may be marked as errors (the WebTechs Validation Service also supports HTML 3.0, the Mozilla, and HotJava DTDs). If you want to continue to use tags that are specific for certain browsers, do it knowing that your page will not look the way you expect on other browsers. Understand also that your pages may not be included properly in Web spider-compiled indexes, depending on which extended tags you use.

Webcrawler may not pick up your Web page if you use the `<!DOCTYPE>` tag with a reference to HTML 3.0, because HTML 3.0 is not officially approved.

Iteration, iteration, iteration

Creating your Web pages and assembling your Web is a repetitive, *build-and-change* process. After you have more than one page, changes on any single page may affect others. Unless you repeat the same tests each time you make a change, you may find out the hard way from your users that errors have crept into your pages. Among the many things that build-and-change requires — unless you have Data's perfect recall — is that you write down your testing procedures and keep track of things as you go.

Written test plans

You actually started the testing and validation of your Web pages when you sketched the layout of each page and your overall Web structure. These sketches are the first documents in your test plan (see — you've already finished something, and you didn't even know you'd started yet).

For your personal Web, your test plan may consist of only a copy of these layout sketches with a checklist of testing steps that you want to use on each page. This effort takes a bit of thinking and some of your valuable time, but the results make you happy later. If you think the Maytag guy is unlucky, you should try things the other way around sometime!

If you're in a business or institutional environment, you are probably more accustomed to formalized, structured development and testing. Familiarity with this environment can help your undoubtedly more complex Web accomplish its goals.

The following section presents a generic alpha test plan. Those of you who have a need to produce this type of document for your organization or anyone who really wants to proceed with testing your Web pages in an extremely orderly fashion may modify it to suit your specific needs. And for the rest of you, it won't strain your brain to read over the plan, too. Remember, do it right the first time or you'll have to take the time to fix it later.

Alpha Test Plan

Introduction

Purpose

Provide a comprehensive plan for testing the accuracy and completeness of the Web page at stages during the development cycle or prior to the release of a new version.

Scope

The test plan will encompass testing the user-level functionality of all features, the accuracy of the data generated, the agreement of the user guide information with the Web page operation, the agreement of the normative data from the manuals and errata sheets with the Web page data, and the compatibility of the Web page with various hardware and software configurations.

Test overview

- ✔ Test all functions of the Web page under expected usage conditions with appropriate hardware and software.

- ✔ Test all functions under abnormal usage conditions, such as inappropriate hardware or software, incorrect or extreme data conditions, and operator errors.

- ✔ Test the accuracy of any data by comparing Webpage-generated values with known values.

Goals

- Determine the level of functionality and performance of the Web page.
- Document all operational abnormalities and Web page errors in an efficient and flexible test-tracking system.
- Verify Web page and user information correlation.

Schedule and resources

Testing begins on (date) and continues until the test plan is completed and there are no correctable errors found on the Web page. The Software Testing and Quality Assurance Department staff (you and your friends) provide full-time testing. Make sure that you draft only people close to you who can keep the location of your pages to themselves. You don't need the aggravation of unwanted testers at this point in your page development. When you get these helpers, you need to give them some instructions on what type of feedback you want. At the simplest, you can just ask them to e-mail you with any problems or suggestions they may have. The e-mail method works if they are conscientious, organized people, which is the only type you want for your alpha test helpers.

Tester form

To really help your testers (and yourself), provide them with a simple text form to complete and e-mail to you with each problem. Request at least the following on your form:

- Tester's name and e-mail address
- Date on which the problem was found
- Page title and URL
- Page version date/time
- Feature/function affected
- Formatting
- Text/data
- Link (URL)
- Image (URL)
- Form (URL)
- Description of problem
- How to duplicate problem
- Comments and suggestions for solutions

Suggest to your testers that it would greatly help you if they would religiously fill in all information on a separate form for each problem. When the forms start clogging up your e-mail in-box, you'll need a place to store them and a method of sorting them. Any reasonable method, from printing each and visually sorting them to importing them into a database program, will work. Use the one method that works for you. Keep in mind that you probably want to use it for the beta test feedback also, so choose a method that can handle the number of messages you expect — then double that number to get ready for the unexpected!

System configurations

Testing is conducted by using the following system configurations as representative of systems in the field:

- **Browsers:** List all browsers to be tested. If possible, try all browsers that you think your target audience may use (or every one you know about, anyway).

- **Computers:** List all computer systems to be tested in conjunction with the browsers. Many browsers work on more than one system (such as, PC with Windows, Macintosh, X-Windows, and so on).

- **Web servers:** List Web-server software to be tested with CGI scripts and forms. You may be limited to your own Internet service provider or your business or institution's Web server, but test it thoroughly and completely.

Test method and evaluation

- Testers evaluate Web page functionality and performance primarily at the user level by performing operations with keyboard and mouse input and evaluating data generated by the Web page.

- Testers document Web page errors and operational abnormalities by recording the following information when a problem is encountered: feature/function affected, page version date/time, date problem found, tester's name, description of problem, method of re-creation, and any other notes that may help the developer understand and resolve the problem. Priorities are assigned to the problems as they are received: priority 1 – system lockup or data corruption; priority 2 – cosmetics (spelling, wording, screens); priority 3 – inconvenient operation.

- The document containing Web page problems is updated as often as possible and is made available to the developers for resolution of the problems.

Performance and functionality testing

Screen appearance: browse through your hard work

Inspect each screen and look for inaccuracies or omissions related to spelling, formatting, and layout. Download and install all the browsers that will run on your own computer and test with them first. Make a deal with Web friends who have different types of computers. Have them test your pages in return for your testing their Web pages with your computer. Turnabout is still fair play, and it exposes you (and them) to new ideas and materials!

Link operation and content

Verify that each link functions correctly and that each destination URL exists and presents the information named in the hyperlink text.

Forms operation

Verify that each form correctly receives, processes, and records the user's responses. Verify that the Web server properly stores the data and delivers it to the appropriate location in the desired format.

Clickable map operation

Verify that clicking on each portion of the map displays the appropriate image or page.

Limits and boundary checking

Test all limit and boundary conditions, such as high and low numerical values and text amounts in forms. Make sure that you test the edges, not just outside the expected limits.

The A-Team's Finished!

Keeping your pages tightly controlled and getting rapid problem reports ensure fast correction of problems. If you've designed your pages well, you don't need a lot of superfluous nitpicking of your style or layout at this point in the testing. You want to make sure the pages display properly and the links work. Even if you perform all the testing discussed above and they do, you really should continue with the next step, beta testing, as discussed in the next chapter. This step is where you find out if anyone but you really likes your Web page(s).

Chapter 16

It Doesn't Matter What YOU Think

In This Chapter

▶ Performing a beta test

▶ Finding the right testers

▶ Keeping your sanity

▶ Promoting feedback

▶ Learning from your users

▶ Wondering when to quit testing

*G*oing out and actively seeking the opinions of strangers about your fantastic Web pages seems like a masochistic act, doesn't it? But because you don't want to keep it all to yourself, you need to know what your potential audience thinks. Additionally, you need to continue to receive feedback from your users throughout the time that you have your pages on the Web. Read on to see how to accomplish this and more. At the end of the chapter we'll even tell you when to stop . . . testing, that is.

Beta Testing

You're not alone in your quest for the perfect Web. Practically everyone on the WWW would like every single page they view to match their vision of perfection. In fact, millions of them will be more than happy to judge your Web. The key is to get a few of them to help you make it better.

During beta testing, you enlist a larger (but still manageable) group of WWW users to help you make your Web pages the best thing since coffee and candy bars. They not only test the performance and functionality, they generously advise you as to how stupid you were to put the image of the sparrow in with the finches, and so on. They spot problems that you didn't even know were problems. What? Things that you looked at every day but ignored can bother enough of your beta testers that you may decide to change them, the problems, that is — not the beta testers!

You can use the same basic technical form that you used during alpha testing for beta testing. However, you should ask at least the following additional questions:

- ✔ Do the pages present the material in the best manner to attract their intended users?
- ✔ Do the pages answer the intended users' questions quickly and obviously?
- ✔ Will the pages cause the users to do whatever they are attempting to get them to do (buy a product, visit a location, call on the phone, and so on)?

Ask them to tell you their specific likes and dislikes, and your beta testers will oblige you; believe us, they really will!

Finding beta testers

We hope that you can find beta testers who are directly interested in the content that your Web pages present. You need feedback on their likes and dislikes from that standpoint as well as their impressions of your Web's functionality. They are your primary audience, albeit a small portion of it, so treat them well.

Find your beta testing participants by posting an invitation in relevant newsgroups. Simply ask for people who are interested in helping you test your new Web page. Filter them by asking them to e-mail their names, addresses, phone numbers, backgrounds in your content area, and some reasons why they think that they would be good beta testers. E-mail immediate thank-yous to everyone who replies with a noncommittal statement that you were overwhelmed by the response and will get back to everyone shortly.

If you decide not to use some respondents, which is unlikely, send each of them a very nice e-mail thanking them profusely and saying that you ran out of your allotted testing spaces before getting to their name, or something equally nice.

Do a good deed for someone and he will tell three friends about it. Do something that makes someone mad and he'll tell 11 people what a jerk you are. You may not be able to make everyone happy, but try your best not to irritate your users!

E-mail each of your beta testers an announcement of each change cycle, with a list of revisions and a copy of the beta test report form you would like them to complete and return. Thank each tester for each problem report. Make sure that you notice the ones whose problem reports resulted in a revision. Take the time to make real friends out of your beta testers and you will benefit from it for a long, long time. Your beta testers are your users. Remember **Rule number 1**? (If you don't, see Chapter 15.)

Cycling ahead of the gremlins

No, a revision cycle isn't something you pedal backward. It's a method of handling problems and changes in your pages in an orderly fashion. Simply stated, you don't fix problems in the order in which you receive them. Sure, you're anxious to clean up your pages, but you must prioritize the problems that you (or others) find. If you don't prioritize, fixing the changes can cost you more time in the long run. You'll find that for a large, complex Web, a one-week revision cycle is probably the shortest time period possible, with a two-week cycle being less anxiety provoking.

Cycling your revisions also helps you keep ahead of the insidious gremlins called *unexpected side effects*. These occur when a seemingly small change is made in one page without enough thought put into its effects and without any testing of the entire Web afterward. An example is changing an image that is linked to every page in your Web. Suppose you put the image in the wrong directory. It wouldn't show up at all and that would be easy to detect. But suppose you change the e-mail address for feedback and make an error. You may not find out about that error for quite a while, unless you use the new address to send yourself mail immediately upon installing the change. (Now that we think about it, this is a good testing technique, too — why don't you try it?)

By batch-processing the prioritized problems, you can give everyone in your testing crew adequate time to thoroughly perform his or her validation. While they are testing your most recent set of revisions, you can be working on the next set. Be sure that you note your fixes on each problem form as completely as the problem itself was noted. Also, you must be careful to change the version number and revision date/time on each page that you change and include this information on the problem fix section of the form or database.

From your testing report database, make and keep an ongoing list of problems. Prioritize them in your own order. Then decide which problem or group of problems to fix. Consider not only the time it takes to revise the HTML documents, but also the time needed to run the changed pages on the entire Web completely through your test checklists on all appropriate browsers and platforms. With this time frame in mind, you'll probably wisely decide that daily changes aren't possible.

Gamma Testing and Beyond?

Although we don't discuss an actual gamma category of testing, you should consider all users who view your Web pages as testers and potential assistants in your ongoing page development. Of course, you understand that the Web is alive, don't you? And your Web pages are a living part of the whole WWW. Therefore, you must feed and nurture your Web to keep it up-to-date, otherwise it loses its users and fades away into the cosmos. To prevent this, you need to use good methods of requesting and encouraging user feedback, right in your Web pages. Your e-mail address suffices at a minimum, but a nice form does the job much better.

There's nothing crazy about a sanity check!

By now you're saying to yourself, "What's all this about two-week revision cycles, fancy forms, and testers all over the place? My pages aren't going to be as buggy as a stray dog." You're probably correct in that sentiment, but you have the idea now that without careful planning and cyclic testing, you may be the one who goes buggy.

To keep this from happening, take the following advice: Keep two separate copies of your Web on your own computer and on your Web server (if the space is available). Perform all changes on the *working* copy while the *published* copy is in use. While you're testing, you can compare the performance and functionality of the working copy to the published copy and see the changes.

When you've completed a revision cycle, copy the working files over the published files — after making a backup of course. If you've used the relative URLs properly, you shouldn't need to change anything in the revised working files before copying them over the old published files. They'll be ready for users instantly.

Stick it to me: the importance of feedback

Ahhhh, users. Funny how they keep popping up here, there, and everywhere. Funny how you feed them your Web pages and ask for feedback from them. User feedback is the lifeblood of your Web, but if you're not careful, it is as useful as the feedback from an amplifier with a microphone in front of the speaker. That is, it makes you sit up and take notice, but it won't give you enough useful information to solve the problem. If you like playing Sherlock Holmes, by all means just put a little message at the bottom of your home page requesting that feedback be sent to your e-mail address.

However, your users may not know exactly how to phrase their wants and needs so that you can instantly understand them. It's up to you to give them a hand with feedback forms, nicely worded requests, and a warm e-mail thank-you when they do respond (no matter what they say). You'll definitely get e-mail when things are broken or awry, and you'll learn to appreciate the occasional pat on the back that comes (all too rarely) from your users.

Building in a report card

If you aren't getting any feedback, you may need to give your users a better method of responding to you, such as a feedback form. There's nothing quite like giving folks a chance to "grade" you to bring out their likes and dislikes. One of the better ways of deciding what kind of feedback form to use is to look around the Web for forms that you like. Check out their source to see how the author created them. If that author used a script that works on your Web server, create one like it for yourself. The server WebMaster (or "god," to you) can probably help you in this area, if you ask nicely.

A simple text form on a page of its own for users to copy, fill in, and e-mail back to you is better than nothing. A real CGI form with questions and response boxes is much better. We talked about these in Chapter 10. Although it's important to be specific in your requests for information, a detailed checkbox form with no place for general comments can miss some valuable information. Give the users space to be creative after you've aroused their interest with your questions or check boxes.

Very serious feedback methods

If you really want information, ask about something specific. Tell users that you're thinking of adding something or changing something and ask them to tell you what they think about your idea. Have a contest in which you give a prize to the person who submits the best or worst feature of your Web and tells why. Get your users involved in your Web and its design, and you'll all benefit. Following are specific methods of getting more feedback.

Hocus-pocus, focus groups

If you're seriously trying to accomplish a set of goals with your Web pages, you may want to try the focus group approach, used so successfully by marketing and advertising companies. This activity can be similar to beta testing, but with a very select group. You would e-mail each group member a request to participate and provide him or her with a special URL to view the pages in question. To make this approach work well, you need to plan it carefully. This can be more of a marketing exercise than Web page testing, but it may be very important to you and your enterprise. You may want to involve your marketing department or advertising consultant in the planning process and in creating the appropriate questionnaires.

Making friends with movers and shakers

Don't just lurk in the newsgroups, PARTICIPATE. Make online friends with the folks who are in-the-know in your industry's newsgroup. If you know the addresses of the important folks in your chosen field of interest, e-mail them an announcement of your Web's grand opening and invite them to drop in. Keep them informed of great new information on your site but don't make a pest of yourself. Ask them if they've been looking for some type of information on the Net but can't seem to find it in your area. Then find it, provide it, and let them know about it while you thank them profusely for their suggestion.

Don't just listen, do something!

When your users lavish you with their feedback, thank them immediately via e-mail. Then use their feedback to better your Web. The best thanks you can give your users is to put their great ideas to use in a timely manner and let everyone know that you appreciate the support.

Be careful, though, in giving credit directly in your Web pages to folks whose feedback you use for a specific change. A few people who don't like the change could blame the feedback provider instead of you. You're the one who is trying to keep your audience happy, so you're the one who has to take the abuse from disgruntled users. It's usually better to thank users personally via e-mail and as a general group in your Web pages, if you feel the need to do so publicly.

Knowing When to Quit (Testing)

Now that you're completely catatonic with fear about opening up your precious Web to the prying eyes of the WWW masses, take solace in knowing that it's only a bunch of electrons running around in wires and silicon. You've nothing to fear from the WWW. No matter how carefully you plan, design, code, and test your Web pages, someone will find something that they don't like. This is a function of the differences in outlook and perspective of millions of people on the WWW.

"You can't please everyone." You can try to please as many of your intended audience as possible within your time and energy limits. Unless you have a deadline imposed by your business or institution that dictates when you open your Web to the Net, you are the sole judge of when it's ready for its grand opening. So open it up when you've tested it thoroughly and can't find any more "real" problems (but never quit testing!). And above all, SMILE; this is supposed to be fun!

Part VI
Going Public: Serving Up Your Web Pages

The 5th Wave   By Rich Tennant

IT'S THEIR BBS ALRIGHT, AND I THINK THEY'VE FIGURED OUT WHO "STRANDED" IS, SO BE CAREFUL WHAT YOU SAY.

In this part . . .

Having survived the rigors of testing and the eye-popping advantages of user feedback, you're finally ready to publish your Web pages and invite the world on in. In this part of the book you find out the brutal truth about getting your message out to the users who stop by to visit your site.

In fact, just because you've got some pages doesn't mean the world will beat a path to your door. You need to be prepared to deliver those pages on a Web server, and you'll want to decide whether that server should be yours or if you should join forces with a service provider to play host to your content. Chapter 17 helps uncover the costs and consequences of the "build versus buy" decision when it comes to Web servers.

When your pages are available for public access, then you can start worrying about how to publicize their availability. Chapter 18 takes you through the kind of public relations blitz you might want to undertake to drag the world to your Web site, hopefully without too much kicking or screaming. Along the way, you learn about acceptable use policies on the Internet and where to draw the line between "tasteful self-promotion" and "shameless hype." Maybe you can prevent a potential flame war just by observing a few discreet rules of netiquette!

After you've lived with your Web pages for a while, you have to learn how to live with change. Your content will get stale and need updating, your links will grow cold, and you'll have to run to keep up with the relentless changes in your content and your users' interests. Chapter 19 helps to brace you for this activity. We hope you'll learn to think of maintenance as an adventure and a way of life rather than as a total waste of time! Just remember, encouraging repeat visits to your pages requires a regular refreshment of the value that they can provide.

All in all, you should be ready to deal with the public on its own terms by the time you've completed this part of the book. If you're ready for change, you'll be ready for anything!

Chapter 17

So You've Woven a Web: What Now?

. . . .

. . . .

*O*kay, so you've decided to go ahead and share your Web pages with God and everybody. After you've made this decision, though, you have to grapple with some interesting issues and get ready to make your pages (and yourself) available to the world at large.

Inviting the World to Your Door

When you start thinking "It's time to publish these pages," you have to decide if they are really ready for prime time. Also, you must be prepared to face scrutiny, the likes of which you may never have faced before. (Remember, there are estimates of 20+ million Internet users!) Then there's the implication of asking for feedback — which we heartily recommend — which means adopting a regular routine of Web page tweaking and fiddling to get (and keep) things current and correct.

Finally, you have the build-versus-buy decision when it comes to serving up Web pages — that is, should you hire a service provider to offer your pages on their server, or should you consider putting up your own server and inviting the world to your very own Web server?

In this chapter, we tackle all these issues, and more, as we investigate how to publish your Web pages. By the time you've read the whole thing, you should be prepared to do some comparison shopping with your friendly neighborhood (and national) service providers. You should also be armed to make the decision whether to have a provider publish your pages or to do it on your own.

Stay Focused on Your Purpose

Before you show your pages to the world, you need to ask yourself yet again, "What it is it that my Web pages are trying to communicate?" Write down your list of objectives and keep them handy.

Next, talk to your beta testers and selected members of your target audience about your pages. Let them look over your pages and then ask *them* what they think that you're hoping to communicate. Write that stuff down, too.

Compare your list of objectives to your informal audience survey. If you don't get at least a 50 percent overlap, it's time to figure out what's not working and why. If you can follow up to get someone you know and trust to give you completely honest feedback, that's the best thing to try next. If you can't, you want to dig through your survey materials to try to figure out what's missing the mark and adjust your content accordingly.

Until you get the overlap you're shooting for, you have to keep testing your pages on your target audience. There's simply no point in going public until you're pretty sure that what you think your pages communicate is what your audience thinks they communicate, too. This may seem incredibly obvious, but take our word for it — this is the most important quality control you can do.

Make Sure Your Users Know Who's in Charge!

The freewheeling nature of the Web poses a nearly irresistible temptation to turn your home page into the crossroads of the world and to make it a meeting place for all and sundry. Don't forget that the main purpose of your site is to communicate the information that you so laboriously developed.

In other words, the key factor in deciding what other links to include on your pages has to be *relevance*. Here are questions you should ask before including links to other people's URLs:

> ✔ Do these other sites have content related to yours?
>
> ✔ Do they appeal to the same audience for more or less the same reasons?
>
> ✔ Do they complement your material or detract from it?
>
> ✔ Can they handle more traffic, or are they already overloaded with hits?
>
> ✔ Are those other sites willing to reciprocate and include pointers to your pages on theirs, as well as the other way around? Don't expect this kind of treatment from CERN, W3, or other large and important sites on the Web, but do expect it from your colleagues and fellows and from organizations with which you're affiliated.

The whole idea is to connect your pages with other resources that enhance the value of your content and that complement your overall goals and objectives. Among other things, this means that if you're trying to sell widgets to your audience, you probably don't want to include links to your competitors' pages. On the other hand, you probably do want to include links to relevant widget standards and to the Institute for Widget Research.

Publish, or Perish the Thought!

But hey, don't let these steps that we recommend for your Web page production process stop you from making your content available on the Internet. If you frequently communicate with your customers or colleagues by using printed materials, the best way to view the Web is as an alternative to print. Just remember that, unlike print, the Web is multidimensional: That is, you don't necessarily need to stick only to the two dimensions so familiar to the "print-obsessed" people in this world.

It's good for business . . .

This is a useful way to think about the Web, if your interests are business-related. If that's the case, you're probably already familiar with the concept of *corporate communications* — that is, the deliberate design and delivery of messages, in whatever medium, to create an image and aid the purchase of products.

For you, the Web can be another way to disseminate your finely crafted messages. Just be sure to observe the antihype leanings of the Internet crowd, and you'll do just fine. Up-front, high-pressure sales tactics aren't appreciated; also a VERY BAD idea is cross-posting an announcement of your Web pages to every newsgroup known to man. (This is called *spamming* in Internet-speak and is universally reviled.)

Another term for publishing a blurb about your company is "hanging your shingle on the Internet." Hanging your shingle is a passive advertisement, not an in-your-face beer commercial between innings. Unless your blurb includes meaningful content and you can appeal to the interest of a fickle, impatient group of Netsurfers, hanging a shingle on the Internet can be a real ho-hum experience!

... and it's good for pleasure!

If yours is a personal page, or you're caught in the grip of what some people — not us! — would call a fond obsession, your reasons for Webbing up may be different from commercial enterprises. In this case, you still want to make sure that a target audience agrees that you're not sending mixed messages to the World Wide Web. But you can give yourself a lot more latitude in focus, goals, and objectives.

Back to the content

Be your focus crassly commercial or pristinely personal, it all comes back to the content. If your pages read well, include a modicum of easily accessible, interesting information, and are easy to navigate, you'll find yourself on the berm of the Information Superhighway with lots of traffic whizzing by. If your pages don't scan, if they're completely idiosyncratic, or if they are totally boring, you'll find yourself in the electronic equivalent of the boondocks, far away from the madding crowds with nary a traveler in sight.

How do you find out which path you're on? It's simple: Ask you target audience! Most of the comments you get back are driven by the content, so that should tell you where to spend the bulk of your efforts.

Dealing and Wheeling: Making Arrangements with an Internet Service Provider

When you're ready to go public, one option to consider is this: Simply transport your Web pages *en masse* to a provider that already offers a Web server.

This process is pretty straightforward, but it does require some planning. It also requires checking some basic compatibility issues. Following are questions you should ask yourself and any Internet service provider whose Web server you might consider jumping onto:

✔ What kind of *httpd* server does it have? Does the server conform to the CERN release, the NCSA release, or neither? Depending on the answer, you'll need to make some script adjustments. Web spaces are not completely portable, so make sure that you're calling the right kind of map-handling application and that your image map files are in a compatible format. Be warned that adapting an existing set of Web documents from one environment to another can be time-consuming, hair-raising, and a downright pain in the you-know-what!

✔ What kind of dependencies do you have in your Web pages? Do you use <BASE> tags to set reference URLs? If so, you'll have to change the URLs to reflect their new location. While you're at it, check every link in every page to make sure that all the proper changes get made. The only good link is a working link, and the only known working link is a tested link!

✔ How much data do you have in your pages? How likely is it that users will download all of your pages? Most service providers charge a per-megabyte transfer fee for Web access in addition to a monthly account fee (and usually setup fees as well). The more data you want to share with the world, the more likely it is that transfer costs will contribute to your build-versus-buy decision.

✔ How much demand will you likely have for your pages? This is just another way of asking, "How big is your audience?" If you already know the audience, you can probably guess at the answer. This will also help to guesstimate the amount of traffic that you generate.

If you decide to work with an Internet service provider, the amount of data transferred from your pages to your users in a month is likely to be a primary determinant of cost.

Most of the vendors that we surveyed indicated monthly account fees of $50 to $150 for a commercial account with Web page services available. The same vendors assessed charges of two to ten cents per megabyte of data transfer per month. This might not sound like much until you stop to figure that only 20 users a day at 2 megabytes apiece account for charges of $12 to $61 a month; only 100 users a day raise those figures to $120 to $610 for the same period!

If your space becomes heavily visited — for example, like the CBS Web site for the NCAA basketball tournament in March, 1995 — it's possible that you could have tens of thousands of visits per day. At the rates listed above, your costs to an outside provider would go from $12,000 to $61,000 *per month* for such service.

Where to draw the line?

Somewhere between 100 and 1,000 users a day, you cross the line between buy versus build. For charges of less than $500 per month, contracting for Web server access makes sense. Consider the analysis in Table 17-1.

Table 17-1
Calculating Monthly Charges for Various Usage Profiles

Web Size (MB):	$Cost Per MB Xfer:	Users Per Day (Avg):	Monthly Account:	Monthly Costs:
2 MB	$0.10	50	$50	$354.16
5 MB	$0.07	50	$100	$632.29
10 MB	$0.05	100	$150	$1,670.83

Assumption: Average of 30.416 days per month used for calculations (30.416 = 365/12).

By the time that you get to the second row in the table, it's time to start thinking about installing your own Web server. By the time that you reach the third row, the numbers make your choice clear (just be sure to adjust these meaningless averages with your own researched numbers before making any rash decisions).

In fact, the closer your projections are to the high end of this scale, the more likely you will be to consider setting up your own Web server. Table 17-2 covers the flip side of this analysis — figuring the costs of doing it yourself — based on the assumptions covered immediately after the table.

Table 17-2   Average Costs for Web Do-It-Yourselfers

Monthly Costs	Server Phone Line	Provider Account	Staff	Monthly Total
$350.00[1]	$36.00[2]	$80.00[3]	$600.00[4]	$906.00
$350.00	$70.00[5]	$150.00[6]	$600.00	$1,170.00
$500.00[7]	$70.00	$150.00	$750.00[8]	$1,470.00
$500.00	$140.00[9]	$300.00[10]	$750.00	$1,690.00

Assumptions (corresponding to the superscript numbers in Table 17-2:)

1. Pentium P90, 64 MB RAM, 2x1.2 GB HD, etc. (Total system cost: $4K, amortized over 36 months at 10% interest; based on equivalent system lease costs.)

2. Average monthly cost for dedicated 28.8 Kbps line to provider (telephone costs).

3. Average monthly cost for dedicated 28.8 Kbps line to Internet access provider.

4. One-fourth time for system administrator earning approximately $30K per year.

5. Average monthly cost for ISDN connection through phone company.

6. Average monthly cost for dedicated ISDN account with Internet access provider.

7. Pentium P133, 64 MB memory, 4 GB disk, etc. (Total system cost: $6K, amortized over 36 months at 10% interest; based on equivalent system lease costs.)

8. One-quarter time for system administrator/Web programmer at $36K per year.

9. Average monthly cost for two "B" channels' ISDN access from the telephone company.

10. Average monthly account cost for a dedicated 128 Kbps line from Internet access provider to support two "B" channels.

The quick-and-dirty restatement of Table 17-2 is, "If the bill from your Internet service provider runs more than $900 a month, it's time to consider putting up your own server." You still want to adjust costs (especially the salary for your Web administrator) to your own figures, but this is a reasonably good rule of thumb.

What to work out with your provider

If your analysis puts you down on the *buy* side of the decision, you want to find an Internet service provider that can host your Web pages. In addition to the questions we mentioned earlier, you want to find out a few more things. It's also reasonable to expect your provider to have some questions for you.

What else you need to find out

✔ Ask the provider for references from individuals and organizations that already have their Web pages on the provider's server. Be sure to check with as many of these references as you can. Ask them questions about the provider's quality of service, their responsiveness to problems, the percentage of the system's overall uptime, and user complaints, if any. You want to find out how good the provider is at providing Internet access, so ask anything else along these lines that you can think of. If the reference accounts use forms or other input-handling programs, ask them to explain how they managed to install and use these programs.

✔ Have the service provider explain its accounting system to you: "How does it know how many users are visiting your pages each day?" and "How does it measure the data transfer it's charging you for?"

✔ Find out how widely distributed this server's links are on the Web: Use a search engine like Lycos or Yahoo! to look for its URL in other pages and see what turns up. More links are better, in this case!

✔ Ask how long it's been in this business and what its growth plan is — in other words, what's its plan to accommodate increased traffic?

✔ Find out how easy it is to run your own CGI scripts or other input-handling programs on their system. Ask for a free trial period and see how things go. Ask about all the tools and other widgets you might need (such as, "How current is their Perl interpreter? Do they have the right version of the map-handling software?"). Ask about consulting services or what other kind of help is available to get your forms and other back-end services working properly.

The whole idea is to figure out what things your users need from your Web pages and then to make sure that you've worked out all these details with your service provider.

What they're going to ask you

From their side of the business, the service providers probably have some questions for you. These mostly concern how URLs are handled in your pages and what services that your users expect the server to provide. On the other hand, if they're not savvy enough to ask you these questions, you should answer them anyway to keep from getting bitten later on because you didn't know the right answers!

✔ You'll probably need a new specification for your <BASE> URL definitions and will have to change these accordingly. You'll also need to know what kind of URL references you use in your pages; if the answer's anything other than "Relative links for all local pages," You have to walk them through your references and figure out how they need to change. If you don't know, ask for help (but be prepared to pay for it).

✔ The service providers should also ask you what kinds of input-handling scripts you need to install on its system and what kinds of languages and services they require. These questions range from queries about programming languages like C or C++, to scripting languages like AppleScript or the C Shell (UNIX), to predefined functions like CERN's htimage or NCSA's imagemap for handling clickable image maps.

✔ Finally, they should ask you if you need help in transferring your Web files (*HTML* documents, maps, graphics files, scripts and other programs, and so on) to their server. This help could be something as simple as setting up special FTP access to a directory inside their Web environment, to outright hand-holding during the transfer process. Warning: The more hand-holding you get, the more this service costs!

Your service provider's goals are simple: get your pages up and running on its server as quickly as possible so that it can start earning money for user access and data transfer. Its ideal customer scenario is someone like you who's thoroughly researched and tested his or her pages, who just wants to get all the links and services working. It doesn't want to spend lots of time holding hands with you, either!

Webbing It Yourself: What's That Mean?

Setting up and managing your own Web server is not easy, assuming you decide that's what you need to do. Besides the costs involved, you should ponder other requirements long and hard before hooking up a server to the Internet — especially if that the server should be up and running 24 hours a day.

Understand the tariffs

Just because we've given you some estimates of what it costs to mount your own server on the Internet doesn't mean that we've determined what your actual costs are going to be. You need to research the options available from your Internet service provider and to calculate your precise costs.

Some considerations vary from one location to another: For example, you might not be able to get an ISDN link to your server, which might require using multiple, slower telephone lines or leasing bandwidth directly from the telephone company (for a fractional or full T-1 connection). Either option could add to the cost and change your decision to buy rather than build.

UNIX, or no UNIX?

We strongly recommend that you use a UNIX or a Windows NT system for your Web server. UNIX offers the greatest variety of *httpd* implementations and the broadest range of Web-related editors and production tools. It also offers some of the best deals on programming languages and scripting tools to provide back-end, input-handling services.

Windows NT, on the other hand, is an exploding operating system (in a good way, that is), and Microsoft's vision of the Internet promises to propel it to deliver outstanding capabilities for serving up the Web on its platform. Plus, it's bundling Web server software with the OS in the next planned release (which doesn't have a release number as of this writing but will be the next release after 3.51, whatever that may be).

Although UNIX runs nicely on Intel-based PCs, UNIX expertise is rare in the PC community, and you may have to import some fairly expensive talent to help deal with a UNIX system. Windows NT expertise is also kind of scarce these days, but that fact is changing rapidly as the system gains more users and proponents.

Try though you might, there's no escaping maintenance!

If you look carefully at the figures in Table 17-2, you'll see that the costs for personnel either equal or exceed all the other costs for a Web connection — that is, personnel costs are greater than or equal to the combined costs of hardware, communication, data transfer, and access. Don't try to skimp on this outlay even if you're contracting most of your Web access.

Change is a sure and wearing constant on the Web. As your information ages, it becomes more and more likely to need patching or replacement. These activities take time and cost money — you're best off if you recognize this up front and factor it into planning your Web presence. Keeping your space current takes time and effort.

Running a server of your own makes you liable to different forms of obsolescence. To stay current, you need to keep tabs on the versions and patches for the following elements on your system:

- ✔ The operating system you're running, be it DOS and Windows, Windows NT, any of the flavors of UNIX, or the Macintosh OS

- ✔ The *httpd* server software and related elements on your server (such as TCP/IP stacks and drivers) that make your Web server run

- ✔ The programming and scripting languages (such as the various UNIX shells or scripting languages available for many types of servers) that make your input-handling and other services run

- ✔ The software and hardware that let the server communicate with the Internet, be it a modem and an asynchronous communications package or a dedicated router and a full-blown T-1 link to your service provider

Here again, these factors argue strongly for making the care and feeding of a Web server at least part of someone's official, paid job responsibilities, if not a full-time task. The level of involvement (and expense) depends on how much business or traffic the Internet brings you, vis-à-vis, how much it costs you. This balance may change with time; we'd argue that the scales always tip in favor of more expenditure over time, not less.

For more information on what's required to roll your own Web server, we recommend some additional reading and some online resources:

Cricket Liu, et al., *Managing Internet Information Resources,* O'Reilly & Associates, Sebastopol, California, 1994 (list price: $29.95) This book offers an excellent overview of providing all kinds of Internet services and includes valuable chapters on tons of Web-related stuff. Excellent coverage of Web-server management and Web-access CGI scripts and programs.

Susan Estrada, *Connecting to the Internet,* O'Reilly & Associates, Sebastopol, California, 1993 (list price: $15.95). This book covers most aspects of selecting an Internet service provider, including contact information for most of the larger regional and all the major national service providers.

Michael Gray and net.Genesis, *Build a Web Site,* Prima Publishing, Rocklin, California, 1995 (list price: $34.95). This book is one of the best available on configuring, installing, running, and maintaining a Web site (the named author, Michael Gray, is the same purveyor of Web growth statistics that we mentioned in Chapter 1).

The following books are also wonderful sources of information about Web servers and creating your own Web pages — check 'em out:

Paul J. Perry, *World Wide Web Secrets,* IDG Books Worldwide, Inc., Foster City, California, 1995 (list price $39.99).

Deborah Morrison, *Building a Better Web Site,* IDG Books Worldwide, Inc., Foster City, California, 1995 (list price $29.99).

Dave Taylor, *Creating Cool Web Pages with HTML* (Mac version) and *Creating Cool Web Pages with HTML,* 2nd Edition (Windows version), IDG Books Worldwide, Inc., Foster City, California, 1995 (list price $19.99 for Mac version and $24.99 for Windows version).

Compiled, ready-to-run *httpd* resources

```
http://hoohoo.ncsa.uiuc.edu/docs/setup/PreCompiled.html
```

Uncompiled, *httpd* source code

```
http://hoohoo.ncsa.uiuc.edu/docs/setup/compilation.html
```

Are You Ready for Success?

Now, we want you to assume that your Web site is up, either through a service provider or by bringing your own server online. What happens if you've struck a collective nerve and your Web site traffic swells to gargantuan levels?

Will you be ready to deal with the onslaught, or will it catch you by surprise? If you are caught by surprise, will the bottleneck frustrate your potential users who would be only too happy to access your information, if only they could get to it?

Barring the element of real surprise, we'd like to suggest that you create some contingency plans to deal with the burden of popularity, should it strike your Web pages. You should be aware that national Internet service providers such as PSI, Delphi, CompuServe, ComNet, ANS, and others can offer services that you probably wouldn't want to finance, let alone manage, on your own.

Even if you don't intend to take advantage of their services immediately, it's a good idea to contact them and start building a relationship for possible future business. That way, if your pages become notorious, you can shift them quickly to an environment that can handle thousands of accesses a day (or more). Even if you decide to bring the kind of capacity online to handle this load, you'll be able to handle your users in the interim, while you're getting the equipment and resources running. If you like, you can simply consider this another subcase of the famous maxim, "Always leave yourself a way out!"

The Answer to the Ultimate Question

If you recall, the central, burning issue of Douglas Adams's five-volume trilogy *The Hitchhiker's Guide to the Galaxy* is the question about "... life, the Universe, and everything..." Well, we hate to disappoint you, but if it isn't "42," we don't know the answer any better than you do!

But when it comes to situating your Web presence, we hope we've given you the ammunition that you need to decide whether to run your own server. Remember, though, that no decision is final — you can always change your mind! In the meantime, we hope that you're ready to decide what to do. If so, it's time to learn how to tell people that your pages are ready for browsing — onward to Chapter 18!

Chapter 18

If You Build It, Will They Come?

. . . .

. . . .

*T*he big day has finally arrived: You've built your pages and tested them thoroughly. Your beta testers are ecstatic, and your survey of the testers shows that your Web site is ready for the world to see. Now, finally, it's time for you to go ahead and publish your stuff on the Web.

At this point, your pages will truly be up and running, ready for access. Although you may expect the world to beat a path to your door, let us give you a few recommendations about how to let the world know where your door is and what's behind it. If nobody knows what wonderful Webs you've woven, you can't be surprised if nobody comes to visit them. In other words, if you don't blow your own horn, nobody else will blow it for you!

In this chapter, we show you how to get the word out. Pretty soon, you should start to see links to your pages popping up here and there, and a trickle of users should begin to flow in. If they like what they see, links will start popping up everywhere, and the trickle could grow to a torrent. In this chapter, we give you some pointers to make sure your chances of success are as good as possible.

Announcing Your Web Site to the World

After you're online and ready to provide your valuable information to the public, you want to spread the word about what you have to offer. In keeping with the Web's chaotic nature, no formal registration or announcement process exists, but you can follow a well-understood process for letting the world know that your site is ready for access.

Write a "semi-formal" announcement

To begin with, you need to write a one-page announcement. If you've ever written a press release, this is a similar kind of document. It should be brief to the point of terseness and cover the following points:

- ✔ Indicate who owns the Web site, be it an organization, a person, or some other kind of legal entity. Be sure to include contact information and a contact name to call or e-mail.

- ✔ Indicate whether the pages are *ready for use* or still *under construction*.

- ✔ Be sure to highlight your home page URL so that interested users can find it.

- ✔ Summarize the content of your pages, emphasizing the value and interest in the materials.

Here's a sample announcement for a hypothetical cookie company:

World Wide Web Information Release
February 1, 1996
New York, NY. Terry's Cookie Company (TCC), a leading purveyor of chocolate chip and other delectable cookies, is pleased to announce the release of its comprehensive collection of cookie information to the World Wide Web. For immediate access, please point your browsers to the following URL:

http://www.tcc.com/

Here's what you can expect to find in our Web pages:

- a fascinating history of cookies, with references to recipes and cookies from pre-Christian times to the present day.

- a comprehensive cookie recipe library, with over 2,000 tested cookie recipes.

- a discussion of cookie-baking tools and techniques, including discussion of ingredients, mixers, baking sheets, cookie guns, and other "cookie technology."

If your research has a cookie in it, we'd like you to be able to find the information you need in the TCC Web pages. Our pages are ready and waiting for you to peruse them!

Terry's Cookie Company also wants its Web pages to become the place for cookie fanciers to meet, so we're setting up a forms-based "Reader's Recipe Exchange." Anyone who browses our pages can submit as many cookie recipes as they'd like. These will be gathered together and published monthly via electronic mail. Individuals wishing to receive the monthly recipe exchange can sign up for the mailing list in the TCC pages, or send an e-mail message to "majordomo@tcc.com" with the following text in the body: "join exchange" (for information on the mailing service put "help info exchange" in the body instead).

While you're visiting our cookie archives, the recipe bank, and the tools and techniques library, be sure to check out our TCC Cookie Catalog. We make it easy for you to order any of our more than 50 varieties of fresh, delicious cookies, or to join our "Cookie of the Month" club. We're sure you'll find a cookie that suits your taste! And if you don't like our cookies, we'll give you your money back!

For more information about the TCC Web pages, or any of TCC's information offerings or products, please contact Gail Shayne at TCC. She can be reached by phone at 212-555-1177; by fax at 212-555-1188, or by e-mail at gshayne@tcc.com. Please visit our Web site soon!

This announcement follows the model we've proposed: It identifies itself clearly, highlights the URL, and stresses the content available in the Web pages. It manages to barely suggest some commercial aspirations toward the end of the announcement, after all the important information's already been stated.

Where to direct your announcement

There are lots of ways to get the word out about your new Web pages, but there are certain bases you'll want to be sure to tag:

✔ Send the announcement to this moderated newsgroup, which publicizes new Web offerings: `comp.infosystems.www.announce`. Make sure your subject line includes a brief, but meaningful, description of the site (not just an unadorned URL). For our preceding press release, this might be "Terry's Cookie Company (`http://www.tcc.com`) delivers cookies, history, and recipes for your delectation."

✔ Advertise your site in the WWW Yellow Pages at `http:/www.yellow.com/cgi-bin/online/`.

✔ Send descriptions of your site and its URL to Cool Site of the Day at `cool@infi.net` or to Spider's Pick of the Day at `boba@www.com`.

Post the announcement to the following mailing lists for inclusion in various What's New information listings:

✔ Send your announcement in HTML format, written in the third person (that is, "Terry's Cookie Company announced their …"), to get included on the Mosaic "What's New" page at `whats-new@ncsa.uiuc.edu`.

✔ To get your announcement on the CERN mailing list for new Web servers (servers only) at `www-announce@W30.cern.ch`.

Other What's New listings worth pursuing include the following:

✔ "What's New" at Netscape home page; download the electronic submission form at URL: `http://www.netscape.com/escapes/submit_new.html` for possible inclusion.

✔ The "Topics" list in the EINet Galaxy for placement on the home pages from the makers of WinWeb and MacWeb, consult the *Galaxy Annotation Help* page at `http://galaxy.einet.net/annotate-help.html`.

Register your URL with a search engine as follows:

✔ For Yahoo!, look for the "Add URL" selection at `http://www.yahoo.com`.

✔ For Webcrawler, look for the "Submit URL" selection at `http://www.webcrawler.com`.

✔ For mass coverage of a list of search engines, newsgroups, and mailing lists visit Promote-It!, a compendium of the Internet's best publicity tools at http://www.cam.org/~psarena/promote-it.html.

The following are sample publications to notify:

✔ *Internet World:* A monthly publication aimed specifically at Internet topics and technology; new Web announcements proliferate here. Send your announcement via e-mail to info@mecklermedia.com or call 1-603-924-7271. Address: 20 Ketchum Street, Westport, CT, 06880.

✔ *IWAY:* A bimonthly publication aimed at the Internet, with coverage for beginning to intermediate users trying to master related tools and technologies. Send your announcement via e-mail to editors@iway.mv.com or call 1-603-924-9334. Address: 86 Elm Street, Peterborough, NH 03458.

✔ *NetGuide:* An online services magazine, it covers all of the major online information services by category. Submit your announcement via e-mail to netmail@netguide.cmp.com or call 1-526-562-5000. Address: 600 Community Drive, Manhasset, NY, 11030.

✔ **Your local newspaper (if applicable):** Fax or mail your announcement to the Business Section editor or the Technology editor, depending on their masthead positions. This helps with local publicity.

✔ **Your local computer magazine (if applicable):** Look for a local news section, or a column or reporter who regularly deals with Web issues. This can help get you more local publicity.

The idea here is to plaster your announcement over as many avenues for potential dissemination as possible. These particular recommendations can reach a large — but potentially disinterested — audience. They may provide some welcome initial exposure, but you'll want to target your publicity more closely to your audience as well. Read on for some more specific advice.

Trolling the Usenet newsgroups

Beyond this basic list, there are sure to be ways to target your information for more precise delivery to your audience. For Terry's Cookie Company, the following additional Usenet newsgroups look appealing:

✔ alt.creative.cook
✔ alt.creative-cooking
✔ alt.food.chocolate
✔ ny.forsale
✔ rec.food.cooking
✔ rec.food.historic
✔ rec.food.recipes

For your own Web pages, you'd want to peruse the list of newsgroups on Usenet, and select those that appear interesting. Before posting anything on a Usenet newsgroup, please locate and read the Frequently Asked Questions list (FAQ) for that newsgroup.

Some newsgroups frown on anything that's even the slightest bit commercial, so you'd want to edit your announcement to eliminate any sales-related information for such groups. Others are pretty freewheeling and laissez-faire. The only way to find out what's what is to read the FAQ and spend a few days skimming the online traffic before posting anything.

If you try to fit into the mindset for the newsgroup, you are less likely to inspire a mail-bombing session or a flame war. It's far better to avoid breaking the rules of local netiquette out of ignorance. Think of these precautions as a way of learning how to communicate with yet another audience for your content!

Niche or industry publications

In addition to the general-purpose magazines we've already mentioned, if you're working in a particular marketplace, or have a specific subject area, chances are good that there will be one or more publications serving that niche.

Find out about these niche publications, and fax them your Web announcement. This can very often provide the best publicity you'll get, especially when the audience you're trying hardest to reach has already been targeted by a publication. If you're interested in the subject matter they cover, your announcement will probably come as welcome news, rather than just another Web announcement, as it might for some of the more broadly focused publications.

Whatever happens with niche publications, it's nice to ride on somebody else's coattails for a change!

The old-fashioned kind of networking

Don't forget that your business and professional contacts form a network of people that you can draw on to get the word out. Local professional societies, informal groups, or other congregations of like-minded people can help broadcast your Web location for you, provided you can appeal to their interest.

Many of these contacts may also have Web sites or pages of their own. If your interests overlap sufficiently, why not ask them to include a link to your new site in their existing pages? You can even offer to return the favor, provided the relevance works both ways. Don't forget to let your colleagues and customers know about your pages, too — send your announcement to these individuals or organizations via e-mail or fax, and update your business card to include your home page URL.

Finally, don't forget to cultivate the gurus, consultants, and other experts in your niche. Many of them have personal Web pages that include links to other pages as well. Again, if there's a fit between what they specialize in and the content on your Web pages, encourage them to check out your materials and ask for their feedback.

Professional organizations are popping up on the Web. Often these groups include a list of members and a link to their Welcome pages. So join a couple and spread your URL even further.

Unless you know these consultants and colleagues really well, it's probably not a good idea to boldly ask them to include a link to your pages. But if you encourage them to look at your content — perhaps by e-mailing them a copy of your announcement — it shouldn't be too surprising if you find your URLs showing up in links on some of their pages.

Staying on the Safe Side of Acceptable-Use Policies

Starting in the late 1970s, but most clearly from the mid-1980s and onward, the issue of "acceptable use" of the Internet has been a difficult one. On the one hand, it's always been a good idea to have a mix of government, research, academic, and business users on the Internet. On the other hand, certain parts of this network are heavily subsidized by us taxpayers.

In the earliest days, the only organizations using the Internet were those that had something to contribute to its development and deployment, or some kind of related effort. Admittedly, the interpretation of *related* was sometimes stretched, and the idea soon emerged that the exchange of information was acceptable on the Internet, but that outright commercial activities, such as advertising, billing, or sales-related information, were not. This also helps to explain an antisales mentality that persists on the Internet to this day, although this is changing dramatically with the development of online transactions.

The charter of the NSFNET Backbone, which once acted as the primary coast-to-coast conduit for Internet information, helps to clarify matters some-what. It clearly states that the Internet's role is to support educational and research activity and to carry only traffic related to those things. Although nobody is censoring each e-mail message or Web page to make sure that these guidelines are honored, the intent of this document is clear:

NSFNET Backbone Acceptable-Use Policy

✔ NSFNET backbone services are provided to support open research and education in and among US research and instructional institutions, plus research arms of for-profit firms when engaged in open scholarly communication and research. Use for other purposes is not acceptable.

Specifically Acceptable Uses:

✔ Communication with foreign researchers and educators in connection with research or instruction, as long as any network that the foreign user employs for such communication provides reciprocal access to US researchers and educators.

✔ Communication and exchange for professional development, to maintain currency, or to debate issues in a field or subfield of knowledge.

✔ Use for disciplinary-society, university-association, government-advisory, or standards activities related to the user's research and instructional activities.

✔ Use in applying for or administering grants or contracts for research or instruction, but not for other fund-raising or public-relations activities.

✔ Any other administrative communications or activities in direct support of research and instruction.

✔ Announcements of new products or services for use in research or instruction, but not advertising of any kind.

✔ Any traffic originating from a network of another member agency of the Federal Networking Council if the traffic meets the acceptable use policy of that agency.

✔ Communication incidental to otherwise acceptable use, except for illegal or specifically unacceptable uses.

Unacceptable Uses:

✔ Use of for-profit activities (consulting for pay, sales or administration of campus stores, sales of tickets to sports events, and so on) or use by for-profit institutions unless covered by the General Principle or as specifically acceptable use.

✔ Extensive use for private or personal business. This statement applies to use of the NSFNET backbone only. NSF expects that connecting networks will formulate their own use policies. The NSF Division of Networking and Communications Research and Infrastructure will resolve any questions about this Policy or its interpretation.

Here's the bottom line: If you're not sure whether what you're sending over the Internet will traverse public sector links, the safest course of action is to honor these guidelines, no matter what you're doing.

It's also wise to be wary of blatantly commercial activity of any kind on the Internet — particularly advertising. As you'll learn, sins of omission provoke far fewer firestorms than do the ones of commission! The best policy, therefore, is the one that minimizes commercial activity while sharing your content freely with all those who visit your Web pages.

Giving Value Means Getting Value

As we've said repeatedly throughout this book, the key to a successful Web presence is quality content. If you provide this to your users, and follow our publicity recommendations, your material will ultimately gain the attention it deserves.

As long as users feel like they're getting information, services, ideas, or anything else of genuine value from your Web pages, they'll not only use them regularly, they too will help spread the word to other users. This should bring considerable value back to you, whether it leads to new customers, new sources of information that's valuable to you, or new contacts who share similar pursuits and interests.

The Web's law of reciprocal value is this: The more value you put into your Web pages, the more you'll get back from the user community in return, no matter how you measure that return value!

Making Sure Your Web Catches the Right Prey

Once your pages are published and the word is out, it's time to relax and kick back, right? WRONG! After publication is when the real work begins: You should be encouraging your users to give you feedback at all times, especially about the value and usefulness of your content. Then you should actively work to incorporate their feedback on an ongoing basis. No matter how good your content is, it can always get better, especially if you're responding to user requests and suggestions.

Also, once your pages are published, the maintenance work begins. You need to stay on top of your own content and materials, to make sure you keep things up to date. Keep checking your links to other sites and sources — they can change without warning, rendering your potentially priceless link to the Widget Research Institute into the worthless error message `404 Unable to contact-server www.wri.com`, which indicates a stale link.

As time goes by, users' tastes and needs for information change, too. If you stay in close touch with your audience, you'll be able to anticipate these changes and keep pace with them. Otherwise, your Web gets all dusty, bestrewn with the corpses of information that have long since been sucked dry. In the next chapter, we help you stay on top of the maintenance effort, with some tips for recognizing and coping with an ever-changing world.

Chapter 19
The More Things Change . . .

*N*ow you can bask in the afterglow of your grand Web achievements. You've published your pages, you've spread the word, and now your hard labor is beginning to bear fruit. Before you pack up your picnic basket and take the rest of the week off, we'd like to remind you that 95 percent of the life cycle for any information product is spent in maintenance mode.

In other words, what you think that you've just finished is really just getting started. In fact, some people would argue that now is when the real fun begins in earnest. You've probably solved the technical problems that you've encountered along the way without having to stress yourself too much or stretch your mind too far from its normal configuration.

But now you have to start dealing with the toughest problems of all: people problems and communication problems. It's almost guaranteed that some of your content won't make sense to some users, that others may disagree with your content (and even be offended by it), and that still others may delight in harping on what you consider to be trivial errors. Don't let negative feedback bring you down; use it, instead, as a reminder that your page can never be perfect and that there's always room for improvement.

In this chapter, you find out about the kinds of problems and feedback you should expect to encounter and how to deal with the day-to-day routine of keeping your Web pages and other resources in tip-top shape.

Quack! Quack! The Two-Dimensional Text Trap Redux

The temptation to add more content and (hopefully) more value grows as you get feedback from users and learn more about the subject matter that drives the content. As pages grow, don't forget that users quickly get tired of scrolling around.

Keep a constant eye on the number of screens in any given page, especially when making changes. Even though you may be tempted to think of a sequence of screens as the same thing as a sequence of printed pages, the two are not the same.

We've all been strongly conditioned by a lifetime of linear printed text, so consider this a reminder that the *H* in HTML stands for *Hypertext*. This means that growing pages must be hyperlinked to remain readable and usable, and to facilitate users who grow bored with one section of your document and want to jump to the next topic. If you don't make it easy for them to jump around, they'll jump ship.

Once the number of screens in an HTML document exceeds three, you should plan on adding internal hypertext links to your pages and break them up into chunks of no more than 20 lines of text. Judicious use of location anchors (`<A NAME="spot">`) and intradocument links (`<A HREF="#spot">`) makes it easy for your users to navigate as the spirit moves them.

Our final word on this topic is that as documents grow in length and complexity, the need for effective structure and navigation grows with them. Don't omit the introduction of these vital elements in some of your pages simply because they started small and grew from there.

Who Says This Stuff Is Stale? (The Mold's a Dead Giveaway . . .)

As we've suggested, the temptation to rest on your laurels can be nearly irresistible after you've overcome the humps of writing, testing, soliciting user feedback, and finally, publicizing your pages. It's amazing how quickly after a "short rest" you go back through your Web pages and exclaim, "Wow, did I really put those pages out there *last August?* Boy, this stuff is really out of date!"

Like leftovers in the refrigerator that have turned to science experiments, stale Web pages can easily become an embarrassment to their owners. The only thing is, they can't alert you to their condition by turning funny colors or starting to smell. You have to keep checking them, just to see how they're holding up against the ravages of time.

Check in on your pages regularly, Doctor Web!

We'd suggest that you take on the job of maintaining your Web pages as if it were a real job instead of something you do in your spare time when the phase of the moon is just right. In other words, make it a part of your scheduled activities to read over your content at least once a month to see how well it's holding up. You'd be surprised how much quality-control difference a little absence can make: We almost always find typos and minor gotchas in our pages whenever we revisit them after a while, and we bet you will, too.

Keep your content current!

But the real work comes from maintaining your content. If all the information on your "What's New" page is six months old, those pages won't be attracting too much notice anymore. If the stunning new advance in widgetry you spend half your pages on has been supplanted by an even more thrilling technological advancement, your coverage will seem old hat. To pick up a newspaper metaphor and mangle it thoroughly, "Yesterday's pages are like yesterday's news; they're only good for lining the bottom of a virtual birdcage!"

Do your links point to nowhere?

In addition to keeping tabs on how current your information is, you should make sure that your links are all still current and correct, too. It only takes one change to make a link useless, but that might be the very link that your users need most. It's probably a good idea to check links weekly or to locate a good Webcrawling robot that can check them for you. Even if you point your users at a "no longer at this location" page with a *click here* (we *hate* that!) anchor to get them to the current location, you can still earn ill will from users for not getting them right where they want to be!

Another ARGH! is to follow a link to find an "Under construction" icon, and that's all that's there. It's a wasted link, and it can really perturb users. Don't fall into this trap: If a link is not ready yet, include the proposed link text but don't link it to anything. Indicate that this will soon be a link, but it is currently under construction. This tells users what you want them to know, without making them follow a link to find out!

Is your HTML passé?

While you're examining your past efforts, check your HTML markup against the standard that browsers are supporting today. If you've set up tables in your pages by using preformatted text, and everybody else is using that newfangled, snazzy-looking HTML table markup, your stuff will look pretty lame by comparison. If some of those Netscape extensions ever get adopted in standard HTML, you may want to dress up your pages with some of their nice features, too.

The whole idea is to keep things on your pages fresh and interesting. If you consider regular checkups the moral equivalent of an open box of baking soda, your Web pages should retain their pristine quality and avoid ending up as the dreaded "science experiments" that they could otherwise become!

If You Ask Them, They'll Tell You

Staying in touch with your users is a really good idea, especially when it comes to Web pages. Make sure that you include a form or two in your pages, if only to capture more information about your visitors and to solicit feedback on what they liked or didn't like about your site. While you're at it, ask them what else they'd like to see there.

Always be sure to include an area on your feedback form for open-ended comments, remarks, criticisms, or whatever else your users feel compelled to share with you. As we mentioned in Chapter 16, the best feedback often comes from completely unexpected quarters and hits you in the least expected places. No matter how well you know a subject or a market, you'll always have a blind spot somewhere. Open-ended feedback can give you the opportunity to shed some light on that blind spot and may even broaden your horizons!

If you treat your pages as an open-ended communications tool with your users, they'll be more inclined to give you feedback. If you then respond to their feedback, you might even develop a relationship with some of your users that might otherwise never have happened. If so, these sources of quality feedback can become part of the group of movers, shakers, and influencers from whom you will always solicit feedback. You may even develop some of your best contacts through the Web.

Keeping Up with Changes

The thing about feedback is that it creates an impetus to change. Whether it's a dynamite suggestion about a better way to structure one of your pages, a request for coverage of a topic that would complement your existing information perfectly, or something that you saw on somebody else's page that you want to emulate, the net result is more work for you.

Because suggestions keep coming, and good ideas are never in short supply, it's easy to get overwhelmed by change. We suggest that planning for change and handling it in bite-size chunks can keep you from becoming a victim of change.

When dealing with suggestions, we recommend that you keep a list of the ideas sent by users and fellow Webheads. If a certain suggestion appears frequently, move this to a "Needed" list, which should be the focus of immediate attention. You can set the threshold to move a common response to "Needed" items to

whatever seems appropriate. We've found that five repeats means the suggestion really belongs on the "Needed" list. We've also learned that our constitu-
ents are a fountain of good enhancement suggestions, so we also keep a "Cool
Ideas" list for future whiz-bang enhancements to our Web site.

Let's assume that you decide to spend every other Tuesday working on your Web
pages. During the interim from one of these Web days to the next, you'd simply
collect and prioritize incoming information. You'd also do your best to monitor
changes and developments in your fields of interest, and you'd keep another list
of things to add to your "What's New" information, possibly culled from the
newsgroups and trade magazines that you follow.

Come the next Web day, you'd pull out your list, select the two or three elements that you wanted to change, and formulate a plan of action to implement
those changes. By incorporating change into your planned activities and
building a process to accommodate it, you can avoid most of the frenzy that
last-minute, ill-considered change can cause. If you know you need to update
your "What's New" information every Web day and add whatever new information or page designs you think are appropriate, this can become just another
part of your ongoing relationship with the Web. Remember, you need to run
your involvement with the Web: Don't let it run you!

Maintenance is an Attitude and a Way of Life!

The whole idea is to make your Web activities a part of your regular daily
round. If working on your Web pages is something that you do only when the
opportunity presents itself, when crunch time comes, that opportunity will
never arrive. If, on the other hand, you make working on your Web pages a part
of your routine, you'll know exactly what you have to deal with, when, and how
long you'll be able to stay at it before you have to move on to something else.
This approach treats your Web pages as a resource in need of regular maintenance, which is exactly the right attitude to take.

Among the many benefits that this kind of approach can confer, it will let you
know when you need to adjust your schedule (or if that's not possible, when
you need to think about hiring or acquiring some extra help). If every-other-
Tuesday isn't enough time, you may have to give up cleaning your wastebasket
on Wednesday and spend a little more time on your Web-related activities. If
you just can't give up this essential task (or delegate it elsewhere, like maybe to
the custodial staff), you may have to hire a helper or a part-time consultant to
assist you with your Web work.

There's a wonderful Latin saying, *Festina lente,* which means *hurry slowly* and
captures the essence of a good maintenance attitude. Although you shouldn't
overdo the time and energy you devote to any of your workaday tasks, it's
important to recognize that regular attention to those tasks can produce the
kinds of results you want. If you can't get to those tasks, you quickly learn to

prioritize and focus on the ones most in need of attention. If that means hiring somebody else to handle your Web pages, so be it. Anything else invites the potential for stale and moldy pages!

When Things Change, They Also Break

While you're involved in maintenance and the gradual process of changing your Web pages, remember that change can introduce unforeseen side effects. In English, this means that every time you change (or add, or delete) information on your Web pages, you need to remember to test your pages as if they were brand new.

You probably won't devote the same painstaking care to testing every little thing about your "old" pages that you did for them when they were still "new." But the sad truth is that you really should take that same care to check and recheck your work every time that you introduce a change.

This means reading (and spell-checking) your content, just to make sure that you haven't introduced another typo for your users to chuckle at. It also means checking and rechecking your links (especially the anchors within documents for link destinations) to make sure that they still connect to the right places.

It's a good idea to make your changes on a set of copied (production) Web pages, rather than in situ on your server. That way, you are free to make as many changes (and mistakes) as you like. Nobody will be able to see your work until you want them to. We'd also suggest showing your new version to a select audience and asking for feedback before switching public access from an old version to the new one. Many a seemingly good idea has blanched in the face of a reality check; it's probably better to get one from somebody who knows how good you really are than from some user who's simply nonplussed by your "strange pages."

We also keep a section on our server where we duplicate our entire Web space utilizing UNIX symbolic links to our entire real Web space. When we're changing a page or adding some others, we can test them thoroughly without disturbing the real Web space. If we're changing a file in our test Web, we delete the file's symbolic link. We then make a copy of the file into the test Web, where we do our edits and validations. After it's passed our visual inspection and survived the rigors of the HTML validator, we copy the new file into the real Web space. We then delete the file from the test Web and replace it with a symbolic link back to the real Web. Voilà! A clean substitution, every time. . . .

Keeping up with change is a real job, so why not treat it like one? If you do, you'll be rewarded with a steady sense of progress in the face of constant changes and course adjustments. As you face these vicissitudes, you may begin to wish for more help from your computer, though. In the next section of the book, we switch to an examination of the tools for building Web pages that may make the mechanics of the job a bit easier. But there's nothing we can do — except prepare you — to buffer you from the unceasing pace of change on the Web.

Part VII

It's Tool Time! HTML Development Tools and More

YOU WILL FORGET YOUR PASSWORD, YOUR HARD DISK WILL CRASH AAAHAHAHAHA

In this part . . .

*U*ntil now you've been slaving in a techno-wilderness, filled with arcane HTML tags and bizarre CGI programming rituals; in this part, you finally find out what kinds of tools are available to help you with this work. Did we wait until near the end of this book-length adventure only to tell you that you could have "automagically" reached Web nirvana just by buying or obtaining the right tools? Fortunately for us, the answer is "No." While there are lots of useful and interesting tools available for use on many different development platforms, nobody's built a completely automatic Web construction kit just yet.

We start this part of the book in Chapter 22 by explaining what kinds of HTML (and Web server) tools are available these days, to give you an idea of what the state of the art is. In the chapters that follow, you have a chance to inspect the offerings for UNIX machines, Macintosh desktops, and finally, the ubiquitous and ever-popular Microsoft Windows environment.

By the time you're finished with this part of the book, you should have a good idea of what kinds of tools are available and where to start looking for them to provide your own favorite authoring environment. Finally, you should have a good feel for what kinds of Web server capabilities are available, and how the various platforms can help to realize them.

Chapter 20

Using UNIX Uniquely

*W*onderful new HTML authoring tools for UNIX-based systems have begun to spring up in recent months. Many are still undergoing testing, but they all look quite promising to UNIX users tired of text-only systems. And for those of you who happen to like text-only, the old EMACS standby is alive and well, with a few added HTML modes to liven it up. To top it off, you can convert or filter almost any file type into or out of HTML using one of the myriad HTML utility programs available for UNIX.

The UNIX mystique is one of sharing resources, so practically all of the UNIX-based HTML authoring systems are freeware. Even commercial UNIX packages typically offer a freeware version for downloading.

But freeware and shareware UNIX HTML authoring tools aren't supported in the same manner as recently released commercial products. Thankfully, they don't cost much, either. These tools are usually easy to learn because they use familiar text-editor metaphors or they act as add-ins to your own UNIX text editors. Either way, if you've ever used any kind of editor, you can learn one of these HTML tools easily.

Diving for Treasure in the UNIX HTML Tools Sea

The sections that follow describe some of the currently popular UNIX-based HTML authoring tools and give you important facts about each one of them. These tools vary in their scope and functionality; but all are designed to help you create HTML documents more easily. Check out the URLs below for complete information on these tools, and many more.

Some tools are standalone UNIX programs that provide structure and error checking while they guide you through the creation of your Web pages. Some tools simply and elegantly provide you with quicker ways of inserting the requisite HTML tags into plain-text documents. Others are comprised of groups of macros for HTML editing to be used by existing UNIX text editors, such as EMACS. File conversion tools take a different approach and change existing text files into HTML-tagged documents.

No matter which kind of tool you choose to try first, remember that the ultimate objective is to create eye-catching, informative Web pages that can function on everybody's browser. If the tool you try doesn't help you meet this objective, try another tool. Rest assured: There's one out there that will do the job for you!

More information on the latest and greatest UNIX authoring tools is readily available starting at the following WWW sites:

```
http://www.exclamation.com/htmlinfo/unixedit.html
http://www.utirc.utoronto.ca/HTMLdocs/unix_tools.html
http://union.ncsa.uiuc.edu/HyperNews/get/www/html/editors.html
http://www.w3.org/hypertext/WWW/Tools/Overview.html
```

Standing Alone Amidst the UNIX HTML Editors

Standalone HTML tools come in flavors that range from plain-text editors to complete WYSIWYG authoring systems with more bells and whistles than an AMTRAK station. The following examples start simply and proceed upward in functionality and cost from there.

The standalone plain-text HTML editors for UNIX, such as A.S.H.E. (A Simple HTML Editor), simply give you a screen that you type your text into. They also provide buttons or menu options from which you select HTML tags, which you must then insert at the proper places in the text. The emphasis in A.S.H.E. is *Simple*. If you understand the UNIX environment, you'll be able to learn A.S.H.E. fairly quickly.

A.S.H.E.

A.S.H.E. (A Simple HTML Editor) was written using C language, Motif, and NCSA HTML Widgets. It is a standalone, unchecked, plain-text HTML editor. It provides active hyperlinks, supports multiple windows, prints text or postscript, and offers automatic file backup. Its menu bar is well designed with File, Edit, HTML, Styles, and Lists. It provides a unique user Message Area while displaying the HTML code in a browser screen view (see Figure 20-1). Unfortunately, it only works under Motif on Sun workstations and requires the NCSA HTML Widget library. It provides very simple but adequate HTML assistance for users of Motif. If that sounds like it's up your alley, please give it a try!

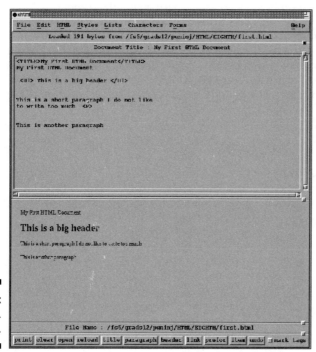

Figure 20-1:
The A.S.H.E.
screen.

The A.S.H.E. beta version was created by John R. Punin, Dept. of Comp. Sci. RPI, Troy, NY 12180; E-mail: `puninj@cs.rpi.edu`. It can be downloaded from

```
ftp://ftp.cs.rpi.edu/pub/puninj/ASHE
```

Several other programs are semi-WYSIWYG in that they provide you with a somewhat standard text-editing screen into which you type your text. The editors then help you place the appropriate HTML tags in your text and keep you from making errors in HTML syntax. These editors also help you with the creation of more complex HTML links and references. HoTMetaL is one example of this type of system.

Phoenix

Phoenix (Alpha 0.1.8) X-Windows-based HTML Editor is freeware from Lee Newberg, Biological Sciences Division, Office of Academic Computing, The University of Chicago, 924 E. 57th Street, Chicago, IL 60637-5415. Phoenix offers true WYSIWYG HTML creation with a built-in browser. It copies and pastes plain, heading, anchor, and/or styled text with the attributes retained. It provides easy anchor (`<A>`) editing with no need to type the URL in most cases. It supports full forms browsing, and copies and pastes images and `ISMAPS` from Web pages. A couple of negatives to remember are that you must register to get into the University of Chicago system and that Phoenix is an academic endeavor in an alpha version that will be developed at an academic pace. So if you're in a hurry for additional features, you'd better try another program. You can download the source directly via anonymous FTP from

```
http://www.bsd.uchicago.edu/ftp/pub/phoenix/phoenix-0.1.8.tar.gz.
http://www.bsd.uchicago.edu/ftp/pub/phoenix/README.html
```

Other editors, such as HoTMetaL and NaviPress, are more or less WYSIWYG HTML authoring systems that let you type your text and format it as it will be displayed by a browser (sometimes yours, sometimes theirs). Then the system not only produces the appropriate HTML-formatted document, but it also lets you cut and paste from other HTML documents, and carries the tags with the copied text. These systems also check your HTML syntax for proper usage. They are the most comprehensive of the HTML authoring systems available for UNIX.

HoTMetaL Pro

HoTMetaL Pro 2.0 is SoftQuad's ($195) commercial HTML editor. A UNIX version for Sun computers is available for free download at various sites. HoTMetaL requires you to edit a document with its embedded HTML codes visible, and then hands off the code to your own browser for viewing. It supports all of the

HTML 2.0 tags and selected 3.0 and Netscape extensions. It can open many document formats — Lotus Ami Pro; Microsoft Word for Macintosh, Windows, and DOS; RTF (Rich Text Format); and WordPerfect for DOS, Windows, and Macintosh — and convert them to HTML.

HoTMetaL (shown in Figure 20-2) performs both syntax checking and HTML validation. With syntax (rules) checking turned on, HoTMetaL helps you enter only valid HTML. If you select HTML validation, it checks your document for conformance to the HTML 2.0 specification. It also provides a list of all HTML 3.0 and Netscape extension tags in your document to alert you to possible incompatibilities with browsers that don't support those codes.

The HTML validation and format conversions are quite useful, but they don't allow you to create image maps nor do they let you see you what your images will look like on the page. You can download the free version from SoftQuad's download site list at

```
http://www.sq.com/products/hotmetal/hm-ftp.htm.
```

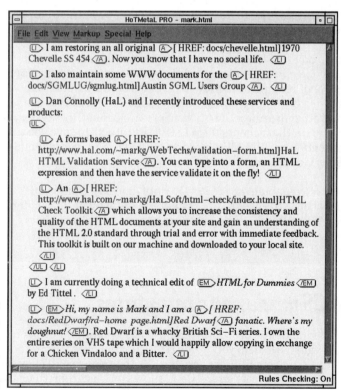

Figure 20-2:
The
HoTMetaL
screen.

NaviPress

NaviPress 1.1 is part of America Online's NaviService, or not, if you don't want the service. Confusing? Yes, it is. The overall service, should you agree to subscribe to it, leads you step-by-step through the Web site creation and maintenance . . . for just a little bit (or more) a month. It may be worth looking into if you want a Web site without much effort and if money isn't a limiting factor.

In any case, the NaviPress program is a good standalone HTML editor. NaviPress's WYSIWYG authoring produces Web pages compliant with the proposed HTML 3.0 standard and specifications. It contains embedded support and friendly interfaces for authoring forms, image maps, all HTML 2.0 elements and formats, and many HTML 3.0 elements. It supports nonstandard HTML extensions via the Special Tag command. NaviPress 1.1 has embedded interfaces for authoring HTML 3.0 pages, including tables.

NaviPress also allows you to create pages, view them, and edit them graphically— all within the same program and without typing a single HTML tag. Very impressive. NaviPress' editing window displays your HTML in close-to-Netscape quality and lets you insert and delete GIF and JPEG graphics directly. NaviPress's point-and-click dialog box for table creation works very well. Also, you can click on NaviPress's color wheels to select background and text colors.

Image map creation is a snap, as long as you only want rectangular hot spots. NaviPress does simple syntax checking but doesn't import any document file formats. NaviPress includes a few megabytes of clip art, such as colored bullets, arrows, icons, and backgrounds with the software. NaviPress can save HTML pages and other files directly to a NaviService account, to NaviServers, or to any Web server that accepts the HTTP PUT protocol to save you the trouble of FTPing them yourself. NaviPress works with AOL's NaviService and other Internet service providers.

NaviPress is available at about $99 for Motif (SunOS), Windows 3.1/3.11/Win95/NT, and Macintosh. The Windows version is 16-bit but it runs under both Windows 95 and Windows NT. For more information please visit

    http://www.naviserver.navisoft.com/index.htm

EMACS modes and templates

The old tried-and-true UNIX EMACS editor has several add-in macro systems (modes) available to help you create HTML documents. These modes vary in their features but generally are very basic in their approach. They save you from typing each tag in its entirety and show you a list from which to choose.

(EMACS users will understand this section, and everyone else will think it's written in E-Greek. But then EMACS is a foreign language to most non-UNIX computer users.)

Various EMACS macro packages are available for editing HTML documents. The first and oldest is Marc Andreesen's *html-mode.el*, was written while he was at the University of Illinois. (Marc is the primary designer of Mosaic and Netscape.) Heiko Muenkel of the University of Hannover, Germany, added pull-down menus (*hm-html-menus.el*) and template handling (*tmpl-minor-mode.el*), which is up to version 4.15. Figure 20-3 shows the *hm-html-menus.el* screen.

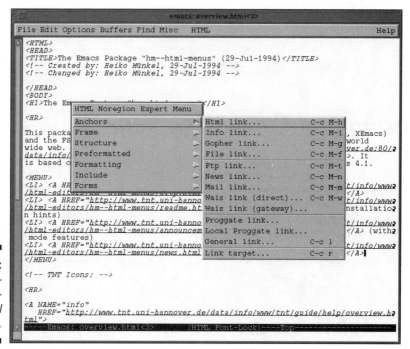

Figure 20-3:
The *hm-html-menus.el* screen.

Nelson Minar of The Santa Fe Institute wrote and continues to improve *html-helper-mode.el* (ver. 1.2.2), which supports Lucid EMACS menu bar and font-lock capabilities and runs under GNU EMACS v18 and v19, Epoch, and Lucid EMACS.

Generally speaking, the various iterations of HTML mode display text and HTML tags alike in fixed-size fonts. By using the *hilit.el* package, tags and references can be colored differently than text. The HTML modes do not support inline display of graphics. The more recent versions of HTML mode can call a Mosaic process to display pages in browser view.

All of the HTML modes work primarily from direct keyboard commands that create paired begin/end HTML tags with an entry point available between the tags. It is possible to select a segment of text and the tags will be inserted around it. None of the modes check the validity of tags or suggest possible tag usage. However, *html-helper-mode* and *tmpl-minor-mode* provide templates for entering multiple fields inside link tags.

For EMACS users, these modes may be just the thing for creating HTML documents. Using them should make HTML tagging easier and less prone to error than manually typing in complete tags. You must still know what tags to use and where to use them. You can obtain information and copies of Muenkel's and Minar's packages, respectively, at

```
http://www.tnt.uni-hannover.de/data/info/www/tnt/soft/info/www/html-
     editors/hm-html-menus/overview.html
http://www.santafe.edu/%7Enelson/tools/
```

Filtering and Converting Your UNIX Files

Because there are so many different file types used on UNIX systems, a long list of HTML filters and converters has accumulated over the past few years. We give you URLs to these lists at the end of this section. These programs transform text, RTF, FrameMaker, or other file types into an HTML-tagged file based on the original file's formatting. Of course these converters are only as good as their HTML rule sets, and their authors' abilities to guess what you really want. Generally, they give you a head start on converting existing files to HTML documents; WebMaker and WebWorks Publisher are two especially promising entries into the FrameMaker conversion arena.

WebMaker 2.1

WebMaker 2.1 from The Harlequin Group Limited is a new and promising FrameMaker converter. At about $99, it's quite a deal for FrameMaker users. WebMaker is a powerful, easy-to-use Web publishing solution for the creation of full-featured Web pages from FrameMaker documents. WebMaker's conversion capabilities convert FrameMaker documents and books to HTML complete with graphics, tables, and equations.

WebMaker takes full advantage of the layout styles you apply in FrameMaker to let you define specialized layout styles for Web publishing. Customization and hyperlinking are easily accomplished and automated to get fast, predictable results. Once you've completed the conversion, the conversion template you create can be used over and over again to automatically convert documents to HTML in the format you've specified. No additional work is required, no matter how many pages, documents, or books you decide to convert.

WebMaker (samples shown in Figure 20-4) is available in several versions of UNIX, as well as Windows and Macintosh platforms, at

```
http://www.harlequin.com/webmaker/2.0/Welcome.html
```

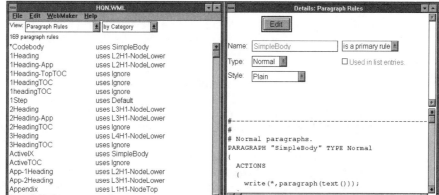

Figure 20-4: Sample WebMaker screens.

WebWorks Publisher

WebWorks Publisher from Quadralay is designed to be used with FrameMaker. WebWorks Publisher is an easy-to-use, full-featured system for the creation and maintenance of professional-quality Web pages and hypermedia documents. It lets you design and maintain your complete documentation base in one single master version, and then produce both high-quality print media and electronic hypermedia tailored to Web distribution, or even online help.

WebWorks Publisher has features to handle complex text, graphics, and hyperlinks. It makes full use of the layout and style information embedded in your original documents to automatically produce HTML documents. When used in conjunction with FrameMaker, you can convert documents from most popular file formats, including Microsoft Word and WordPerfect. It is available for HP-UX 9.x, MacOS 7.1, SunOS 4.1, Sun Solaris 2.3, and Windows 3.1 or NT.

You may obtain more information and download an evaluation copy from

```
http://www.quadralay.com
```

Lists of UNIX helper and filter programs are available at

```
http://www.utirc.utoronto.ca/HTMLdocs/UNIXTOOLS unix_doc_man.html
http://www.w3.org/hypertext/WWW/Tools/Word_proc_filters.html
```

UNIX Web Server Search

A WWW (or HTTP) server is a daemon program constantly running on an Internet-attached computer that responds to an incoming TCP connection and provides a service to the caller. The vast majority of WWW servers (about 83 percent) run on UNIX platforms around the world. And as everyone knows, there are more flavors of UNIX than ice cream at Baskin-Robbins. Consequently, there are also many different kinds of WWW servers on those UNIX platforms.

Big surprise: Free servers are the most popular with 82 percent of the servers being free or proprietary. Most of these run on UNIX, but not all do. The NCSA HTTPD server is used by about 45 percent of the WWW sites in the world, with the CERN server second at about 15 percent, and Apache third at about 5 percent. Several commercial servers are rapidly gaining popularity, due primarily to their ease of use and support for secure transactions. The major commercial player in the UNIX market is Netscape, with about 7 percent of the sites worldwide. For the most recent information on UNIX-based WWW (HTTP) servers, check out these sites and follow their links:

```
http://www.proper.com/www/servers-chart.html
http://www.w3.org/hypertext/WWW/Servers.html
http://www.yahoo.com/Computers_and_Internet/Internet/
    World_Wide_Web/HTTP/Servers/Unix/
```

This chapter has provided you with a brief overview of the major UNIX-based HTML-authoring systems as well as some of the ancillary packages. The Web itself is the best place to obtain the latest and greatest UNIX Web tools, so "the Web's up. Let's go surfin' now." In the next chapter, we drop UNIX like a hot potato and get tight with the Macintosh.

Chapter 21

More Macintosh Madness

A plethora of excellent HTML authoring tools for the Macintosh is available for downloading from numerous online sites. All but a couple of these tools are freeware or shareware, and most of them are appropriate for beginning to advanced HTML authors. Because of their low-cost or no-cost status, these freeware/shareware tools don't offer the kind of hand-holding you might expect from commercial products. But then, they don't cost much, either. Most of them ship with very good to pretty good documentation, and some even have online or "balloon" help. Thankfully, these tools are easy to learn because they use familiar Macintosh word-processing or text-editor models and the Macintosh menuing system.

Surveying the Orchard of Macintosh HTML Tools

In the subsections that follow, you encounter information on several types of Macintosh HTML authoring tools that are available to help you create Web pages. These tools vary in their scope and functionality, but all of them can provide solid HTML help.

Many Macintosh HTML authoring tools have the capability to display a WYSIWYG or semi-WYSIWYG view of your HTML documents internally. Along with this capability comes a certain amount of error checking, because these programs' internal display mechanisms can simulate a browser and recognize HTML tags. The best tools let you see both WYSIWYG and tagged views of your documents, and all of the truly complete implementations provide balloon help as well.

Several standalone WYSIWYG programs let you check your HTML code and keep you from making syntax or placement mistakes. Some of these tools add to the functionality of existing word processing and text editors, thereby giving them the ability to help you include HTML tags. Some go as far as converting existing files from their normal formats to HTML, and vice versa.

While you're trying out one or more of these tools, ask yourself, "Does this program make writing HTML any easier?" If your answer is "No," try another tool. Regardless of the kind of tool you choose, you can reasonably expect it to make your HTML creation job easier, not harder.

You can find the most up-to-date information on Macintosh HTML tools by starting at these sites:

```
http://www.comvista.com/net/www/htmleditor.html
http://www.yahoo.com/Computers_and_Internet/Internet
    World_Wide_Web/HTML_Editors/Macintosh/
http://www.w3.org/hypertext/WWW/Tools/Overview.html
```

Biting into Standalone HTML Editors for Macintosh

The standalone authoring tools for the Macintosh range in complexity from the Simple HTML Editor (SHE) to the complete Web-creation environments of PageMill and NaviPress. The simple, generally plain-text HTML editors like HTML Editor, HTML.edit, and Simple HTML Editor (SHE) basically let you type your text and give you buttons or menu options to select tags at appropriate insertion points. These are being superseded by the completely WYSIWYG environments, such as the freeware Webtor, and partially WYSIWYG shareware, such as HTML Pro. The packages discussed below are the most popular and perhaps the easiest to use of the myriad of standalone Macintosh HTML creation tools.

Webtor

Jochen Schales at the Fraunhofer Institute for Computer Graphics in Darmstadt, Germany created this outstanding-looking freeware package. It displays inline graphics and provides a full WYSIWYG environment for editing multiple documents with no tags showing. You can send your documents to a browser to test them or to a text editor to see the HTML tags.

It's virtually impossible to make HTML mistakes while using Webtor because it performs HTML level 2.0 checking of all text. It includes a configurable DTD which lets you use HTML extensions. It also includes a document outliner. This should be a winner for novice to intermediate Web makers. You may download it from:

```
http://www.igd.fhg.de/~neuss/webtor/webtor.html
```

HTML Pro

HTML Pro is a relatively new Macintosh product from Niklas Frykholm. In this beginner-oriented program, editing is accomplished in one window on the HTML coded text and simultaneously viewed in another window with a near-WYSIWYG view. The document can be edited in both windows, and all menu options — such as copying, pasting, and formatting text—apply in both windows. To switch between the two windows you can either use the View menu or simply click on the window. You can click or type your codes and then get an instant look at the result in the other window. It only edits one 32K document at a time. Download a copy of this ($5) shareware program from:

```
http://www.ts.umu.se:80/~r2d2/computers/package/
    htmlpro_help.html
```

PageMill

PageMill from Adobe is hot, hot, hot! It provides an easy-to-understand word processing environment where you don't type HTML tags or look at them. (Can you spell WYSIWYG?) Your Web pages look like they would appear in a browser (except their contents are editable), and PageMill writes the HTML code for you.

PageMill makes good use of Macintosh drag-an-drop to paste in links, text snippets, and graphics. You can drag links directly from your Netscape browser and drop them into your own pages. It also converts from JPEG or PICT to GIF graphics and creates imagemaps directly in the page. Of course, you expect and receive only the best in graphics manipulation from Adobe in PageMill.

You can get Version 1.0 for your Macintosh or Power Macintosh for $149. Take a look for yourself at their Web site. They even have screen shots on the site like the one shown in Figure 21-1. When you graduate from novice to Webspert, Adobe also offers SiteMill as an upgrade from PageMill.

```
http://www.adobe.com/Apps/PageMill/
```

HoTMetaL Pro

HoTMetaL Pro 2.0 is SoftQuad's ($195) commercial HTML editor. A Macintosh version is available for free downloading at various sites. HoTMetaL requires you to edit a document with the embedded HTML codes visible; then it hands the code off to your own browser for viewing. It provides all of the HTML 2.0 tags and selected 3.0 and Netscape extensions. It can open many document formats — Lotus Ami Pro; Microsoft Word for Macintosh, Windows, and DOS; RTF (Rich Text Format); and WordPerfect for DOS, Windows, and Macintosh — and convert them to HTML.

HoTMetaL does both syntax checking and HTML validation. With syntax (rules) checking turned on, HoTMetaL helps you enter only valid HTML. If you select HTML validation, it checks your document for conformance to the HTML 2.0 specification. It also provides a list of all HTML 3.0 and Netscape extension tags in your document to alert you to possible incompatibilities with browsers that don't support those codes.

The HTML validation and format conversions are quite useful, but this editor doesn't allow you to create image maps, nor does it let you see you what your images will look like on the page (see Figure 21-2). You can download the free version from SoftQuad's download site list at:

```
http://www.sq.com/products/hotmetal/hm-ftp.htm
```

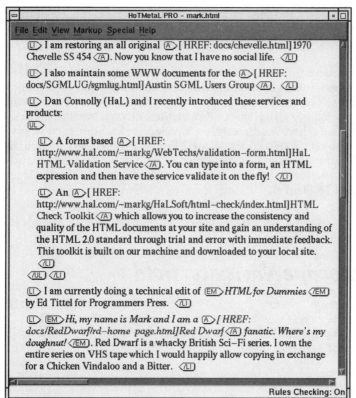

Figure 21-2:
The
HoTMetaL
Screen.

NaviPress

NaviPress 1.1 is part of America Online's NaviService, or not, if you don't want the service. Confusing? Yes it is. The overall service, should you agree to subscribe to it, will lead you step-by-step through the Web site's creation and maintenance . . . for just a little bit (or more) a month. It may be worth looking into if you want a Web site without much effort, and money isn't a limiting factor.

In any case, the NaviPress program is a good standalone HTML editor. NaviPress' WYSIWYG authoring produces Web pages compliant with the proposed HTML 3.0 standard and specifications. It contains embedded support and friendly interfaces for authoring forms, image maps, all HTML 2.0 elements and formats, and many HTML 3.0 elements. It supports nonstandard HTML extensions via the Special Tag command. NaviPress 1.1 has embedded interfaces for authoring HTML 3.0 pages, including tables.

It allows you to create pages, view them, and edit them graphically — all within the same program and without typing a single HTML tag. Very impressive. NaviPress' editing window displays your HTML in close-to-Netscape quality and lets you insert and delete GIF and JPEG graphics directly. NaviPress' point-and-click dialog box for table creation works very well. Also, you can click on NaviPress' color wheels to select background and text colors.

Image map creation is a snap, as long as you only want rectangular hot spots. NaviPress does simple syntax checking but doesn't import any document file formats. NaviPress includes a few megabytes of clip art, such as colored bullets, arrows, icons, and backgrounds with the software. NaviPress can save HTML pages and other files directly to a NaviService account, to NaviServers, or to any Web server that accepts the HTTP PUT protocol to save you the trouble of FTPing them yourself. NaviPress works with AOL's NaviService and other Internet service providers. NaviPress is available at $99 for the Macintosh System 7 and up at:

```
http://naviserv.navisoft.com/index.htm
```

Netscape Navigator Gold

Of course you've read the hype from Netscape about NSGold; but because it hasn't been released in even beta in January of 1996, it's still a maybe. If it lives up to expectations and works as well as Netscape Navigator, it may be a real winner. Keep track of it at:

```
http://home.netscape.com/comprod/products/navigator/
    version_2.0/gold.html
```

Tackling Text Editor Extensions and Templates

Editor or word processing add-in functions are templates and programs that are installed into your existing editor or word processing program. These extensions appear in the editor's menus as HTML functions which insert tags, create forms, and the like. Some extensions give the program the ability to open and save HTML-tagged documents.

The HTML add-ins for BBEdit and BBEditLite are quite extensive and provide a well-rounded HTML authoring system. Tools of this kind can cause the editor to open a standard text file and save it with HTML tags automatically. To use these add-ins, you must first have the editor or word processing software on your computer to which the add-in installs.

If you use BBEdit, two excellent sets of add-ins for HTML editing are available. They are BBEdit HTML Extensions by Carles Bellver and BBEdit HTML Tools by Lindsay Davies. They will be discussed together here because they are so similar in form and function.

Using either of these add-ins with BBEdit or BBEditLite gives you access to most, if not all, of the HTML authoring functions that you probably need for most Web pages. Because you may already use BBEdit or BBEditLite, you may be able to get going very quickly with these add-ins. It won't take you much time to try one of these and see if you like it.

BBEdit HTML Extensions

Carles Bellver's extensions work well with BBEdit and are distributed along with many packages (including BBEdit and some Apple CDs). They are freeware (see Figure 21-3). The latest release is Version 12 (11/8/95) as of January 1996. Download them from:

```
http://www.uji.es/bbedit-html-extensions.html
```

Figure 21-3:
The BBEdit
with HTML
Extensions
Screen.

BBEdit HTML Tools

Lindsay Davies' extensions (with BBEdit 3.1.x) provide a good method of creating HTML documents for current BBEdit users. The tools are very complete, including their balloon help inside the dialog boxes. They help you create templates, check your HTML syntax, translate special characters in both directions, and the like. These tools also help you with -includes and create special insertion tags that make updating pages quick and easy. The Version 1.3.1 (6/1/95) files are freeware and can be downloaded from:

```
http://www.york.ac.uk/~ldll/BBEditTools.html
```

Magnificent Miscellaneous Mac Tools

Numerous tools for assisting you to create maps, forms, CGI applications, and more are readily available for your Macintosh. An extensive list of these tools is provided at the following site:

```
http://www.comvista.com/net/www/WWWDirectory.html
```

Web Server Primer

A WWW or HTTP server is a program constantly running a computer that responds to an incoming TCP connection and provides a service to the caller. There are several varieties of HTTP server software for the Macintosh. The most popular is WebStar although it only represents a small percent of the overall HTTP servers in use on the WWW. Of course, most of the HTTP servers (over 80 percent) are UNIX based.

Here's a brief look at the Macintosh Web server software, which you aren't ready to tackle anyway. We just wanted to help you broaden your world wide horizons a bit. You can find more information on servers by starting at the ComVista or Yahoo! sites:

```
http://www.comvista.com/net/www/server.html
http://www.yahoo.com/Computers_and_Internet/Internet/
    World_Wide_Web/HTTP/Servers/Macintosh/
```

WebSTAR / MacHTTP Web server

WebSTAR, from StarNine Technologies, is the commercial successor to MacHTTP, building on the same code base with the same great programming by Chuck Shotton. The latest release (Version 1.0) of WebSTAR is several times faster than MacHTTP and has the same features as commercial servers on other platforms.

MacHTTP, by Chuck Shotton of BIAP Systems, was the first HTTP server for Macintosh computers. It is still a full-featured server and is currently sold by StarNine Technologies, which just recently became a subsidiary of Quarterdeck Corporation. The latest release is Version 2.2.

Quarterdeck recently announced two add-ons for WebSTAR: the Commerce Kit and the Security Kit. The Commerce Kit provides the ability to accept online payments for products or services (via a link to First Virtual) by using either credit cards or a custom commerce interface. The Security Kit provides secure transmission of data between client and server using the Secure Sockets Layer (SSL) protocol. Have a look at more information at:

```
http://www.starnine.com/http://www.qdeck.com
```

NetWings

NetWings is a full-featured HTTP server for Macintosh built on the 4D database system. It was released in 1995 by NetWings Corp. It uses the HTTP 1.0 standard, supports CGI applications through AppleEvents, has site protection, can load documents from any drive on the network, and can serve either documents and files or pages built on-the-fly from information in its 4D databases. The software is available now, and a demo version should also be available. Have a look for yourself at:

```
http://netwings.com/
```

Chapter 22
Webbing Up to Windows

● ●

In This Chapter

▶ Gazing through Windows HTML authoring tools

▶ Exploding numbers of standalone editors

▶ Burgeoning word processor plug-ins

▶ Sailing through file converters

▶ Searching for Windows Web servers

● ●

*A*stounding new HTML authoring tools for Windows-based systems have sprung up in recent months. Many are still undergoing testing, but they all look quite promising to Windows users who are tired of text-only systems. To top it off, you can convert or filter almost any file type into or out of HTML by using one of the myriad HTML utility programs available for Windows.

The Windows mystique is one of sharing resources; so in that vein, many of the Windows-based HTML authoring systems are shareware. Even some of the commercial Windows HTML authoring packages offer a freeware version for downloading.

The freeware and shareware Windows HTML authoring tools aren't supported in the same manner as the recently released commercial products. But, then, they don't cost much either. These tools are usually easy to learn because either they use familiar text editor metaphors or they are add-ins to your own Windows word processors. Either way, if you've ever used a Windows-based word processor, you'll be able to learn one of these HTML tools easily.

Surveying the Field of HTML Software Tools

The sections that follow describe some of the currently popular Windows-based HTML authoring tools and give you important facts about each of them. These tools vary in their scope and functionality, but all of them are designed to help you create HTML documents more easily. Check out the URLs at the end of each section for complete information on these tools and many more.

Some of these tools are standalone Windows programs that provide structure and error checking while they guide you through the creation of your Web pages. Some simply and elegantly provide you with quicker ways of inserting the requisite HTML tags into plain-text documents. Others comprise groups of macros for HTML editing for use in existing Windows word processors, such as Word for Windows or Word Perfect. File-conversion tools take a completely different approach and transform existing text files into HTML-tagged documents.

No matter which kind of tool you choose to try, remember that the objective is to create eye-catching, informative Web pages that will function on everybody's browser. If the tool you try doesn't help you meet this objective, try another tool. Rest assured: there's one out there that will do the job for you!

More information on the latest and greatest Windows HTML authoring tools is readily available from the following WWW sites:

```
http://www.techsmith.com/community/htmlrev/index.html
      (Carl's comparison table is great.)
http://www.yahoo.com/Computers_and_Internet/Internet/
      World_Wide_Web/HTML_Editors/MS_Windows/
http://union.ncsa.uiuc.edu/HyperNews/get/www/html/editors.html
http://www.w3.org/hypertext/WWW/Tools/Overview.html
```

Looking at Standalone HTML Authoring Systems for Windows

As we're writing this chapter, new standalone HTML authoring systems continue to pop up almost daily. It seems as if everyone is trying to produce a better mousetrap for Windows-based HTML authoring tools. Standalone HTML authoring systems provide complete editing and tag insertion assistance and sometimes much more. Most contain their own WYSIWYG pseudo-browser to show you how your Web screens should look, or they'll run your own browser to test your HTML work.

Some of the tools that we surveyed appear to be well-constructed and low on bugs, but we've decided it would be more fun to cover the cheesy, buggy ones instead. (If you believe that, we have a deal for you on some swampland in . . . never mind.) We wouldn't waste your time or ours discussing anything but the best we could find. Here they are.

HoTMetaL Pro / HoTMetaL Free

HoTMetaL Pro 2.0 is SoftQuad's ($195) commercial HTML editor. Windows (3.1, 95, and NT) versions of the Free edition are available for free downloading at various sites. HoTMetaL requires you to edit the document with the embedded HTML codes visible, and then it hands the code off to your own browser for viewing. It provides all of the HTML 2.0 tags and selected 3.0 and Netscape extensions. It can open many document formats — Lotus Ami Pro; Microsoft Word for Macintosh, Windows, and DOS; RTF (Rich Text Format); and WordPerfect for DOS, Windows, and Macintosh — and convert them to HTML.

HoTMetaL does syntax checking and HTML validation. With syntax (rules) checking turned on, HoTMetaL helps you enter only valid HTML. If you select HTML validation, it checks your document for conformance to the HTML 2.0 specification. It also provides a list of all HTML 3.0 and Netscape extension tags in your document in order to alert you to possible incompatibilities with browsers that don't support those codes.

HoTMetaL's HTML validation and format conversions are quite useful, but the program doesn't allow you to create image maps, nor does it let you see you what your images will look like on a page (see Figure 22-1). You can download the free version from a site on SoftQuad's download site list at:

    http://www.sq.com/products/hotmetal/hm-ftp.htm.

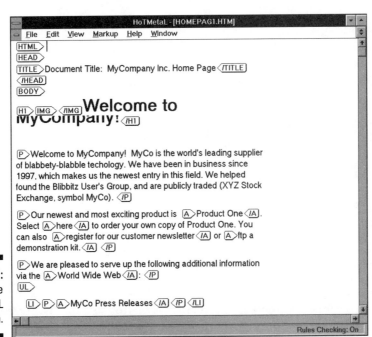

Figure 22-1:
The
HoTMetaL
screen.

FrontPage

FrontPage 1.0, from Vermeer Technologies Inc. of Cambridge, Massachusetts, is much more than just an HTML editor (see Figure 22-2). It's a complete Web site manager that lets you customize your Web server without CGI (common gateway interface) programming. The package contains the FrontPage Editor — an HTML (hypertext markup language) authoring tool; the FrontPage Explorer, which provides a tree-structured view of your Web site; and the FrontPage Personal Web Server, based on NCSA (National Center for Supercomputing Applications) code, which comes in 16-bit and 32-bit versions for Microsoft Windows (3.1, 95, and NT).

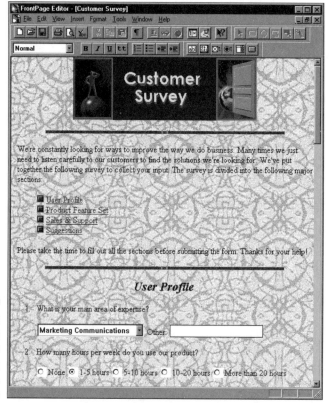

Figure 22-2:
The
FrontPage
editing
screen.

FrontPage's WYSIWYG editor doesn't let you directly edit HTML code, and the 1.0 version doesn't support HTML tables. It's claim to fame is its *WebBots*. WebBots are fragments of code, hidden inside HTML comments, that the Web server executes when the page is accessed. Unfortunately, the Web server needs Vermeer's FrontPage Server Extensions to use WebBots. Currently only the FrontPage server contains these, but Vermeer is developing extensions for other Web servers.

FrontPage 1.1 and a developers' kit for creating custom WebBots should be available early in 1996. The FrontPage package lists for $695. Although it's more than most beginning Web page authors may need, FrontPage may be a way for non-programmers to produce a complex Web site quickly and easily. You can find out more about FrontPage from Vermeer's Web site at:

```
http://www.vermeer.com/
```

NaviPress

NaviPress 1.1 is part of America Online's NaviService, or not, if you don't want the service. Confusing? Yes, it is. The overall service, should you agree to subscribe to it, will lead you step-by-step through the Web site creation and maintenance . . . for just a little bit (or more) a month. It may be worth looking into if you want a Web site without much effort and money isn't a limiting factor. NaviPress and the NaviService package may be compared with the FrontPage system for entire Web site construction and management by non-programmers and non-computer experts.

In any case, the NaviPress program is a good standalone HTML editor. NaviPress' WYSIWYG authoring produces Web pages compliant with the proposed HTML 3.0 standard and specifications. It contains embedded support and friendly interfaces for authoring forms, image maps, all HTML 2.0 elements and formats, and many HTML 3.0 elements. It supports nonstandard HTML extensions via the Special Tag command. NaviPress 1.1 has embedded interfaces for authoring HTML 3.0 pages, including tables.

It allows you to create pages, view them, and edit them graphically — all within the same program and without typing a single HTML tag. Very impressive. NaviPress' editing window displays your HTML in close-to-Netscape quality and lets you insert and delete GIF and JPEG graphics directly. NaviPress' point-and-click dialog box for table creation works very well. Also, you can click on NaviPress' color wheels to select background and text colors.

Image map creation is a snap, as long as you only want rectangular hot spots. NaviPress does simple syntax checking but doesn't import any document file formats. NaviPress includes a few megabytes of clip art (such as colored bullets, arrows, icons, and backgrounds) with the software. NaviPress can save HTML pages and other files directly to a NaviService account, to NaviServers, or to any Web server that accepts the HTTP PUT protocol to save you the trouble of FTPing them yourself (see Figure 22-3). NaviPress works with AOL's NaviService and other Internet service providers.

NaviPress is available at $99 for Motif (SunOS), Windows 3.1/3.11/Win95/NT, and Macintosh. The Windows version is 16-bit, but it runs under both Windows 95 and Windows NT.

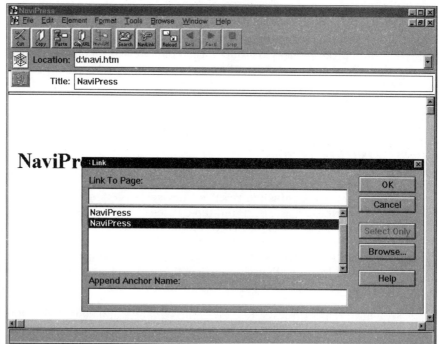

Figure 22-3:
The
NaviPress
editing
screen.

http://naviserver.navisoft.com/index.htm

HTMLed Pro

HTMLed Pro is a substantially improved version of HTMLed. It shows the tags, text, and entities in different colors. Its table and form editors are easy to use. The form editor displays the elements as they would appear inside a browser. It provides customizable ten-button toolbars and includes provisions for opening files on a remote server by saving a copy to the local drive and then using FTP to upload them to the server.

HTMLed Pro comes with a standard document outline that simplifies starting a new Web page by allowing the user to select standard elements to be included and to enter important information (see Figure 22-4). This simplifies starting a new document. These user templates can be saved and reused. Also, HTML 3.0 and Netscape-specific tags are supported. This product is definitely worth looking at. You can get a free, limited-time demo or the real thing for $99 at:

http://www.ist.ca

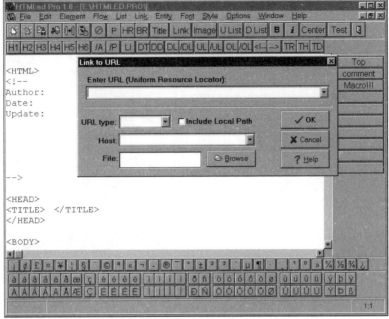

HotDog

HotDog is rapidly growing in popularity due to its large number of easy-to-use features and low cost. For a text-based HTML editor with no HTML syntax checking, it's very well designed (see Figure 22-5). It provides an intuitive (for Windows users) interface for character and tag scrolling list windows, clear dialogs for images and links, table and form editor screens, and an automated method of preparing a Web page for the Web server.

HotDog supports both HTML 3.0 and Netscape's extensions. HotDog is available at the following URL for a 30-day trial (full standard version) and may be purchased for $30; the Professional version is also available from Sausage Software for $99.95 at:

```
http://www.sausage.com
```

InContext Spider

InContext Spider's ability to view the structure and links of a document undoubtedly help beginning Web authors. The editing window shows a graphical representation of the HTML structure with the HTML displayed in an adjoining window. It provides several display options. A simplified interface with only

common tags accessible from the standard toolbar makes it easy for the beginner. This can irritate power-users because some useful tags are nearly hidden within the menu system.

InContext Spider (see Figure 22-6) relies on the NCSA Mosaic browser for direct viewing, although any browser can view finished HTML documents. It contains a built-in HTML 2.0 validator. This should be one of the packages you test if you're just starting your Web weaving. An evaluation version of InContext Spider and the complete $99 version are available from InContext Systems at:

```
http://www.incontext.ca/
```

Netscape Navigator Gold

Of course you've read the hype from Netscape about NSGold; but because it hasn't been released (even in a beta form) as we're writing this chapter, as far as we're concerned it's a definite "maybe." If NSGold lives up to its expectations and works as well as Netscape Navigator, it could be a real winner. Keep track of it at:

```
http://home.netscape.com/comprod/products/navigator/
        version_2.0/gold.html
```

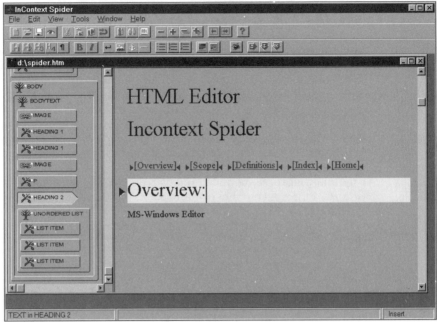

Figure 22-6:
The
Incontext
Spider
editing
screen.

Word Processor Plug-Ins

If you're joined at the hip to either Word for Windows or WordPerfect for Windows, you may be interested in trying their Internet plug-in packages. These are Word Internet Assistant (Word IA) and WordPerfect Internet Publisher, respectively. They are essentially sets of macros that alter Word and WordPerfect so that they can create and view HTML documents. They provide adequate HTML assistance but aren't really in the same ballpark as the better standalone HTML systems. They're both free at the following locations and at many other mirror sites (a mirror site is a Web or FTP site that copies the contents of another site somewhere else on the Internet, to give users multiple places to download from; most of the really popular Web and FTP sites have mirrors, some have as many as 30 or more).

Internet Assistant for Microsoft Word (6.0 or Word95) is available at:

```
http://www.microsoft.com/msoffice/freestuf/msword/download/ia/
      default.htm
```

WordPerfect Internet Publisher is available at:

```
http://wp.novell.com/elecpub/inttoc.htm
```

Filters and File Converters

You can find numerous options for automatic conversion of existing text documents into HTML. Such services are available from several of the standalone HTML editors, from word processor HTML plug-ins, and from new standalone converters, such as HTML Transit, WebMaker, and WebWorks Publisher. They work quickly and easily. For example, if you use Word for Windows with the Word IA plug-in, you simply open a standard Word document, save the file in HTML format by using the Save As command, and presto! it's converted. Most of the formatting that really counts, including headings, is converted.

Of the following three standalone converters, HTML Transit imports and converts the largest number of file formats. This is somewhat unfair to the other two, because they're designed specifically to convert FrameMaker files. If you have formatted files that you'd like to convert to HTML for Web display, check into these systems.

HTML Transit

HTML Transit from InfoAccess, Inc., reads the structure of the source document and recognizes elements such as headings, subheads, bullets, images, and so on. It then creates a default template based on this structure, which becomes the foundation for one-button generation of HTML documents. HTML Transit offers direct translation for all major word processing formats, including Microsoft Word, WordPerfect, WordPro (AmiPro), FrameMaker, and Interleaf. PageMaker and Quark formats are supported through RTF. Conversion of all major graphics formats is also supported.

HTML Transit is based on over a decade of electronic publishing experience by InfoAccess (formerly OWL International), which produced the industry's first commercially available hypertext product ten years ago. Their $45,000 GUIDE Professional Publisher was the model for HTML Transit's template-based architecture.

With a well-formatted word processor or page layout file and HTML Transit, you may not need an HTML "editor" at all. It's a bit expensive ($495), but it may just be what you're looking for. Have a look for yourself at:

http://www.infoaccess.com/

WebMaker 2.1

WebMaker 2.1 from The Harlequin Group Limited is a new and very promising FrameMaker converter. At $99, it's quite a deal for FrameMaker users. WebMaker is a powerful, easy-to-use Web-publishing solution for the creation of full-featured Web pages from FrameMaker documents. WebMaker's conversion capabilities convert FrameMaker documents and books to HTML complete with graphics, tables, and equations.

WebMaker (shown in Figure 22-7) takes full advantage of the layout styles you apply in FrameMaker to let you define specialized layout styles for Web publishing. Customization and hyperlinking combine to produce fast, predictable results. After you've completed a conversion, you can reuse the conversion template that you create as many times as needed to automatically convert documents to HTML from the format you've specified. No additional work is required, no matter how many pages, documents, or books you decide to convert!

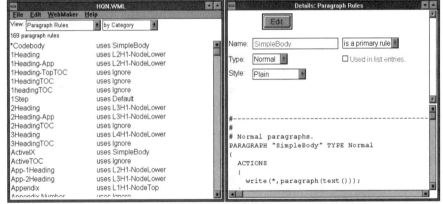

Figure 22-7: Sample WebMaker screens.

WebMaker is available for Windows at:

```
http://www.harlequin.com/webmaker/2.0/Welcome.html
```

WebWorks Publisher

WebWorks Publisher from Quadralay was also designed to be used with FrameMaker. WebWorks Publisher is an easy-to-use, full-featured system for the creation and maintenance of professional-quality Web pages and hypermedia documents. It lets you design and maintain your complete documentation base in one single master version and then produce both high-quality print media and electronic hypermedia tailored to Web distribution (or even online help).

WebWorks Publisher has features to handle complex text, graphics, and hyperlinks. It makes full use of the layout and style information embedded in your original documents to automatically produce HTML documents. When used in conjunction with FrameMaker, documents can be converted from most popular file formats including Microsoft Word and WordPerfect. It is available for HP-UX 9.x, MacOS 7.1, SunOS 4.1, Sun Solaris 2.3, and Windows 3.1 or NT. You can obtain more information and download an evaluation copy of WebWorks Publisher from:

```
http://www.quadralay.com
```

For a look at the myriad of other HTML converters and filters, start your surfing at these sites:

```
http://www.w3.org/hypertext/WWW/Tools/Filters.html
http://www.yahoo.com/Computers_and_Internet/Internet/World_Wide_Web/
      HTML_Converters/
http://union.ncsa.uiuc.edu/HyperNews/get/www/html/converters.html
```

A Windows Web Server Primer

Here's a brief look at Web server software for Windows and at sites where you can find more information. A W3 (or HTTP) server is a program on the Web Server computer that responds to an incoming TCP connection and provides a service to the requester. There are many varieties of HTTP server software that can serve incoming Web requests.

We've noticed a recent upsurge in the number of HTTP servers for Windows-based computers, especially for Windows NT servers. The ComVista site that follows lists twenty-one different sites for NT-based HTTP server programs. We'll discuss the most popular and let you surf the Net for the others. The ComVista and Yahoo! sites at the following URLs will start you in the right direction, or the left direction, whichever you prefer:

```
http://www.comvista.com/us/lea/servers.html
http://www.yahoo.com/Computers_and_Internet/Internet/
      World_Wide_Web/HTTP/Servers/Microsoft_Windows_Windows_95/
```

If you are determined to set up your own Web server, here are a few suggestions for possible Windows-based servers:

- Common Lisp Hypermedia Server (CL-HTTP) by MIT
- FrontPage Personal Web Server by Vermeer
- Windows (3.1) HTTPD and TCP

The following are Windows NT servers:

- NaviServer by NaviSoft
- Netscape Commerce Server
- Netscape Communications Server
- Freeware HTTP Server for Windows NT
- Internet Office Web Server by CompuServe
- Windows NT Server 3.51 by Microsoft

You sure are a glutton for information if you've read this far! Congratulations, you must be *really* stuck on the Web. Grab one of these HTML editors or authoring systems and get cracking on your own super Web site or pick up a server and see what it can do. See ya on the Web. Next, get ready for our recap of the book, in "The Part of Tens," which combine humor and summary for a fabulous finish to your Web adventures!

Part VIII
The Part of Tens

The 5th Wave   By Rich Tennant

In this part . . .

Here are some *lists of ten* designed to add to your HTML experience. The chapters that follow explore some important dos and don'ts for HTML. We also remind you of the most important considerations for good page design, for testing your work, and for making the sometimes difficult "build-versus-buy" decision when it comes to choosing a Web server.

We'd like you to think of these final chapters as a way of reviewing what you've already learned, and a way of reminding you of what's really important. Along the way, expect to find our tongues firmly planted in our cheeks — if you can't get a laugh out of what we hope by now is familiar territory, maybe you can get a laugh out of the incongruous juxtaposition of strange and wonderful ideas!

Chapter 23

The Top Ten HTML Do's and Don'ts

• •

• •

*B*y itself, HTML is neither excessively complex nor overwhelmingly difficult. As better wags than we have put it, "This ain't rocket science!" Nevertheless, it's good to have a set of guidelines to help you make the most out of HTML without stepping away from your need to communicate effectively with your users.

This chapter attempts to underscore some of the fundamental points that we've made throughout this book regarding proper and improper use of HTML. Hopefully, you'll adhere to the prescriptions and avoid the maledictions. But, hey, they're your pages, and you can do what you want with them. The users will decide the ultimate outcome! (Just don't make us say, "We *told* you so!")

Remember Your Content!

Darrell Royal, the legendary coach of the University of Texas Longhorns football team in the '60s and '70s, is rumored to have said to his players, "Dance with who brung ya." In normal language, we think this means that you should stick to the people who've supported you all along and give your loyalty to those who've given it to you.

We're not sure what this means for football, but for Web pages it means keeping the content paramount. If you don't have strong, solid, informative content, the users will quickly realize that your Web pages are relatively content free. Then they'll be off elsewhere on the Web, looking for the content your pages may have lacked.

Above all, this means placing your most important content on the site's major pages and placing frills and supplementary materials on secondary pages. The short statement of this principle for HTML is, "Tags are important, but what's between and around the tags — the content — is what really counts." Make your content the very best that it can possibly be!

Structuring Your Documents

Providing users with a clear road map and to guide them through your content is as important for a home page as it is for an online encyclopedia. But the longer or more complex the document, the more important a road map becomes. This will ideally take the form of a flowchart showing page organization, or it could even be represented as a graphic for inclusion on an orientation page for your site.

We're strong advocates of top-down page design. You should start the construction of any HTML document or collection of documents with a paper and pencil (or with whatever modeling tool you like best). Sketch out the relationships within the content and the relationships among your pages. Don't start writing content or placing tags until you understand what you want to say and how you want to organize your materials.

Good content flows from good organization. It helps you stay on track during page design, testing, delivery, and maintenance. It helps your users find their way through your site. Need we say more?

Keeping Track of Tags

While you're building documents, it's often easy to forget to use closing tags where they're required (for example, the </A> that closes the opening anchor tag <A>). Even when you're testing your pages, some browsers can be so forgiving that they'll compensate for your lack of correctness, leading you into possible problems from other browsers that aren't quite so understanding (or lax, as the case might be).

There are lots of things to say on this subject, so we'll try to stick to the ones that count:

✔ Keep track of yourself while you're writing or editing HTML. If you open an anchor or text area or whatever, go back through and find the closing tag for each opening one.

✔ Use a syntax-checker to validate your work as part of the testing process. These are mindless, automatic tools that will find missing tags for you and also find other ways to drive you crazy along the way!

Here's a URL that's a jump page for HTML validation tools:

```
http://www.charm.net/~web/Vlib/Providers/Validation.html
```

✔ Try to obtain and use as many browsers as you possibly can when testing your pages. This will not only alert you to the "missing tag" problem; it will also point out potential design flaws and remind you of the importance of providing alternate text for users with nongraphical browsers.

✔ Always follow the rules of HTML document syntax and layout. Just because most browsers don't require the use of structure tags like <HTML>, <HEAD>, and <BODY> doesn't mean that it's okay to leave them out; it just means that they don't care if you break the rules. Your users may (and we certainly don't) want you writing any improperly structured HTML, either!

Although HTML isn't exactly a programming language, it still makes sense to treat it like one. Therefore, following formats and syntax will help avoid trouble, and careful testing and rechecking of your work will ensure a high degree of quality and standards compliance.

Making the Most from the Least

More is not always better, especially when it comes to Web pages. Try to design and build your pages by using the least amount of ornament and complex layout that you can rather than by overloading pages with lots of graphics, as many levels of headings as you can cram in, and links of every possible description.

Remember that structure exists to highlight the content. The more the structure dominates, the more it takes away from content. Therefore, use structure sparingly, wisely, and as carefully as possible. Anything more will become an obstacle to delivering your content. This means that you should stay away from excessive use of graphics, links, and layout tags!

Building Attractive Pages

Working within a consistent framework lets users learn how to view and navigate your pages. Making them easy to navigate only adds to their appeal. If you're in need of inspiration, cruise the Web and look for layouts and graphics that work for you. If you take the time to analyze what you like about them, you can work from other people's design principles without having to steal the details of their layout and look.

When designing your Web documents, start with a fundamental layout for your pages. Pick a small but interesting set of graphical symbols or icons and adopt a consistent navigation style. Use graphics sparingly and tune them to be as small as possible (by reducing size, number of colors, shading, and the like), while still retaining their "eye-candy" appeal. Use simple, easy-to-use, consistent navigation tools throughout. It's possible to make your pages both appealing and informative if you're willing to invest the time and effort to create the right look and feel.

Avoiding Browser Dependencies

When building Web pages, the temptation to view the Web in terms of your favorite browser can prove nearly irresistible. That's why you should always remember that users view the Web in general, and your pages in particular, from many different perspectives and through many different browsers.

During the design and writing phase, it's common to ping-pong between the HTML text and a browser's-eye-view of that text. At this early point in the process, we recommend switching among a group of browsers, including at least one character-mode browser. This will help balance your viewpoint on your pages and usually helps to maintain a focus on the content as well.

During testing and maintenance, it's even more important to browse your pages through as many different viewports as you can. Make sure to work from multiple platforms and to try both graphical- and character-mode browsers on each one. This takes time but will repay itself with pages that are easy for everyone to read and follow. It will also help those viewers who come at your materials from a different platform than your own native one, and it will help your pages achieve true platform (as well as browser) independence.

Evolution, Not Revolution

Over time, Web pages will change and grow. Keep looking at your work with a fresh eye (or keep recruiting fresh eyes from the ranks of those who haven't seen your pages before) to avoid the process of what we call "organic acceptance."

This is best explained by the analogy of your face and the mirror: You see it every day, you know it intimately, so you might not be as sensitive to the impact of change over time as someone else. Then you see yourself on videotape or in a photograph or through the eyes of an old friend. At that point, changes obvious to the entire world become obvious to you: "My hairline's really receded," or "I've gone completely gray," or "My spare tire could mount on a semi!"

Just as with the rest of life, changes to your Web pages are evolutionary, not revolutionary. That is, they usually proceed by small daily steps, not big radical ones. Nevertheless, you need to remain sensitive to the supporting infrastructure and readability of your content as things evolve on your pages. Maybe the lack of on-screen links to each section of the Product Catalog didn't matter when you only had 3 products to deal with; now that you have 25, it's a different story. Over time, structure needs to adapt to follow the content. If you regularly reevaluate your site's effectiveness at communicating the content, you know when it's time to make changes, both large and small.

This is where user feedback is absolutely crucial. If you don't get feedback through forms and other means of communication, you should go out and aggressively solicit some from your users. "If you don't ask them," the common wisdom goes, "you can't tell how you're doing!"

Navigating Your Wild and Woolly Web

A key ingredient for building quality Web pages is the inclusion of navigational aids. In Chapter 11, we introduced the concept of a "navigation bar" that provides users with a method to avoid or minimize scrolling. By judicious use of intratext links and careful observation of what constitutes a "screenful" of information, use of text anchors makes it easy to move to the "previous" or "next" screens as well as to the "top," "index," and "bottom" of a document. We believe pretty strongly in the "low scroll" rule: That is, users should have to scroll more than one screenful in either direction from a point of focus or entry without encountering a navigation aid to let them jump (rather than scroll) to the next point of interest.

We don't believe that navigation bars are required or that the names of the controls should always be the same. We do believe that the more control you give users over their reading, the better they like it (and the more traffic your Web pages get). The longer any particular document, the more important such controls become. We find they work best if they occur about every 20 lines in longer documents.

Beating the Two-Dimensional Text Trap

Conditioned by centuries of printed material and the linear nature of books, our mindsets about hypertext can always use some adjustment. When building your documents, remember that hypermedia should add interest, expand on the content, or make a serious impact on the user. Within these constraints, this kind of material can vastly improve any user's experience of your site.

If you can avoid old-fashioned linear thinking, you may not only succeed in improving your users' experience, you may even make your information more readily available to your audience. That's why we encourage careful consideration of document indexes, cross-references, links to related documents, and other tools to help users navigate within your site. Keep thinking about the impact of links and looking at other people's materials, and you may yet shake free of the linear trap imposed by Gutenberg's great legacy (the printing press)! If you're looking for a model for your site's behavior, don't think about your great new trifold four-color brochure, think about how your customer service people interact with new customers on the telephone ("What can I do to help you today?").

Overcoming Inertia Takes Constant Vigilance

Finally, when dealing with your Web materials postpublication, remember that your tendency will be to come to rest regarding future efforts. Maintenance is nowhere near as heroic, inspiring, or remarkable as creation, yet it represents the bulk of activity needed to keep a living document alive and well.

Make maintenance a positive term and look for ways to improve its perception. If you start with something valuable and keep adding value, your materials appreciate over time. If you start with something valuable and leave it alone, your materials will become stale and lose value. Keeping up with constant change is a hallmark of the Web; ignore this trend with your materials and they'll quickly be ignored.

In terms of behavior, this translates into the creation of (and adherence to) a regular maintenance schedule. Make it somebody's job to spend time on the Web site regularly and check to make sure the job is getting done. If someone is set to handle regular site updates, changes, and improvements, he or she will start flogging the other participants to give them things to do when scheduled site maintenance rolls around. The next thing you know, everybody is involved in keeping the information fresh, just as they should be. This also keeps your visitors coming back for more!

Chapter 24

Ten Design Desiderata

*W*hen building a Web site, it's always essential to know what you're trying to communicate. The content should always remain king. Nevertheless, we'd like to suggest a bevy of design desiderata to consider when assembling the frames and devices for your pages.

Creating Page Layouts

The first thing to decide is a common layout (template) for your Web pages. Layout involves deciding whether to use text links or graphical controls, and it also involves setting a style for page headings and footers.

Headings may incorporate text navigation bars or other information that you want to make consistent for your users. Footers should include contact information and the original URL for reference, possibly preceded by a horizontal rule.

Some organizations have gone so far as to lay down a border for each page, with the area above the frame used as the header, and the area below as the footer. Whatever layout you choose, make it as attractive as you can (without making it distracting) and use it consistently. Doing this helps to create a welcome feeling of familiarity across your pages that, in turn, helps users find their way around your site.

Building a Graphical Vocabulary

If you decide to use graphics as navigation links, keep the icons or buttons as small and simple as possible. Using small, simple graphics reduces transfer time and makes them faster for browsers to render.

Building a small, consistent set of graphical symbols (what we've called a *vocabulary*) also improves browser efficiency: Most browsers cache graphics so that they don't have to be downloaded after the first time they appear. It's much faster to reuse an existing graphic than to reference a new one. That's why we advocate a fairly limited graphics vocabulary.

Remember to supply ALT text definitions for these elements when you reference them. Doing this keeps users with character-mode browsers from being left in the lurch. These graphical elements should be simple enough that a single word or short phrase can substitute for them, and still deliver the same meaning and impact.

Using White Space

Although content may be king in Web pages, it's still possible to have too much of a good thing. Don't try to limit the amount of scrolling by eliminating headings and paragraph breaks.

White space is the term used by page designers to describe the space on a page that's unoccupied by other things like graphics and type. A certain amount of white space is critical for the human eye. In general, the more complex or convoluted the images or content, the more positive the effect of white space on a page.

Be sure to give your content and images room to breathe by leaving at least 20 percent of any screen unoccupied. You can build white space into your documents with extra paragraph tags, or by regularly using headings to separate regions of text and graphics. Whatever method you use, be sure to give readers enough room to follow your lead through your pages!

Formatting for Impact

HTML includes a variety of descriptive (`<EM>`, `<STRONG>`, `<CITE>`, and so on) and physical (`<I>`, `<B>`, `<TT>`, and so on) character tags. It also employs larger fonts and text styles to set headings off from ordinary text. When you're using these tools, remember that emphasis and impact are relative terms: In fact, the less often such tags are used, the more impact they have.

Overuse of character handling, whether descriptive or physical, can blunt the impact of your entire document. Be sure to use such controls judiciously, only where impact is critical.

When trying to decide whether to use a descriptive or physical character tag, be aware that certain browsers may provide wider latitudes in rendering descriptive tags. Physical tags usually are associated with certain fonts (for example, a monospaced Courier font is typical for the typewriter tag `<TT>`). Descriptive tags can be associated with the same characteristics, but they can also be represented through other fonts or text colors, especially for graphical browsers. Thus, it's important to consider whether the rendering or the emphasis is important: If it's the rendering, use a physical style; if it's the emphasis, use a logical one.

Enhancing Content

If a picture is worth a thousand words, are a thousand words worth a picture? When combining text and graphics in Web pages, be sure to emphasize the relationship between the two in the content. Graphics can be especially useful in diagramming complex ideas, in representing physical objects or other tangible phenomena, and in compressing large amounts of content into a small space.

Yet the surrounding text also needs to take cognizance of the graphics, use them as a point of reference, and refer back to key elements or components as they're being discussed. This makes labels, captions, and other methods of identifying particular elements on a graphic almost as important as the graphic itself. Careful integration of text and graphics enhances the content of a page.

The same is true for other hypermedia within Web pages. Beyond the novelty of including sounds or music, animation, or video, the content of these other media needs to be integrated with the text to have the greatest impact.

Rather than explaining a leitmotif only in words, it becomes possible to define and then discuss a leitmotif around a musical phrase from a symphony or string quartet. Likewise, discussion of film editing techniques, such as dissolves, can be amplified with examples taken from the work of classic directors.

Whatever materials appear in or through your Web pages, they need to be solidly integrated and share a common rhetorical focus. This fact applies as strongly to hypermedia as it does to text, but the possibilities of enhancing content in this way should never be overlooked.

Making Effective Use of Hypermedia

Strong integration of hypermedia with the other content on a page is the most important ingredient for effective use. It's also necessary to understand the potential bottlenecks that some users face.

Effective use of hypermedia, therefore, implies asking your users for *informed consent* before inflicting such materials on them. For graphics, this means preparing thumbnails of larger images, labeling them with size information, and using them as clickable maps to let users request a download of the full-sized image. In other words, the user who decides to pull down a full-color image of *The Last Supper* cannot be dismayed when he or she already knows that it's a 1.2MB file that may take several minutes to download. By the same token, including such an image right on a Web page may irritate people who were merely looking for information about the picture.

This principle applies equally to sounds, video, and other kinds of hypermedia. Remember to ask for informed consent from your users, and you can be sure that only those individuals who are willing to wait are subjected to delays in delivery.

Aiding Navigation

By including outlines, tables of contents, indexes, or search engines within your Web documents, you can make it much easier for users to find their way around your materials. So why not do it?

Forming Good Opinions

We think that no Web site is complete without an interactive HTML form to ask users for their feedback. Not only does this give you a chance to see your work from somebody else's perspective, it can be a valuable source of input and ideas for enhancing and improving your content. Just remember: "If you don't ask them, they won't tell you!"

Knowing When to Split

As pages get larger and larger, or as your content shows itself to be more complex than you originally thought, you come to a point where a single long document could function better as a collection of smaller ones.

How can you decide when it's time to split things up? By trading off convenience against impatience. A single long document takes longer to download and read than any individual smaller one, but each time that a user requests an individual document, it may have to be downloaded on the spot. The question then becomes, "One long wait, or several short ones?"

The answer lies in the content. If your document is something that's touched quickly and then exited immediately, delivering information in small chunks makes sense. The only people who have to pay a delay penalty are those who choose to read through many pages; in-and-outers don't have to pay much at all. If your document is something that's downloaded and then perused in detail, it may make sense to keep large amounts of information within a single document.

By using the materials frequently yourself (make sure to use them over a slow link as well as a fast one) and by asking users for feedback, you should be able to strike the happy medium between these extremes, as soon as one wanders by!

Adding Value for Value

Obtaining feedback from users is incredibly valuable and makes HTML forms all the more worthwhile. But responding to that feedback in a visible, obvious way can make the experience as good for the users as it should be for you.

It's a good idea to publicly acknowledge feedback that causes change, whether for reasons good or ill. The "What's New" page that links to many home pages (and maybe should on yours, too) is a good place to make this acknowledgment. We also believe in acknowledging strong opinions by e-mail or letter to let the user know you heard what they said and thank them for their input.

If you can develop your users as allies and confederates, they can help you improve and enhance your content. These improvements could lead to improved business or maybe just to improved communications. Either way, by giving valuable information and acknowledging the value of other people's contributions, you've added to the total of what the Web delivers to the world!

Chapter 25

Decimating Web Bugs

. . . .

. . . .

*W*hen you've put the finishing touches on a set of pages, it's time to put them through their paces. Testing is a key ingredient for controlling the quality of your content. It should include a thorough content review, a complete check of your HTML syntax and semantics, investigations of every possible link, and a series of sanity checks to make doubly and triply sure that what you've wound up with is what you really wanted to build. Read on for some gems of testing wisdom for ridding your Web pages of bugs, errors, and other undesirable elements.

Making a List and Checking It Twice

Your document design should include a roadmap that specifies all of the individual HTML documents in your Web, and the relationships among them. If you're smart, you've kept this map up to date as you moved from design into implementation (and in our experience, things always change when you go down this path). If you're not smart, don't berate yourself — just go out and update this map now. Be sure to include all intradocument links as well as interdocument ones.

This road map can serve as the foundation for a testing plan, wherein you systematically investigate and check every page and every link. You just want to make sure that everything works like you think it does and that what you've built has some relationship, however surprising, to what you designed. This road map becomes your list of things to check, and as you go through the testing process, you'll be checking it (at least) twice.

Mastering the Mechanics of Text

By the time any collection of Web pages comes together, you're typically looking at thousands of words, if not significantly more. Yet the number of Web pages that are published without even a cursory spelling check is astonishing. That's why we suggest — no, demand — that you include a spelling check as a step in testing and checking your materials.

You can use your favorite word processor to spell-check your pages. As you check them, you're able to add all of the HTML markup to your custom dictionary, and pretty soon, the program only pukes on the URLs and other strange strings that occur from time to time in HTML files.

Or, if you'd prefer, you can try out one of the several HTML-based spell-checking services now available on the Web. We like the one you can find at

```
http://imagiware.com/RxHTML.cgi
```

If this spell-checker doesn't cut it for you, visit one of the search engines we mention in Chapter 14 and use `spell-check` as a search string. For us, a recent visit to Yahoo! turned up over a half dozen likely candidates.

Nevertheless, you should persist and root out all the real typos and misspellings. Your users may not thank you, but they will have a higher opinion of your pages if they don't find them full of errors!

Lacking Live Links Leaves Loathsome Legacies

Nothing is more irritating to users than to see a link to some Web resource on a page that they're just dying to follow, only to get the dread `404 Server not found` error instead. Our admittedly unscientific and random sampling of Webheads shows us unequivocally that users' impressions of a set of pages are strongly proportional to the number of working links they contain.

The moral of this survey is: Always check your links. This is as true after you've published your pages as it is before they've been subjected to the limelight of public scrutiny. Checking links is as important for page maintenance as it is for testing initial pages for release. If you're smart, you'll hire a robot to do the job for you: They work incredibly long hours, don't charge much, and faithfully check every last link in your site (or beyond, if you let them loose). We're rather fond of a robot named MOMspider, created by Roy Fielding of the W3C. Visit MOMspider's home page at

```
http://www.ics.uci.edu/WebSoft/MOMspider
```

This spider takes a bit of work to get to know, but you can set it to check only local links, so it can do a bang-up job of catching stale links before your users do. If you don't like this particular tool, try a search engine with `robot` or `spider` as your search term. There are definitely lots to choose from! The best thing about robots is that you can schedule them to do their jobs at regular intervals: They always show up on time, they always do a thorough job, and they never complain, either.

Another hint: Just because a URL has a pointer in it to where the real content is located doesn't mean it's okay to leave the original link alone. If your link checking shows something like this, do yourself and your users a favor and update the URL to its current location. You'll save them time and lower the number of bogus packets on the Internet, too.

Looking for Trouble in All the Right Places

When it comes time for beta testing your pages, you want to bring in as rowdy and refractory a crowd to bang on them as you possibly can. If you have customers or colleagues who are picky, opinionated, pushy, or argumentative, be comforted to know that such people make ideal beta testers.

They'll use your pages in ways you never imagined possible. They'll interpret your content to mean things you never intended, in a million years. They'll drive you crazy, and crawl all over your most cherished beliefs and principles.

They'll also find gotchas, big and small, that you never knew were there. They'll catch the typos that the word processors couldn't. They'll tell you things you left out, and things you should have omitted. They'll give you a whole new perspective on your Web pages, and they'll help you to see them from all kinds of extreme points of view.

The results of all this suffering, believe it or not, is positive. Your pages emerge clearer, more direct, and more correct than they would have if you'd tried to do all the testing yourself. If you don't believe us, try skipping this step, and see what happens when the real users start banging on your materials! Beta testing is a must for a well-rounded Web site, especially one intended for business use.

Covering All the Bases

If you're an individual user with a simple home page, or a collection of facts and figures on your private obsession, this step may not apply. But go ahead and read along anyway — you just may learn something.

If your pages represent the views and content of an organization of some kind, chances are 100 percent that you'll want to subject your content to some kind of peer and management review before publishing it to the world. In fact, we recommend that you build reviews into each step along the way toward building your pages — starting with overall design, to writing copy for each page, to reviewing the final assembly of pages — to avoid hitting any potential stumbling blocks. If you have any doubts about copyright protection (or violation), references, logo usage, or other such important details, you probably should get the legal department involved as well (if you have one, that is).

It may even be a good idea to build some kind of sign-off process into reviews, so that you can later prove that the materials were reviewed and approved by responsible parties. We hope you don't have to be that formal about publishing your Web pages, but it's far, far better to be safe than sorry. Is this covering the bases, or covering something else? You decide . . . and take appropriate action.

Tools of the Testing Trade

When you're grinding through your Web pages, checking your links and your HTML, remember that there is automated help available. If you check the validation tools in Chapter 15, you'll be well on your way to finding some computerized assistance in making sure your HTML is as clean and standards-compliant as the freshly driven snow (do we know how to mix a metaphor, or what?).

Likewise, it's a good idea to investigate the Web spiders covered in Chapter 14, and use them regularly to check the links in your pages. They are able to get back to you if something isn't current, so you know where to start looking for the real links you need. Remember to make this a regular part of your maintenance routine, while you're at it. The best way to do that is to use a spider, and schedule it to run at regular intervals.

Fostering Feedback

You might not think of user feedback as a form (or consequence) of testing, but it represents some of the best reality checks your Web pages are ever likely to get. That's why it's a good idea to do everything you can — including offering prizes or other tangible inducements — to get users to fill out HTML forms on your Web site.

That's also why it's an even better idea to read the feedback you get, and to go out and solicit as much as you can handle (or more). And finally, the best idea of all is to carefully consider the feedback you get and implement the things that may improve your Web offerings.

Making the Most of Your Audience

Asking for feedback is an important step toward developing a relationship with your users. Even the most finicky and picky of your users can be an incredible asset: Who better to pick over your newest pages, and to point out all the small, subtle errors or flaws that they revel in discovering? Working with your users can mean that, over time, some become more involved in your work and in helping guide the content of your Web pages (if not the rest of your professional or obsessional life). Who could ask for better than that?

Chapter 26

Ten Ways to Decide to "Build or Buy" Your Web Services

*W*hen the time comes to publish your Web pages, you'll have to make one of the toughest and most important decisions about where the pages should live. Should you set up your own server, and handle this yourself? Or should you find a friendly national, regional, or local Internet service provider and let them do it for you?

These are good questions, indeed. Answering them will tell you whether you want to buy or build, or perhaps buy now and build later (or even build now and buy later). Stick with us as we take you through the numbers and the reasons why you might choose to roll your own or to get underneath somebody else's Web umbrella.

Understanding Objectives

The most important thing to understand is your overall objectives. If your organization is planning on making a major move onto the Internet and views the Web as a key ingredient to its future success and well-being, building your own server might be a natural extension of other plans.

If your organization simply views the Web as yet another way to disseminate news and information along with existing media and techniques, having your own Web server might add no strategic value. At that point, you could perform some simple analyses and figure out whether building or buying makes more sense.

Point 1: If the Web is a paramount method for communicating with your audience, having your own server helps to establish your organization as a legitimate, full-time Web presence.

Counting Your Pennies

For a detailed analysis of the costs and considerations, please refer back to Chapter 17. The quick-and-dirty formula is the following: If Web-related costs from a provider average $1,000 a month or more, it's worthwhile considering a server of your very own. If average costs are less than $1,000 a month, it's probably not worthwhile, unless there are other compelling factors to consider. For example, an Internet service provider may not use its Web server as heavily as its clients might, yet it'd look kind of lame if it didn't have one!

When calculating costs, figure that at least one-fourth of a system administrator's time is required to run a Web server. Remember also that costs include monthly communications fees, Internet access charges, and maintenance-related expenditures. And you have to amortize the hardware and software costs to set up the system in the first place. It's not at all unusual for the after-purchase costs to add up to ten (or more) times the initial costs over the life of a system.

Point 2: At $1,000 a month or more for Web services, it's reasonable to start thinking about building, rather than buying, a Web server.

Projecting and Monitoring Traffic

One of the key elements in determining Web service costs is figuring the download fees that are usually assessed by service providers. Normally, such costs run from two to ten cents per megabyte of data that's downloaded. This might not sound like much, but let's stop to crunch some numbers: If your pages are 2MB in size and you average 30 users per day, that translates into $36.50 to $182.50 for an average month. Raise the amount of data to 5MB, and the costs go from $91.25 to $456.25 for an average month.

None of these costs is prohibitive, though, nor would they add up to enough, including telephone or access line costs and monthly account fees, to exceed our $1,000 monthly ceiling. Things really get expensive, though, when hundreds to thousands of users a day start downloading your data. At that point, multiplying costs three- to thirtyfold really can get prohibitive. That's why some initial testing and an audience survey can be important in making usage projections.

Point 3: If you're expecting (or even hoping for) lots and lots of traffic, you're better off building your own server instead of buying space on somebody else's. Don't forget to hire an experienced WebMaster or to train somebody in-house right away!

How Much is Too Much?

The principle of parsimony argues that you'd better try to limit the amount of data you publish on your Web pages, especially if you're paying by the megabyte of data transferred from your provider's server. It's important to keep an eye on the amount and kind of data that your Web server offers.

If you've got numerous large files or images that some, but not all, users find interesting, you might consider making them available through other means. This could include finding an anonymous `ftp` site on the Internet and directing users to pick up these large files there, or it might mean setting up an e-mail-based file delivery system like that provided by `listserv` or `majordomo`.

Point 4: Keep an eye on the data that users download and try to make large, infrequently accessed files or documents available by other means.

Managing Volatility

The Web is an ever-changing galaxy of information. Keeping up with change means regular effort and a fair amount of volatility in your Web page offerings. Many providers charge extra when you change your materials, but even if they don't, the effort of making and testing changes has an associated cost.

We recommend that you manage and schedule changes on your server. Plan on regular updates and stick to the plan. Gather up incremental and incidental changes in the meantime and apply them when the schedule or external factors say it's the right time. While you're at it, keep tabs on your materials' freshness, and regularly check your off-server links to other pages and locations for currency and correctness.

If you have loads of content that change frequently, you might want the extra control over the server that you get with building your own. Convenience and access to your data have value, too, and may influence you to build your own server even if your costs appear to hover below the $1,000 monthly cut-off.

Point 5: Constant, unceasing change is much more expensive than planned change. Whether you build or buy your Web server, you'll still have to manage change, or it will manage you! Where change is frequent and regular, the convenience of access to your own server can have significant value.

Communicating Corporately

If your organization has a well-planned communications strategy, effective use of the Web will complement other channels of communication already in use — like the trade press, the news media, and the industry analysts and pundits who follow your industry. In this kind of environment, Web documents usually reflect and coordinate with documents of many other kinds, including advertisements, collateral, and a full range of other corporate publications.

In environments where tight controls over corporate or organizational communications must be maintained, it's pretty normal to find Web servers under the purview of a public relations or corporate communications department. Likewise, in environments where internal and external communications are formal and carefully managed, you might even find one set of servers for internal materials (not available to the public) and another set of servers for external materials.

Point 6: In tightly managed organizations, especially those with carefully orchestrated communications, control over the Web server may be an absolute requirement, irrespective of other considerations.

Reaching Your Audience

If you decide to build your own server, and connect up to the Internet via a 28.8 Kbps modem through a provider, you've limited the number of users who'll be able to access your Web pages at any given time (probably to one to three users for each such connection). If, on the other hand, you attach a full 1.44 Mbps T-1 link to your server, you've increased the size (and the cost) of your pipe significantly, but you'll still be limited to under 100 simultaneous users.

Projecting traffic, as it turns out, is not only important to understanding costs, it's also important to matching the size of the Web server pipe against the number of potential users. It's wasteful to use a large pipe for low-traffic situations, but it can be catastrophic to provide a small-to-medium pipe when a tsunami of interest is heading your way. Frustrate your users long enough, and they may decide to meet their interests elsewhere.

Monitoring usage and demand is the only way to cope with this phenomenon, but you'll be far better off if you start out with extra, unused capacity than if your pipes are clogged from the word "Go!" Because operating your own server gives you the flexibility of negotiating the right-sized pipe to the Internet with a telecommunications company and a service provider, many large-volume operations prefer to do it themselves. Even though these costs can be quite high, they're generally lower than if you paid someone else to provide them. Just don't expect to be able to add or expand pipes at a moment's notice, and you'll be able to avoid getting too, too frustrated when it's time to add more capacity.

Point 7: Make it easy for the audience to browse your materials, and they'll do just that. Make it difficult or impossible, and they'll go away . . . forever!

"Web-ifying" Commerce

Companies of many commercial stripes are hungrily eyeing the millions of Internet users as another customer base, ripe for electronic commerce. Today, there are several ways to conduct commercial transactions over the Internet, ranging from so-called digital cash to a variety of secure credit card handling operations.

We don't want to take on the responsibility of recommending a particular approach (even though several of the principals at First Virtual Holdings, Inc., are friends of ours). We'll just say that electronic commerce via the Web is a trendy phenomenon whose potential still vastly outweighs its current use.

But if your company is thinking seriously about adding electronic commerce on the Web to its existing sales channels, you'll probably want to carefully consider building your own Web server. Issues of control, of access to customer information, and of managing the details of financial transactions all argue that the best hands for your Web server to be in are your own!

Point 8: If you're thinking about doing business via the Web, you'll probably want to control your own server, for a variety of good business reasons.

Understanding Your Options

Whether you're building or buying your Web services, you must clearly understand how those pages operate. This is especially true for forms handling, or other Common Gateway Interface-related programs that run on the server to handle user information requests or submissions.

It's imperative that the server that runs your pages is compatible with the services that you want to provide and the programs that you want to run on your users' behalf. This means specifying the kind of `httpd` implementation you need, and it also means understanding the names and versions of surrounding standard services that CGI programs may call on (like the differing clickable image map implementations on the NCSA and CERN implementations of `httpd`, for example).

Point 9: When selecting the server for your Web pages, compatibility with CGI programs, related libraries and other collections of widgets and data is an absolute must. Don't build or buy the wrong kind of server!

Overcoming Success

Finally, you may have to cope with what many people would consider an enviable problem: What happens if your Web pages become the latest rage, and your server gets completely inundated by users trying to avail themselves of your magnificent content?

If that happens, you'll want to make arrangements for fallback services. In this extreme case of demand, working with a national Internet service provider — like ANS, PSI, Delphi, CompuServe, etc. — will be an absolute must. If you can afford what these companies can offer, you'll be able to buy as much capacity from them as you can stand to pay for.

Point 10: If you're smitten with boundless success, be prepared to suffer (especially in the checkbook) for your fame, but make alternative arrangements with a national provider to avoid the perils of Point 7.

Glossary

● ●

absolute When used to modify pathnames or URLs, it means a full and complete specification (as opposed to a relative one).

acceptable use A doctrine originally formulated by the National Science Foundation restricting the Internet to research and academic, but not commercial, use.

alpha test The testing on software performed by the developers, usually during the development process; also, the first of several stages in the software testing process (*see* beta test).

anchor In HTML, an anchor is a tagged text or graphic element that acts as a link to another location inside or outside a given document, or it may be a location in a document that acts as the destination for an incoming link. The latter definition is how we usually use it in this book.

animation A computerized process of creating moving images by rapidly advancing from one still image to the next.

anonymous ftp A type of Internet file access that relies on the File Transfer Protocol service, where any user can typically access a file collection by logging in as *anonymous* and supplying his or her username as a password.

AppleScript The scripting language for the Macintosh operating system, used to build CGI programs for Macintosh-based Web servers.

Archie An Internet-based archival search facility, based on databases of filenames and directory names taken from anonymous ftp servers around the Internet.

ARPA (Advanced Research Projects Administration; *see* DARPA).

attribute In HTML tags, an attribute is a named characteristic of an associated tag. Some attributes are required, while others are optional. Some attributes may also take values (if so, the syntax is ATTRIBUTE="value") or not, depending on the tag and the attribute (*see* Chapter 5 for tag details in alphabetical order).

AUP (Acceptable Use Policy; *see* acceptable use).

authoring software In the context of HTML, authoring software refers to programs that understand HTML tags and their placement. Some such programs can even enforce HTML syntax; others can convert from word-processing or document-formatting programs to HTML formats.

awk A powerful scripting language included with most implementations of UNIX, *awk* supplements the file-processing capabilities of the UNIX shells, including pattern matching of fields and C-like structured programming constructs.

back end The server-side of client/server is called the *back end* because it is usually handled by programs running in obscurity on the server, out of sight (and mind) for most users.

bandwidth Technically, bandwidth is the range of electrical frequencies that a device can handle; more often, it's used as a measure of a communications technology's carrying capacity.

Basic (Beginner's All-purpose Symbolic Instruction Code) A programming language, Basic (also called BASIC) is easy to learn and use. The most popular implementation is Microsoft's QuickBasic.

beta test The phase of software testing where a program or system is turned over to a select group of users outside the development organization for use in more or less real-life situations.

body The body is one of the main identifiable structures of any HTML document. It is usually trapped between the head information and the footer information.

bookmark Most Web browsers include a facility for building a list of URLs that users want to keep for future reference. Netscape calls such references *bookmarks* in its browser.

browser A Web access program that can request HTML documents from Web servers, and render such documents on a user's display device (*see also* client).

BSD (Berkeley Software Distribution) A flavor of UNIX that was particularly important in the late 1970s and 1980s when most of the enhancements and add-ons to UNIX appeared first in the BSD version (like TCP/IP).

BTW Acronym for *By The Way*; commonly used in e-mail messages.

bugs Small verminous creatures that sometimes show up in software in the form of major or minor errors, mistakes, and gotchas. Bugs got their name from insects that, having been attracted to the glow of the filament in a tube, were found in antiquated tube-based computers of the late '50s and early '60s.

C A programming language developed at AT&T Bell Laboratories, C remains the implementation language for UNIX and the UNIX programmer's language of choice.

case sensitive Means that the way computer input is typed is significant; for example, HTML tags can be typed in any mixture of upper- and lowercase, but because HTML character entities are case sensitive, they must be typed exactly as shown in this book.

CD-ROM (Compact Disc-Read-Only Memory) A computer-readable version of the audio CD; CD-ROMs can contain up to 650 MB of data, making them the distribution media of choice for many of today's large (some would even say bloated) programs and systems.

CERN (Centre European Researche Nucleare). The Center for High-Energy Physics in Geneva, Switzerland; the birthplace of the World Wide Web.

character entity A way of reproducing strange and wonderful characters within HTML, character entities take the form `&string;` where the ampersand (&) and semicolon (;) are mandatory metacharacters, and `string` names the characters to be reproduced in the browser. Because character entities are case sensitive, the string between the ampersand and the semicolon must be reproduced exactly as written in Chapter 6 of this book.

character mode When referring to Web browsers, character mode (also called *text mode*) means that such browsers can reproduce text data only. They cannot produce graphics directly without the assistance of a helper application.

clickable map A graphic in an HTML file that has had a pixel coordinate map file created for it, to allow regions of the graphic to point to specific URLs for graphically oriented Web navigation.

client The end-user side of the client/server arrangement, the term *client* typically refers to a consumer of network services of one kind or another. A Web browser is therefore a client program that talks to Web servers.

client/server A model for computing that divides computing into two separate roles, usually connected by a network: The client works on the end-user's side of the connection and manages user interaction and display (input and output, and related processing), while the server works elsewhere on the network and manages data-intensive or shared-processing activities, like serving up the collections of documents and programs that a Web server typically manages.

common controls When designing HTML documents, most experts recommend that you build a set of consistent navigation controls and use them throughout a document (or collection of documents), providing a set of common controls for document navigation.

Common Gateway Interface (CGI) The specification governing how Web browsers can communicate with and request services from Web servers; also the format and syntax for passing information from browsers to servers via forms or document-based queries in HTML.

computing platform A way of referring to the kind of computer someone is using, this term encompasses both hardware (the type of machine, processor, etc.) and software (the operating system and applications) in use.

content For HTML, content is its *raison d'etre;* although form is important, content is why users access Web documents and why they keep coming back for more.

convention An agreed-upon set of rules and approaches that allows systems to communicate with one another and work together.

DARPA (Defense Advanced Research Projects Administration) A U.S. Department of Defense funding agency that supplied the cash and some of the expertise that led to the development of the Internet, among many other interesting things.

dedicated line A telephone line dedicated to the purpose of computerized telecommunications; a dedicated line may be operated continuously (24 hours a day) by its owner. In this book, such lines usually provide a link to an Internet Service Provider.

default In general computer-speak, a default is a selection that's made automatically in a program, instruction, or whatever, when no selections are made explicitly. For HTML the default is the value assigned to an attribute when none is supplied.

desktop (also called *desktop machine*) The computer a user typically has on his or her desktop; a synonym for *end-user computer* or *computer*.

dial-up A connection to the Internet (or some other remote computer or network), made by dialing up an access telephone number.

directory path The device and directory names needed to locate a particular file in any given file system; for HTML, UNIX-style directory paths usually apply.

DNS (Domain Name Server; *see* domain names).

document The basic unit of HTML information, a *document* refers to the entire contents of any single HTML file. Because this doesn't always correspond to normal notions of a document, we refer to what could formally be called *HTML documents* more or less interchangeably with *Web pages*, which is how such documents are rendered by browsers for display.

document-based queries One of two methods of passing information from a browser to a Web server, document-based queries are designed to pass short strings of information to the server by using the `METHOD="GET"` HTTP method of delivery. This method is typically used for search requests or other short lookup operations.

document headings The class of HTML tags that we generically refer to as `<H*>`, document headings allow authors to insert headings of various sizes and weights (levels 1 through 6) to add structure to their documents' contents. As structural elements, headings should identify the beginning of a new concept or idea within a document.

document structure For HTML, this refers to the methods used to organize and navigate within HTML documents or related collections of documents.

DoD (Department of Defense) The folks who paid the bills for and operated the earliest versions of the Internet.

domain names The names used on the Internet as part of a distributed database system for translating computer names into physical addresses and vice versa.

DOS (Disk Operating System; *see also* OS) The underlying control program used to make most Intel-based PCs run. Microsoft's MS-DOS is the most widely used implementation of DOS and provides the scaffolding atop which its (equally widely used) MS-Windows software runs.

DTD (Document Type Definition) A formal SGML specification for a document, a DTD lays out the structural elements and markup definitions that can then be used to create instances of documents.

dumb terminal A display device with attached keyboard that relies on the intelligence of another computer to drive its display and interpret its keyboard inputs. Such devices were the norm in the heyday of the mainframe and minicomputer and are still widely used for reservation systems, point of sale, and other specialized-use applications.

e-mail An abbreviation for *electronic mail*, e-mail is the preferred method for exchanging information between users on the Internet (and other networked systems).

electronic commerce The exchange of money for goods or services via an electronic medium; many companies expect electronic commerce to do away with mail order and telephone order shopping by the end of the century.

encoded information A way of wrapping computer data in a special envelope to ship it across a network, encoded information refers to data-manipulation techniques that change data formats and layouts to make them less sensitive to the rigors of electronic transit. Encoded information must usually be decoded by its recipient before it can be used.

error message Information delivered by a program to a user, usually to inform him or her that things haven't worked properly, if at all. Error messages are an ill-appreciated art form and contain some of the funniest and most opaque language we've ever seen (also, the most tragic for their unfortunate recipients).

Ethernet The most common local-area networking technology in use today, Ethernet was developed at about the same time (and by many of the same people and institutions) as the Internet.

FAQs (Frequently Asked Questions) Usenet newsgroups, mailing list groups, and other affiliations of like-minded individuals on the Internet usually designate a more senior member of their band to assemble and publish a list of frequently asked questions, in an often futile effort to keep from answering them quite as frequently.

file extension In DOS, this refers to the three-letter part of a filename after the period; for UNIX, Macintosh, and other file systems, this refers to the string after the rightmost period in a filename. File extensions are used to label files as to their type, origin, and possible use.

flame Used as a verb ("He got flamed."), it means to be the recipient of a particularly hostile or nasty e-mail message; as a noun ("That was a real flame."), it refers to such a message.

flamewar What happens when two or more individuals start exchanging hostile or nasty e-mail messages; this is viewed by some as an art form, and is best observed on Usenet or other newsgroups (where the *alt.flame* . . . or *alt.bitch* newsgroups would be good places to browse for examples).

footer The concluding part of an HTML document, the footer should contain contact, version, date, and attribution information to help identify a document and its authors.

forms In HTML, forms are built on special markup that lets browsers solicit data from users and then deliver that data to specially designated input-handling programs on a Web server. Briefly, forms provide a mechanism to let users interact with servers on the Web.

front end In the client/server model, the front end part refers to the client side; it's where the user views and interacts with information from a server; for the Web, browsers provide the front end that communicates with Web servers on the back end.

FTP (sometimes ftp; File Transfer Protocol) An Internet file transfer service based on the TCP/IP protocols, FTP provides a way to copy files to and from FTP servers elsewhere on a network.

gateway A type of computer program that knows how to connect to two or more different kinds of networks, to translate information from one side's format to the other's, and vice versa. Common types of gateways include e-mail, database, and communications.

GIF (Graphics Information File) One of a set of commonly used graphics formats within Web documents. It is used frequently because of its compressed format and compact nature.

Gopher A program/protocol developed at the University of Minnesota, Gopher provides for unified, menu-driven presentation of a variety of Internet services, including WAIS, telnet, and FTP.

graphics In HTML documents, graphics are files that belong to one of a restricted family of types (usually GIF or JPEG) that are referenced via URLs for in-line display on Web pages.

grep (general regular expression parser) A standard UNIX program that looks for patterns found in files and reports on their occurrences. The *grep* program handles a wide range of patterns, including so-called "regular expressions," which can use all kinds of substitutions and wildcards to provide powerful search-and-replace operations within files.

GUI (Graphical User Interface) Pronounced *gooey.* GUIs are what make graphical Web browsers possible; they create a visually oriented interface that makes it easy for users to interact with computerized information of all kinds.

heading For HTML, a heading is a markup tag used to add document structure. The term is sometimes be used to refer to the initial portion of an HTML document between the <HEAD> . . . </HEAD> tags, where titles and context definitions are commonly supplied.

helper applications Today, browsers can display multiple graphics files (and other kinds of data); sometimes, browsers must pass particular files — for example, motion picture or sound files — over to other applications that know how to render the data they contain. Such programs are called helper applications because they help the browser deliver Web information to users.

hierarchical structure A way of organizing Web pages using links that make some pages subordinate to others. (*See* tree-structure[d] for another description of this kind of organization.)

history list Each time a user accesses the Web, his or her browser normally keeps a list of all the URLs visited during that session; this is called a history list, and provides a handy way to jump back to any page that's already been visited while online. History lists normally disappear when the user exits the browser.

hotlist A Web page that consists of a series of links to other pages, usually annotated with information about what's available on that link. Hotlists act like switchboards to content information, and are usually organized around a particular topic or area of interest.

HTML (HyperText Markup Language) The SGML-derived markup language used to create Web pages. Not quite a programming language, HTML nevertheless provides a rich lexicon and syntax for designing and creating useful hypertext documents for the Web.

http or **HTTP** (hypertext transfer protocol) The Internet protocol used to manage communication between Web clients (browsers) and servers.

httpd (http daemon) The name of the collection of programs that runs on a Web server to provide Web services. In UNIX-speak, a *daemon* is a program that runs all the time and listens for service requests of a particular type; thus, an *httpd* is a program that runs continually on a Web server, ready to field and handle Web service requests.

hyperlink A shorthand term for hypertext link, which is defined in its own entry.

hypermedia Any of a variety of computer media — including text, graphics, video, sound, etc. — available through hypertext links on the Web.

hypertext A method of organizing text, graphics, and other data for computer use that lets individual data elements point to one another; a nonlinear method of organizing information, especially text.

hypertext link In HTML, a hypertext link is defined by special markup that creates a user-selectable document element that can be selected to change the user's focus from one document (or part of a document) to another.

image map A synonym for clickable image, this refers to an overlaid collection of pixel coordinates for a graphic that can be used to locate a user's selection of a region on a graphic, and in turn, used to select a related hypertext link for further Web navigation.

IMHO Acronym for *In My Humble Opinion,* mostly used in e-mail messages.

Infobahn A psuedo-Teutonic synonym for Information Superhighway (taken from autobahn, the German highway system), commonly used because it's shorter and "cooler" than Information Superhighway.

Information Superhighway The near-mythical agglomeration of the Internet, communications companies, telephone systems, and other communications media that politicians seem to believe will be the "next big thing" in business, academia, and industry. Many people believe that this highway is already here, and that it's called *the Internet*.

input-handling program For Web services, a program that runs on a Web server designated by the ACTION attribute of an HTML <FORM> tag, whose job it is to field, interpret, and respond to user input from a browser, typically by custom-building an HTML document in response to some user request.

Internaut Someone who travels using the Internet (like *astronaut* or *argonaut*).

Internet A worldwide collection of networks that began with technology and equipment funded by the U.S. Department of Defense in the 1970s that today links users in nearly every known country, speaking nearly every known language.

IP (Internet Protocol; *see* TCP/IP) IP is the specific networking protocol of the same name used to tie computers together over the Internet; IP is also used as a synonym for the whole TCP/IP protocol suite.

ISDN (Integrated Services Digital Network) An emerging digital technology for telecommunications that offers higher bandwidth and better signal quality than old-fashioned analog telephone lines. Not yet available in many parts of the U.S. or in the rest of the world.

ISO (International Standards Organization) The granddaddy of standards organizations worldwide, the ISO is a body made up of standards bodies from countries all over the place. Most important communications and computing standards — like the telecommunications and character code standards mentioned in this book — are the subject of ISO standards.

JPEG or **JPG** JPEG stands for Joint Photographic Experts' Group, an industry association that has defined a particularly compressible format for image storage that is designed for dealing with complex color still images (such as photographs). Files stored in this format usually take the extension .JPEG (except DOS or Windows machines, which are limited to the three-character .JPG equivalent). Today, JPEG is emerging as the graphics format standard of choice for use on the World Wide Web.

Kbps (Kilobits per second) A measure of communications speeds, in units of 210 bits per second (2^{10} = 1024, which is just about 1,000 and explains the quasi-metric K notation).

KISS (Keep It Simple, Stupid!) A self-descriptive philosophy that's supposed to remind us to "eschew obfuscation," except it's easier to understand!

LAN (Local Area Network) Typically, one of a variety of communications technologies used to link computers together in a single building, business, or campus environment.

layout element In an HTML document, a layout element is a paragraph, list, graphic, horizontal rule, heading, or some other document component whose placement on a page contributes to its overall look and feel.

linear text Shorthand for old-fashioned documents that work like this book does: by placing one page after the other, *ad infinitum* in a straight line. Even though such books have indexes, pointers, cross-references, and other attempts to add linkages, they must be applied manually (rather than by clicking your mouse).

link For HTML, a link is a pointer in one part of a document that can transport users to another part of the same document or to another document entirely. This capability puts the *hyper* into hypertext. In other words, a link is a one-to-one relationship/association between two concepts or ideas, similar to cognition (the brain has triggers such as smell, sight, and sound that cause a link to be followed to a similar concept or reaction).

list element An item in an HTML list structure tagged with the ⟨LI⟩ (list item) tag.

list tags HTML tags for a variety of list styles, including ordered lists ⟨OL⟩, unordered lists ⟨UL⟩, menus ⟨MENU⟩, glossary lists ⟨DL⟩, or directory lists ⟨DIR⟩.

listserv An Internet e-mail handling program, typically UNIX-based, that provides mechanisms to let users manage, contribute and subscribe to, and exit from named mailing lists that distribute messages to all subscribed members daily. A common mechanism for delivering information to interested parties on the Internet, this is how the HTML working group communicates among its members, for example.

logical markup Refers to any of a number of HTML character-handling tags that exist to provide emphasis or to indicate that a particular kind of device or action is involved. (*See* Chapter 4 for a discussion of HTML tags by category that includes the details on descriptive versus physical markup.)

Lynx A widely used UNIX-based character-mode Web browser.

MacWeb A Macintosh-based graphical-mode Web browser implemented by MCC (*see also* MCC).

maintenance The process of regularly inspecting, testing, and updating the contents of Web pages; also, an attitude that such activities are both inevitable and advisable.

majordomo A set of Perl programs that automates the operation of multiple mailing lists, including moderated and unmoderated mailing lists, and routine handling of subscribe/unsubscribe operations.

map file A set of pixel coordinates on a graphic image that corresponds to the boundaries of regions that users might select when using the graphic for Web navigation. This file must be created by using a graphics program to determine regions and their boundaries, and then stored on the Web server that provides the coordinate translation and URL selection services.

markup A way of embedding special characters (metacharacters) within a text file to instruct a computer program how to handle the contents of the file itself.

markup language A formal set of special characters and related capabilities used to define a specific method for handling the display of files that include markup; HTML is a markup language that is an application of SGML and is used to design and create Web pages.

Mbps (Megabits per second) A measure of communications speeds, in units of 2^{20} bits per second (2^{20} = 1,048,576, which is just about 1,000,000 and explains the quasimetric M notation).

MCC (Microelectronics and Computing Corporation) A computing industry consortium based in Austin, Texas, that developed the WinWeb and MacWeb browser programs.

metacharacter A specific character within a text file that signals the need for special handling; in HTML the angle brackets (< >), ampersand (&), pound sign (#), and semicolon (;) can all function as metacharacters.

MIME (Multipurpose Internet Mail Extensions) http communications of Web information over the Internet rely on a special variant of MIME formats to convey Web documents and related files between servers and users, and vice versa.

modem An acronym for **mo**dulator/**dem**odulator, a modem is a piece of hardware that converts between the analog forms for voice and data used in the telephone system and the digital forms for data used in computers. In other words, a modem lets your computer communicate using the telephone system.

Mosaic A powerful graphical Web browser originally developed at NCSA, now widely licensed and used for a variety of commercial browser implementations.

MPEG or **MPG** An acronym for Motion Picture Experts' Group, MPEG is a highly compressed format designed for use in moving pictures or other multi-frame-per-second media (such as video). MPEG can not only provide tremendous compression (up to 200 to 1), it also updates only elements that have changed on-screen from one frame to the next. This feature makes it extraordinarily efficient as well — .MPEG is the common file extension to denote files using this format, and .MPG is the three-letter equivalent on DOS and Windows systems (which can't handle four-letter file extensions).

MPPP (Multilink Point-to-Point Protocol) An Internet protocol that allows simultaneous use of multiple physical connections between one computer and another, to aggregate their combined bandwidth and create a "larger" virtual link between the two machines.

multimedia A method of combining text, sound, graphics, and full-motion or animated video within a single compound computer document.

MVS (Multiple Virtual Storage). A file system used on IBM mainframes and clones.

navigation In the context of the Web, navigation refers to the use of hyperlinks to move within or between HTML documents and other Web-accessible resources.

navigation bar A way of arranging a series of hypertext links on a single line of a Web page to provide a set of navigation controls for an HTML document or a set of HTML documents.

NCSA (National Center for Supercomputing Applications) A research unit of the University of Illinois at Urbana, where the original Mosaic implementation was built, and where the NCSA *httpd* Web server code is maintained and distributed.

nesting In computer terms, one structure that occurs within another is said to be nested; in HTML, nesting happens most commonly with list structures, which may be freely nested within one another, regardless of type.

netiquette A networking takeoff on the term *etiquette,* netiquette refers to the written and unwritten rules of behavior on the Internet. When in doubt if an activity is permitted or not, ask first, and then act only if no one objects (check the FAQ for a given area, too — it often explicitly states the local rules of netiquette for a newsgroup, mailing list, etc.).

network link The tie that binds a computer to a network; for dial-in Internet users, this is usually a telephone link; for directly attached users, it is whatever kind of technology (Ethernet, token-ring, FDDI, etc.) is in local use.

numeric entity A special markup element that reproduces a particular character from the ISO-Latin-1 character set, a numeric entity takes the form `&#nnn;` where `nnn` is the one, two, or three-digit numeric code that corresponds to a particular character (Chapter 6 contains a complete list of these codes).

on-demand connection A dial-up link to a service provider that's available whenever it's needed (on demand, get it?).

online A term that indicates that information, activity, or communications are located on, or taking place in, an electronic, networked computing environment (like the Internet). The opposite of online is *offline,* which is what your computer is as soon as you disconnect from the Internet.

OS (Operating System) The underlying control program on a computer that makes the hardware run and supports the execution of one or more applications. DOS, UNIX, and OS/2 are all examples of operating systems.

packet A basic unit (or package) of data used to describe individual elements of online communications; in other words, data moves across networks like the Internet in packets.

pages The generic term for the HTML documents that Web users view on their browsers.

paragraphs The basic elements of text within an HTML document, <P> is the markup tag used to indicate a paragraph break in text (the closing <P> tag is currently optional in HTML).

path, pathname *See* directory path.

PC (personal computer) Today, PC is used as a generic term to refer to just about any kind of desktop computer; its original definition was as a product name for IBM's 8086-based personal computer, the IBM PC.

Perl A powerful, compact programming language that draws from the capabilities of languages like C, Pascal, *sed, awk,* and BASIC, Perl is emerging as the language of choice for CGI programs. Its emergence is partly owing to its portability and the many platforms on which it is currently supported, and partly owing to its ability to exploit system services in UNIX quickly and easily.

physical markup Any of a series of HTML markup tags that specifically control character styles (bold <B> and italic <I>) or typeface (<TT>, for typewriter font).

pick list Generally, a list of elements displayed for user selection of one or more choices; in HTML, the result of the <SELECT> and <OPTION> tags to construct such a list for use in a form.

pipe As used in this book, pipe generally refers to the bandwidth of the connection in use between a user's workstation and the Internet (or the server on the other end of the connection, actually).

plain text Usually refers to vanilla ASCII text, as created or viewed in a simple text-editing program.

platform Synonym for computer.

port address TCP/IP-based applications use the concept of a port address to know which program to talk to on the receiving end of a network connection. Because there may be many programs running on a computer at one time — including multiple copies of the same program — the port address provides a mechanism to uniquely identify exactly which process the data should be delivered to.

POTS (Plain Old Telephone System) The normal analog telephone system, just like the one you probably have at home.

PPP (Point-to-Point Protocol) A modern, low-overhead serial communications protocol, typically used to interconnect two computers via modem. Most Web browsers require either a PPP or SLIP connection in order to work.

protocol A formal, rigidly defined set of rules and formats that computers use to communicate with one another.

provider *See* service provider.

RAM (Random-Access Memory) The memory used in most computers to store the results of ongoing work and to provide space to store the operating system and applications that are actually running at any given moment.

relative When applied to URLs, relative means that in the absence of the <BASE> tag, the link is relative to the current page's URL in which the link is defined. This makes for shorter, more compact URLs and explains why most local URLs are relative, not absolute.

resource Any HTML document or other item or service available via the Web. Resources are what URLs point to.

return (short for *carriage return*) In text files, a return is what causes the words on a line to end and makes the display pick up at the leftmost location on the display. As used in this book, it means don't press the Enter or Return key on your keyboard in the middle of a line of HTML markup or a URL specification.

robot A special Web-traveling program that wanders all over the place, following and recording URLs and related titles for future reference (like in search engines).

ROM (Read-Only Memory) A form of computer memory that allows values to be stored only once; after the data is initially recorded, the computer can only read the contents. ROM is used to supply constant code elements such as bootstrap loaders, network addresses, and other more or less unvarying programs or instructions.

router A special-purpose piece of internetworking gear that makes it possible to connect networks together, a router is capable of reading the destination address of any network packet. It can forward the packet to a local recipient if its address resides on any network that the router can reach, or on to another router if the packet is destined for delivery to a network that the current router cannot access.

screen The glowing part on the front of your computer monitor where you see the Web do its thing (and anything else your computer might like to show you).

search engine A special Web program that can search the contents of a database of available Web pages and other resources to provide information that relates to specific topics or keywords supplied by a user.

search tools Any of a number of programs (*see* Chapter 14) that can permit HTML documents to become searchable, using the <ISINDEX> tag to inform the browser of the need for a search window and behind-the-scenes indexing and anchoring schemes to let users locate particular sections of or items within a document.

sed A powerful UNIX-based text-editing program that makes it easy to locate and manipulate text elements within any of a number of files.

server A computer on a network whose job is to listen for particular service requests and to respond to those that it knows how to satisfy.

service provider An organization that provides individuals or other organizations with access to the Internet. Service providers usually offer a variety of communications options for their customers, ranging from analog telephone lines, to a variety of higher-bandwidth leased lines, to ISDN and other digital communications services.

setup When negotiating a network connection, the phase at the beginning of the communications process is called the *setup*. At this point, protocol details, communication rates, and error-handling approaches are worked out, allowing the connection to proceed correctly and reliably thenceforth.

SGML (Standard Generalized Markup Language) An ISO standard document definition, specification, and creation mechanism that makes platform and display differences across multiple computers irrelevant to the delivery and rendering of documents.

shell *See* UNIX shell.

SLIP (Serial Line Interface Protocol) A relatively old-fashioned TCP/IP protocol used to manage telecommunications between a client and a server that treats the phone line as a slow extension to a network.

SMTP (Simple Mail Transfer Protocol) The underlying protocol and service for Internet-based electronic mail.

spider (also called Web spider, Webcrawler) A Web-traversing program that tirelessly investigates Web pages and their links, while storing information about its travels for inclusion in the databases typically used by search engines.

stdin (UNIX standard input device) The default source for input in the UNIX environment, *stdin* is the input source for CGI programs as well.

stdout (UNIX standard output device) The default recipient for output in the UNIX environment, *stdout* is the output source for Web browsers and servers as well (including CGI programs).

superstructure In HTML documents, we refer to superstructure as the layout and navigational elements used to create a consistent look and feel for Web pages belonging to a document set.

syntax Literally, the formal rules for how to speak, we use syntax in this book to describe the rules that govern how HTML markup looks and behaves within HTML documents. The real syntax definition for HTML comes from the SGML Document Type Definition (DTD).

syntax checker A program that checks a particular HTML document's markup against the rules that govern its use; a recommended part of the testing regimen for all HTML documents.

tag The formal name for an element of HTML markup, usually enclosed in angle brackets (< >).

TCP (Transfer Control Protocol; *see also* TCP/IP) The transport layer protocol for the TCP/IP suite, TCP is a reliable, connection-oriented protocol that usually guarantees delivery across a network.

TCP/IP (Transfer Control Protocol/Internet Protocol) The name for the suite of protocols and services used to manage network communications and applications over the Internet.

teardown When a network communication session is ending, the two computers agree to stop talking and then systematically break the connection and recover the port addresses and other resources used for the session. This process is called teardown.

technophobe Literally, someone who's afraid of technology, this term is more commonly applied to those who simply want to use technology without understanding it.

telnet The Internet protocol and service that lets you take a smart computer (your own, probably) and make it emulate a dumb terminal over the network. Briefly, telnet is a way of running programs and using capabilities on other computers across the Internet.

template Literally, a model to imitate, we use the term template in this book to describe the skeleton of a Web page, including the HTML for its heading and footer, and any consistent layout and navigation elements for a page or set of pages.

terminal emulation The process of making a full-fledged, stand-alone computer act like a terminal attached to another computer, terminal emulation is the service that telnet provides across the Internet.

test plan The series of steps and elements to be followed in conducting a formal test of software or other computerized systems; we strongly recommend that you write — and use — a test plan as a part of your Web publication process.

text controls Any of a number of HTML tags, including both physical and logical markup, text controls provide a method of managing the way that text appears within an HTML document.

text-mode A method of browser operation that displays characters only. Text-mode browsers cannot display graphics without the assistance of helper applications.

throughput Another measure of communications capability, this term refers to the amount of data that can be "put through" a connection in a given period of time. It differs from bandwidth in being a measure of actual performance, instead of a theoretical maximum for the medium involved.

thumbnail A miniature rendering of a graphical image, used as a link to the full-sized version.

title The text supplied between `<TITLE> . . . </TITLE>` defines the text that shows up on that page's title bar when displayed; it is also used as data in many Web search engines.

token-ring The second most common type of local-area networking technology in use, token-ring is always and forever associated with IBM, because it helped to develop and perfect this type of network. It takes its name from passing around special permits to transmit called *tokens,* in a ring-shaped pattern around the network, to give all attached devices a fair chance to broadcast information whenever they need to.

transparent GIF A specially rendered GIF image will takes on the background color selected in a browser capable of handling such GIFs. This makes the graphic blend into the existing color scheme and provides a more professional-looking page.

tree structure(d) (*see* hierarchical structure) Computer scientists like to think of hierarchies in graphical terms, which make them look like upside-down trees (a single root at the top, multiple branches below). File systems and genealogies are examples of tree-structured organizations that we're all familiar with, but they abound in the computer world. This type of structure also works well for certain Web document sets, especially larger, more complex ones.

UNIX The operating system of choice for the Internet community at large and the Web community, too, UNIX offers the broadest range of tools, utilities, and programming libraries for Web server use.

UNIX shell The name of the command-line program used to manage user-computer interaction, the shell can also be used to write CGI scripts and other kinds of useful programs for UNIX.

URI (Uniform Resource Identifier) Any of a class of objects that identifies resources available to the Web; both URLs and URNs are examples of URIs.

URL (Uniform Resource Locator) The primary naming scheme used to identify Web resources, URLs define the protocols to be used, the domain name of the Web server where a resource resides, the port address to be used for communication, and the directory path to access a named Web file or resource.

URL-encoded text A method for passing information requests and URL specifications to Web servers from browsers, URL encoding replaces spaces with plus signs (+) and substitutes special hex codes for a range of otherwise unreproducible characters. This method is used to pass document queries from browsers to servers (for the details, please consult Chapter 13).

URN (Uniform Resource Name) A permanent, unchanging name for a Web resource, URNs are seldom used in today's Web environment. They do, however, present a method guaranteed to obtain access to a resource, as soon as the URN can be fully resolved (it sometimes consists of human or organizational contact information, instead of resource location data).

Usenet An Internet protocol and service that provides access to a vast array of named newsgroups, where users congregate to exchange information and materials related to specific topics or concerns.

V.32 CCITT standard for a 9.6 Kbps two-wire full duplex modem operating on a regular dial-up or two-wire leased lines.

V.32bis Newer higher-speed CCITT standard for full-duplex transmission on two-wire leased and dial-up lines at rates from 4.8 to 14.4 Kbps.

V.34 The newest high-speed CCITT standard for full-duplex transmission on two-wire leased and dial-up lines at rates from 4.8 to 28.8 Kbps.

V.42 CCITT error correction standard that can be used with V.32, V.32bis, and V.34.

V.42bis CCITT data compression standard, capable of compressing files on the fly at an average rate of 3.5:1. It can yield speeds of up to 38.4 Kbps on a 9.6 Kbps modem, and up to 115.2 Kbps on a 28.8 modem. If your modem can do this, try to find an Internet Service Provider that also supports V.42bis. This feature can pay for itself very quickly.

VAX/VMS The VAX is a Digital Equipment Corporation computer in wide use; VMS (Virtual Memory System) is the name of the proprietary operating system that many of these machines run. Today, many VAXes run UNIX instead of VMS.

Veronica A search tool for navigating the global collection of Gopher servers, collectively referred to as *Gopherspace*.

WAIS (Wide-Area Information Service) A collection of programs that implements a specific protocol for information retrieval, able to index large-scale collections of data around the Internet. WAIS provides content-oriented query services to WAIS clients, and is one of the more powerful Internet search tools available.

Web Shorthand for the World Wide Web (or W3), we also use Web in this book to refer to a related, interlinked set of HTML documents.

Web pages Synonym for HTML documents, we use Web pages in this book to refer to sets of related, interlinked HTML documents, usually produced by a single author or organization.

Web server A computer, usually on the Internet, that plays host to *httpd* and related Web-service software.

Web site An addressed location, usually on the Internet, that provides access to the set of Web pages that correspond to the URL for a given site; thus a Web site consists of a Web server and a named collection of Web documents, both accessible through a single URL.

white space The breathing room on a page, this refers to the parts of a document or display that aren't occupied by text or other visual elements. A certain amount of white space is essential to make documents attractive and readable.

Windows (also called MS-Windows) Microsoft's astonishingly popular (and sometimes frustrating) GUI environment for PCs, Windows is the GUI of choice for most desktop computer users.

WinWeb The Windows version of a popular Web browser developed at MCC.

World Wide Web (also called WWW or W3) The complete collection of all Web servers available on the Internet, which comes as close to containing the "sum of human knowledge" as anything we've ever seen.

WYSIWYG (What You See Is What You Get) A term used to describe text editors or other layout tools (such as HTML authoring tools) that attempt to show their users on-screen what final, finished documents will look like.

X Windows The GUI of choice for UNIX systems, X Windows offers a graphical window, icon, and mouse metaphor similar to (but much more robust and powerful than) Microsoft Windows.

Index

(continued)

(continued)

(continued)

IDG BOOKS WORLDWIDE LICENSE AGREEMENT

4. Limited Warranty. IDGB warrants that the Software and disk are free from defects in materials and workmanship for a period of sixty (60) days from the date of purchase of this Book. If IDGB receives notification within the warranty period of defects in material or workmanship, IDGB will replace the defective disk. IDGB's entire liability and your exclusive remedy shall be limited to replacement of the Software, which is returned to IDGB with a copy of your receipt. This limited warranty is void if failure of the Software has resulted from accident, abuse, or misapplication. Any replacement Software will be warranted for the remainder of the original warranty period or thirty (30) days, whichever is longer.

5. No Other Warranties. To the maximum extent permitted by applicable law, IDGB and the author disclaim all other warranties, express or implied, including but not limited to implied warranties of merchantability and fitness for a particular purpose, with respect to the Software, the programs, the source code contained therein and/or the techniques described in this Book. This limited warranty gives you specific legal rights. You may have others which vary from state/jurisdiction to state/jurisdiction.

6. No Liability For Consequential Damages. To the extent permitted by applicable law, in no event shall IDGB or the author be liable for any damages whatsoever (including without limitation, damages for loss of business profits, business interruption, loss of business information, or any other pecuniary loss) arising out of the use of or inability to use the Book or the Software, even if IDGB has been advised of the possibility of such damages. Because some states/jurisdictions do not allow the exclusion or limitation of liability for consequential or incidental damages, the above limitation may not apply to you.

7. U.S. Government Restricted Rights. Use, duplication, or disclosure of the Software by the U.S. Government is subject to restrictions stated in paragraph (c) (1) (ii) of the Rights in Technical Data and Computer Software clause of DFARS 252.227-7013, and in subparagraphs (a) through (d) of the Commercial Computer—Restricted Rights clause at FAR 52.227-19, and in similar clauses in the NASA FAR supplement, when applicable.

About the Disk

●●●

*1*n this section of the book, we explain what you find on the *HTML For Dummies,* 2nd Edition, disk. In a nutshell, it contains the following goodies:

- ✔ A collection of Web documents built just to help you find your way around the book's materials

- ✔ A hotlist of all the URLs mentioned in the book, to make it easy for you to access any of the Web resources we've mentioned

- ✔ An online version of the book's glossary, to help you look up all the strange and bizarre terminology Webheads are prone to use from time to time

- ✔ Copies of all the HTML examples, easily accessible by chapter and heading, along with any graphics they use

- ✔ A hyperlinked table of contents for the book, to help you find your way around its many topics and treasures

- ✔ A collection of HTML documents that describe HTML tags for draft standards (Beyond HTML 2.0), and for Netscape and Internet Explorer Extensions

- ✔ A specially-compressed archive of Common Gateway Interface (CGI) programs, built especially for you, to help add functionality to your own Web server (and to provide what we hope are sterling examples of the art of CGI programming)

All of this and more will be available on your own hard disk, if you simply follow the installation instructions in the next section. We also explain a few other odds and ends along the way

Installing the Disk

Installing for Windows users

Installing the *HTML For Dummies* disk is a completely straightforward process. If you have a PC running Windows 3.1 or later (such as Windows for Workgroups 3.11, the Windows 3.11 update, or Windows 95), you can install in a few easy steps:

1. **Insert the disk into the floppy drive on your PC.**

2. **Windows 3.x: From the Program Manager, click on File and then Run.**
   Windows 95: Click on the Start button and then choose Run.

3. **Type in H4D2E.EXE and then click on OK. Follow the instructions on the screen.**

That's all there is to it!

Windows 95 alters the folder and file names of the extracted contents of the archive on your computer. This is normally only a cosmetic feature of Windows 95, but sometimes this feature may cause some programs to improperly handle file and folder names. After the installation is complete, use the Windows Explorer to look at the names of the folders created by the *HTML For Dummies* installation. For safety's sake, you should manually replace the initial uppercase letters of folders and files with a lowercase letter. Directories should appear as: `dummies`, `h4d2`, `graphics`, `template`, and `graphics` (inside the `template` folder). We apologize for this inconvenience, but this is a quirk of the Windows 95 system and cannot be corrected by the installation utility.

Installing for Mac or UNIX users

The *HTML For Dummies* disk also contains files for use on a Macintosh or on a UNIX machine. You do, however, need to have the proper software on your system to mount and read a PC-formatted 1.44MB floppy in order to access the contents. This means you need the program named PC Exchange in order to read this diskette.

For Macintosh users, the files are in a compressed format under the filename `H4D2ESEA.HQX`. You need to use StuffIt Expander or BinHex (version 4.0 or higher) to this file, to change from a hexadecimal format into a binary format. This produces a StuffIt self-extracting archive which, when double-clicked, unpacks itself for you. The files extract to a folder named `DUMMIES`.

The files included for use on a UNIX system are not on the disk, but you can download them from our Web site at

```
http://www.outer.net/html4dum/html4dum.htm.
```

Once you download the archive, create your root directory where you can unarchive the files (we recommend the name `html_for_dummies`). You need an unpack utility that knows how to decompress files saved in the *tar* format, using the following system command:

```
tar -xv html4dum.tar.
```

The disk's inside story

If you look at the contents of the *HTML For Dummies* disk, here's what you see:

```
CGIS.TAR        compressed CGI programs and related files
H4D2E.EXE       self-extracting file for Windows
H4D2ESEA.HQX    BinHexed, compressed files for Macintosh systems
README.TXT      latest disk information
REGISTER.TXT    text-only version of the HTML For Dummies
                registration form
```

When you execute H4D2E.EXE, or unpack one of the other compressed files for Macintosh or UNIX, the contents of the self-extracting file are unpacked; only then can you see what is on the disk – except now it's on your hard disk, instead!

The HTML For Dummies Files

Once unpacked, you find that the installation program has created directories in the following arrangement:

```
Directory Tree              Full Directory Specification
_____                      _____
C:
 |-other directories
 |-\DUMMIES                 C:\DUMMIES
 |-H4D2                     C:\DUMMIES\H4D2
       |-GRAPHICS           C:\DUMMIES\H4D2\GRAPHICS
       |-TEMPLATE           C:\DUMMIES\H4D2\TEMPLATE
            |-GRAPHICS      C:\DUMMIES\H4D2\TEMPLATE\GRAPHICS
```

By describing the contents of each of these directories and naming the important files in each one, we can provide an excellent road map to what's on the disk.

You probably won't need to interact with too many of the individual files in these directories because most of them are linked together as HTML documents that you can explore using almost any Web browser. Because this includes most of the major players in this field — like Netscape, WinWeb, Mosaic, WebSurfer, and so on — you shouldn't have too much difficulty using your browser to help you look around. To give you an idea of what's there, we cover the files according to their home directory (assuming, of course, that you've accepted the installation defaults and the files actually live where we say they do).

C:\DUMMIES\H4D2

This directory contains the majority of the *HTML For Dummies* files, both in terms of importance and capturing key components of the book. Nearly every file in this directory ends with the extension .HTM, indicating that it is an HTML document.

The files in this directory fall into three categories:

1. Those that begin with CHnn, where *n* is a digit between 0 and 9, are keyed to chapters in the book. Thus, CH07 indicates that the file in question is related to Chapter 7 of the book (the HTML Markup Reference chapter, in fact). These filenames continue on with the notation -Enn, where again, *n* is a digit between 0 and 9. This keys the file to a specific figure number for the chapter. Thus, the file named CH07-E14.HTM keys to figure 7-14, which illustrates the capabilities of the HTML paragraph tag (<P>). For other chapters, like 13, CH13CERN.MAP indicates the clickable map file supplied for the CERN httpd implementation, while CH13NCSA.MAP represents its NCSA counterpart.

2. Those files that begin with something other than CHnn are HTML documents that belong to a collection of *HTML For Dummies* sample pages that we've constructed as a teaching aid and as a navigational tool, to help you find your way around the materials we've assembled for the book. The next few pages show a partial listing of what's what.

3. Those files with names that range from T0001.HTM through T0117.HTM contain information about a variety of HTML tags, for advanced standard HTML, and for the Netscape and Internet Explorer extensions.

COMMENT.HTM	E-mail form to send messages to the HTML4DUM authors
CONT-<chapnum>	Contents for Chapter <chapnum>
CONT-01.HTM	Contents for Chapter 1
. . .	Contents for Chapters 2 through 25
CONT-26.HTM	Contents for Chapter 26
CONTACT.HTM	Listing of email, home page and bio page links for the authors and related people
CONTBLAH.HTM	Non-table version of contents page
CONTENTS.HTM	Contents page layed out using a table
COVRTEXT.HTM	Text from the cover of the 1st edition

EDBIO.HTM	Ed Tittel's bio page
ERRATA.HTM	list of errors and mistakes from the 1st edition
ERRATA.TXT	text version of the errata page
EX-<chapnum>.HTM	Chapter chapnum example jump page
EX-<chapnum>-<exnum>.HTM	Example exnum Chapter chapnum
EX-05-02.HTM	Example from Chapter 5
FTPSTUFF.HTM	FTP page to download disk contents and CGIs
GLOS-A.HTM	Glossary words *a*
. . .	Glossary words *b* through *w*
GLOS-X.HTM	Glossary words *x*
HOTLIST.HTM	List of a few good search engines and related sites
HTML4DU2.HTM	Non-imagemap version of the home page
HTML4DUM.HTM	Imagemap version of the home page
ISOLATIN.TXT	Text of the ISO Latin character set
JMSBIO.HTM	James Michael Stewart's bio page
MEBIO.HTM	Mike Erwin's bio page
MGBIO.HTM	Mark Gaither's bio page
NAVIGATE.HTM	Infomation about the navigation controls used
PART1.HTM	Book excerpt
. . .	Book excerpts, parts 2 through 7
PART8.HTM	Book excerpt
REGISTER.TXT	Text version of the online registration page
REGISTRN.HTM	Online registration page
SEARCH4D.HTM	List of main pages and online search utility
SHBIO.HTM	Sebastian Hassinger's bio page
SJBIO.HTM	Steve James' bio page
T0001.HTM	<A> Anchor
T0002.HTM	<ABBREV> Abbrev
T0003.HTM	<ABOVE> Math Line Above
T0004.HTM	<ACRONYM> Acronym
T0005.HTM	<ADDRESS> Address

T0006.HTM	\<ARRAY\> Math Array
T0007.HTM	\<ATOP\> Math Box Atop
T0008.HTM	\<AU\> Author
T0009.HTM	\<B\> Bold
T0010.HTM	\<BANNER\> Document Banner
T0011.HTM	\<BASE\> Document Base
T0012.HTM	\<BELOW\> Math Line Below
T0013.HTM	\<BIG\> Big Print
T0014.HTM	\<BODY\> Document Body
T0015.HTM	"\<BODY\>, \<BODYTEXT\> Body Text"
T0016.HTM	\<BOX\> Math Box
T0017.HTM	\<BQ\> Blockquote
T0018.HTM	\<BR\> Line Break
T0019.HTM	\<BT\> Bold Upright
T0020.HTM	\<CAPTION\> Caption
T0021.HTM	\<CHOOSE\> Math Box Choose
T0022.HTM	\<CITE\> Citation
T0023.HTM	\<CODE\> Code
T0024.HTM	\<CREDIT\> Credit
T0025.HTM	\<DD\> Definition List Definition
T0026.HTM	\<DEL\> Deleted Text
T0027.HTM	\<DFN\> Definition
T0028.HTM	\<DIR\> Directory List
T0029.HTM	\<DIV\> Document Divisions
T0030.HTM	\<DL\> Definition List
T0031.HTM	\<DT\> Definition List Term
T0032.HTM	\<EM\> Emphasis
T0033.HTM	\<FIG\> Figure
T0034.HTM	\<FIGTEXT\> Figure Text
T0035.HTM	\<FN\> Footnotes
T0036.HTM	\<FORM\> Form
T0037.HTM	\<H*\> Document Headings

T0038.HTM	\<HEAD\> Document Head
T0039.HTM	\<HR\> Horizontal Rule
T0040.HTM	\<HTML\> Main Document Head
T0041.HTM	\<I\> Italics
T0042.HTM	\<IMG\> Image
T0043.HTM	\<INPUT\> Form Input
T0044.HTM	\<INS\> Inserted Text
T0045.HTM	\<ISINDEX\> Is Indexed
T0046.HTM	\<ITEM\> Math Array Item
T0047.HTM	\<KBD\> Keyboard Text
T0048.HTM	\<LANG\> Language
T0049.HTM	\<LEFT\> Math Box Left
T0050.HTM	\<LH\> List Heading
T0051.HTM	\<LI\> List Item
T0052.HTM	\<LINK\> Document Link
T0053.HTM	\<MATH\> Mathematics
T0054.HTM	\<MENU\> Menu List
T0055.HTM	\<META\> Meta
T0056.HTM	\<NEXTID\> Next ID
T0057.HTM	\<NOTE\> Admonishments
T0058.HTM	\<OF\> Math Root Of
T0059.HTM	\<OL\> Ordered List
T0060.HTM	\<OPTION\> From Select Option
T0061.HTM	\<OVER\> Math Box Over
T0062.HTM	\<OVERLAY\> Overlay
T0063.HTM	\<P\> Paragraph
T0064.HTM	\<PERSON\> Person
T0065.HTM	\<PRE\> Preformatted Text
T0066.HTM	\<Q\> Quotation
T0067.HTM	\<RANGE\> Range of a Document
T0068.HTM	\<RIGHT\> Math Box Right
T0069.HTM	\<ROOT\> Math Root

T0070.HTM	\<ROW\> Math Array Row
T0071.HTM	\<S\> Strikethrough
T0072.HTM	\<SAMP\> Sample
T0073.HTM	\<SELECT\> Form Select
T0074.HTM	\<SMALL\> Small Print
T0075.HTM	\<SPOT\> Spot ID
T0076.HTM	\<SQRT\> Math Square Root
T0077.HTM	\<STRONG\> Strong
T0078.HTM	\<STYLE\> Style Notation
T0079.HTM	\<SUB\> Subscript
T0080.HTM	\<SUP\> Superscript
T0081.HTM	\<T\> Upright
T0082.HTM	\<TAB\> Horizontal Tab
T0083.HTM	\<TABLE\> Tables
T0084.HTM	\<TD\> Table Data Cell
T0085.HTM	\<TH\> Table Header Cell
T0086.HTM	\<TEXT\> Math Text
T0087.HTM	\<TEXTAREA\> Form Textarea
T0088.HTM	\<TITLE\> Title
T0089.HTM	\<TR\> Table Rows
T0090.HTM	\<TT\> Teletype
T0091.HTM	\<U\> Underline
T0092.HTM	\<UL\> Unordered List
T0093.HTM	\<VAR\>
T0094.HTM	"\<VEC\>, \<BAR\>, \<DOT\>, \<DDOT\>, \<HAT\>, \<TILDE\> Math Vectors"
T0095.HTM	\<BASEFONT\> Basefont
T0100.HTM	\<BR\> Line Break
T0096.HTM	\<CENTER\> Center
T0097.HTM	\<FONT\> Font Size
T0101.HTM	\<HR\> Horizontal Rule
T0102.HTM	\<IMG\> Image

T0103.HTM	<ISINDEX> Is Indexed
T0105.HTM	<LI> List Item for <OL>
T0107.HTM	<LI> List Item for <UL>
T0098.HTM	<NOBR> No Break
T0104.HTM	<OL> Numbered List
T0106.HTM	<UL> Bulleted List
T0099.HTM	<WBR> Word Break
T0108.HTM	<AREA> Image Map Area
T0109.HTM	<BGSOUND> Background Sound
T0112.HTM	<BODY> Body
T0113.HTM	<CAPTION> Table Caption
T0114.HTM	<FONT> Font
T0115.HTM	<IMG> Image
T0110.HTM	<MAP> Client Side Image Map
T0111.HTM	<MARQUEE> Marquee
T0116.HTM	<TABLE><TD><TH><TR> Table and Elements
T0117.HTM	<!— HTML comment tags —>
TAGINDEX.HTM	Master Tag Jump Page with Table
TAGBLAH.TXT	Master Tag Jump Page without Table
TEMPLATE.HTM	Jump Page to the Templates
URLS-01.HTM	Chapter URLs
. . .	URLS for Other Chapters, by Number (chapters without URLs do not have entries here)
URLS-25.HTM	Chapter URLs
WHATSNEW.HTM	Lists All Alterations and Changes Made to the Web Site

All in all, the best way to explore the *HTML For Dummies* Web pages is to fire up your browser and point it at the file named `C:\DUMMIES\H4D2\HTML4DUM.HTM`, the home page for the whole collection. As an initial run-through, if you simply select the "NEXT" (the right-hand pointing arrow) link at the bottom of each page, you can take a guided tour of the whole shebang and get a pretty good idea of what's available and how you might use it.

We're especially proud of the online glossary and your ability to use our "Web-ified" Table of Contents pages to locate the HTML documents for all the examples that appear in the book. But you'll probably find some other things to like in here as well. . . .

If you see anything you don't like or don't understand, please send us e-mail: as our book recommends, we believe in asking for, listening to, and reacting to our users' feedback — this means you! (Thanks in advance, by the way.)

C:\DUMMIES\H4D2\GRAPHICS

This is the graphics subdirectory for the graphics used in the HTML documents for the *HTML For Dummies* pages themselves. As its name implies, this is where all the .GIF (Graphics Information Files) files for images in our sample HTML documents reside. If we used it in an example (or on the *HTML For Dummies* Web pages), you can find it in here. All we can say further is "Help yourself!"

For the incurably curious, here are some of the details:

AT_WORK.GIF	under construction icon
BACK.GIF	navigation button back
BOGUSB.GIF	example image
DOTBLUE.GIF	blue dot
DOTRED.GIF	red dot
DOTWHITE.GIF	white dot
H4D-SM.GIF	H4D cover art icon
HOME.GIF	navigation button home
HT4CONTI.GIF	main navigation image contents icon
HT4FILEI.GIF	main navigation image file icon
HT4LOGOI.GIF	main navigation image logo icon
HT4MENUM.GIF	main imagemap
HT4NEWI.GIF	main navigation image new icon
MBOX.GIF	mailbox icon

MENU.GIF	navigation button menu
NEW.GIF	new icon
NEW_LG.GIF	large new icon
NEXT.GIF	navigation button next
OPENDOOR.GIF	open door icon
PHONE.GIF	telephone icon
RAINBOLG.GIF	another rainbow bar
README.GIF	newspaper icon
SPACE.GIF	transparent spacer graphic
TRANS001.GIF	example graphic of a smiley face
VALDHTML.GIF	HTML validation icon

At the very least this small collection of graphical items should give you some interesting raw material to draw on for your own Web creations!

C:\DUMMIES\H4D2\TEMPLATE

For your pleasure and convenience, we've included a few simple templates to get you started on your HTML authoring adventures. Don't limit yourself to just these few files located in this directory, however. You can use any page we include that ends in ".HTM" as a template. Here's our collection of HTML documents, designed specifically as templates:

BASIC.HTM	our most basic HTML page template, suitable for any kind of use
PERSONAL.HTM	a ready-to-complete personal home page of your very own
FRSTPAGE.HTM	an initial or welcome page for a company, organization, or topical Web site
TABLES.HTM	a page example that includes a pre-defined <TABLE> ready for use
NOTDONE.HTM	the infamous "under construction" page; the name of this file should tell you how we feel about its use!

DISPLAY.HTM

a collection of widgets and graphics that you can use to spruce up your own Web pages. Use this page to look up the file name for the widget you want to use, to drop it into your own pages!

Once you understand HTML's basic concepts, you soon find that the only template you use is the BASIC.HTM template, or a similar basic HTML document you create on your own. Nevertheless, we've supplied this set to give you some ideas, and to help you get started with the authoring process. Remember, too, that the files in the TEMPLATE directory are not your only sources for examples of working HTML documents. Every file in the main *HTML For Dummies* directory (DUMMIES/H4D2) can be used as a template as well. Simply open that file in your favorite text editor, save it under another name, delete our information. and replace it with your own. The "save under another name" instruction is VERY important: otherwise, you'll trash one of the original *HTML For Dummies* pages and will have to go back to the diskette (or to our Web site) to replace it, if you ever want to use it again!

Remember, you can view the source code for any HTML document to learn how a design element was incorporated or some unique layout was created. You are always welcome to learn from the work of others, but be careful not to plagiarize. If you plan to closely copy someone else's work, take time to ask their permission before appropriating their work (and don't forget, copyright violation is against the law).

C:\DUMMIES\H4D2\TEMPLATE\GRAPHICS

These are the graphics files used in the templates (as distinct from the graphics used in the *HTML For Dummies* Web pages, located in C:\DUMMIES\H4D2\GRAPHICS). You should spend some time exploring here, too, because you'll find some useful goodies; the file named DISPLAY.HTM is especially useful, because it includes all of the graphics in this subdirectory, along with the filename for each one, as a kind of "reference page" for each and every graphic here. Instead of listing those files again here, we just encourage you to open that page with your browser, where you can see all of them displayed in their full-color glory!

Working with the CGI programs

The reason why the CGI programs are stored in a tar file is that the names of the files for those programs exceed the DOS 8.3 filename limitations. In plain English, it's because the filenames are too long for poor DOS to handle. The reason why that's OK is that CGI programs have to run on a Web server, not on your workstation. Because 70-plus percent of all the Web servers in use today are UNIX, and the bulk of the remainder are either Macintoshes or Windows NT, long filenames for CGI programs are the norm, rather than the exception. While you can obtain Web server software that runs on Windows 95 or Windows 3.x for use on your desktop machine, we don't imagine that you want to spend $99 (the retail price for Quarterdeck's excellent WebServer software, available for 16-bit Windows environments). That's why we didn't worry about using long filenames here, either.

The CGI archive contains three subdirectories, one for each of the programming languages we used. Here's the annotated list of CGI files you find in the CGIS.TAR archive file, divided into those subdirectories:

\APPLESCRIPT

COUNTCGI.TXT	readme for counter script
RIGHT.HTML	test page for ismapper script
MAP_DEFAULT.HTML	test page for ismapper script
MAP.GIF	test image for ismapper script
LEFT.HTML	test page for ismapper script
ISMAP-TEST.HTML	test page for ismapper script
ISMAPPER-AS.CGI.HQX	ismapper script
COUNTER.ACGI.HQX	counter script
TIME-AS.CGI.HQX	current time script

\C

COUNTER-CGI.C	counter script
TIME_NOW	compiled current time script
ISMAPPER.C	ismapper script
ISMAPPER	compiled ismapper script
TIME-CGI.C	current time script

\PERL

COUNTER.FORM.HTML	test page for counter script
RIGHT.HTML	test page for ismapper script
MAP_DEFAULT.HTML	test page for ismapper script
MAP.GIF	test image for ismapper script
LEFT.HTML	test page for ismapper script
ISMAP-TEST.HTML	test page for ismapper script
ISMAPPER-CGI.PL	ismapper scirpt

ISMAPPER.LOG	ismapper log file
ISMAPPER.CONF	ismapper conf file
COUNTER-CGI.PL	counter script
COUNTER.LOG	counter log file
TIME-CGI.PL	current time script

To use any of these CGIs, you have to get in touch with the system administrator for the Web server you use and let him or her know that you've got a CGI you'd like to use with your pages. Chances are good you can get permission to use one of these programs, if it's appropriate for that server (for example, putting an AppleScript file on a UNIX machine, or a shell script on a Macintosh, is pretty much guaranteed not to work), or that your administrator will tell you how to use a similar CGI that's already installed there. Just remember, you may not have the right file system access privileges to move CGIs around on your Web server, so the right way to start is by asking your local system administrator or Webmaster about how CGIs work on their system, and tell them what you're trying to do. That way, you won't get in trouble (or waste your time trying to do something you simply don't have the rights to attempt on your Web server).

Where to Go from Here

We really can't make you go anywhere from this point in your reading, but we hope you decide to install the *HTML For Dummies* disk and experience its contents first-hand. We also hope that you might read this book while you're at it! Enjoy!

IDG BOOKS WORLDWIDE REGISTRATION CARD

RETURN THIS REGISTRATION CARD FOR FREE CATALOG

Title of this book: **HTML For Dummies®, 2nd Edition**

My overall rating of this book: ❏ Very good [1]   ❏ Good [2]   ❏ Satisfactory [3]   ❏ Fair [4]   ❏ Poor [5]

How I first heard about this book:

❏ Found in bookstore; name: [6]

❏ Advertisement: [8]

❏ Word of mouth; heard about book from friend, co-worker, etc.: [10]

❏ Book review: [7]

❏ Catalog: [9]

❏ Other: [11]

What I liked most about this book:

What I would change, add, delete, etc., in future editions of this book:

Other comments:

Number of computer books I purchase in a year: ❏ 1 [12]   ❏ 2-5 [13]   ❏ 6-10 [14]   ❏ More than 10 [15]

I would characterize my computer skills as: ❏ Beginner [16] ❏ Intermediate [17] ❏ Advanced [18] ❏ Professional [19]

I use ❏ DOS [20] ❏ Windows [21] ❏ OS/2 [22] ❏ Unix [23] ❏ Macintosh [24] ❏ Other: [25]_____
(please specify)

I would be interested in new books on the following subjects:
(please check all that apply, and use the spaces provided to identify specific software)

❏ Word processing: [26]

❏ Data bases: [28]

❏ File Utilities: [30]

❏ Networking: [32]

❏ Other: [34]

❏ Spreadsheets: [27]

❏ Desktop publishing: [29]

❏ Money management: [31]

❏ Programming languages: [33]

I use a PC at (please check all that apply): ❏ home [35] ❏ work [36] ❏ school [37] ❏ other: [38] _____

The disks I prefer to use are ❏ 5.25 [39] ❏ 3.5 [40] ❏ other: [41]_____

I have a CD ROM: ❏ yes [42]   ❏ no [43]

I plan to buy or upgrade computer hardware this year: ❏ yes [44]   ❏ no [45]

I plan to buy or upgrade computer software this year: ❏ yes [46]   ❏ no [47]

Name: _____   Business title: [48] _____   Type of Business: [49] _____

Address (❏ home [50] ❏ work [51]/Company name: _____)

Street/Suite# _____

City [52]/State [53]/Zipcode [54]: _____   Country [55] _____

❏ **I liked this book!** You may quote me by name in future
   IDG Books Worldwide promotional materials.

My daytime phone number is _____

IDG BOOKS

THE WORLD OF
COMPUTER
KNOWLEDGE

 # YES!

Please keep me informed about IDG's World of Computer Knowledge.
Send me the latest IDG Books catalog.